LOST LIBERTIES

D0067219

323.4909
L

LOST LIBERTIES

Ashcroft and the Assault on Personal Freedom

EDITED BY CYNTHIA BROWN

THE NEW PRESS

NEW YORK
LONDON

© 2003 by The New Press.
Individual essays © by each author.
All rights reserved.
No part of this book may be reproduced, in any form, without written permission
from the publisher.

Published in the United States by The New Press, New York, 2003
Distributed by W. W. Norton & Company, Inc., New York

ISBN 1-56584-829-2
CIP data available

The New Press was established in 1990 as a not-for-profit alternative to the large,
commercial publishing houses currently dominating the book publishing industry.
The New Press operates in the public interest rather than for private gain, and is committed
to publishing, in innovative ways, works of educational, cultural, and community value
that are often deemed insufficiently profitable.

The New Press, 38 Greene Street, 4th floor, New York, NY 10013
www.thenewpress.com

In the United Kingdom: 6 Salem Road, London W2 4BU

Composition by dix!

Printed in Canada

2   4   6   8   10   9   7   5   3   1

3 1327 00415 9505

CONTENTS

Introduction
Aryeh Neier   1

I. TOOLS FOR A NEW KIND OF WAR

1. The Course of Least Resistance: Repeating History in the War on Terrorism
David Cole   13

2. How Democracy Dies: The War on Our Civil Liberties
Nancy Chang   33

3. After 9/11: A Surveillance State?
Reg Whitaker   52

II. THE ASHCROFT APPROACH

4. Secret Arrests and Preventive Detention
Kate Martin   75

5. Racial Profiling Post–9/11: Old Story, New Debate
Tanya E. Coke   91

6. Living in Fear: How the U.S. Government's War on Terror Impacts
American Lives
Anthony D. Romero   112

7. The War on Terrorism: Guantánamo Prisoners, Military Commissions,
and Torture
Michael Ratner   132

8. Breaking the Code: Or, Can the Press Be Saved from Itself?
Michael Tomasky   151

III. PRIVACY, SECRECY, AND PUBLIC HEALTH

9. Balancing in a Crisis? Bioterrorism, Public Health, and Privacy
Janlori Goldman   161

10. The Public Health Fallout from September 11: Official Deception and
Long-Term Damage
Joel R. Kupferman   184

IV. GLOBAL THREAT, GLOBAL CITIZEN

11. Axis of Antagonism: U.S.–European Relations and the War on Terror
Gary Younge   209

12. The "War on Terror" and Women's Rights: A Pakistan-Afghan Perspective
Farida Shaheed   222

13. Human Rights, the Bush Administration, and the Fight against Terrorism:
The Need for a Positive Vision
Kenneth Roth   237

Notes   255
Index   303

LOST LIBERTIES

INTRODUCTION
ARYEH NEIER

Within hours after the collapse of the World Trade Center and the destruction of a portion of the Pentagon, most of us knew that civil liberties would be under fire. After all, as David Cole and other contributors to this volume point out, we have been down this road before. The historical events of the past century that inspired the worst violations of civil liberties—aside from those that are endemic in our treatment of racial minorities—share certain characteristics.

The crackdown against pacifists and other opponents of World War I, against suspected anarchists and Reds after the war, against Japanese Americans during World War II, and against alleged Communists, sympathizers, and dupes during the early years of the Cold War all involved Americans thought to be aiding foreign conspiracies or undermining the country's resolve in a foreign conflict.

Though the consequences were not comparable in stifling dissent, an assault against civil liberties took place again during the Vietnam War. Hundreds of conscientious objectors were imprisoned; scores of thousands of peaceable demonstrators were arrested and some of them were punitively reclassified in the draft to speed up their induction into the armed services; federal grand juries conducted wide-ranging investigations of critics of U.S. foreign policy; prominent opponents of the war such as Dr. Benjamin Spock and the Reverend William Sloane Coffin were prosecuted for conspiring against the draft; President Richard Nixon established a personal secret police, "the Plumbers," operating outside the constraints of the law, to plug "leaks" such as the information that the U.S. had invaded Cambodia; the U.S. Army was deployed to spy on civilians; the federal government sought to enjoin the *New York Times* and the *Washington Post* from publishing information about the origins of the war; and so on.

The anti-immigrant aspects of public policy since September 11, as manifested particularly in the secret arrests, secret detentions, and secret immigration proceedings discussed in Kate Martin's essay, and of some of the past century's most significant violations of civil liberties, had counterparts even earlier in American history. It is only necessary to mention the Alien and Sedition Acts of the end of the eighteenth century and the "Know-Nothing" movement of the middle of the nineteenth century. While Americans rightly celebrate our tradition of freedom, it is useful to recall that it is a tradition that has been sustained only because those committed to it have periodically fought back and overcome the forces in American society that—pretending to speak in the name of patriotism—would take the country in the opposite direction.

Though it is not surprising that the devastating events of September 11 should inspire a new round of attacks on civil liberties, it is nevertheless dismaying. As one looks back at the previous periods when rights were systematically violated, it is difficult to discern any resulting gain for national security. The prosecutions of critics of World War I did nothing for the war effort and did not hasten Germany's defeat and agreement to an armistice. So far as we know, none of those responsible for the letter bombs or the other terrorist *attentats* of the post–World War I era was netted by the Palmer raids. America's victory in the war in the Pacific was not hastened by the internment of the Japanese-Americans. The loyalty and security investigations and purges of the late 1940s and the 1950s in Hollywood, the universities, and other sectors of public life appear not to have had an impact on the course of the Cold War. And, the efforts by the Johnson and Nixon administrations to curb dissent did nothing to stave off the ignominious end to the war in Vietnam.

That is not to say that governmental authorities are unjustified in taking certain steps to protect public safety in the current circumstances. It is a nuisance to take off one's shoes before boarding an airplane, but the longer wait to get through the security checks seems rationally related to our interest in enhanced safety aloft. One hopes that more safeguards are in place for the transport of hazardous materials, and that precautions are being taken against efforts to blow up the bridges and tunnels. Vaccinations against smallpox that could be lethal to some people seem an extreme measure. Yet if the government makes a case that the risk is real that bioterrorists could acquire the capacity to spread this dread disease, and appropriate steps are taken—as Janlori Goldman proposes in her essay here—to protect the vulnerable and to limit the availability of data on testing and screening, most of us would readily go along.

The case that has not been made, and probably cannot be made, is that abrogations of civil liberties make us safer. It did not happen in the past. What is it this time about the USA PATRIOT Act, John Poindexter's Total Information Awareness (TIA) proposal, John Ashcroft's secret detentions and immigration proceedings, or Donald Rumsfeld's denial of either prisoner-of-war status or of charges, attorneys, and hearings to the prisoners at Guantánamo that makes us more secure? Is it that the current generation of officials is wiser and more trustworthy than A. Mitchell Palmer, J. Edgar Hoover, Joseph McCarthy, Richard Nixon, and John Mitchell? What have they done to prove it? Or, as seems more likely, are some of these measures mainly intended to cover up government misconduct or incompetence? Closed-door immigration hearings merely hide the Justice Department's utter failure to connect those caught up in these proceedings to terrorism. Similarly, denying the prisoners at Guantánamo lawyers and hearings prevents us from finding out the absence of evidence justifying their detention. Until proven otherwise, these measures should be regarded as failures of the war against terrorism.

Looking back at what was done to curb civil liberties in earlier periods of national danger or perceived danger, one wonders whether the real purpose was in fact to increase security. No doubt this was the main consideration for many proponents of restrictions on rights, even if that was not the effect. Yet one also detects a punitive or vengeful strain in American history. That is, it is not only important to ensure safety; it also seems to be important to some that those living among us enjoying the fruits of American society whose presumed political sympathies or demographic characteristics are similar to those who have caused trouble for the country should pay a price. They are regarded as part of a wider conspiracy. Measures that violate civil liberties are inherently divisive. For those intent in separating not only the world but also Americans between those who are "with us" or "with the terrorists," such measures apparently serve a salutary purpose.

It is important, of course, to give credit where credit is due. President George W. Bush has made significant efforts to avoid violence along religious or ethnic lines. Were it not for his efforts against vigilantism starting immediately after the events of September 11, the situation undoubtedly would be far worse than it is today. One thinks of the horrendous carnage in Gujarat, India, after the episode in February 2002 in which a few harassed Muslim vendors set fire to a train carrying Hindu nationalists, causing some fifty-eight deaths. With Gujarati government officials standing by or egging them on, and with national leaders refusing to interfere, Hindu mobs destroyed Muslim shops and homes throughout the province, forcing scores of thousands to flee their homes. As many as 2,000 Muslims were slaughtered, with no effort by the authorities to apprehend and punish the guilty. That no mass violence took place in the United States despite the vastly greater death toll of September 11 than on the train is due not only to differing traditions between the United States and India, it is also attributable to the president's leadership in steering the country away from communal strife.

Unfortunately, the president's praiseworthy and successful efforts to avoid ethnic and religious violence were not matched by a comparable attempt to protect constitutional rights. Major new violations of rights have already become a part of American law and practice. We are at risk of entering another of those dark periods of American history when the country abandons its proud tradition of respect for civil liberties.

To say that we are at risk, however, is not to say that the struggle to preserve our rights is hopeless. We have a chance to succeed again as we did three decades ago in beating back the assault on civil liberties that was aimed at suppressing dissent over the Vietnam War. In that era, not only did Americans continue to speak out about the war despite all efforts to silence them, the president of the United States was forced to resign for his violations of rights. Immediately following his resignation, Congress adopted such significant protections for civil liberties as the Privacy Act of 1974, the Federal Education Rights and Privacy Act (FERPA), and the 1974 amendments to the Freedom of Information Act (FOIA). Congress also adopted the main laws that continue today to commit the United States to promote human rights internationally, passing certain measures over President Gerald Ford's veto. Most important, in the latter part of the 1970s and the beginning of the 1980s, the federal courts dismantled much of the political surveillance system that had developed not only during the Vietnam War but since the early years of the twentieth century. These developments made the post-Vietnam era a high point for civil liberties protection in American history.

Several factors combined, I believe, to beat back the assault on civil liberties of the late 1960s and early 1970s. One of them was the availability of a large number of skilled advocates to represent those arrested and prosecuted for dissent or made targets of political surveillance. Some of the lawyers involved had played a part in the civil rights struggles of a slightly earlier period. Others were themselves of the generation that was most active in protesting the war. Many took on cases under the auspices of the American Civil Liberties Union or other civil liberties groups. In that period, literally thousands of lawyers were ready to take on the defense of First Amendment or due process rights without cost, an incommensurably greater number than had ever been available at any previous period.

Another factor was the receptivity of the judiciary, particularly in the federal courts, to efforts to protect civil liberties. This should not be overstated. Richard Nixon's imprint on the U.S. Supreme Court was already evident by 1972, as when it considered *Laird v. Tatum*,[1] a challenge to the U.S. Army's spying on civilians. In an opinion by one of Nixon's appointees, Chief Justice Warren Burger, that also reflected the views of his newest appointee, Justice William Rehnquist, the Court held that the targets of the spying lacked standing to bring the matter before the judiciary. Notwithstanding such significant setbacks, the courts did much to restrain excesses in the exercise of executive power, as in the Supreme Court's 1972 decision that warrants are required for all domestic security wiretaps,[2] and its 1971 decision rejecting the effort of the Nixon administration to prevent the *New York Times* and the *Washington Post* from publishing the Pentagon Papers.[3]

The discovery of the Watergate burglary by an alert security guard and the subsequent cover-up by President Nixon and his associates that gradually unraveled under probing by the press, the courts, and Congress was yet another factor that turned back the onslaught against civil liberties. Watergate gave its name to the entire panoply of Nixon's abuses, thereby tending to obscure the fact that, of itself, the bugging of the telephones at the headquarters of the Democratic National Committee was a relatively minor and peripheral example of what was going on during the Vietnam War era. Yet it did open the eyes of the country and helped to persuade most Americans that the Nixon administration was willing to resort to any means against those it saw as its critics and opponents. Thereby, it greatly strengthened public insistence that individual rights should be protected by legal process.

Perhaps the most important factor in safeguarding civil liberties during the Vietnam War era was the unwillingness of many millions of Americans to be intimidated. There was never a moment when wiretaps, grand jury investigations, arrests, prosecutions or convictions, and prison sentences stopped those critical of the war from speaking out. In that respect, the period differed markedly from earlier times when civil liberties were under attack. As one who attended college in the 1950s, I recall that we were known as "the silent generation." The term was justified. Though Joseph McCarthy's star was already fading when I entered my freshman year in September 1954—the Army-McCarthy hearings had taken place about three months earlier—we did not find our voice. It wasn't until the sit-ins and freedom rides of the civil rights movement took place several years later that college campuses began again to make themselves heard on matters of public policy.

Not all these factors are present today, of course. Nothing has happened or is likely to happen that is comparable to the fortuitous discovery of the Watergate break-in to discredit those promoting the violation of civil liberties. Whatever one thinks of the Bush administration's assaults on the rights of Americans, it is hard to imagine that it would engage in Nixon-style "dirty tricks," or that the president's men would stoop to burglaries to find information to discredit their opponents. Also, of course, the federal courts, while not a lost cause, have undergone major changes. Though probably still reliable where many freedom of expression issues are concerned, the courts cannot be counted upon for robust defense of civil liberties in a number of other areas where claims of national security are invoked. A crucial question for the courts will be to what extent they are ready to protect us against new forms of political surveillance made possible by advances in technology. Will they simply ratify the arrangements worked out in the complex interactions between corporate interests and government described by Reg Whitaker in his essay in which he refers to a new "security-industrial complex"? Or, can we expect them to safeguard privacy as they did two decades ago? Unfortunately, if President Bush has a chance to make new appointments to the U.S. Supreme Court, as seems likely, the situation is likely to worsen. As it is, the appointments he is making to the federal district and appellate judiciary with the advice and consent of a U.S. Senate now controlled by his party are shifting the balance further against the protection of civil liberty.

On the other hand, even in a difficult judicial environment, the availability of skilled advocacy can mitigate abuses. As in the Vietnam War era, there is no shortage today of lawyers to take on civil liberties assignments. The defense of rights is as well organized at present as at any time previously. Moreover, although advocates for those denied their rights face a challenging task in the courts, that is not their only forum. The organizations that sponsor legal representation in civil liberties cases are also participants in broader public debates.

As always, the decisive factor in determining how badly the country fares in the current period of assault on civil liberties will be its effectiveness in cowing Americans into going along. Will universities turn their backs on students from the Middle East or South Asia? Will Muslim women fear to go in the streets wearing head scarves? Will the government's renewed passion to collect dossiers on Americans make us fearful of associations that could arouse suspicions? Will we balk if an attempt is made—as some have advocated—to require national identity cards? Is unfettered discussion and debate of sensitive topics such as the war in

Afghanistan, the war against Iraq, and America's treatment of the Guantánamo detainees possible in the secondary schools?

The early signs are not consistent. It was distressing that only one United States senator, Russell Feingold of Wisconsin, voted against the USA PATRIOT Act that was passed in great haste just four weeks after the September 11 attacks and that, as Michael Tomasky notes in his essay, no major newspaper opposed it editorially before it was adopted. The act, as Nancy Chang's essay makes clear, is one of the most comprehensive assaults on civil liberties in American history. Similarly, it was sad to read in the *New York Times* in December 2001 that the publisher of the *Sacramento Bee* was booed off the stage as she tried to deliver a commencement address at California State University about the importance of preserving civil liberties even as the country wages the war against terrorism.[4] The widespread public support for racial profiling against Middle Easterners on national security grounds, discussed in Tanya Coke's closely reasoned and nuanced essay, is disturbing. On the other hand, it is reassuring to learn of the trend cited in Anthony Romero's essay here in which local communities are adopting resolutions calling for the protection of civil liberties. As the *Times* reported a year after its account of the ugly incident in Sacramento, "Nearly two dozen cities around the country have passed resolutions urging federal authorities to respect the civil rights of local citizens when fighting terrorism. Efforts to pass similar measures are under way in more than 60 other places."[5] Though lacking legal force, such resolutions nevertheless signify much about the public spirit. Some of the communities adopting the resolutions are predictable: college towns such as Ann Arbor and Berkeley. Others, such as Flagstaff, Arizona—the dateline at the head of the *Times* story—and Chicago, are a bit more unexpected. Also, it is heartening to note, as Romero points out, that the proposed Terrorism Information and Prevention System (TIPS) was dropped from the Homeland Security Act of 2002 in Congress at the insistence of conservative former House Majority Leader Richard Armey. If civil liberties are to be protected, those committed to constitutional rights on both sides of the political spectrum will have to be prominent in the struggle.

One argument that ought to carry weight with conservatives and liberals alike is made by Kenneth Roth in his essay: that the United States will be more effective in the fight against terrorism if it upholds human rights both at home and abroad. Farida Shaheed, writing from a Pakistani perspective, points out that this is particularly significant in circumstances where the United States is intent on dividing the world between those who are with America or with the terrorists. Noting that "U.S. foreign policy has far too often bolstered and protected dictators and authoritarian regimes," she argues that "forced to choose, people may elect to be counted amongst those against the U.S., irrespective of the character and qualities of those they end up being associated with." Needless to say, this would be disastrous for the United States. We have long proclaimed to the world that our country stands for freedom, and President Bush has portrayed the terrorists as archenemies of the values that America represents. Yet unreadiness to uphold the standards of freedom at home, or in dealing with those apprehended in the struggle against terrorism overseas, or in relations with other governments that claim they, too, are engaged in the war against terrorism, inspires cynicism and the increased resentment against the United States that Shaheed describes.

No one imagines that, by being more respectful of civil liberties domestically or more consistent in promoting human rights internationally, the United States will persuade would-be terrorists to undergo a change of heart and renounce violence. But the climate within which terrorists operate is important. As should be obvious, the struggle to defeat them or to thwart their intentions will be far more difficult if antagonism against the United States is pervasive in the societies in which they plan their attacks. As Roth notes, the international sympathy for the United States immediately following September 11 was quickly squandered. Yet it can be recaptured, but not by pursuing a course that makes the United States seem duplicitous when it asserts its commitment to freedom. The image of prisoners held incommunicado at Guantánamo beyond the reach of any court, perhaps forever—discussed in Michael Ratner's essay—clashes sharply with such assertions.

United States Attorney General John Ashcroft has portrayed the effort to protect civil liberties as support for the terrorists. He told the United States Senate Judiciary Committee that: "To those who scare peace-loving people with phantoms of lost liberty, my message is this: Your tactics only aid terrorists, for they erode our national unity and diminish our resolve. They give ammunition to America's enemies and pause to America's friends."[6] It is a statement that echoes similar comments uttered over the course of the past century by such officials as J. Edgar Hoover, Joseph McCarthy, and Richard Nixon who led earlier assaults on civil liberty. Over time, Americans rejected such efforts to smear the proponents of rights. "McCarthyism" is now a term of opprobrium used by those across the political spectrum to denote such assertions as these by Ashcroft that attempt to link those who uphold constitutional principles with those out to destroy the United States.

Subsequent to this December 2001 Senate Judiciary Committee testimony, the Bush administration seemed to exercise tighter control over Attorney General Ashcroft, the leading present-day embodiment of what historian Richard Hofstadter referred to as "the paranoid style in American politics."[7] Ashcroft's public appearances during 2002 were less frequent and more circumscribed. It appeared that the White House recognized his potential for becoming a political liability to the president. Yet the failure of the president to repudiate publicly such comments, the leeway given to Vice Admiral John Poindexter to develop his appalling Total Information Awareness program, and the many violations of constitutional principles that characterize the policies and practices of the Bush administration suggest that it considers that attacks on civil liberties will secure broad public support only if they are not accompanied by the rhetorical extremes to which Ashcroft would take them. As the Bush administration seems to have its ear close to the ground and has demonstrated its acute sensitivity to public opinion, its judgment on this matter is especially disturbing. It may be that the only way to alter its policies is to ensure that Americans are more outspoken in demanding that their rights, and the rights of others, should be respected. That is the purpose of this book. In bringing together essays by leading proponents of rights that tell what has happened since September 11 and what the country's current policies portend, we hope to give all those concerned about our civil liberties the information they need to turn up the volume.

PART I

TOOLS FOR A NEW KIND OF WAR

1. THE COURSE OF LEAST RESISTANCE: REPEATING HISTORY IN THE WAR ON TERRORISM

DAVID COLE[1]

The idea of progress is a powerful one. In 1958, in the midst of the Cold War, Yale Law Professor Ralph Brown published a comprehensive study of the federal government's loyalty and security program, and opened his discussion by claiming that censorship, "a traditional device for curbing dangerous speech, . . . is worthy of mention chiefly because, in the political sphere, the times have passed it by." [2] Similarly, as the Bush administration launches a war on terrorism in response to the horrific attacks of September 11, 2001, scholars, government officials, and pundits repeatedly remind us that the administration has avoided the mistakes of the past: it has not locked up people for merely speaking out against the war, as we did during World War I; it has not interned people solely for their racial identity, as the military did during World War II; and it has not punished people for membership in proscribed groups, as we did during the Cold War.[3]

But as a nation, we should be careful about too quickly congratulating ourselves. As Brown went on to argue in his book about the Cold War loyalty program, "the decline of conventional censorship has been more than offset by a new development, censorship of the speaker rather that the speech." [4] Similarly, while many argue that the nation has avoided the mistakes of the past in this crisis, it would be more accurate to say that the Bush administration has adapted the mistakes of the past, substituting new forms of political repression for old ones. As in the McCarthy era, the government has offset the decline of traditional forms of repression by developing new forms of repression. A historical comparison reveals not so much a *repudiation* as an *evolution* of political repression.

Periods of great fear inevitably produce calls for "preventive" law enforcement; we seek not merely to punish perpetrators after the fact, but to prevent the next disaster from occurring. Attorney General John Ashcroft has proudly proclaimed the "preventive" features of his campaign against terrorism.[5] The FBI, reportedly, is eagerly reprogramming its agents to act in a "preventive" mode. And especially when one has lived through an attack like that of September 11, the desire for prevention is eminently rational and sensible.

But preventive justice and criminal justice are not an easy mix. The criminal law's strong presumption of innocence until guilt is proven beyond a reasonable doubt, and related constitutional safeguards, make it an unwieldy mechanism for prevention. Prevention is not impossible to achieve through the criminal process. In theory, deterrence operates to prevent crimes, although when perpetrators are willing to sacrifice their own lives, deterrence is not very realistic. And the crimes of conspiracy and attempts—as in attempted murder or attempted assault—mean that we do not have to wait for the bomb to explode before arresting individuals and invoking criminal sanctions. Sheikh Omar Abdel Rahman is currently serving multiple life sentences for his role in planning to bomb the tunnels and bridges around Manhattan—the bombs never went off, yet the government was able to prosecute the planners on conspiracy charges and incarcerate them for the rest of their lives.[6]

Still, the criminal process undoubtedly makes preventive law enforcement more difficult. Accordingly, in times of fear, government often looks for ways to engage in prevention without being subject to the rigors of the criminal process. History reveals that three methods in particular are invoked in virtually every time of fear. The first involves a *substantive* expansion of the terms of responsibility, as government indulges in group-based presumptions of guilt or suspicion, targeting individuals not for what they do or have done, but based on predictions about what they might do, often based on the color of their skin, their nationality, or their political and religious associations. The second method is *procedural*—the government invokes administrative processes to effect control, precisely so that it can avoid the guarantees associated with the criminal process. The third method is *directional*—the government tends to target the most vulnerable among us first, only expanding measures of control to other groups later. In hindsight, these responses are virtually always considered mistakes. They invite excesses and abuses, as many innocents suffer without any evident gain in security. And, most significantly, they compromise our most basic principles: commitments to equal treatment, political freedoms, individualized justice, and the rule of law.

CRIMINALIZING OPPOSITION—SUBVERSIVE SPEECH, GUILT BY ASSOCIATION, AND MATERIAL SUPPORT

The most direct way to authorize preventive law enforcement is to sufficiently redefine liability broadly so that authorities can sweep up large numbers of people without having to prove that individuals have engaged in specific harmful conduct. In our history, this has been accomplished in two principal ways: by targeting people for what they say, before they act; and by targeting people for their associations. In today's war on terrorism, these ends are served by targeting people for "material support" to proscribed groups.

In the beginning, we targeted words. In World War I, Congress made it a crime to utter "any disloyal, profane, scurrilous, or abusive language . . . as regards the form of government of the United States, or the Constitution, or the flag."[7] Over 2,000 persons were prosecuted, essentially for speaking out against the war.[8] Eugene Debs, the Socialist Party candidate for president, was sentenced to ten years in prison for merely praising some draft resisters in a speech. The Supreme Court affirmed the sedition law's constitutionality in his and several other cases at war's end.[9] Few groups or individuals were even willing to criticize this state of affairs. When Harvard Law Professor Zechariah Chafee did so, the university, prompted behind the scenes by the Justice Department, brought him up on charges of being unfit to be a professor. He was acquitted, but only by the narrowest of margins, 6-5.[10]

By the Cold War, however, as Professor Brown reported, we had largely repudiated criminal censorship. In its place arose guilt by association. In the Cold War, "radicals" were generally punished not for their speech, but for their membership, affiliation, or sympathetic association with the Communist Party.[11] The infamous Alien Registration Act of 1940, better known as the Smith Act, made it a crime to be a member of the Communist Party, or to organize a group to advocate overthrow of the government. President Truman's executive order creating a loyalty program focused on association with Communists as the principal evidence of disloyalty. The government could claim that it was avoiding the mistakes of World War I censorship, even as it was effectively suppressing political dissent by targeting Communist associations and sweeping a wide range of progressive political groups under the "Communist" label. In November 1950, for example, the attorney general had nearly 200 groups on a list of Communist and other subversive organizations, affiliation with which could lead to being called before the House Un-American Activities Committee (HUAC), loss of a job, or being subjected to vigilante violence.[12]

From the government's point of view, both censorship and guilt by association facilitate preventive law enforcement. In World War I, antiwar protesters could be silenced and suppressed before their words were actually translated into any antiwar action. Similarly, if the government can target people for their associations, it can disrupt the organization of movements that might someday lead to criminal activity, without having to prove that particular individuals intended to further illegal activity of any kind. The Communist Party never actually sought to overthrow the United States government by force or violence, but because its rhetoric was interpreted as so advocating, the government was able to control and ultimately decimate the party, and many other organizations on the left accused of Communist sympathies, through the imposition of guilt by association.

Today, of course, the punishment of dissent during World War I and of political association during the Cold War are both seen as grave errors. The Supreme Court, to its credit—although largely after the fact—has developed constitutional doctrines that make these particular mistakes difficult to repeat. On the question of subversive speech, the Court first drew an important line, in 1957, between abstract advocacy, and advocacy of illegal conduct, thereby putting an end to prosecution of Communists for their group's advocacy.[13] In 1969, the Court further developed the test in *Brandenburg v. Ohio*,[14] requiring the government to show that an individual's speech was intended and likely to produce imminent illegal conduct, a threshold that for all practical purposes requires proof of an actual criminal conspiracy.

And in a series of cases beginning as the Cold War was winding down, the Supreme Court prohibited guilt by association, ultimately declaring it to be "alien to the traditions of a free society and to the First Amendment itself."[15] The prohibition has its genesis in *Scales v. United States*,[16] which effectively ended prosecutions for Communist Party membership under the 1940 Smith Act. As the Court stated:

> In our jurisprudence guilt is personal, and when the imposition of punishment on a status or on conduct can only be justified by reference to the relationship of that status or conduct to other concededly criminal activity . . . , that relationship must be sufficiently substantial to satisfy the concept of personal guilt in order to withstand attack under the Due Process Clause of the Fifth Amendment.[17]

The Court explained that groups often engage in both lawful and unlawful activities, and that both the Due Process Clause and the First Amendment forbid punishing individuals who support only a group's lawful ends.[18] Driven by these constitutional concerns, the Court interpreted the Smith Act to require proof that an individual specifically intended to further the unlawful ends of the Communist Party.

These constitutional bulwarks, however, have not ended the desire for preventive law enforcement in times of crisis. Government officials who are pressed by the public to prevent the next terrorist attack but are barred by history and the Constitution from targeting people for their speech or associations have sought to develop other ways of implementing preventive law enforcement.

The principal substantive innovation in today's war on terrorism has been the targeting of "material support" to terrorist groups. The targeting of "material support" is the linchpin of the government's current war on terrorism. With the enactment of the Antiterrorism and Effective Death Penalty Act of 1996 and the USA PATRIOT Act of 2001, federal law now makes it both a crime and a deportable offense to provide "material support" for terrorist organizations, and the United States has vigorously pushed other nations to enact similar laws of their own.[19] Virtually every criminal "terrorism" case that the government has filed since September 11 has included a charge that the defendant provided material support to a terrorist organization.[20] And the government has effectively closed down three of the largest Muslim charities in the United States based on broad allegations about potential terrorist financing.[21]

The reason the "material support" laws have proven so popular with federal prosecutors is that, like the speech and membership provisions of World War I and the Cold War, they do not require proof that an individual intended to further any terrorist activity. Under the criminal "material support" statute, for example, it is a crime to provide material support—defined expansively to include any "physical asset," "personnel," "training," or "expert advice and assistance"—to a designated terrorist organization, without regard to the purpose or effect of the actual support provided.[22] Under this law it would be a crime for a Quaker to send a book on Gandhi's theory of nonviolence—a "physical asset"—to the leader of a terrorist organization in hopes of persuading him to forego violence. Indeed, the Quaker would have no defense even if he could show that his efforts had *succeeded* in convincing the group to end its violent ways. Similarly, if this law had been on the books in the 1980s, the thousands of Americans who donated money to the African National Congress (ANC) for its lawful political struggle against apartheid would face lengthy prison terms, because during those years the ANC was designated as a terrorist organization by our State Department.

The "material support" law is a classic instance of guilt by association. It imposes liability regardless of an individual's own intentions or purposes, based solely on the individual's connection to others who have committed illegal acts.

Moreover, it imposes liability highly selectively. The law does not neutrally prohibit all material support to foreign organizations, or even all material support to foreign organizations that use violence. Rather, it selectively prohibits material support only to those groups that the secretary of state in his discretion chooses to designate. The statute gives the secretary of state a virtual blank check in designating groups; he can designate any foreign organization that has ever used or threatened to use a weapon against person or property, and whose activities are contrary to our foreign policy, national defense, or economic interests.[23] There are undoubtedly thousands of groups around the world that meet the first criterion, and therefore the second criterion does virtually all the work in selecting the handful that actually get designated.[24] Yet because the secretary of state defines our foreign policy, his determination that a group's activities undermine our foreign policy is literally unreviewable.[25]

The government contends that the "material support" statute does not violate the principle established in these cases because it does not criminalize membership per se, but only material support.[26] But the distinction is illusory. Groups literally cannot exist without the material support of their members and associates. If the right of association means only that one has the right to join organizations that no one can support, the right would be empty. Indeed, if this view were correct, all the laws that the Supreme Court faulted for imposing guilt by association could have been cured simply by hinging penalties not on the fact of membership, but on the payment of dues, the volunteering of one's services, or monetary contributions—the very evidence generally advanced to prove membership. Surely the Supreme Court did not insist so strongly on the prohibition on guilt by association for it to be vulnerable to such a formalistic end run. Indeed, the Court has said, "[t]he right to join together 'for the advancement of beliefs and ideas' . . . is diluted if it does not include the right to pool money through contributions, for funds are often essential if 'advocacy' is to be truly or optimally 'effective.'" [27]

Some argue that the guilt by association principle ought not apply to the provision of material support to terrorist groups because money is fungible, and therefore any support of a terrorist group will at a minimum have the indirect effect of furthering terrorism.[28] Money is, of course, fungible. But that is true of all money and all groups, domestic or foreign, political parties or militant terrorists. And for that reason, the argument proves far too much. If accepted, it would mean that legislatures could penalize material support of any organization that has ever engaged in any illegal activity, without regard to the purpose and use of any particular material support. The state could make it a crime to provide newspapers or social services to gang members, to pay dues to the Communist Party, or to make a donation to the Republican Party, on the grounds that each of these organizations has engaged and may engage in the future in illegal activity, and that giving them material support will free up resources that could then be used to further the group's illegal ends. The United States made just such a broad "freeing up" argument to the Supreme Court in 1967 in the Smith Act case of *United States v. Scales* as a reason for rejecting the specific intent test, without success.[29]

Finally, the freeing up argument overstates the extent to which donations to a group's lawful activities are in practice translated into illegal activities. Although advocates of targeting funding often seem to assume that it is so, most "terrorist organizations" do not exist for the *purpose* of engaging in terrorism. They generally have a political purpose or goal—ending apartheid in South Africa, or obtaining self-determination for the Palestinians in the Occupied Territories or the Kurds in Turkey—and use a variety of means to attain that end. Some of those means may be terrorist, and some may be perfectly lawful. But it simply does not follow that all organizations that use or threaten to use violence will turn any donation that supports their lawful activities into money for terrorism. No one would seriously suggest, for example, that the millions of dollars donated to the African National Congress in the 1980s to support its lawful antiapartheid work were simply transformed into bombs and weapons for its military wing.

Cutting off material support for terrorist *activity* is undoubtedly a worthy and appropriate goal. But that can be done without indulging in guilt by association. When the Antiterrorism and Effective Death Penalty Act of 1996 added the current "material support" provision, it was already a federal crime to provide material support to anyone—individual, group, or government—for the purpose of engaging in terrorist activity. Similarly, as the war on organized crime demonstrated, racketeering and money laundering laws authorize the government to criminalize "fronts" when used to support criminal activity.[30] If a charitable organization is used fraudulently to raise money for terrorism, those responsible for doing so can be prosecuted for supporting terrorist activity, money laundering, or racketeering without relying on guilt by association.

Al Qaeda itself may present a special case, for it does not appear to have many legal purposes at all. Unlike, say, the IRA, the ANC, or the PLO, groups with political agendas that used violent among many other means, Al Qaeda appears to do little more than plot, train for, and conduct terrorism. But if that is the case, we don't need "guilt by association." It ought to be a relatively simple matter to establish what the Supreme Court has said is constitutionally required: namely, that when an individual affirmatively supports Al Qaeda, he intends to support its terrorist ends, because it has few if any other ends.

The extent to which the "material support" statute imposes guilt by association is illustrated by two current cases. In the first, the Humanitarian Law Project (HLP) has sued the attorney general to challenge the constitutionality of the "material support" statute as it applies to the HLP's conduct.[31] The HLP, a long-standing human rights organization based in Los Angeles, had been providing training and other assistance to the Kurdistan Workers' Party (PKK) in Turkey before the material support statute was passed. In particular, they had been training the PKK in human rights advocacy and peace negotiation skills, in the hopes that they could support the Kurds, a much abused minority in Turkey, while encouraging peaceful resolution of the conflict there between Kurds and the Turkish government. Once the "material support" statute was passed and the secretary of state designated the PKK as a "terrorist organization," the HLP and its members would have faced lengthy prison terms had they continued their training.

In the second case, federal prosecutors have charged five young men from Lackawanna, New York, with providing material support to Al Qaeda by attending one of its training camps in Afghanistan.[32] To the government, the five are part of a "sleeper cell," ready and willing to engage in terrorism as soon as the call comes. To the defense, they are a group of misguided religious idealists who found themselves in the training camp but returned from the trip never intending to engage in any violent action of any kind. But under the material support statute's expansive reach, the government wins whichever version is true, because it need not prove that the individuals actually intended to undertake or even to further any terrorist act.

Like the sedition laws of World War I and the Communist membership provisions of the Cold War, the "material support" law allows the government to imprison individuals without proving that they ever sought to further a single act of terrorism. This makes preventive law enforcement much easier, because it frees the government to go after "suspicious" individuals even where it lacks sufficient evidence to charge them with actually perpetrating or even planning a terrorist crime. But as the Cold War so vividly demonstrated, for the same reasons it makes it virtually inevitable that the government will target and penalize many wholly innocent persons.

SUBSTITUTING ADMINISTRATIVE PROCESS
FOR CRIMINAL JUSTICE

Expanding the substantive scope of criminal prohibitions is only the most obvious way to effect preventive law enforcement. Far more insidious, and far more common, is the exploitation of administrative procedures in order to avoid the rigors of the criminal process altogether. Administrative processes have proven highly effective in chilling activities of which the government disapproves, in large part because they can be applied without affording their targets the rights of a criminal defendant. But because the rights that attach to the criminal process are for the most part intended to ensure that we do not imprison innocent people, to resort to administrative processes carries with it the potential for widespread abuse.

ENEMY ALIENS

The paradigmatic example of an administrative mechanism for preventive law enforcement is the Enemy Alien Act of 1798.[33] This law—enacted along with, but unlike, the Alien and Sedition Acts, which are still with us more than two hundred years later—authorizes the president during a declared war to lock up, deport, or otherwise restrict the liberty of any person over fourteen years of age who is a citizen of the country with which we are at war. It requires no individualized finding of culpability, dangerousness, or even suspicion. Because the law provides for deportation and detention without any process at all, it gives the government substantial power to engage in preventive detention. Detainees need not be provided hearings or lawyers, and the government need not prove anything beyond the fact of enemy citizenship. It represents the ultimate form of administrative control over potential threats.

Presidents have invoked the Enemy Alien Act during the War of 1812, World War I, and World War II to regulate the activities of all "enemy aliens," and to detain and deport some of them.[34] It hasn't been invoked since World War II, because it requires a formally declared war. The dangers of such authority were dramatically illustrated in World War II, when the government extended the rationale of the Enemy Alien Act to U.S. citizens of Japanese descent, and ultimately interned some 110,000 persons solely for their Japanese descent, regardless of citizenship, and without any individualized hearings or trials.[35] We have since formally apologized for that action and paid reparations to survivors. But as illustrated below, the temptation to use administrative processes for preventive detention continues.

In times of crisis that do not reach the level of a formally declared war, the government cannot invoke the Enemy Alien Act. Instead, it has relied on another form of administrative detention, also targeted at foreign nationals: immigration law. The most infamous example of the use of immigration authority for preventive detention purposes was the Palmer raids during the winter of 1919–20.[36] The raids were sparked by a series of terrorist bombings in the United States, including mail bombs addressed to Supreme Court Justice Oliver Wendell Holmes, Jr., and numerous other government officials, and a bomb that went off outside Attorney General A. Mitchell Palmer's home in Washington, D.C. The government responded by mounting a mass, nationwide roundup of foreign nationals, not for their role in the bombings, but for their political associations with the Communist Party, the Communist Labor Party, and the Union of Russian Workers. The raids focused on foreign nationals because, lacking a peacetime sedition law, the immigration laws were the only authorization for targeting individuals for their politics; as Acting Secretary of Labor Louis F. Post observed, "the force of the delirium turned in the direction of a deportation crusade with the spontaneity of water flowing along the course of least resistance."[37]

The government ultimately arrested somewhere between 4,000 and 10,000 individuals, many without any warrant, conducted illegal searches and seizures in doing so, detained many in overcrowded and unsanitary conditions, and interrogated them without counsel.[38] The last tactic, which was seen as critical to obtaining the admissions of political association that would then form the basis for deportation, was made possible by a last-minute rule change, effected one business day before most of the arrests took place, which delayed the alien's right to a lawyer (and to confrontation with the evidence upon which the arrest was based) until the case had "proceeded sufficiently in the development of the facts to protect the Government's interests."[39] Ultimately, more than 500 foreign nationals were deported for their political associations; no one was charged with the bombings.[40] Louis Post, who oversaw most of the deportations, and who courageously cancelled several thousand deportations, later noted that "In no instance was it shown that the offending aliens had been connected in any way with bomb-throwing or bomb-placing or bomb-making. No explosives were found, nor any firearms except four pistols personally owned and some guns in the 'property room' of an amateur theatrical group."[41] Nonetheless, there was a limit to what

Post could do; as he complained, the laws forced him "to order deportations of many aliens whom not even a lynching mob with the least remnant of righteous spirit would have deported from a frontier town." [42]

Immigration proceedings are preferable to criminal proceedings from the government's standpoint for a number of reasons. The Supreme Court has long ruled that deportation is not punishment, and that therefore the rights that attach to criminal trials do not automatically extend to deportation hearings. [43] Aliens in deportation proceedings have no constitutional right to a lawyer, and have a statutory right to a lawyer only if they can find and afford one. [44] They have no constitutional right to a presumption of innocence beyond a reasonable doubt, to a jury trial, or to confront witnesses. The Supreme Court has insisted that aliens living in the United States have a due process right to a fundamentally fair hearing, but the contours of that right have not been very clearly articulated. [45] The rules of evidence do not apply, and the government asserts the right not only to rely on hearsay, but also to deport, detain, and deny immigration benefits to noncitizens on the basis of secret evidence presented in camera and ex parte to the judge, so that neither the noncitizen nor his attorney have any right to confront or rebut it. [46]

ADMINISTRATIVE DETENTION

Immigration detention and enemy alien detention are, of course, by definition limited to foreign nationals. Given the judgment of history on the Japanese internment of World War II, one might think that the notion of extending administrative detention to citizens would have been quickly abandoned. But preventive detention is a powerful and tempting tool for law enforcement. In 1948, in the immediate aftermath of the war, the Justice Department secretly and unilaterally adopted a program, known as "the Portfolio," for interning "dangerous persons" during an emergency declared by the president. [47] Under this program, which applied to citizens and foreigners alike, the president would suspend the writ of habeas corpus, and mass arrests would be made under a single "master warrant" issued by the attorney general. The single warrant would also authorize widespread searches and seizures. Those detained would have no right to seek judicial review, but would be limited to an administrative hearing before specially constituted boards of review not bound by the rules of evidence. Their only appeal would be to the president. [48]

In September 1950, as part of an omnibus Cold War Internal Security Act,

Congress independently created its own detention plan.[49] This statute, which remained on the books until 1971, also authorized emergency detention of dangerous persons, albeit under slightly more restrictive terms than "the Portfolio" provided. As Richard Longaker described Congress's detention program:

> [It authorized] detention without arraignment before a judge, the possibility of bail, or a jury trial. . . . Apprehension and incarceration were based on an administrative finding of prospective guilt in which non-judicial officers utilized a standard of reasonable belief, not probable cause, that a suspect should be held. . . . The authority of the Attorney General was uncontrolled. He could issue warrants at will and withhold evidence selectively, including the identity of the detainee's accusers, thus bypassing the right of a defendant to confront and cross-examine his accusers.[50]

In 1952, Congress authorized and funded six detention centers for suspected subversives in Arizona, California, Florida, Oklahoma, and Pennsylvania.[51]

No one was ever detained under "the Portfolio" or the Internal Security Act programs, because no emergency arose. But the very fact that, for more than a generation after World War II, the federal government planned to detain "dangerous" citizens and foreigners wholly outside the criminal process illustrates how far the notion of substituting administrative process for criminal justice had spread. In addition, the mere existence of these authorities justified the FBI in undertaking widespread political spying for decades, not for any criminal law purpose but simply so that it could maintain lists of suspicious persons to be detained in a future emergency. At its peak in 1954, the FBI's "Security Index" of people to be detained numbered 26,174 persons.[52] In the 1960s, the FBI's list included civil rights and antiwar movement activists, including Dr. Martin Luther King, Jr.[53] In the late 1960s, the FBI instructed its agents to investigate for potential inclusion on the lists Students for a Democratic Society, other "pro-Communist New Left–type groups," and even all persons living in "communes."[54]

It was not until 1971 that Congress repealed the emergency detention provisions and enacted a provision stating that "no citizen shall be imprisoned or otherwise detained by the United States except pursuant to an Act of Congress."[55] Yet the FBI continued to maintain lists of subversive persons until at least 1975, when it revealed the existence of the list to a congressional committee investigating intelligence abuses and abandoned the list.[56]

LOYALTY REVIEW BOARDS AND CONGRESSIONAL INVESTIGATIONS

The vast majority of those harmed by the excesses of the Cold War were targeted not through the criminal process, and not, as above, through administrative

detention, but by two other "administrative" mechanisms: loyalty review procedures and congressional committee hearings. In both settings the government
was able to inflict a kind of guilt by association while denying its targets critical
criminal protections, such as the presumption of innocence and the right to confront the evidence against one.

Loyalty review processes were applied to every federal employee, and to many
nonfederal employees through copycat programs implemented by state and local
governments and private employers seeking to do business with the government.
Here, the ostensible targets were disloyal employees. But disloyal was for all practical purposes reduced to "Communist," and one could lose one's job not only for
membership in the party, but even for "sympathetic association" with suspected
Communists.[57] As in the immigration process, the government successfully argued that it need not provide the rights that would apply in a criminal process, because denying someone a job did not constitute punishment. Indeed, the courts
generally went even further, holding that because employees did not have a liberty
or property interest in retaining their jobs, they were not even entitled to due
process.[58]

Consider, for example, the case of Dorothy Bailey. In 1949, Bailey, a personnel
trainer with the Civil Service Commission in Washington, D.C., lost her job. A
"loyalty review board" had found that there were "reasonable grounds" to suspect
that she was disloyal to the United States. Ms. Bailey never learned the source of
those grounds. She was told only in the most general terms that she was suspected
of having been associated with the Communist Party, the American League for
Peace and Democracy, and the Washington Committee for Democratic Action,
all organizations that had been designated by the attorney general as suspect. At
her hearing, she was represented by three of the nation's leading lawyers: Thurman Arnold, Abe Fortas, and Paul Porter. All had had high government posts, and
Fortas would become a Supreme Court justice. They put on a vigorous defense.
Bailey admitted past membership in the American League, but denied all other
charges. She asserted her loyalty, offered seventy supporting affidavits and four
witnesses to attest to her character, and submitted to all questioning by the hearing examiners. No witness offered evidence against her. As the court of appeals for
the D.C. Circuit later summarized it, "the record consists entirely of evidence in
her favor."[59] Yet the hearing board ruled against her, on the basis of undisclosed
secret FBI reports relaying accusations by unidentified informants. The court of
appeals found nothing illegal or unconstitutional about the process, reasoning

that since she had no right to a government job, she was entitled to no due process in her termination.[60] The Supreme Court affirmed the decision by an equally divided vote. In the end, the best her high-powered lawyers could do was hire her as their office manager.[61]

Dorothy Bailey did not stand alone. Thousands of public and private employees were fired as disloyal during the Cold War. And Professor Ralph Brown estimated that because loyalty review programs were adopted by federal, state, and local governments, and often extended to private employers who sought to do business with the government as well, as many as one in five working Americans were subjected to the loyalty review process in one way or another—by having to take an oath, fill out loyalty disclosure forms, or be subjected to full-scale loyalty review hearings.[62]

The infamous House Un-American Activities Committee's hearings provided yet another way to effect preventive law enforcement without having to provide the safeguards of the criminal process. HUAC subpoenaed thousands of witnesses to testify about their alleged Communist sympathies and to name names.[63] It operated on the theory of guilt by association, which, as Alan Barth described it, went in two directions: "An organization was contaminated by any 'subversive' individual who entered it. And, conversely, every member of the group became 'subversive' by the mere fact of membership."[64] Again, because a congressional hearing is not a criminal trial, and does not take any liberty or property interest from the witness, the government did not need to provide witnesses with the rights they would be entitled to even in a civil trial. Witnesses were frequently confronted with accusations from unidentified informants, and denied any opportunity to confront their accusers or to present their own witnesses. Yet the exposure of such proceedings often led private employers to fire those who appeared there, and therefore, HUAC's chilling effect was substantial.[65]

All of the administrative measures for prevention described above are now seen as having spawned grave and widespread abuses of civil liberties. The Palmer raids were condemned contemporaneously by a blue-ribbon panel of lawyers, including Roscoe Pound, the dean of the Harvard Law School, and Professor Felix Frankfurter,[66] and history has only confirmed their judgment. History has also decried the Japanese internment, the loyalty review boards, and HUAC. These events have taught us the not altogether surprising lesson that when the government is allowed to avoid the safeguards designed to protect the innocent, many innocents suffer. Yet today, our government has once again invoked similar administrative shortcuts in its pursuit of preventive justice.

ADMINISTRATIVE PROCESS IN TODAY'S WAR ON TERRORISM

Perhaps the most dramatic instance of the resort to administrative process in today's war on terrorism is the indefinite and virtually incommunicado detention of foreign nationals and U.S. citizens alike as "enemy combatants."[67] The Enemy Alien Act does not apply, by its terms, to the war on terrorism, because we have not declared war on any nation; there are no citizens of Al Qaeda. But the government has nonetheless sought to invoke military authority to bypass the criminal process, asserting unreviewable authority to detain in military custody any person whom the president identifies as an "enemy combatant." Under this authority, the government maintains, it may detain foreign nationals and U.S. citizens alike indefinitely, without a hearing, without access to a lawyer, and without judicial review, simply on the president's say-so. The military has used that authority to hold more than 600 foreign nationals at a military base on Guantánamo Bay, Cuba, and to hold two U.S. citizens—Yaser Hamdi and Jose Padilla—in naval brigs here in the United States.[68]

The government has also dusted off the Palmer raids tactics, exploiting immigration authority to arrest and detain large numbers of persons without any showing that they are connected to terrorism. Shortly after September 11, 2001, Attorney General John Ashcroft announced he would use every law on the books, including immigration law, to target "suspected terrorists" and get them off the street and into detention, in order to prevent future acts of terrorism.[69] As of this writing, the Justice Department refuses to say how many persons have been detained in this preventive detention campaign, but a conservative estimate would number the detentions at approximately 2,000 as of December 2002, fifteen months after the campaign began.[70]

As will be described in other essays in this book, the bulk of the detainees have been held and tried in secret on immigration charges[71] and have been denied essential legal protections; this has been possible only because the immigration process is administrative in nature. And just as the Palmer raids turned up no actual bombers and the McCarthy era tactics identified few spies or saboteurs, so the government's yield of actual terrorists from its current preventive detention program has been staggeringly small. According to Ashcroft, all of the detainees were "suspected terrorists." Yet of the approximately 2,000 persons so detained, only four have been charged with any crime relating to terrorism.[72] None has been charged with involvement in the crimes of September 11. And the vast majority of the detained individuals not only have not been charged with a terrorist crime, but have been affirmatively cleared of any criminal charges by the FBI. As noted above, the government's policy has been to release and/or deport detainees only after the FBI has cleared them. Yet as of October 2002, Attorney General Ashcroft announced that the Immigration and Naturalization Service (INS) had deported 431 detainees, and in July 2002 the Justice Department reported that only eighty-one individuals remained in immigration detention.[73] Thus, by the government's own account, virtually none of those detained as "suspected terrorists" turned out to be terrorists.

Still a third administrative mechanism for "preventive" law enforcement in today's war on terrorism, and an increasingly important one, is the freezing of assets linked to terrorists under the authority of the International Emergency Economic Powers Act (IEEPA).[74] This law, designed to authorize the president to impose economic sanctions on foreign countries in emergency situations, has in recent years been adapted by executive order to the task of cutting off funds for designated "terrorist" groups and individuals. President Bill Clinton initiated the extension of IEEPA to embargo political organizations rather than nations in 1995, when he declared a national emergency with respect to the Middle East peace process, and designated twelve organizations—ten Palestinian organizations opposed to the peace process and two Jewish extremist groups—as Specially Designated Terrorists (SDTs).[75] The executive order also permits the secretary of state to designate additional SDTs if they are found to be "owned or controlled by, or to act for or on behalf of" an entity designated by the president.[76] Shortly after the attacks of September 11, President Bush issued an executive order imposing similar financial restrictions on Specially Designated Global Terrorists, or SDGTs, and also authorizing the secretary of the treasury to add to the list anyone who "assist[s] in, sponsor[s], or provide[s] . . . support for," or is "otherwise associated" with, an SDGT.[77]

Designation results in the immediate blocking of all of the entity's assets, and makes it a crime to engage in any economic transactions with the designated entity. Yet the statute specifies no substantive criteria for identifying which entities shall be designated, leaving that critical decision entirely to the president's discretion. The statute affords those designated by the president no opportunity to contest the designation. And those groups and individuals subsequently identified by the secretary of treasury need only be found to be in some way "associated" with the initially designated entities.

This executive transformation of IEEPA essentially resurrects the Cold War practice of generating official lists of proscribed organizations. As in the Cold War, the lists are created in secret, using secret criteria. The president may selectively blacklist disfavored political groups without substantive standards or procedural safeguards, and the secretary of the treasury may extend those sanctions to individuals based solely on "associations," without regard to the character of the associations.

Moreover, a little-noticed provision in the USA PATRIOT Act, enacted in October 2001, amended IEEPA to authorize the Treasury Department to freeze all assets of any organization merely on the assertion that it is under investigation for potentially violating IEEPA, and further authorizes the government to defend that freeze order if challenged in court on the basis of secret evidence, presented to the court in camera and ex parte.[78] Under the investigative provision, the Treasury Department after September 11 froze the assets of two Muslim charities, Global Relief Foundation, Inc., and Benevolence International Foundation. In both cases, it did so without a hearing, and without any specific charges; the groups were told only that they were "under investigation." And in both cases, the government searched the organizations' offices and seized all of their records, books, and computers. Both organizations have since been listed as Specially Designated Terrorists and Specially Designated Global Terrorists, again based not on allegations of criminal conduct, but on their alleged associations with other groups designated by the president.

Global Relief Foundation challenged on multiple constitutional grounds both the search and seizure of its offices and the freezing of its assets. In June 2002, a district court rejected all of the challenges. It found that the freezing order did not constitute punishment, and that therefore protections associated with the criminal process were not applicable. And it upheld both the search and seizure and the freezing order on the basis of secret information submitted ex parte and in camera to the court, and not provided to Global Relief Foundation or its lawyers.[79] The third designated charity, The Holy Land Foundation, also challenged its designation, and in August 2002 a district court also rejected its challenges, using similar reasoning.[80]

TARGETING THE MOST VULNERABLE

In today's war on terrorism, as in past times of fear, many argue that the balance between liberty and security needs to be recalibrated. Our increased sense of vulnerability makes the polity place greater value on being secure, and in theory warrants reductions in liberty if and where they might in fact make us more secure. At the same time, we want to be both secure and free. So when government officials adopt security measures, they often construct them in ways that do not require the majority to forfeit their own rights and liberties, but instead selectively sacrifice the liberties of a vulnerable minority for the purported security interests of the majority. In this way, the majority need not confront the hard question of which of their own liberties they are willing to sacrifice in the name of security.[81]

Evidence of this trend is consistent throughout American history. In the Alien and Sedition Acts of 1789, for example, Congress subjected all persons, citizens included, to criminal sanctions for speech that criticized the government, but at the same time it subjected foreign nationals to the even more draconian punishment of detention simply on the president's say-so, without regard even to subversive speech. At the turn of the century, when an American citizen with a foreign-sounding last name assassinated President William McKinley, Congress responded by making foreign nationals excludable for advocating anarchism, while rejecting similar proposals to criminalize citizens' anarchist speech. In 1919, as described above, the government responded to a series of terrorist bombings by carrying out a mass roundup of foreign nationals based on their political associations. At the time, Attorney General Palmer and President Woodrow Wilson asked Congress for a peacetime sedition law that would allow the government to target radical citizens as well, but Congress repeatedly balked. And in the Cold War, many of the government's first anti-Communist initiatives were targeted at foreign nationals, using the immigration law. The federal government tried for twenty years, for example, to deport Australian labor organizer Harry Bridges for his alleged ties to the Communist Party.

The same trend can be seen in today's war on terrorism, which has largely targeted foreign nationals, especially those of Arab or Muslim identity. Most of those incarcerated in Attorney General Ashcroft's campaign of preventive detention have been foreign nationals; the government has explicitly exploited immigration law to do to foreign nationals what it could not do to citizens. The worst provisions of the USA PATRIOT Act are those directed at noncitizens, resurrecting ideological exclusion, authorizing deportation for innocent associational activity, and giving the attorney general unilateral authority to detain foreigners simply by signing a slip of paper. President Bush's military tribunal order was limited to noncitizens, even though there was no legal impediment to applying it to citizens as well. And foreign nationals from Arab countries have been subjected to discriminatory interviews, registration requirements, and deportation policies, simply because they are from Arab countries.

History also suggests that measures initially targeted at noncitizens will not be limited to noncitizens, but will simply serve as the first step in ever-increasing assertions of government authority. In the Japanese internment of World War II, the anti-Communist fervor of the Cold War, the COINTELPRO and other domestic spying initiatives of the 1960s and 1970s, and in today's war on terrorism as well, the line between noncitizen and citizen has been crossed, and citizens, too, have been subjected to the measures of political repression initially targeted at foreign nationals.

CONCLUSION

Those who claim that the United States has avoided the mistakes of the past in its current war on terrorism have failed to look beneath the surface. Although it is true that the scope of the wrongs done during World War I, World War II, or the Cold War has not yet been equalled, we are only in the initial stages of this war, a war that is likely to be as permanent as the war on drugs or the war on crime. And when one looks not at the quantity but at the quality of the Bush administration's response, it is clear that it has resurrected the very techniques that invited abuses in the past—namely, expanding the substantive definitions of wrongdoing to encompass otherwise innocent political activity, reliance on group identity rather than individual conduct for suspicion, the adoption of administrative measures to avoid the safeguards associated with the criminal process, and targeting the most vulnerable among us.

If the past is any guide, these mistakes will come at substantial cost to the targeted communities, as many innocent persons are swept up in the government's preventive net. But the mistakes may also undermine the war on terrorism itself. Professor Oren Gross has argued that the greatest threat that terrorists pose to a democratic state is not to its physical survival, but to what one might call the survival of principle.[82] He argues that what the terrorists want is to provoke the state into (over)reacting in ways that violate its own principles, and thereby undermine the state's legitimacy and create sympathy for those allied with the terrorists.[83] If that is the case, it is all the more critical that we learn from our past mistakes and adhere to the principles that distinguish us from terrorists as we respond to the threats they pose. Otherwise we might well be playing right into Al Qaeda's hands.

At this writing, a little more than one year after the United States suffered one of the worst attacks on civilian life in modern history, one might expect to find widespread sympathy and support for the United States around the world. But instead, reports of anti-Americanism suggest that hostility to the United States has grown substantially since September 11.[84] No doubt much of this resentment is attributable to President Bush's unilateral foreign policy. But it is likely also due at least in part to the fact that as the president insists that the nation is fighting a war for freedom—Operation Enduring Freedom—his administration has denied those basic freedoms to many persons treated as suspicious for little more than the fact that they are foreign nationals of Arab origin and/or Muslim faith. When the nation sacrifices the very principles that allegedly distinguish us from the terrorists, and particularly when we do so in ways that appear to discriminate, we forfeit much of the legitimacy of our efforts, and that in turn may undermine security even further.

It is certainly understandable that in times of fear, the citizenry defers to authority and closes its eyes to the wrongs perpetrated in the name of their protection. But history reveals that blind faith is wholly unwarranted. Now more than ever it is critical that we remain true to our principles. There is nothing wrong with prevention when it consists of protecting potential targets, or in stepping up security at borders, airports, and other vulnerable points. But when prevention translates into the punishment of individuals for what the government suspects they may do, rather than for what they have done, it cannot be justified in a democratic society. The safeguards of the criminal process are there for a reason, and whenever a democratic government imposes punishment or deprives persons of their liberty without adhering to these principles, it does more harm than good. The success of the war on terrorism, and indeed of our democratic experiment, requires us to reconsider the shortcuts that we have too swiftly and predictably adopted. Thus far, it seems that all we have learned from history is how to mask the repetition, not how to avoid the mistakes.

2. HOW DEMOCRACY DIES:
THE WAR ON OUR CIVIL LIBERTIES

NANCY CHANG[1]

Since the tragic events of September 11, 2001, our democracy has come under threat from a growing arsenal of antiterrorism measures that cede to the executive branch of government the unprecedented, and largely unchecked, powers to conduct its operations in secret, to repress peaceful political dissent, to conduct surveillance even where it has no basis for suspecting criminal activity, to compile, analyze, and share sensitive personal information, and to detain both citizens and noncitizens for investigatory purposes.

Perhaps the best known of these measures are the USA PATRIOT Act,[2] which President George W. Bush signed into law on October 26, 2001, only six weeks after the September 11 attacks, and the Homeland Security Act,[3] which did not take effect until November 25, 2002, fourteen months after the attacks. Both laws were passed by a Congress under such intense pressure to act decisively in the face of crisis that it abdicated its responsibility to ensure that civil liberties infringements are justified by compelling national security interests.

The USA PATRIOT Act, the Orwellian acronym for the Uniting and Strengthening America by Providing Appropriate Tools Required to Intercept and Obstruct Terrorism Act of 2001, comprises a long-standing executive branch wish list of aggressive law enforcement tools.[4] Congress passed this legislation with breathtaking speed at a moment when it was exiled from its anthrax-contaminated offices and the nation was on edge from Attorney General John Ashcroft's predictions of more terrorist attacks.

In a last-minute exercise of brute force, the Republican House leadership jettisoned an antiterrorism bill that raised far fewer civil liberties concerns and that had been unanimously approved by the House Judiciary Committee, and replaced it with the 342-page USA PATRIOT Act.[5] Legislators complained that they did not have time to obtain, much less read, a copy of the act before it was brought to a vote.[6] To make matters worse, this complex and far-reaching legislation was accompanied by little public hearing or debate and by no conference or committee report. In the House, the act passed by the wide margin of 356 to 66. In the

Senate, Senator Russell Feingold cast the lone opposition vote. As he did so, he warned the nation, "Preserving our freedom is one of the main reasons that we are now engaged in this new war on terrorism. We will lose that war without firing a shot if we sacrifice the liberties of the American people."[7]

The Homeland Security Act, which had languished in the Senate for months over the issue of civil service protections, was rushed into law in just two weeks by the lame duck Congress that returned from the November 2002 midterm election. While on the campaign trail, President Bush had lashed out against the Democratic legislators who had blocked his ambitious plan to consolidate twenty-two federal agencies and 170,000 government employees into a single Department of Homeland Security.[8] To the surprise of the pundits, the midterm election narrowly handed a Republican president control of both houses of Congress for the first time since 1952. The Democratic congressional leadership, interpreting the election results as a "mandate" for the president's agenda, swiftly submitted to his demand for this monumental legislation. The act, which weighs in at 484 pages, passed the House by a vote of 299 to 121, and the Senate by a vote of 90 to 9.[9]

The Homeland Security Act exempts from public disclosure under the Freedom of Information Act (FOIA) "critical infrastructure information" that has been voluntarily submitted by a private entity to a covered federal agency when the submission includes a written statement asserting an expectation of privacy.[10] The exemption applies even when the information describes a danger to the public health and safety. In addition, the Homeland Security Act exempts advisory groups established and maintained by the Department of Homeland Security to assess law enforcement technology needs from the public meeting, disclosure, and reporting requirements of the Federal Advisory Committee Act.[11] At the same time that the act limits public access to government information, it promotes government access to sensitive personal information and the sharing of that information among federal, state, and local authorities, making for a dangerous combination.[12] Furthermore, the act is riddled with provisions that protect special interest groups with no pretense of enhancing security.[13]

The USA PATRIOT Act and the Homeland Security Act are accompanied by a plethora of other antiterrorism measures.[14] When Congress has failed to grant the Bush administration the powers it has desired, the administration has not hesitated to issue executive orders, interim agency rules, and policy guidelines granting those powers to itself. These executive measures—which, to the extent that they have been disclosed to the public, have been implemented without prior public notice and comment—are responsible for some of the most egregious civil liberties violations in the history of our nation. Through a web of Justice Department interim rules and policy guidelines, more than a thousand Muslim nationals of Arab and South Asian countries with no terrorist ties have been targeted for arrest based on their religion and ethnicity and detained for weeks and months under punishing conditions.[15] Notably, not one of these men has been charged with a terrorist crime relating to the September 11 attacks. And through sheer executive fiat, the Department of Defense has asserted the authority to hold United States citizens it has unilaterally designated as "enemy combatants" indefinitely, in military brigs, without providing them access to counsel or any of the other constitutional protections that must be afforded those charged with crimes.[16]

The cumulative impact of these legislative and executive antiterrorism measures has been a radical shift of power to the executive branch that has placed the Bill of Rights—with its First Amendment guarantees of freedom of speech, political association, religion, and the press, its Fourth Amendment protections against unreasonable searches and seizures, its Fifth Amendment guarantees of due process and equal protection, and its Sixth Amendment guarantees to criminal defendants of a fair and speedy trial and the right to confront adverse witnesses—in danger of becoming yet another casualty of the "war on terrorism." And as our personal freedoms have given way, so, too, have the democratic values that define us as a nation: the rule of law, government accountability, public participation in decision making, and tolerance for the expression of unpopular views.

The suspension of civil liberties during times of crisis has been a constant refrain in our nation's history. The past century saw the Red Scare of 1919 with its arrests and deportations of anarchists and Socialists, the internment of more than 110,000 individuals of Japanese ancestry following the bombing of Pearl Harbor, the Communist witch hunts of the Cold War, and J. Edgar Hoover's concerted efforts to disrupt and destroy the civil rights movement and other peaceful political movements during his extended tenure as FBI director. But with the easing of tensions, each of these chapters came to a close. And with a deep sense of shame and regret, the nation every time has vowed not to repeat its mistakes of succumbing to prejudice and hysteria.

Unlike past crises, the terrorist threat that confronts us today, along with the measures that have been erected in response, seem destined to become permanent features of American life. Although Congress has scheduled a dozen or so of the most instrusive surveillance provisions in Title II of the USA PATRIOT Act to "sunset," or expire, on December 31, 2005, any foreign intelligence investigations that began before that date, and any investigations of offenses that began or occurred before that date, will not sunset.[17] Given the fact that the Bush administration vigorously lobbied Congress to make all of the USA PATRIOT Act's provisions permanent, in the event that President Bush is reelected in 2004, he can be expected to exert intense pressure on Congress to reenact the provisions that are scheduled to sunset.

SECRET GOVERNMENT

The framers of our Constitution understood from firsthand experience that "[t]he accumulation of all power, legislative, executive, and judicial in the same hands . . . may justly be pronounced the very definition of tyranny."[18] But rather than heed this caution, the Bush administration has exacerbated the dangers inherent to wartime enhancements of executive power by shielding their exercise from public and press scrutiny.[19]

A month after the September 11 attacks, contempt for openness in government and the informed citizenry that it fosters became the standard operating procedure throughout the federal bureaucracy. In a memorandum dated October 12, 2001, Attorney General Ashcroft encouraged agency heads to withhold information requested under the Freedom of Information Act[20] (FOIA) by promising them: "When you carefully consider FOIA requests and decide to withhold records, in whole or in part, you can be assured that the Department of Justice will defend your decisions unless they lack a sound legal basis or present an unwarranted risk of adverse impact on the ability of other agencies to protect other important records."[21]

In keeping with the spirit of Ashcroft's memorandum, the Department of Justice (DOJ) has steadfastly refused to comply with a FOIA request filed in October 2001 by public interest organizations for the identities of the many hundreds of noncitizens who were arrested and detained by the Immigration and Naturalization Service (INS) in the wake of September 11. In support of its claimed need for secrecy, the DOJ argued, "bits and pieces of information that may appear innocuous in isolation, when assimilated with other information . . . will allow [terrorists] to build a picture of the [government's] investigation and to thwart the government's attempts to investigate and prevent terrorism."[22] But in an opinion issued in August 2002, Judge Gladys Kessler of the federal district court in Washington, D.C., rejected the government's grandiose "mosaic theory," as it "would permit the Government to lump together all information related to an ongoing government investigation and withhold it solely because innocuous parts of data might be pieced together by terrorist groups." Judge Kessler ordered the government to release the INS detainees' names under supervised conditions, declaring that "secret arrests are 'a concept odious to a democratic society,' and profoundly antithetical to the bedrock values that characterize a free and open one such as ours."[23] But the DOJ would not be swayed by Judge Kessler's admonition. Rather than release the detainees' names, it obtained a stay of her order and appealed her decision.[24]

In a similar vein, the DOJ's chief immigration judge, Michael Creppy, issued a blanket directive on September 21, 2002, barring the press and the public—including family members and friends—from attending the immigration hearings of noncitizens designated by the government as "special interest detainees," and barring his staff from disclosing any information about their cases to the public. A set of lawsuits challenging the Creppy directive on First Amendment grounds have elicited widely divergent views from two federal appellate courts on the role of the judiciary in our constitutional democracy when it is confronted with complaints of executive branch overreaching during a time of crisis. The Court of Appeals for the Sixth Circuit in Cincinnati ruled in August 2002 that the press has a First Amendment right of access to the hearings encompassed by the Creppy directive unless the immigration judge assigned to hear the matter makes an individualized determination that secrecy is required to protect national security. Judge Damon Keith, the author of the Sixth Circuit opinion, eloquently proclaimed: "Democracies die behind closed doors. . . . When government begins closing doors, it selectively controls information rightfully belonging to the people. Selective information is misinformation."[25] In marked contrast, in November 2002 the Court of Appeals for the Third Circuit in Philadelphia declined the opportunity "to conduct a judicial inquiry into the credibility of [the] security concerns" proffered by the government in support of the Creppy directive.[26] The Third Circuit recognized that the government's concerns were merely speculative; it nevertheless concluded that "national security is an area where courts have traditionally extended great deference to Executive expertise."[27] This split of opinion between two appellate courts makes it likely that the Supreme Court will soon rule on the constitutionality of the Creppy directive.

At the same time that the Bush administration has sought to hide its actions from public and press scrutiny, it has also sought—in direct defiance of the separation of powers doctrine on which our Constitution was constructed—to avoid oversight by its co-equal branches of government, Congress and the judiciary. Since September 11, the administration has routinely refused to cooperate with Congressional requests for information on its anti-terrorism activities. On October 5, 2001, President Bush ordered his cabinet to limit briefings on classified and sensitive national security matters to eight Congressional leaders. This move prompted Senator John Kerry, a member of a Senate subcommittee responsible for overseeing intelligence matters, to complain, "We just cannot do our job as U.S. senators without updated briefings and relevant information."[28]

And during the summer and fall of 2002, as the one-year anniversary of the USA PATRIOT Act approached, the DOJ repeatedly stonewalled a June 13, 2002, request from the House Judiciary Committee for information regarding the DOJ's implementation of the act. The chair of the committee, Representative James Sensenbrenner, was so angered by the DOJ's lack of cooperation that he threatened to "blow a fuse" and break with tradition by subpoenaing Attorney General Ashcroft to appear before the committee if the requested information was not provided promptly.[29]

The Bush administration has also routinely sought to escape judicial review of its actions. On October 31, 2001, the DOJ issued an interim rule authorizing it to monitor communications between federal prison inmates and their counsel without court approval.[30] This rule has had the effect of chilling communications between inmates and their counsel that are essential to a well-prepared defense. In addition, in the summer of 2002, the administration began to advance the extraordinary position that the courts lack jurisdiction to consider the propriety of the military's designation of United States citizens as "enemy combatants." And tucked away in the USA PATRIOT Act is a provision that will allow the government to obtain a stay of any civil lawsuit challenging the government's willful violation of specified provisions of the act where "the court determines that civil discovery will adversely affect the ability of the Government to conduct a related investigation or the prosecution of a related criminal case."[31]

In 1829, James Madison observed that "[t]he essence of Government is power;

and power, lodged as it must be in human hands, will ever be liable to abuse."[32] Several recent disclosures confirm the obvious: Madison's observation holds true today. In August 2002, the Foreign Intelligence Surveillance Court, which hears behind closed doors the government's applications for warrants under the Foreign Intelligence Surveillance Act (FISA) of 1978 to conduct clandestine wiretaps and physical searches, released its first public opinion in its twenty-four-year history.[33] This opinion disclosed that the government had "confess[ed] error in some 75 FISA applications related to major terrorist attacks directed against the United States, including misstatements and omissions of material facts."[34] In addition, an FBI memo that surfaced in October 2002 documented at least ten incidents in the first quarter of 2001 alone in which FBI agents had illegally videotaped suspects, intercepted e-mail messages after court permission had expired, and recorded the telephone conversations of an innocent person who had taken over the cell phone number of a terrorism suspect.[35]

These disturbing revelations of law enforcement malfeasance represent only a small fraction of the government wrongdoing that takes place under the cover of secrecy afforded by criminal investigations and foreign intelligence operations. Inevitably, covert government actions nurture and conceal official misconduct as they breed public distrust. The framers of our Constitution wisely recognized that secrecy in government runs contrary to our democratic norms, and that its best antidotes are transparency and public accountability in government operations.

THE SUPPRESSION OF POLITICAL DISSENT

When the security of the nation is endangered, our commitment to the rights guaranteed by the First Amendment is at its most essential. Such moments force decisions on matters of consequence that demand a vigorous and informed public debate and a full airing of diverse viewpoints. Yet, ironically, it is precisely at such moments that First Amendment values are most likely to be abandoned in favor of authoritarian rule.

The present moment is no exception. As discussed above, the Bush administration, in its effort to maintain a free hand in the exercise of its new powers, has drastically restricted public access to government information by broadly claiming a wartime need for secrecy. In addition, the administration has raised the costs of political activism. Section 802 of the USA PATRIOT Act defines a new federal crime of "domestic terrorism" that stretches beyond recognition the common understanding of the term "terrorism" as premeditated and politically motivated violence targeted against a civilian population.[36] The new crime's ambit extends to any "acts dangerous to human life that are a violation of the criminal laws . . . [if they] . . . appear to be intended . . . to influence the policy of a government by intimidation or coercion . . . [and] . . . occur primarily within the territorial jurisdiction of the United States."[37]

Social movements in the United States have had a time-honored tradition of engaging in civil disobedience—acts of moral conscience in which individuals publicly and deliberately violate a law to protest government policy. Our nation's independence from Great Britain, the abolition of slavery, suffrage for women, the passage of federal civil rights legislation, and the withdrawal of American troops from Vietnam were achieved not by academic debate but by vibrant mass movements that took their messages to the streets. But the vagaries in the USA PATRIOT Act's definition of domestic terrorism grant the government license to lump nonviolent civil disobedience in the tradition of Henry David Thoreau, Gandhi, and Martin Luther King, Jr., together with the Al Qaeda network's ruthless murders of innocent civilians under the single banner of terrorism. As a result, protest activities that, prior to the enactment of the USA PATRIOT Act, would have ended in a simple charge of disorderly conduct under a local ordinance might now lead to federal prosecution and conviction for domestic terrorism. We know from experience that when prosecutors are entrusted with the discretion to file inflated charges for minor crimes, politically motivated prosecutions and the exertion of undue pressure on activists to turn state's witness and to serve as government informants are not far behind.

As the result of guidelines issued by Attorney General Ashcroft on May 29, 2002, that ease FBI restrictions on domestic intelligence gathering, activists who engage in civil disobedience—as well as the entirely law-abiding individuals and organizations with whom they associate—are now more likely than ever to become the targets of government monitoring, surveillance, and infiltration of their political activities.[38] The Ashcroft guidelines broadly permit the FBI to open a full investigation of a political group based on no more than a "reasonable indication" that the group has engaged in or aims to engage in a specified set of crimes that includes the new crime of domestic terrorism.[39] In addition, the FBI may consider a group's advocacy of nonimminent violence, which the Supreme Court held in *Brandenburg v. Ohio* to be speech that is protected by the First Amendment except when it is directed to inciting imminent lawless action and is likely to produce such action, in deciding whether to initiate a full investigation.[40] Once a group is under investigation, the guidelines authorize the FBI to collect information on its members, finances, geographical dimensions, and past and future activities and goals, and to use confidential agents and employ such investigative techniques as undercover activities and operations, electronic surveillance, searches and seizures, and the opening of mail.[41]

Furthermore, the Ashcroft guidelines permit the FBI to take affirmative steps in furtherance of a terrorism investigation. These steps include conducting surveillance at political meetings, mosques, and other places and events open to the public, considering illegally obtained information voluntarily provided from private sources, drawing on nonprofit and commercial data-mining services, and visiting Web sites and Internet electronic bulletin boards and chat rooms.[42]

The increase in government secrecy, the creation of a sweeping federal crime of domestic terrorism, and the relaxation of FBI domestic surveillance guidelines are ominous developments. They join the Antiterrorism and Effective Death Penalty Act of 1996, which makes it a crime to provide any material support to groups designated by the secretary of state as foreign terrorist organizations, even when the support takes the form of humanitarian aid or activities that promote a peaceful resolution of conflict.[43] Taken as a whole, these measures portend a return of the politically motivated spying on peaceful social movements that marked J. Edgar Hoover's troubled tenure as FBI director, and they will cause many who disagree with government policies to engage in self-censorship.

BIG BROTHER IS WATCHING

Alarmingly, antiterrorism measures threaten the privacy of all Americans, and not just those who have come to the attention of the government because of their political associations or dissident viewpoints, or because they are suspected of criminal or terrorist activity. As will be explained below in Reg Whitaker's essay, advances in surveillance technology have exponentially increased the government's ability to monitor our everyday activities.

As remarkable as these technologies may be, they are but a prelude to the technologies of the future. The Total Information Awareness (TIA) Project, which is currently under development by the Department of Defense, has as its stated objective the collection of information on our activities—including our credit card purchases, banking and financial transactions, airline and hotel reservations, car rentals, tollbooth records, medical appointments, school activities, real estate transfers, marriages and divorces, births and deaths, and telephone and Internet usage—in "a virtual, centralized grand database" that can be instantaneously searched to identify individuals who fit profiles of suspicious activity.[44] It seems appropriate that TIA's shadowy objectives have been entrusted to Vice Admiral John Poindexter, President Ronald Reagan's infamous national security adviser who used proceeds from the sale of arms to Iran to fund the Contra rebels in Nicaragua. Unless Congress acts swiftly to constrain the executive branch from unleashing Big Brother technologies like TIA, our privacy will soon be a relic of the past.

At the same time, the USA PATRIOT Act and the Homeland Security Act increase the executive branch's authority to conduct surveillance. Many of these powers are conferred by Title II of the USA PATRIOT Act, which authorizes the executive branch to evade the probable cause requirement of the Fourth Amendment, obtain sensitive personal records and other tangible things from third parties, conduct "sneak-and-peek searches" of homes and offices, track e-mail and Internet usage, and conduct nationwide roving wiretaps. In addition, Titles III and V of the act expand the government's access to banking, financial, educational, and business records.[45]

Information concerning the government's use of its surveillance powers has been extremely difficult to come by. Court orders demanding the production of third-party records routinely include "gag orders" threatening their recipients with being held in contempt of court in the event that they disclose the order's existence or its contents. In addition, in keeping with the Bush administration's penchant for secrecy, the DOJ has classified its responses to the House Judiciary Committee's June 13, 2002, request for information concerning the DOJ's implementation of the USA PATRIOT Act.[46]

But DOJ reports, which by statute are required to be released to the public, reveal that the number of warrants for wiretaps and searches in 2001 was nearly as high as the number in 2000.[47] Significantly, warrants issued under the USA PATRIOT Act pack a far stronger punch than did their predecessors. For starters, the act widens the scope of the government's surveillance powers by permitting warrants to cover multiple individuals and multiple locations, and by extending the reach of warrants beyond the geographical limits of the issuing court. The act also lengthens the life span of many warrants. In addition, with advances in information technology, a single request for computerized records can easily result in the production of electronic information concerning millions of people.[48]

Also, the government has found it easier to obtain third-party records through agency-issued subpoenas and requests for voluntary cooperation, neither of which are subject to mandatory reporting requirements.[49] Law enforcement agencies have easily pressured companies to turn over customer records without a court order "with the idea that it is unpatriotic if the companies insist too much on [legalities]."[50]

Perhaps the most controversial of the enhanced surveillance provisions in Title II of the USA PATRIOT Act is Section 218. This section amends the Foreign Intelligence Surveillance Act, which authorizes the government to conduct surreptitious wiretaps and physical searches for foreign intelligence surveillance purposes. FISA permits the government to sidestep the Fourth Amendment's requirement that it demonstrate probable cause to believe that the target of a search or seizure is engaged in criminal conduct.[51] Courts may issue FISA surveillance orders as long as the government has probable cause to believe that the target of surveillance is a foreign power or its agent.

Before FISA was amended by Section 218, foreign intelligence surveillance orders were available only when the gathering of foreign intelligence information was "the purpose" of the surveillance.[52] With the introduction of Section 218, however, FISA orders can be issued as long as the gathering of foreign intelligence information is "a significant purpose" of the surveillance.[53]

In November 2002, Section 218 became the subject of the only ruling that the Foreign Intelligence Surveillance Court of Review has issued in its entire twenty-four-year history.[54] This highly secretive court, which consists of three sitting Court of Appeals judges handpicked by Chief Justice William Rehnquist, considers appeals from decisions by the equally secretive, but far more prolific, Foreign Intelligence Surveillance Court. Both courts employ an entirely one-sided process in which the government's arguments are heard behind closed doors. Its decisions authorizing FISA surveillance are never revealed to the public except in those rare situations when the government seeks to use the information it has gathered as evidence in a criminal prosecution.

The Court of Review reversed the lower court's first decision to deny a government application for a foreign intelligence surveillance order after an otherwise unbroken string of some 14,000 approvals.[55] The Court of Review interpreted Section 218 as permitting the government to obtain a FISA surveillance order even when the government's primary purpose is criminal investigation, as long as the government "entertains a realistic option of dealing with [the target of investigation] other than through criminal prosecution."[56] This ruling has torn down the procedural wall separating law enforcement operations from foreign intelligence operations that, for two decades, had served the vital function of ensuring that the government did not use its intrusive FISA surveillance powers as an end run around the Fourth Amendment's requirement of probable cause when the government's primary interest in the target of surveillance was to prosecute him.

Attorney General Ashcroft hailed the Court of Review's ruling as "a giant step forward" that "revolutionizes [the DOJ's] ability to investigate terrorists and prosecute terrorist acts."[57] And he wasted no time in assigning teams of lawyers and FBI agents to take advantage of the government's expanded ability to conduct surveillance under the lax FISA rules.[58] Because the DOJ has no reason to seek Supreme Court review of the Court of Review's ruling in its favor and no other party has standing to do so at this time, the Court of Review's ruling will control FISA surveillance for the foreseeable future. While Section 218 is one of the small handful of provisions in Title II of the USA PATRIOT Act that is scheduled to sunset on December 31, 2005, foreign intelligence investigations that began before that date and investigations of offenses that began or occurred before that date are exempt from the sunset provision.

Another controversial provision of Title II of the USA PATRIOT Act is Section 215, which, like Section 218, extends FISA's reach.[59] Under Section 215, the director of the FBI and any of his designees with the rank of assistant special agent in charge or higher may apply for a court order requiring the production of "any tangible things (including books, records, papers, documents, and other items)" upon a written statement that these items are being sought for an investigation "to protect against international terrorism or clandestine intelligence activities."[60] A judge presented with an application under Section 215 is required to enter an order if he finds that the application meets these simple requirements.[61]

Section 215 repealed a restriction that had required the government to specify in its applications for court orders that there were "specific and articulable facts giving reason to believe that the person to whom the records pertain is a foreign power or an agent of a foreign power."[62] While Section 215 bars investigations of United States citizens and lawful permanent residents "solely upon the basis of activities protected by the First Amendment to the Constitution," it does nothing to bar investigations based on any other activities that tie such persons, no matter how tangentially, to an international terrorism investigation.[63]

In addition, Section 215 repealed a restriction that had confined its reach to "records" in the possession of "a common carrier, public accommodation facility, physical storage facility, or vehicle rental facility."[64] Section 215 extends to the far larger universe of all "tangible things" and places no limits on the parties from whom the production of tangible things may be compelled.[65] Even records held by libraries and booksellers identifying the books read by their patrons are fair game under Section 215.

While the DOJ has adamantly refused to provide the public with information on its use of Section 215, a survey conducted by the University of Illinois's Library Research Center of 906 public libraries reveals that, in the year since the September 11 attacks, federal and local law enforcement agencies visited at least 545 libraries to request information on patrons.[66] Approximately 10 percent of the requests that were reported referenced Section 215 of the USA PATRIOT Act.[67] And the vast majority of the requests that were reported sought a library's voluntary cooperation.[68] Section 215 is scheduled to sunset on December 31, 2005.

Yet another controversial provision of Title II of the USA PATRIOT Act is Section 213, which authorizes federal agents to conduct "sneak-and-peek searches," or covert searches of a person's home or office without providing the person with notice of the execution of the search warrant until after the search is completed. Section 213 allows notice of the execution of the search warrant to be delayed upon a showing of "reasonable cause to believe that providing immediate notification . . . may have an adverse result," and it fails to set a time limit by which notice must be provided.[69] In addition, Section 213 allows notice of the execution of a warrant for the seizure of items to be delayed upon a showing of a "reasonable necessity."

"Sneak-and-peek searches" contravene the common law principle that law enforcement agents must "knock and announce" their arrival before they conduct a search—a requirement that forms an essential part of the Fourth Amendment's reasonableness requirement.[70] When notice of a search is delayed, the subject of the search will be foreclosed from pointing out mistakes and deficiencies in the warrant to the officer executing the warrant and from timely contesting the search in court. In addition, he will be prevented from monitoring whether the search was conducted in accordance with the warrant's requirements and from tracking the whereabouts of property removed from his premises pursuant to the warrant. Section 213 is not scheduled to sunset. Moreover, Section 213 is not limited to terrorism investigations, but extends to all criminal investigations.

In addition, our privacy has been placed in jeopardy by antiterrorism measures that vastly expand the government's power to compile and analyze our personal information and to disseminate it widely. The Department of Homeland Security's Directorate for Information Analysis and Infrastructure Protection, which is charged with amassing law enforcement, intelligence, and other information toward the goal of identifying terrorist threats against the United States, has the potential to become a full-fledged domestic intelligence operation.[71] Its information sources include the FBI, the CIA, and the National Security Administration, in addition to other federal agencies, state and local governments, and the private sector.[72] In the course of fulfilling its responsibilities, the directorate is authorized to employ data-mining techniques to sift through databases and pinpoint individuals who meet patterns of conduct that are associated with suspicious activity.[73] Unfortunately, such techniques tend to rely on ethnic profiling and, as a result, subject many innocent individuals to unwanted and unnecessary attention from law enforcement. The chasing of bad leads wastes scarce government resources and antagonizes the very communities whose cooperation and trust we will need to fight terrorism effectively.

Notwithstanding the fact that the Homeland Security Act requires the Department of Homeland Security to maintain a Privacy Office, it is difficult to imagine what this office could possibly do to ensure that the rich stores of personal information at the department's disposal are not leaked out to the public.[74] The number of individuals who will have access to this information will be large, making unauthorized disclosures inevitable. Foremost among the department's priorities is the sharing of information among governmental agencies at the federal, state, and local levels.[75] In addition, the department has the authority to share information with the private sector.[76]

The FBI's Project Lookout fiasco demonstrates how easily sensitive information can leak to the public and wreak havoc on the lives of innocent persons. In the days following the September 11 attacks, the FBI shared, on a confidential basis, with a select group of car rental companies, airlines, trucking companies, security guard companies, and banks, a watch list that it had compiled of several hundred people it wanted to question in connection with its terrorism investigation.[77] Many of the people on the list were believed to have information useful to the investigation and, once they were interviewed and cleared of suspicion, they were removed from the list. Nevertheless, outdated versions of the list containing the names of innocent persons have been in wide circulation, both in the United States and abroad, and the FBI has conceded that it has lost control over the list's distribution.[78] Private businesses have used the list for a range of unintended purposes, from screening out prospective customers and job applicants, to running security checks on employees.[79] Those whose names appear on the list, as well as those whose names have been confused with names on the list, have been treated with hostility and suspicion and have suffered a wide range of irreparable harms.

INVESTIGATORY DETENTIONS

On October 25, 2001, the day before the USA PATRIOT Act went into effect, Attorney General Ashcroft outlined his bone-chilling plan to detain individuals while investigating them for terrorist connections. In a speech delivered to the nation's mayors, he announced:

> It has been and will be the policy of this Department of Justice to use . . . aggressive arrest and detention tactics in the war on terror. Let the terrorists among us be warned: If you overstay your visa—even by one day—we will arrest you. If you violate a local law, you will be put in jail and kept in custody as long as possible. We will use every available statute. We will seek every prosecutorial advantage. We will use all our weapons within the law and under the Constitution to protect life and enhance security for America.[80]

Ashcroft has certainly fulfilled his pledge to unleash the full power of the state against terrorism suspects. In the course of doing so, however, he has inflicted tremendous harm on more than a thousand innocent detainees and the families and communities from which they were uprooted. As detailed in Kate Martin's essay below, many of these detainees were held virtually incommunicado for extended periods—with little or no access to families, attorneys, consular officials, and public interest organizations concerned for their welfare—as they endured severe physical and psychological abuse at the hands of prison guards and inmates.

Ashcroft has also inflicted tremendous violence on the Bill of Rights. With the cooperation of the INS and local law enforcement agencies, the FBI has rounded up in excess of a thousand men, nearly all of whom have been Muslim nationals of Arab and South Asian countries.[81] The manner in which many in this group were arrested leaves little doubt that they were discriminated against on the basis of their ethnicity and religion rather than on individualized suspicion of criminal or terrorist activity. Some of the detainees came to the attention of law enforcement agents in the course of traffic stops and other chance encounters, while others were reported to law enforcement authorities by neighbors and acquaintances who were quick to mistake men with a Middle Eastern appearance for terrorists.[82] The DOJ subsequently acknowledged that "most of the people arrested in the weeks after the terror attacks have since been cleared of any connection to the attacks or terror groups."[83] And with the exception of Zacarias Moussaoui, who was arrested prior to the attacks, not one of them has been charged with, much less convicted of, a terrorist crime relating to the September 11 attacks.

With rare exceptions, the government has lacked the probable cause required by the Fourth Amendment to hold these detainees on criminal charges, and it has been forced to devise alternative rationales for holding them. To expand its power to detain noncitizens on the pretext of minor immigration violations, the INS has issued an astounding collection of executive measures. One such measure is an interim rule issued by the DOJ on September 17, 2001, that authorizes the INS to hold noncitizens in custody without filing charges against them for forty-eight hours or, in the event of an "emergency or other extraordinary circumstance," for an uncapped "reasonable period of time."[84] By permitting the INS to hold noncitizens without charge indefinitely without evidence that they are engaged in suspicious activity, this rule contravenes Section 412 of the USA PATRIOT Act, which limits to seven days the time the attorney general may hold noncitizens without charge when he has certified that he has "reasonable grounds to believe" that they are engaged in terrorist activities.[85] The custody rule also contravenes the Due Process Clause, which protects "all persons" in the United States, including deportable noncitizens, from indefinite detention for violation of the immigration laws,[86] and the Fourth Amendment, which requires the government to formally charge criminal suspects and provide them with a probable cause hearing before a neutral magistrate within forty-eight hours of arrest.[87]

In addition, since September 11, the INS has instituted a policy of detaining noncitizens who have final orders of deportation, and are ready to leave the country, and has held them for additional months while the FBI clears them of terrorist ties.[88] In April 2002, a group of detainees challenged this policy in a class-action lawsuit filed in the federal district court in Brooklyn, New York.[89] The suit, *Turkmen v. Ashcroft,* accuses the government of turning the Constitution on its head by presuming the detainees guilty until the FBI's investigation has proved them innocent.

Nor has the INS confined its roundups to those arrested in the days and months immediately following September 11. Pursuant to the PATRIOT Act, the agency has put in place a National Security Entry-Exit Registration System (NSEERS),[90] which currently requires male nonresident aliens over the age of sixteen who are from one of twenty countries—nineteen of which are Arab or Muslim—to report to the INS within a tight deadline to be photographed, finger-printed, and interrogated. Those who fail to comply with these requirements place themselves at risk of being deported. On December 16, 2002, the INS office in Los Angeles arrested around 400 noncitizens, most of whom were Iranian and Iraqi exiles with minor visa violations, who had voluntarily come to that office to comply with the "special registration" requirements of NSEERS. But the NSEERS program offers a false sense of security. Terrorists are not likely to report them-selves to the INS. And the arbitrary and unwarranted mass arrests that took place in Los Angeles will discourage many nonresident aliens who are seeking lawful residency in the United States from reporting. Moreover, as Tanya Coke explores in her essay below, national origin profiles are a poor substitute for individualized suspicion of wrongdoing, and their use erodes public confidence in law enforce-ment while it contravenes the Constitution's Equal Protection Clause.

The DOJ has also pursued a policy of detaining individuals as "material witnesses" to grand jury proceedings since September 11, without disclosing their names or whereabouts.[91] A 1984 statute provides that the government may, under tightly prescribed conditions, keep individuals whose testimony is material to a "criminal proceeding" in detention until such time as their testi-mony is secured.[92] Based on its expansive reading of this statute, the government has locked up terrorism suspects when it lacks probable cause to hold them on criminal charges and cannot detain them for immigration violations because they are either United States citizens or noncitizens whose immigration status is lawful.

In a decision issued in April 2002, Judge Shira Scheindlin of the federal district court in Manhattan concluded that the material witness statute "carve[s] out a carefully limited exception to the general rule that an individual's liberty may not be encroached upon unless there is probable cause to believe that he or she has committed a crime."[93] Accordingly, she construed the statute narrowly and ruled that it did not apply to grand jury proceedings.[94] In July 2002, however, Judge Michael Mukasey, who sits on the same court as Judge Scheindlin, reached a dif-ferent conclusion. Finding that "[t]he duty to disclose knowledge of crime rests upon all citizens" and "is so vital that one known to be innocent may be detained, in the absence of bail, as a material witness," Judge Mukasey concluded that the application of the material witness statute to grand jury proceedings did not run afoul of the Fourth Amendment.[95] The government has appealed Judge Scheindlin's ruling to the Second Circuit Court of Appeals.[96]

The DOJ's defiance of constitutional norms in rounding up and detaining more than a thousand innocent Muslims and Arabs has been breathtaking. But the Department of Defense (DOD), too, has claimed extraordinary powers to detain individuals caught up in its investigation outside the criminal justice system under the war powers that are reserved to the executive branch by Article II of the Constitution. The DOD is holding at least two American citizens—Yasser Hamdi, who was captured in Afghanistan, and Jose Padilla, who was arrested at a Chicago airport in June 2002—in incommunicado detention as "enemy combatants." The government has argued that these men may be held in military custody without being charged and without being provided access to counsel or the outside world until the end of hostilities. The government has also argued that courts lack jurisdiction to conduct a factual inquiry on whether its designation of the men as enemy combatants is supported by the evidence.[97] A December 2002 opinion of Judge Mukasey in *Padilla v. Rumsfeld* and a January 2003 opinion of the Fourth Circuit Court of Appeals in *Hamdi v. Rumsfeld* largely accepted the DOD's arguments, though Judge Mukasey's opinion would grant Padilla limited access to counsel.[98] One day after the Fourth Circuit issued its ruling, the government filed a motion asking Judge Mukasey to vacate the portion of his opinion granting access to counsel on the grounds that such access would interfere with its interrogation of Padilla.[99]

FIGHTING FOR OUR CIVIL LIBERTIES

Our hopes for protecting our civil liberties from executive and congressional overreaching rest in part with the federal judiciary, whose members are insulated from the political fray by their lifetime tenure. While the judiciary tends to defer to the political branches of government on national security matters, it is unlikely to abdicate entirely its traditional role under our Constitution as a check on executive and congressional abuses of power. The Supreme Court has yet to issue a ruling on the merits of any of the more than one dozen lawsuits that challenge post–September 11 antiterrorism measures. A number of lower court judges, however, have scrutinized the national security justifications proffered by the government for these measures and have found them to be wanting.[100]

Unfortunately, with the return of the Senate to Republican control, such displays of judicial independence are likely to be less frequent. Proclaiming the 2002 midterm election a victory for his political agenda, President Bush announced plans to pack the courts with conservative jurists cut in the mold of Supreme Court Justices Antonin Scalia and Clarence Thomas, starting with eighty vacancies on the federal bench.[101]

Ultimately, the fight to defend the Bill of Rights must be won in the political arena. Already, organized efforts by grassroots movements have produced important victories. With the support of Representative Dick Armey, civil libertarians successfully pressured Congress into adding two provisions to the Homeland Security Act: one that prohibits the activities of Operation TIPS, a surveillance program proposed by the Bush administration to promote citizen spying, and one that bars the development of a national identification system.[102] In addition, by the end of 2002, close to two dozen cities had passed resolutions urging that the fight against terrorism not be conducted at the expense of civil liberties, and many more cities were poised to pass similar resolutions.[103] Although these resolutions do not bind the federal government, they send a powerful message to Congress and the president that Americans will not stand by idly while democracy dies behind closed doors.

3. AFTER 9/11: A SURVEILLANCE STATE?

REG WHITAKER

In the aftermath of the terrorist attacks of September 11 2001, the government of the United States has armed itself with new and extended intrusive powers of surveillance over electronic and other forms of communications, and over both public and private databases, both inside and outside the United States. This enhanced surveillance capacity obviously has significant implications for civil liberties and constitutional rights. Supporters of tough security measures dismiss or downplay concerns about the misuse of intrusive surveillance. Critics, who interestingly appear on both the left and the libertarian right of the political spectrum, sometimes tend to be equally dismissive about the need for enhanced surveillance, seeing it more as a pretext than a context for state inroads into the autonomy of civil society. In assessing the use, or misuse, of these new powers, it is important to situate the government's actions in relation to the specific challenges posed by 9/11.

HOW 9/11 DIFFERS FROM PAST CRISES

September 11 marked a new phase in America's international relations, a "war on terrorism," as proclaimed by President George W. Bush. Like the two most recent historical antecedents of this war, World War II and the Cold War, the war on terrorism has ramifications for domestic politics, especially for civil liberties and minority communities. The forcible relocation of the Japanese-American population from the West Coast in 1942 and the excesses of McCarthyism in the early Cold War offer notorious examples of how the search for security can generate injustices. More worrisome is the potential long-term damage to the fabric of civil liberties that may persist long after the emergency passes.

The historical cycle in which violent threats generate the expansion of arbitrary and intrusive powers of government is being repeated. Once again, the constitutional protection of rights is being dismissed, sometimes from the highest offices in the land, as an inconvenient impediment to safety. And yet again a panicked public is encouraged to trust in action over deliberation, results over due process.

In certain ways, the present crisis bears even more dangerous potential than earlier wartime emergencies. The terrorist threat is a qualitatively different one from the threats posed in previous emergencies. As Washington struggles to find the most effective response to a new and, in many ways, unprecedented, threat, the very novelty and uncertainty of the situation tempts government to reach for new powers while heedlessly discarding old forms and conventions. Phrases such as "thinking outside the box," and "connecting the dots," may be appropriate for policy makers moving in unfamiliar and uncharted territory, but they can be dangerous guides for encroaching upon constitutional rights.

During the Cold War, after an initial period of high anxiety, even paranoia, in the late 1940s and early 1950s, East-West relations settled into an uneasy but durable modus vivendi. This allowed space for the reemergence of vigorous dissent and debate in American society after the McCarthy-era repression. It is difficult to imagine any such form of persistent quasi-stability developing in the war on terrorism, and thus the prolongation of a climate of repression seems more likely—especially if further acts of terrorism with high casualty rates are successfully carried out on American soil.

There is much that is novel about the organizational structure and operating methods of the terrorists. Al Qaeda is a contemporary product of globalization: flexible, adaptable, diversified, transnational, de-centered, a network of networks. Like transnational organized criminal networks, Al Qaeda operates very much as a paradigm "new economy" corporation. As part of the "dark side" of globalization, terrorist networks assiduously cover their global tracks, evading the scrutiny of law enforcement and security agencies rooted in national jurisdictions. As borderless enterprises, they utilize the most up-to-date technologies of communication that facilitate the instantaneous transfer of ideas, capital, and financial resources across national borders and continents. The intelligence and security failure of 9/11 clearly signaled the need for agencies like the CIA and the FBI to modify, if not reinvent, new and more appropriate intelligence-gathering mechanisms. Just as clearly, emphasis on new information technologies and more intrusive and extensive surveillance was inevitable.

DISAPPEARING BOUNDARIES BETWEEN
PUBLIC AND PRIVATE

In response to the borderless terrorist threat, the U.S. government has tried to dissolve, or at least to weaken, a series of boundaries that had previously been erected to demarcate spheres that were believed best kept as distinct from one another as possible. Foremost among these are national jurisdictions, demarcating national sovereignties. The Bush administration has actively and aggressively moved in numerous ways since 9/11 to extend its surveillance and its coercive reach across national boundaries, to the extent that many of its allies have become increasingly resentful.

Of more immediate concern within the United States is the concerted drive to break down various firewalls that been maintained in the past to protect the private sector from government control. The tracking of those directly responsible for 9/11—the biggest single criminal investigation in history—pointed to private sector databases (involving, for instance, credit card, telephone, and air miles data) for essential clues in reconstructing the trail of the terrorists. Money laundering investigations, involving the reporting and automatic surveillance of a very wide range of private financial transactions, had already begun in relation to criminal activities, but since 9/11 have been greatly stepped up to track terrorist financing trails.

The appropriation of private sector data has proved useful in the investigation of terrorist trails. More subtly, a series of internal firewalls that had separated data banks held within government itself have also fallen under attack. The most notable of these is the distinction between counterintelligence investigations of foreign espionage operations in America and criminal law enforcement, with lower standards with regard to legal safeguards for the targets of surveillance in the former. In general, faced with borderless threats, government has sought to gain access to a seamless web of information on citizens and noncitizens drawing on all potential sources.

This thrust has plausible arguments in its favor, rooted in the specific nature of the terrorist threat, with a ready constituency among a fearful public. It is also important to point to the inherent dangers. There are very good reasons why the various firewalls have been erected around data collected for different purposes by different agents, and why restraints have been imposed historically on government access to personal information. The right to privacy has long been viewed as a fundamental element of a free society, but one that is increasingly in question in the era of new information technologies.

The technological capacity to achieve a global surveillance regime has been known for some time. The last two decades of the twentieth century witnessed remarkable developments in surveillance technologies. The daily lives of people everywhere, but particularly in the most industrially developed nations, are now tracked and recorded. Electronic eyes scan the globe, from closed-circuit cameras on the ground, to satellites gathering sophisticated imagery from space. Voice communication is scooped out of the sky by electronic listening posts. Sophisticated search engines troll through e-mail traffic and Internet use. The global positioning system based on satellites can yield the precise location of targeted individuals anywhere on earth. Unique biometric identifiers, such as palm- and fingerprints, iris patterns, facial and gait characteristics, and DNA sequencing, are increasingly being recorded and stored in data banks—and demanded to gain access to services or pass security screenings. Virtually every daily economic transaction adds to an electronic trail that can potentially construct a unique social profile of an individual. Detailed medical records and significant genetic information can profile individuals in a remarkably intimate manner.

What is particularly alarming to privacy advocates is that the new information technologies, based on the universal language of digitization, permit the seamless transfer and matching of information gathered by different agents for different purposes. Databases can "talk" to one another, and in so doing, create the capacity for decentralized "dataveillance," a surveillance society in which the "files" exist in no central location, and are perhaps under no central control, but which in their totality may exercise far more intrusive capacity to gaze into the private space of individuals than the Big Brother surveillance state of the past. Yet these same technologies offer numerous benefits that must be balanced against the threats they pose to privacy: to take one instance alone, the potential benefits to health of detailed medical and genetic databases are immense. The same developments that alarm some, excite others. Indeed, most typically, they both alarm and excite the same people.

The political and administrative problem of privacy protection in the era of dataveillance has generally been posed as: how best to constrain and control this technical potential so as protect a reasonable degree of personal privacy, while at the same time retain the economic and social benefits promised by the new technologies?

Prior to 9/11, there seemed good reason to believe that there were structural impediments to total surveillance. The new information technologies, although often originating in the defense sector, owe their rapid global diffusion primarily to private sector research, development, and marketing. Their commercial potential had been best exploited by the corporate sector, with governments by and large reaping the benefits as technological spinoffs. But a paradox had appeared in the 1990s. The toolbox of surveillance was increasing exponentially while the totalitarian surveillance state that had been so threatening a feature of the twentieth century, whether in Fascist or Communist form, was in dissolution, and even the liberal capitalist state that had borrowed, in less virulent form, many of the surveillance capacities of the authoritarian state, appeared to be in retreat before the forces of the market.

If states collect and use information on their citizens primarily as a means of social and economic control, corporations collect personal data primarily for marketing purposes. There is a long tradition, especially in the United States of resisting government threats to personal privacy. More recently, different concerns have been raised about threats to privacy arising from the vast, unregulated, and rapidly accumulating corporate data banks. These concerns can be best described as a shift from the Big Brother surveillance state to the Little Brothers surveillance society.[1] Legal responses have varied. Europe and Canada have adopted public regulatory regimes that stipulate that personal data collected by private entities for a specific commercial purpose may not be sold or traded to third parties without the express consent of the individuals from whom the information was drawn. The United States with its antigovernment traditions, has so far tended to rely more on corporate self-regulation, enforced by private litigation. In both cases, the emphasis is on firewalls separating public from private data collections, and separating different private data collections from one another. In the absence of effective barriers, data matching and linkage quickly threatens personal privacy. Yet despite the ominous growth trajectory of panoptic technologies, the de-centered and dispersed quality of the electronic eyes and ears diminished their totalizing potential. Nobody, public or private, seemed to have the will or capacity to put it all together—until 9/11.

Even with the attention paid to the private sector, it was already apparent well before 9/11 that states, and the United States preeminently among them, did have some impressive, but underused, surveillance capacity. Two examples illustrate the potential for a renascent Big Brother state. Since the late 1940s, the English-speaking countries under the leadership of the U.S. National Security Agency (NSA) have maintained an extensive electronic eavesdropping partnership known as the UKUSA alliance. During the Cold War, listening posts across the globe closely monitored communications within the Soviet bloc. Today, the UKUSA countries tap into the Intelsat communications satellite system that relays most of the world's phone calls, faxes, telexes, Internet, and e-mail communications around the world. A system called ECHELON links all the computers among the UKUSA agencies using a set of key words in a dictionary contributed by all the agencies; flagged messages are automatically routed to the country or countries that entered the particular key word flag. In the United States, the FBI had, before 9/11, begun deploying CARNIVORE, a super search engine that, when installed on Internet service providers, is capable of trolling through e-mail traffic and flagging communications of interest to the agency based on the identities of senders and receivers, key word recognition, etc.

A second example of state surveillance capacity is the machinery for tracking money laundering trails centered in the U.S. Treasury Department in the Financial Crimes Enforcement Network (FinCEN), which "links the law enforcement, financial and regulatory communities together for the common purpose of preventing, detecting and prosecuting money laundering and other financial crimes."[2] FinCEN relies on the worldwide monitoring of large financial transactions, and reportedly has at its disposal sophisticated artificial intelligence software capable of detecting anomalous or suspicious patterns in the vast daily volume of transactions, flagging transactions that might require closer attention, or criminal investigation. Technology permits the instantaneous flow of capital across national borders by computer keystroke, which has assisted in the rapid development of transnational financial networks. Governments, the bankers and financiers assert, cannot interfere effectively in this globalizing process, and should stay out. Yet these networks are also threatened by illicit financial flows, funding criminal or terrorist enterprises, and here, the private sector needs and demands the intervention of governments. The same technologies that foster licit financial flows also enable national states working together, under U.S. leadership, to monitor and investigate illicit flows.

Prior to 9/11, these powerful state surveillance systems faced certain limitations, both legal and political. Each of the participating UKUSA agencies was constrained by domestic law or practice from listening in on its own citizens. The awesome potential of the ECHELON system drew the critical attention of the European Parliament, especially of its French members who complained about a global "Anglophone spy network" that might be used against European economic interests.[3] FinCEN's potential was limited by the reluctance of many countries to cooperate fully with new disclosure laws, and of many transnational financial corporations to open their books and their clients' financial data to Uncle Sam's prying eyes. Nevertheless, the need to control the dark side of globalization, whether organized criminal or terrorist networks, had given greater urgency to the deployment of international policing and surveillance. The return of Big Brother could be discerned, just over the horizon.

As the twin towers of the World Trade Center collapsed on the morning of September 11, so too did many of the scruples that had limited the scope of state surveillance. With money laundering trails identified as a crucial link in the terrorist organizational structure, foot dragging among many participants gave way to greater cooperation. The Bush administration acted quickly and decisively to take advantage of the opening offered by 9/11 to transform the legal and institutional structure of policing and to break down barriers that had previously limited the state's surveillance reach.

ELECTRONIC SURVEILLANCE POWERS
IN THE USA PATRIOT ACT

Introduced within a week of the 9/11 attacks and rushed through Congress under great pressure, the USA PATRIOT Act was signed into law on October 26, 2001.[4] Its provisions significantly expand the electronic surveillance powers of federal law enforcement authorities, often without providing appropriate checks and balances to protect civil liberties. Most of what the administration wanted survived hasty congressional scrutiny, although sunset clauses were introduced on some of the electronic surveillance provisions. Ideas that had been put forward previously by the executive branch and subjected to strenuous criticism were whisked through the legislative process after 9/11.

This act introduces sweeping changes to more than a dozen federal statutes. The complexity of the changes and the relative lack of debate surrounding their passage make analysis of the implications somewhat difficult and, in some cases, controversial.[5] Civil libertarian critics have excoriated its extension of state powers.[6] Others have suggested that the critics have overstated their case.[7] What follows is a quick summary of the major changes that avoids the more complicated interpretive legal issues, while focusing on new powers and extensions of existing powers.

There are three broad sections of the act that are of relevance to this discussion: communication surveillance in criminal investigations; foreign intelligence investigations; and money laundering.

With regard to communication surveillance, the act relaxes restrictions around required warrants and court orders. With regard to court authorization of pen registers and trap-and-trace devices (these are technical terms that refer to methods of identifying senders and receivers of telephone communications), Section 216 extends court orders to cover e-mail messages and Internet use, and extends court orders to cover the entire United States, as opposed to being limited to the judicial district in which the court has jurisdiction as in the past. Critics point out that, even though the capture of message content is specifically prohibited, e-mail header information, which may include subject headings, or the addresses of specific Web sites visited, may be much more revealing than the simple telephone numbers previously captured. There is, however, provision for judicial oversight.

This provision may provide sanction to the FBI's CARNIVORE program, even though once installed by an Internet service provider, CARNIVORE may monitor all the communications of all subscribers, not just those targeted by a court order.[8] Service providers are immunized from legal liability for surrendering their customers' privacy when they cooperate in "good faith" with government, even before court orders have been obtained, and they are promised reasonable compensation for the costs of assisting authorities. Although the act imposes no positive obligation on service providers to modify their systems to accommodate law enforcement needs, anecdotal information suggests that after 9/11, Internet service providers have come under increasing pressure to assist, even in the absence of specific court orders.[9] However, to what extent providers have installed CARNIVORE is not known, since public disclosure of such information is prohibited.

Under this act, some agencies gain enhanced access to communications records and the content of stored e-mail required under search warrants, and requirements for notification of the subjects have been reduced. Warrants here, too, may now be issued "without geographic limitation" in the U.S.A.

The act lowers the barriers between criminal investigations and foreign intelligence information. Facilitating closer cooperation between criminal investigators and foreign intelligence collectors is probably not a controversial intention in itself, but the extension to criminal investigations of the much laxer standards of protection required under the Foreign Intelligence Surveillance Act (FISA) is debatable. FISA was originally a response to concerns about domestic spying that surfaced during the 1970s. While the need for special surveillance powers and secret evidence in relation to foreign espionage activities in the United States was widely accepted, it was generally believed that such methods were unacceptable against American citizens, especially those engaged in First Amendment activities, as with the Vietnam War protests. Under FISA, government operates on a lower threshold for gaining authorization for intrusive surveillance against targets suspected of espionage and foreign intelligence operations in the U.S.A. than is the case for criminal investigations. For instance, under FISA, investigators gain access to records from car rental agencies, motel accommodations, and storage facilities, as well as easier recourse to physical searches and pen register and trace-and-trap orders. Special FISA courts meet in camera, with nondisclosure of evidence deemed to be of a sensitive intelligence nature.

Under the PATRIOT Act, FISA is amended in certain crucial and significant ways. Originally, a FISA surveillance order required certification that "*the* purpose for the surveillance is to obtain foreign intelligence information." If evidence of a criminal offence was uncovered from FISA surveillance, prosecution could not be based on FISA surveillance, but would have to be based on a surveillance order under Title III of the Omnibus Crime Control and Safe Streets Act of 1968, a narrower and more restrictive authorization for wiretap orders. After 9/11, the Justice Department sought to amend FISA to read simply that "*a* purpose" was to obtain foreign intelligence. Congress balked at this very low threshold, but instead provided in Section 218 that foreign intelligence gathering be a "*significant* purpose" to trigger a FISA surveillance or search order. Less threatening to privacy than the Bush administration's proposal, this compromise nevertheless departs significantly from the clear distinction originally drawn between surveillance for criminal law enforcement, and surveillance for foreign intelligence. The act encourages cooperation between law enforcement and intelligence investigators; but in blurring the line between the two, it invites the Justice Department to opt for the lower threshold. Finding a "significant" foreign intelligence component to terrorist investigations will probably not unduly tax the resources of law enforcement officials.

Not content with lowering the threshold, the PATRIOT Act widens FISA's powers. It permits "roving surveillance," that is, orders that are not tied to a particular place or particular means of communication. While it is not unreasonable to point out that those seeking to evade surveillance will constantly shift their means and location of communication, there are obvious dangers that roving surveillance will capture communications among persons not named in the order. The act extends FISA pen register and trace-and-trap orders to cover e-mail as well as telephone communication. It extends the duration of surveillance and physical search orders, in some cases providing extensions of up to a year. It expands the scope of access to certain kinds of business records to include seizure of any "tangible items," regardless of the nature of the business in possession of the records.

Balancing these provisions are others that impose and, in some cases, expand safeguards against abuse. Anticipating an increased work load for FISA courts, the number of judges is raised from seven to eleven. Prohibitions against FISA orders based solely on the target's exercise of First Amendment rights are expanded. And finally, Congress inserted a sunset provision for the FISA amendments.

Questions about how government would use expanded access to FISA orders were raised in 2002 when the FISA court issued a stunning rebuke to the Justice Department, a rebuke later made public by Congress.[10] The court identified more than seventy-five cases in which it says it was misled by the FBI in documents in which the bureau attempted to justify its need for wiretaps and other electronic surveillance. The FBI and the Justice Department were said to have violated the law by allowing information gathered from intelligence eavesdrops to be used freely in bringing criminal charges, without court review, and criminal investigators were improperly directing the use of counterintelligence wiretaps. In August 2002, the Justice Department appealed this opinion to the little known Foreign Intelligence Surveillance Court of Review, arguing that the USA PATRIOT Act now permitted FISA to be used to obtain evidence for a prosecution if the government also has a significant non–law enforcement foreign intelligence purpose.[11]

On November 18, the Review Court, in its first ever decision, concluded that FISA, as amended by the PATRIOT Act, supports the government's position, and that the restrictions imposed by the FISA court are not required by FISA or the Constitution."[12] "Proclaiming a major victory in the war on terrorism, Ashcroft said the decision 'revolutionizes our ability to investigate and prosecute terrorists' because it permits criminal investigators and intelligence agents to work together and to share information."[13] The *New York Times* called the decision "a Green

Light to Spy."[14] As if in confirmation, the attorney general announced plans to intensify secret surveillance, including the designation of special intelligence prosecutors in every federal court district, and the creation of a new FBI unit to seek intelligence warrants.[15]

Nor has the appetite of the executive branch and Congress for intrusive surveillance powers been exhausted by the language of the PATRIOT Act. The Homeland Security Act, signed by the president in November 2002, contains additional powers for electronic surveillance. Section 225 includes the entire text of the Cyber Security Enhancement Act, which earlier passed the House, permitting Internet service providers voluntarily to provide government agents with access to the contents of their customers' private communications without those persons' consent based on a "good faith" belief that an emergency justifies the release of that information. Under the same section, law enforcement may install pen register and trap-and-trace devices without a court order where there is an ongoing attack on a "protected computer" (any computer involved in interstate commerce or communications). Section 225 introduces fines and twenty-year prison terms for computer hackers who recklessly cause or attempt to cause serious bodily injury—a threat based on the idea that hackers could maliciously break into and disrupt the computer systems of critical infrastructures like nuclear power plants or air traffic control systems. Section 891 contains the entire text of the Homeland Security Information Sharing Act, another measure that passed the House earlier in the year, facilitating the sharing of sensitive intelligence information and the content of electronic intercepts with state and local authorities. There are some limited privacy protections in the Act.[16]

The final section of the PATRIOT Act that raises issues about privacy protection is the expanded authority of the treasury secretary to regulate and probe the activities of financial institutions, especially their relations with foreign entities, in pursuit of money laundering. New money laundering crimes are defined in the act, mainly to extend the existing legislation to include a wider range of terrorist and cybercrime activities, and to extend U.S. jurisdiction to prosecute money laundering offences abroad. The most controversial aspect of the expanded surveillance powers in the act is the concerted attempt to extend the cooperation of financial institutions, securities dealers and brokers, as well as commodity merchants, etc., to include not merely automatic reporting of cash transactions over $10,000, but an obligation to file "suspicious activity reports" and to follow more rigorous "due diligence" requirements. Financial institutions are encouraged to cooperate closely with law enforcement agencies with regard to suspected terrorist-associated money laundering. They are required to maintain anti–money laundering programs meeting certain standards, such as appointing a designated compliance officer, maintaining an employee training program, developing internal procedures and controls, and conducting an independent audit. They must also establish minimum customer identification standards. In effect, the act seeks to enlist financial institutions as active participants in the government's surveillance program, yet another example of the tendency to break down barriers between the public and private sectors. The objective of identifying and rolling up the financial networks that fund terrorist activity is widely shared, but financial institutions may not be entirely comfortable with the requirement for active compliance in reporting their clients' "suspicious" financial transactions, especially when failure to do so may result in severe penalties, including seizure of assets.

SURVEILLANCE IN PRACTICE

The attorney general has released new investigative guidelines for the Justice Department reflecting its mission to "neutralize terrorists before they are able to strike," and to shift emphasis from criminal investigation to crime "prevention." Among these guidelines is authorization given to the FBI to conduct "online research" for counterterrorism purposes, "even when not linked to an individual criminal investigation." Moreover, the FBI is authorized to use "commercial data mining services to detect and prevent terrorist attacks, independent of particular criminal investigations." The FBI is further enabled to establish its own databases drawn from multiple sources, and to operate "counterterrorism information systems"—although the guidelines prohibit the FBI from "using this authority to keep files on citizens based on their constitutionally protected activities."[17] Of course, if such activities are suspected of being carried out in association with terrorist activities, this protection is presumably waived.

One of the surveillance spinoffs from the PATRIOT Act that has come to partial notice is its application to libraries and bookstores. FISA court orders requiring pen register and trace-and-trap disclosure is now extended to e-mail on online communication, apparently including records of URLs visited in Web surfing, or the detailed information such as keywords recorded in search engines consulted online. Persons seeking anonymity in Internet use may use library online facilities. Libraries have consequently been visited by the FBI seeking records of usage and identification of users, citing "roving" warrants. The FBI also may have sought to have their surveillance software, like CARNIVORE, installed on library systems. Nor do these intrusions stop at online monitoring. Section 215 of the PATRIOT Act requires any person or business to produce any books, records, documents, or "tangible items." Libraries and bookstores may be required to provide records of books borrowed, or purchased, by persons under suspicion. The incidence of such requests, and the degree of compliance, is not known: the Catch-22 is that the FBI prohibits disclosure regarding such orders. This has led one commentator to suggest that Attorney General Ashcroft may have been reading Kafka in his local library.[18] This is uncomfortably reminiscent of the notorious FBI "Library Awareness Program" from the 1960s to the late 1980s, which attempted to bully librarians into snooping into the reading habits of patrons deemed left-wing or anti-American by the FBI.[19] Could we now be seeing attempts to track and identify persons reading about Islam or terrorism? Protestations by the Justice Department about the protection of First Amendment rights may or may not be sincere, but in the absence of any possibility of monitoring and evaluating their actions, skepticism seems a wise rule.

This raises another serious problem in evaluating the impact of the new powers: the administration is resistant to providing Congress access to information on the implementation of the act. Congress, which was pressured into passing the USA PATRIOT Act without due deliberation, did add sunset clauses to many key sections, under which authority is terminated by December 31, 2005, unless extended by Congress. If sunset provisions are to have any real force, Congress must have access to sufficient information to make informed judgments on whether the extension of new powers is justified. Yet when a request was made in July 2002 by House Judiciary Chairman James Sensenbrenner (R-WI) and ranking minority member John Conyers (D-MI) that a wide range of questions concerning the implementation of the PATRIOT Act be answered by the executive branch, the government failed to respond to most of their questions. Even threats of subpoenas have not succeeded in dislodging much more information. In early November, 2002, the president signed a bill authorizing Justice Department appropriations, including statutory authorities relating to federal law enforcement activities. The bill contains a number of clauses inserted by Congress imposing substantial obligations on the executive branch for reporting information on a wide array of matters related to law enforcement. In signing, the president attached a "Signing Statement" that indicated his interpretation of the reporting obligations, asserting his right to withhold information "the disclosure of which could impair foreign relations, the national security, the deliberative processes of the Executive, or the performance of the Executive's constitutional duties," as defined in each case by the president.[20]

The American Civil Liberties Union (ACLU), the Electronic Privacy Information Center, the American Booksellers Foundation for Free Expression, and the Freedom to Read Foundation filed a Freedom of Information request on August 21, 2002, seeking general information about the use of new surveillance powers, including the number of times the government has:

- directed a library, bookstore, or newspaper to produce "tangible things," e.g, the titles of books an individual has purchased or borrowed, or the identity of individuals who have purchased or borrowed certain books;
- initiated surveillance of Americans under the expanded Foreign Intelligence Surveillance Act;
- conducted "sneak-and-peek" searches, which allow law enforcement to enter people's homes and search their belongings without informing them until long after;
- authorized the use of devices to trace the telephone calls or e-mails of people who are not suspected of any crime;
- investigated American citizens or permanent legal residents on the basis of activities protected by the First Amendment (e.g., writing a letter to the editor or attending a rally).

Following failed negotiations with Justice Department officials, on November 13, 2002, the ACLU asked a federal court to order the department to respond immediately to their FOIA lawsuit.[21] At the time of this writing, the court had yet to issue a decision.

Resistance to disclose information about government actions has been taken further yet in the Homeland Security Act. The new Department of Homeland Security will be permitted to exempt from the FOIA information about critical infrastructures[22] received from the private sector (most of America's critical infrastructures, such as power grids and communication and transportation networks are under private ownership). According to the Society of Professional Journalists, this would have the effect of removing large amounts of information that is now potentially open to public access, and of shielding from lawsuits any industry mistakes that threaten public health or safety.[23]

There are plausible arguments in favor of secrecy when issues of security against terrorist attack are at stake. But most of the critics of government stonewalling do not challenge the reasonableness of keeping genuinely sensitive and potentially damaging information out of the public realm. Their expectations are simply for a level of information that will permit democratic accountability, and allow the public informed judgments on government's performance in the war on terrorism. The excessive secrecy and the active resistance to requests for information, even from the legislative branch, can only stoke suspicious that the executive branch has things it would prefer to hide from the public.

TOWARD "TOTAL INFORMATION AWARENESS"?

This discussion has focused on the Justice Department and its legal powers. But the American government's surveillance plans are not confined to domestic law enforcement. Foreign intelligence agencies, despite the setback administered by their failure to anticipate and prevent 9/11, possess surveillance capacities, previously directed at targets abroad, that are tempting tools for an aggressive government to employ at home as well. After all, the logic goes, the terrorists operate across borders, so why should the United States deny itself the awesome powers of foreign surveillance for homeland security? Since the administration has made every effort to break down the barriers between criminal investigation and intelligence collection,[24] it is a simple step further to reduce the barriers set up against intelligence agencies spying on Americans. Close cooperation between the FBI and the CIA has been encouraged since 9/11 at the top level. The CIA is reportedly "expanding its domestic presence, placing agents with nearly all of the FBI's fifty-six terrorism task forces in U.S. cities, a step that law enforcement and intelligence officials say will help overcome some of the communications obstacles between the two agencies that existed before the September 11, 2001, attacks."[25] The NSA, which shares some of the blame for the 9/11 intelligence failure, has access to the vast surveillance capacities of the UKUSA network and its ECHELON system, but is barred by law from snooping on Americans. Should tracking terrorists abroad come to a halt at the U.S. border, when it is America that is squarely in the terrorist sights? The NSA director has mused on this question in an appearance before the Senate.[26]

There were of course very good reasons why agencies like the CIA and the NSA were barred from domestic spying, and these reasons have not vanished since 9/11. There may be compelling and plausible arguments in favor of greater coop-eration, but a domestic role for foreign intelligence collection agencies must at the very least be accompanied by rigorous checks and balances, and strong ac-countability mechanisms—unfortunately, the very kinds of safeguards that the Bush administration has been assiduously limiting since 9/11.

The true visionary for a post–9/11 surveillance state might be neither John Ashcroft nor the directors of any of the existing security and intelligence agencies. Instead, he may be Vice Admiral John M. Poindexter, of the Iran-Contra affair no-toriety. Admiral Poindexter, whose conviction for lying to Congress was reversed in 1991 by a federal appeals court because he had been granted immunity for his testimony, has been rehabilitated by the Bush administration and made director of the Information Awareness Office in the Defense Advanced Research Projects Agency (DARPA). DARPA has a distinguished lineage in the information age. It was from this office that the Internet sprang. In 1969, DARPA set up a pioneer computer network among defence scientists called ARPANET, which, after a se-ries of transformations, and freed of its original sponsor, eventually evolved into the Internet.[27] DARPA has a mandate to develop and apply new surveillance tech-nologies post–9/11.

Admiral Poindexter's vision is a program called Total Information Awareness (TIA). Under the slogan *scientia est potentia* ("knowledge is power"), his office is putting together a series of research teams working on advanced surveillance technologies of various kinds, from biorecognition technologies to sophisticated translation systems to biosurveillance providing early warning of attacks of bio-logical agents. He envisages a cutting-edge system for detecting, classifying, iden-tifying, and tracking terrorists. To do this, he intends to "punch holes in the stovepipes" that separate different data collections, and develop a seamless global system that mines data from all possible sources, public and private, American and foreign. One of the "significant new data sources that needs to be mined to discover and track terrorists is the *transaction space*." Terrorists move easily un-dercover, but they leave an "information signature. We must be able to pick this signal out of the noise."[28] The *Washington Post* editorialized that "anyone who de-liberately set out to invent a government program with the specific aim of terrify-ing the Orwell-reading public could hardly have improved on the Information Awareness Office."[29] Even the conservative columnist William Safire denounced this "supersnoop's dream."[30] Congress in early 2003 held up funding for TIA until the administration explains it to Congress, including its impact on civil liberties, and barred any deployment of the technology against U.S. citizens without prior Congressional approval.

It may not even be necessary. There is a consensus among informed experts that the intelligence failure of 9/11 is attributable less to a collection deficit than to an *analytical* deficit. There were many bits and pieces of information concerning the threat from Al Qaeda, and even the imminence of a major attack on American soil. The key failing of the intelligence community was its inability to put the pieces together and make sense of the bigger picture. It has been widely observed in the United States and elsewhere that as a general rule, the collection capacity of intelligence agencies has outstripped their analytical capacities. Schemes such as Total Information Awareness actually threaten to worsen this imbalance, swamping overworked analysts with too much information, almost all of it irrelevant, but requiring processing. The idea that, out of a deluge of detailed information from banking, credit, debit, air miles, and other databases, actionable profiles of potential terrorists will somehow emerge is more a matter of faith than of science (not perhaps entirely unlike the touching faith in computers and American know-how that fuels the scientifically dubious scheme for a fail-safe antimissile shield).

It is possible to become overalarmed about the Orwellian prospect, especially if one accepts too readily the techno-hype behind it. The intentions may be alarming, but the means of delivering Total Information Awareness are as yet more suspect than enthusiasts like Admiral Poindexter believe. There are questions surrounding many of the technologies that are being promoted by the private sector to the U.S. government as quick fixes for terrorism. When the Defense Department tested face-matching technologies, their results were less impressive than the figures claimed by the companies pedaling them. Effective surveillance is very costly. This may help explain the very large number of detentions and deportations of illegal immigrants suspected of terrorist links since 9/11. The FBI faces a dilemma: should they watch, or simply deport, suspects? A Sacramento FBI agent is quoted: "A lot of times it comes down to dollars and cents. . . . We just can't afford [surveillance] for as many people as we suspect might have bad intentions." A federal prosecutor adds: "The prevailing sentiment is, 'Just get them the hell out.' "[31]

There are also some important technological limitations on Big Brother's surveillance capacities. Chief among these is the universal accessibility of encryption systems that defeat the decryption capabilities of the NSA and all other intelligence agencies, American or foreign. Clumsy and unsuccessful attempts were made during the Clinton administration to impose a "Clipper Chip" that would offer government a trapdoor entry into encrypted messages, and to embargo the export of encryption software outside North America. There are programs, such as the FBI's "Magic Lantern" (a virus sent to capture encryption keys from a remote targeted computer), that look to technical fixes of this problem, but government snoopers are by and large resigned to living with an inability to read intercepted e-mail messages.[32] The UK government, prior to 9/11, went so far as to legislate criminal sanctions for persons who refuse to disclose their encryption keys to police or security officials who demand them, but the U.S. government has declined to follow this example. The reason for U.S. reticence is not hard to find: opposition to the British legislation came not only from civil libertarians, but, more influentially, from e-commerce interests irritated at government intrusion into security systems, the integrity of which is essential to e-commerce transactions.

This points to an inherent contradiction in the relations between public and private actors as barriers between state and corporate surveillance systems are lowered. There are two very different, and sometimes antagonistic, concepts of "security" at work. To the public sector, security comes from accessing and controlling the "transaction space." To the private sector, security means guaranteeing the integrity of transactions with clients, whether consumers or other businesses. In the face of the terrorist threat as embodied in 9/11, there is good reason for businesses to buy into government surveillance programs to make their own operations more secure—indeed, there is a lot of money to be made by private companies in equipping government surveillance operations. Yet corporations are not always on the same page as government, or indeed on the same page as each other. These confusions lead to a peculiar, stuttering dynamic in the development of government surveillance programs.

Nowhere are these confusions more apparent than in the operations of the office of special adviser to the president on cyber security, Richard Clarke, a former adviser on terrorism to President Clinton, who unusually survived to serve his Republican successor. On September 18, 2002, the White House officially released its draft *National Strategy to Secure Cyberspace,* which had emerged from Clarke's office.[33] It is an anodyne document—full of good intentions and good advice to the private sector about how to maintain security against hackers and cyberterrorists, but with no teeth to enforce the advice. The economic damage to national security that might be exacted by a concerted cyber attack on the U.S. private sector and critical infrastructures has been the subject of many warnings. Yet many in the private sector do not wish to assume the costs associated with adopting stricter security systems, and do not wish to shake consumer confidence by pointing to the vulnerability of their existing security systems. Hence, the gutting of Mr. Clarke's report.

Actually, the contradictions are even more acute. The vulnerabilities of private sector security are hyped and indeed overhyped by the private security industry that has a vested interest in advancing sales of its software and hardware systems. The very notion of cyberterrorism has been characterized as overblown and alarmist.[34] Dire predictions of "an electronic Pearl Harbor" almost certainly run ahead of the actual potential for damage. Many critical infrastructures, such as air traffic control and power systems, communicate within "intranets," not connected to the Internet, and are "air-gapped" to provide protection from malicious hackers cruising the Net looking for targets. Yet, alleged vulnerabilities are deliberately exaggerated by those with security systems to sell credulous government officials. Government is thus being pushed in different directions by different private interests, at the same time that it extends its surveillance of the private sector.

A SECURITY-INDUSTRIAL COMPLEX

To assess the impact of 9/11 and the future direction of the surveillance state, it is necessary to look at the relations of government with the private sector, or, more precisely, with various private sectors. The Bush administration has sought to dramatically extend its surveillance reach as a counterterrorist strategy. In doing so, it has constructed close links with certain corporate interests in the high-tech, dotcom sector. Homeland security is quickly shaping up as the biggest government contract bonanza since the end of the Cold War. If President Eisenhower warned in his farewell address in 1961 of a military-industrial complex, the war on terrorism has generated an emergent security-industrial complex.[35] Homeland Security Secretary Tom Ridge has been an enthusiastic advocate of public-private partnership: "We look to American creativity to help solve our problems and to help make a profit in the process."[36] Tens of billions of dollars are on the table, and are being snapped up by companies that, like the Cold War defense industries, have in the first instance a single customer, Uncle Sam. This has been a godsend for a sector recovering from the huge hit of the dotcom collapse prior to 9/11. Their profitability rests on a continued market in government for new surveillance and security technologies, and on the hope for commercial spinoffs as business and society look for technological security fixes. In both cases, the security-industrial complex has a stake in joining with government in pumping up the threat level, just as the defense interests and the government pumped up anxiety over the Soviet threat in the past—including "missile gaps" that never were.

Yet it is also reported that "While the Bush administration has waged its campaign to strengthen homeland security since the Sept. 11 terrorist attacks, many of the nation's largest and most influential businesses have quietly but persistently resisted new rules that would require them to make long-term security improvements."[37] Corporations in the banking, retail sales, chemical manufacturing, and nuclear power industries are balking at government efforts to impose tougher and more expensive security standards. The private sector wants security, but is traditionally suspicious of government regulation and intrusion. Ironically, the Republican Party tends to share this suspicion, even as a Republican administration imposes unparalleled government intervention in the name of national security. Although many qualms about big government may have been swallowed in the wake of 9/11, there are ideological contradictions within the governing party that are bound to intensify with time.

This is the complex context in which the Bush administration's efforts to amass new and intrusive surveillance powers must be assessed. In the end, it may well be that privacy protection laws, resistance by both civil libertarians and sections of the private sector, as well as overreliance on technology, may ensure that the administration's reach exceeds its grasp.

PART II

THE ASHCROFT APPROACH

4. SECRET ARRESTS AND PREVENTIVE DETENTION

KATE MARTIN[1]

> To bereave a man of life . . . or by violence to confiscate his estate, without accusation or trial, would be so gross and notorious an act of despotism, as must at once convey the alarm of tyranny throughout the whole nation but confinement of the person, by secretly hurrying him to jail, where his sufferings are unknown or forgotten, is a less public, a less striking, and *therefore a more dangerous* engine of arbitrary government.
>
> ALEXANDER HAMILTON, FEDERALIST NO. 84 (EMPHASIS IN ORIGINAL)[2]

In the four months following September 11, the U.S. government secretly arrested and jailed nearly 1,200 individuals, both citizens and noncitizens.[3] One was charged as a terrorist; virtually all were either Arabs or Muslims. More than 600 people charged with immigration violations, most of whom probably had no lawyer, were subjected to secret hearings where the government excluded family and friends.[4] As of January 2003, Attorney General John Ashcroft had still refused to release their names or transcripts of the closed hearings. In June 2002, Ashcroft announced that a U.S. citizen arrested at Chicago's O'Hare Airport was being held incommunicado in a military brig as an "enemy combatant." The president claimed the power to order the U.S. military to jail indefinitely citizens and noncitizens, unilaterally deemed by him to be "terrorists" or "enemy combatants."[5]

The government has told the various federal courts that have been asked to review these policies that they have no role in judging the legality of its actions in the war on terrorism. If the courts do not reject the Bush administration's arguments, the executive branch will have succeeded in arrogating to itself the power to arrest someone in the United States in secret and hold him incommunicado without meaningful access to a court. It will have done so without ever even asking Congress for such extraordinary powers.

PREVENTIVE DETENTION IN THE USA PATRIOT ACT

Before September 11, there was a basic understanding in the United States that the government could jail an individual only if it had evidence to charge him with a crime or, in some circumstances, a violation of the immigration laws. In the name of antiterrorism, the Bush administration has engineered a dramatic and dangerous erosion of that fundamental principle of due process.

Within a week of September 11, the Bush administration sent a draft antiterrorism bill to the Congress. Named the USA PATRIOT Act, it was passed four weeks later, after the attorney general and the Republican leadership in the Congress warned that further terrorist attacks were imminent and that if these new powers were not authorized, those attacks would be the fault of the Democrats in Congress.[6]

One of the most controversial provisions sought by the Bush administration was authority from Congress for preventive detention of noncitizens, who had not been charged with anything, on the sole say-so of the attorney general. The administration's initial proposal contained no limits on how long an individual could be detained and would have prevented any court review of the detention. This was one of the few provisions on which the Congress did require some safeguards for individual rights. The final law provided that a noncitizen may be detained without charges for seven days initially if the attorney general's certifies that he is a threat to national security.[7] At the end of those seven days, the government must charge the individual in order to continue to detain him. However, if an individual is cleared of such charges and has the right to remain in the United States, the PATRIOT Act gave the attorney general the power to certify the noncitizen as a threat to national security and jail him indefinitely, subject only to recertification every six months.[8]

SECRET ARRESTS

Although the administration demanded and received new detention powers from Congress in the USA PATRIOT Act, claiming that such authority was urgently needed to counter an imminent terrorist threat, as of early 2003 it had not used those new statutory powers. Instead, while the Congress and the public debated under what limited circumstances, and with what necessary safeguards, preventive detention might be appropriate, Attorney General Ashcroft ordered hundreds of secret arrests—not of suspected terrorists, but simply of Arabs or Muslims, both citizens and noncitizens.

Within days of September 11, the attorney general and the FBI announced that hundreds of people had been arrested. In those uncertain and chaotic days, it seemed reassuring that the government was rounding up terrorists, but frightening that so many terrorists were hiding in the country. But very soon, government announcements raised doubts about the arrests. While trumpeting the number of arrests in an apparent effort at reassurance, the Justice Department refused to provide the most basic information about who had been arrested and what the charges were against them. They said only that people were being held either on criminal or immigration charges or under a little-known or little-used authority to jail "material witnesses." We later learned that on September 21, the attorney general had ordered the immigration service to keep secret all information concerning the noncitizens being picked up.[9]

At the same time, very disturbing press reports described people simply having disappeared for days, and kept without access to counsel or the courts, for apparently no reason other than their ethnicity or religion.[10] A father and son, both U.S. citizens, were arrested as they returned from a business trip in Mexico, because their passports looked suspicious. The father was released after ten days and was sent home wearing a leg monitor, but the son spent two more months in jail until a federal judge determined that the plastic covering on his passport had split.[11] The key factor in their arrest appeared to be their Arabic-sounding names.

On October 11, Tarek Abdelhamid Albasti was arrested at the restaurant he owned in Evansville, Indiana. Born in Egypt, Albasti was an American citizen with a two-year-old daughter and a father-in-law who was a former U.S. Foreign Service officer. FBI agents had shown up at his restaurant twice after the September 11 attacks, asking about his political beliefs and the flying lessons that he had been given as a birthday present. Mr. Albasti was arrested with his uncle and seven other Muslim men from Evansville and flown to Chicago in shackles. They were not charged, but were detained as material witnesses. After a week in jail, where they staged a hunger strike, Albasti and the others were released without ever testifying about anything.[12]

Ali al-Maqtari, born in Yemen, studied in France and came to the United States on a tourist visa hoping to become a French teacher. He met and married Tiffany Hughes, a native of North Carolina and a convert to Islam. On September 15, 2001, he drove his wife, a member of the National Guard, to Fort Campbell, Kentucky, to report for duty. At the gate, the two were ordered out of their car and were questioned while the car was searched. Mr. Maqtari was detained and jailed for more than a month; his wife was harassed into leaving the Guard. Court papers show that Mr. Maqtari was detained because authorities found two box cutters in his car, along with postcards of New York City. He had used the box cutters when working in his uncle's supermarket. His lawyer, Michael J. Boyle, of New Haven, said a photo of Ms. Hughes had already been posted at the guardhouse at Fort Campbell when they arrived because she had picked up her military orders in Massachusetts on September 13 wearing an Islamic head covering.[13]

These reports raised fears that the secrecy was not for national security purposes but to shield government misconduct. The suspicion arose that the government was jailing, without trial, Arabs and Muslims who had no links to terrorism. In mid-October, a coalition of more than forty civil liberties, civil rights, human rights, and legal assistance organizations—including the organization I direct, the Center for National Security Studies—made a request under the Freedom of Information Act and the First Amendment for the names of those jailed and the charges against them.

All the major press covered the coalition's demand for the names as they reported our worry that individuals had been disappeared.[14] The editorial pages of major newspapers called for release of the names, as did members of Congress, including Senator Patrick Leahy, who demanded that the attorney general explain the detentions before the Senate Judiciary Committee.[15] On November 27, 2001, the day before that hearing, the attorney general released a list of ninety-three individuals who had been charged under federal criminal laws,[16] but refused to release any other names. In December 2001, the coalition sued the Justice Department to obtain the identities of the other 900 detainees under the First Amendment and the Freedom of Information Act.[17]

The understanding that "'secret arrests,' [are] a concept odious to a democratic society," has always been fundamental in U.S. law.[18] As one court explained:

> If there is no official arrest record at the jail, except the private log of the jailer, how is it to be determined if there was unnecessary delay in according the person arrested his rights? How is his family or a friend going to learn of his arrest if, on inquiry, they are advised there is no official record? The constitutional foundation underlying these rights is the respect a state or city must accord to the dignity and worth of its citizens. It is an integral part of constitutional due process that a public record of such arrests be maintained.[19]

And Thomas Jefferson outlined the importance to the public: "The functionaries of every government have propensities to command at will the liberty and property of their constituents. There is no safe deposit for these but with the people themselves, nor can they be safe with them without information."[20]

In court, the Justice Department conceded that the Constitution prohibits secret arrests on criminal charges.[21] But without ever explaining how secret arrests on immigration charges—or no charges at all—could be constitutional, the government advanced two rationales for its secrecy.[22] First, it argued that producing the list of those it had jailed would be useful information to Al Qaeda. But the government claimed at the same time that if any Al Qaeda associates did happen to be among those who were jailed, they were free to communicate from jail with whomever they pleased. Not being able to explain this inconsistency, the government resorted to claiming that giving out the list of those who had no connections to Al Qaeda would reveal something of significance to terrorist groups, namely the "mosaic" of its terrorism investigation. But again, the government never explained what the list of names would reveal, beyond the already well-known fact that the investigation focused on Arab and Muslim males.[23] And FBI Director Robert Mueller himself publicly announced that while they had found certain sleeper cells in the United States, whom they had under surveillance, they had not found anyone in the United States, other than the alleged twentieth hijacker, who knew about the attacks in advance.[24]

Second, the government made the ironic claim that it was refusing to release the names out of concern for the individuals' privacy. But rather than protecting the privacy of these individuals, the attorney general and others repeatedly implied—falsely—that they were terrorist suspects.[25] Thus, the government's statements led the employers and neighbors of the detainees, who knew that they had disappeared for months, to assume that their employees or neighbors might well be terrorist suspects. Nor did the government show any concern for the privacy of those individuals who were deported back to repressive countries with a note from the U.S. government that they had been picked up as part of the September 11 investigation.[26]

After secretly arresting and jailing hundreds, the government held secret immigration hearings for at least 611 individuals, from which it excluded not only journalists and human rights observers but also family and friends.[27] Even open immigration hearings lack many basic due process protections: a noncitizen is not entitled to a court-appointed lawyer—she only has a lawyer when she has the opportunity and money to find one; and the judge is not an independent member of the judiciary but an employee of the Justice Department. Thus, in immigration proceedings, the most important protection against government abuse is public scrutiny and accountability. But instead of requiring an individualized determination at each hearing, as to whether there was some need to close a part of the hearing, for example, to protect classified information, the attorney general simply ordered that all the hearings would be completely secret. The only rationale for this blanket order could have been to keep secret the identifies of the individuals who had been secretly jailed.

In early 2002, media and civil liberties groups challenged the closed hearing order as unconstitutional.[28] In one case, the government defended its policy by submitting sworn affidavits claiming grave national security harm if the public were allowed to attend the immigration hearing of a leading figure in the Detroit Muslim community, Rabih Haddad. But after losing in the trial court, the national security harm evidently evaporated as the government released the hearing transcript and didn't appeal that particular order.[29]

As of this writing, the government has still refused to release the names of the other detainees or their lawyers, and the various lawsuits appear headed for the Supreme Court. On August 2, 2002, the trial court ruled in the secret arrests case that the government must release the names of the detainees and their lawyers, and pointed out the constitutional responsibility of the judiciary "to ensure that our Government always operates within the statutory and constitutional constraints which distinguish a democracy from a dictatorship."[30] The government appealed that ruling. While recognizing the importance of the government's effort to keep the public safe, one appeals court ruled the blanket order closing immigration hearings unconstitutional, noting that "democracies die behind closed doors"; another disagreed.[31]

The victory on secret arrests was front-page news in even the smallest papers around the country.[32] And editorial writers wrote that it sent a message to the Bush administration that its antiterrorist campaign risked trampling on the Constitution.[33] Nevertheless, the Justice Department attempted to institutionalize secret arrests by unilaterally issuing a rule that no state could release the names of INS detainees held in its jails, even when required to do so by state sunshine laws.

DISCRIMINATORY DRAGNET

Although we do not yet have the names, at this writing enough information has been revealed through the lawsuits and the attendant public pressure to make it clear that the roundup of hundreds of individuals was not focused on terrorist suspects but was a dragnet aimed at Arabs and Muslims. While Attorney General Ashcroft's public pronouncements misleadingly suggested that those who were jailed were suspects,[34] the lawsuit forced the government to describe under oath its basis for jailing people. The Justice Department never claimed to the courts that any of the detainees were terrorist suspects or that they even knew anything about the 9/11 attacks.[35] Only a mere handful appear to have had any connection at all to terrorism or the hijackers.[36] (Even those alleged connections were often nothing more than the use of a public computer terminal, or being at the same motor vehicle bureau as one of the hijackers.[37]) While the government lawyers could not explain the basis for the decision to jail these particular individuals,[38] virtually all of them appear to be either Arabs or Muslims.[39] In court, the Justice Department was forced to admit that many of the individuals had been "cleared of any wrongdoing" and, as of March 2003, almost 300 had been released into the U.S.[40]

Although the Bush administration evidently had no information linking the nearly 1,200 detainees to terrorism, it nevertheless jailed them before trial, before they had been found guilty of anything.[41] Many of the criminal defendants were jailed on minor charges, which, when proved, carried sentences no longer than the length of time for which the defendants were locked up before trial. The government's list of charges included such crimes as document fraud, which typically might not even be prosecuted. Press reports showed that many individuals jailed as part of the investigation ended up pleading guilty to such charges and receiving sentences equal to the time already served pretrial.[42]

Similarly, those who were charged with violations of the immigration laws would not have found themselves in jail prior to September 11. Immigration violations—which may range from overstaying a visa to not having received the necessary paperwork to secure legal residency because of government delays—historically have not resulted in arrest, much less jail before any hearing. But those immigrants swept up in this dragnet were routinely denied pretrial bail,[43] and some were held for weeks or months before even being charged.[44]

In November 2001, Ashcroft had proclaimed that terrorists would be arrested for spitting on the sidewalk.[45] Like authoritarian regimes, instead of providing the due process of charge, indictment, and trial, the government simply labeled people as criminals and locked them up. The Justice Department policy was to jail first and then ask questions. Even when individuals had agreed to leave the country or were to be deported, they were still held in jail until the FBI had "cleared" them of terrorist connections.[46] Such a policy of preventive detention turns the presumption of innocence on its head: the government now jails individuals it deems suspicious until the FBI "clears" them.[47]

The administration's policy has sown fear and mistrust in the very communities within the United States that the Justice Department is looking to for assistance and information in the antiterrorism efforts. A leading Arab-American civil rights organization, for example, felt it important to counsel people to talk to the FBI only with a lawyer present, rather than agree to the kind of voluntary informal interview possible where the community shares a sense of common objectives and trust with the police.[48] Such suspicion is warranted given the government's jailing and deportation of those who came forward to help with information after the attacks.[49]

VIOLATIONS OF INDIVIDUAL RIGHTS

While Attorney General Ashcroft repeatedly claimed that the government had not violated any individual's rights, the Justice Department has refused to release the information necessary for the public to know whether that is true. But Amnesty International and Human Rights Watch have both published reports detailing numerous serious violations of detainees' rights.[50] Detainees were held for long periods without being charged. Many were transferred across the country, held in maximum security facilities—sometimes in solitary confinement—and prevented from telephoning anyone, even lawyers.[51] People were beaten in jail, kept with the lights on for twenty-four hours a day, and prevented from observing their religious practices.[52] The Justice Department's own inspector general found the allegations sufficiently compelling to launch an investigation.[53]

SECRET ARRESTS OF "MATERIAL WITNESSES"

In addition to secretly arresting individuals charged with crimes or immigration violations, the government also secretly jailed an unknown number of people as "material witnesses." Under a little-known and previously little-used law, the government may jail someone not charged with any crime if it can show a court that jailing the person is necessary in order to obtain his testimony at an upcoming trial.[54] The use of this material witness authority since September 11 has been shrouded in secrecy. The press has located at least forty-four people, both citizens and noncitizens, who have been jailed, some for many months, but the government has refused to say how many people have been detained on this basis.[55]

While the material witness law allows individuals to be jailed without being charged with any crime when their testimony is needed at trial and the government shows that it is likely that otherwise they will not show up, the law nowhere allows the government to do so in secret. But the Bush administration invoked grand jury secrecy rules to jail individuals in secret, claiming they were needed as grand jury witnesses. Not only is such use of the material witness law to jail grand jury witnesses rather than trial witnesses questionable,[56] some substantial number of individuals jailed as material witnesses never even testified before a grand jury or any other proceeding.[57]

Those cases suggest that the government simply used the material witness law to jail people whom it thought "suspicious" but had no evidence to charge with a crime. While some argue that the threat of terrorism is so great that such extreme measures are called for, the government has other means of protecting against future crimes. It can wiretap and put twenty-four-hour surveillance on individuals suspected of plotting terrorist attacks. But allowing the government to jail individuals without making the constitutionally required showing to a judge that there is "probable cause" that the individual has committed a crime means that there is no method for determining whether that person has in fact done something wrong. Whether such measures might be appropriate for terrorists, the strength of our constitutional system has always been that something more than the attorney general's say-so is needed to jail someone as a terrorist.

Nevertheless, in the months following September 11, the government apparently used the material witness authority to secretly jail and interrogate some number of actual criminal suspects, perhaps only a handful, and to secretly jail and interrogate some larger number of innocent people. In both instances the government acted not in accordance with the rule of law, but like a dictatorship. Since then, the government has embarked on an even more ambitious detention program aimed at immigrants.

TREATING IMMIGRANTS LIKE CRIMINALS

In November 2001, a top Ashcroft deputy, Michael Chertoff, told Congress that looking for a terrorist in the United States is like "looking for a needle in a haystack."[58] In addition to the secret arrests, the government has undertaken a whole series of detention measures not aimed at terrorists but at Arab and Muslim immigrants. As also noted in an essay above, the Justice Department, on its own, without seeking authority from Congress, has changed the rules to make it easier to jail immigrants, all without any independent court review—an effort to intimidate an entire community.

Immigration violations exist in a unique area of the law: the Supreme Court has declared that they are a civil, not a criminal, matter—even though the immigration laws can be used to jail people for months and then deport them from the only country they may ever have known. Although, on the one hand, this is consistent with the historical understanding in the United States that not having your papers in order does not make one a criminal, on the other hand it has the additional effect that when the government now chooses to treat immigrants like criminals, they have none of the due process protections otherwise accorded to people accused of a crime, including the right to a court-appointed lawyer if they cannot afford one.

In the wake of September 11, the Justice Department unilaterally instituted a series of changes taking advantage of this legal anomaly to make it easier to detain immigrants without any independent court review. On September 20, 2001, the Justice Department extended the length of time that a noncitizen can be detained without charges.[59] On October 31, the Justice Department decreed that even when individuals have been granted bond on immigration violations, it can unilaterally keep them in detention, while it appeals; this move sparked protests from Republican Senator Arlen Specter, among others.[60] Also on October 31, the Justice Department announced that it would eavesdrop on the attorney-client conversations of detainees without obtaining any court-authorized warrant, simply on the attorney general's determination that they were a terrorist.[61]

On January 25, 2002, the Justice Department began an Absconder Apprehension Inititative to enter the names of 6,000 men from Arab and Muslim countries, against whom a final deportation order had been issued, into the National Crime Information Center (NCIC) database.[62] Overlooked was the fact that many such orders had been obtained without the noncitizen having the opportunity to challenge them, as mandated by due process. The local police with access to the NCIC, who might stop a person for running a red light, could then be ordered to arrest him immediately. No justification was given for focusing on this subset of the 314,000 noncitizens who have been issued such orders. The explicit aim was to secure the immediate detention and deportation of these individuals, who would have no opportunity to obtain counsel or any court hearing whatsoever. Whole families—from Afghanistan, for example—who had lived in the United States for years, whose members had married Americans, had had children, worked, paid taxes, and applied for residency were hauled off to jail.[63]

This initiative was followed in the fall of 2002 by a requirement that all men from twenty-five mostly Arab and Muslim countries report to the immigration service offices to register and be fingerprinted and photographed. Those whose papers were not in order were immediately led away in handcuffs.[64] This program again sparked widespread community protest, but as of March 2003, had not been stopped.[65]

Finally, there is every reason to fear that the Justice Department has been compiling a database of persons who could be detained because of their ethnicity or religion in the event of another terrorist attack in the United States.[66] In November 2001, the department began interviewing thousands of men from Middle East and South Asian countries. While the announced purpose was to find information about terrorism, the nature of the questions made clear that the real purpose was to amass as large a database as possible, on as many Americans and immigrants as possible. The interviews asked for the names and addresses of all those in the United States with whom the noncitizen had had contact, including American family and friends, even when there was no suspicion of any terrorist link. Creating a database of individuals not suspected of any crime but simply known to have associated with Middle Eastern men can have no benign purpose. If, as predicted by Commissioner for Civil Rights Peter Kirsanow, there are many more detentions after another attack,[67] this new database will no doubt be used to identify people to be detained.

All of these programs raise serious questions about the effectiveness of the Justice Department's efforts. Is it carrying out a focused investigation, doing the difficult work necessary to identify and detain actual terrorists; or is it using this threat as an opportunity for an anti immigrant dragnet? Such an approach not only betrays American values but has little chance of success. The fact that 1,000 or even 5,000 individuals in a country with 8 million undocumented immigrants are arrested is no assurance that the truly dangerous ones are among them.

MILITARY DETENTIONS AND "ENEMY COMBATANTS"

While the government has used aggressively every shred of preexisting legal authority to detain people for belonging to a certain ethnic or religious group, it has also claimed extraordinary authority to detain, without charges, indefinitely, individuals suspected of terrorism without access to counsel and with only the most limited and pro forma review by any court. President Bush has claimed that he possesses such authority, regardless of any congressional authorization and indeed even in the face of an explicit congressional prohibition on detention of U.S. citizens. Although this unbounded authority has been used sparingly and was originally invoked only against noncitizens, it has now been used to jail two Americans incommunicado and indefinitely, as described below.

On November 13, 2001, the president issued a military order authorizing the military to detain indefinitely, without charges or trial, noncitizens deemed terrorists by the president.[68] The order applied to any noncitizen found either within the United States or abroad whom the president decided was involved in terrorism or harbored a terrorist, without limiting it to Al Qaeda or even any terrorist group attacking Americans.

The president's order was widely criticized for authorizing secret military trials and detentions, the latter also criticized as being a secret end-run around the provisions of the just-enacted PATRIOT Act that had strictly limited when noncitizens could be detained without charges. As a result of the public outcry, the Defense Department issued regulations that scaled back some of the most objectionable parts of the order concerning secret military trials, and as of this writing, neither the military trial nor detention authority for noncitizens found in the U.S. has been used.[69]

Instead, the government has detained two U.S. citizens in a military brig, held them incommunicado, and denied them access to counsel. In April 2002, the government announced that one of the prisoners captured in Afghanistan and held at Guantánamo Bay in Cuba had been born in the United States and was being transferred to a military prison in South Carolina.[70] When the public defender attempted to file a habeas corpus action on behalf of Yasser Hamdi, the government argued that he was being held as an "enemy combatant" and as such had no right to see a lawyer or anyone else.[71]

Then in June 2002, Attorney General Ashcroft announced that a U.S. citizen named Jose Padilla, who had been arrested at Chicago's O'Hare Airport and initially held as a material witness in federal prison, was being transferred to military custody to be held as an "enemy combatant."[72] Although the government did not charge Padilla with any crime, the attorney general said that he had returned from

Afghanistan to scout out information about setting off a radioactive "dirty bomb" in the United States. When the lawyer who had been assigned to represent him as a material witness filed a habeas corpus petition on his behalf, the government made the same arguments as in the Hamdi case.[73] It refused to let the lawyer meet with Padilla, claiming that it can hold him indefinitely and that the courts may not overrule the president.[74]

The government argued that because the United States is at war, the president has unilateral authority as commander in chief to detain even U.S. citizens if he, in his sole discretion, decides that they are "enemy combatants." It argued that under the law of war, such "enemy combatants" can be detained without being tried, at least until the end of the conflict, and gave conflicting answers as to whether the conflict was the military one in Afghanistan or some more difficult-to-gauge conflict with Al Qaeda or terrorism.

While it is certainly true that the law of war authorizes military commanders to capture and detain enemy soldiers on the battlefield, the U.S. recognized the law of war only selectively in the conflict with Al Qaeda, as described below by Michael Ratner. While invoking the authority to detain captured soldiers until the end of the war, the Bush administration denied that the Geneva Conventions apply to the individuals captured in Afghanistan and held in Guantánamo.[75] If the government had followed the Geneva Conventions, Yasser Hamdi would have had at least some opportunity to show whether, as his father claims, he was only in Afghanistan doing relief work, not fighting. The government's "enemy combatant" scheme provides no forum for an individual like Hamdi to show that he was mistakenly arrested, that he was not an enemy soldier, even though picked up on the battlefield.[76]

Even more troubling is the government's extending the notion of captured enemy soldiers on a battlefield to apply to a U.S. citizen arrested at a Chicago airport. Under the government's rationale that the laws of war, not criminal law, apply to Al Qaeda (or other terrorist) suspects found in the United States, the military, not law enforcement officials like the FBI, would be authorized to "capture" and detain any American or noncitizen in the United States on the president's say-so. Indeed, this legal rationale would authorize shooting them, just as it is legal to shoot enemy soldiers during war.[77] It would authorize holding citizens indefinitely, incommunicado, while interrogating them, without any judicial authorization, much less oversight.

To date, the administration has used this authority sparingly. But the government has cleverly positioned these two "test" cases in one of the most conservative courts in the country, and has made a very strong argument that the courts should defer to the president in this "time of war." According to this sophisticated argument, while Hamdi and Padilla are entitled to file habeas petitions in court, the court's role is extremely limited: to review only the legal basis advanced by the government, not to look at the underlying facts of what these individuals have actually done or planned. The Justice Department has further argued that because the role of the court is so limited, there is no need for the lawyers representing Padilla and Hamdi to actually communicate with them, and that such communication would interfere with the government's interrogation of them.[78] If the Supreme Court eventually decides this issue, the government can expect a sympathetic hearing from at least some justices when it argues that the Court should follow its historic—although misguided—practice of allowing a free hand to the president during time of war.

Indeed, after the Republican electoral victories in November 2002, Solicitor General Theodore Olson argued that the only protection for individual liberties is in the political choices of the electorate; there is no role for the courts but to defer to the president.[79] But not only is there no political authorization by Congress for such detentions of U.S. citizens, Congress has explicitly prohibited their detention except when explicitly authorized by the legislature, not the president.[80] The administration's argument would eliminate the constitutional separation of powers that give the courts the responsibility to enforce the Bill of Rights, and thus protect individuals from the tyranny of the majority. As James Madison wrote: "The accumulation of all powers, legislative, executive, and judiciary, in the same hands whether, of one, a few, or many, and whether hereditary, self appointed, or elective, may justly be pronounced the very definition of tyranny."[81]

CRIMINAL PROSECUTIONS

The government claims that these extraordinary measures—secret arrests, widespread immigration detentions, military detention without charges—are necessary because existing criminal law is inadequate to deal with the threat of terrorism. But the record is completely to the contrary. Even before September 11, the government had a perfect record of indicting and convicting those terrorists whom it had identified and caught, for example, for the U.S. embassy bombings in Africa. Since September 11, it has also successfully prosecuted individuals charged as Al Qaeda terrorists: Richard Reid, "the shoe bomber," and John Walker Lindh, the American fighting with the Taliban in Afghanistan.[82]

Terrorism is a unique crime in that, by definition, it is tied to religious or political motivation and, therefore, it is crucial, even if difficult, to draw careful lines between those who engage in criminal terrorist activities and those innocents who may share the political or religious beliefs or ethnic background of terrorists. (Of course, it is difficult to view the World Trade Center attacks as motivated by a political agenda, but there is a long history of terrorist violence aimed at legitimate political ends.) There is evidence that the Justice Department is not drawing those lines but instead is using the criminal law not only against terrorists, but also to target First Amendment–protected political and religious speech and association and to engage in discriminatory enforcement targeted against Muslims and Arab-American activists who are not charged with or linked to terrorism.

Serious questions have been raised about several pending criminal cases. Lynn Stewart, a left-wing New York lawyer who had represented an Egyptian cleric convicted of terrorism, has been criminally charged for making public statements on behalf of her jailed client in circumstances that raise the specter of criminal prosecution of dissent and government interference with the attorney-client relationship.[83] The government also indicted six Yemeni-Americans living in Lackawanna, New York, for providing "material support to terrorism" by traveling to Afghanistan before September 11.[84] While the defendants claim that they went for religious reasons and had nothing to do with terrorism, the government's position is that their trip would still be a crime.[85] Such a broad reading of the crime of material support for terrorism would sweep in innocent and protected religious associations. The government's indictment of a prominent Arab-American businessman in Florida on criminal charges regarding the hiring of illegal immigrants has raised questions about selective enforcement based on religion and ethnicity. The government sought to keep him in jail before trial without bond, citing his contributions to Muslim charities and a letter he wrote a newspaper. In granting bond, the judge criticized the government: "There is a great danger that connections and associations can be used to paint with a very broad brush. Simply because someone meets or knows someone . . . or shares the same characteristics does not make him responsible for somebody else's actions."[86]

Given the actions to date of the Ashcroft Justice Department, there is reason to fear that it will increasingly use the criminal law—along with the other authorities described above—to target individuals who have innocent First Amendment–protected associations with groups considered suspicious by the government, from pro-Palestinian or antiwar groups to radical environmentalists and Muslim charities. It is a terrible reflection on the times that at least criminal defendants, unlike those secretly jailed for immigration violations or held by the military as enemy combatants, will be afforded some basic due process before being jailed.

CONCLUSION

Since September 11, President Bush and Attorney General Ashcroft claim that they alone can write the rules for when individuals will be jailed and then decide who comes within those rules, all with no outside appeal. These detentions, undertaken without congressional authorization, public debate about their propriety or necessity, or judicial review, violate not only fundamental due process for individuals, but the very constitutional structure of our government, the separation of powers created as the "essential precaution in favor of liberty."[87]

In a nation defined by adherence to the principles of freedom and individual liberty, national security must include the security to be free of arbitrary detention; to know that one will not be secretly carted off to jail in the middle of the night and held incommunicado. That security must be extended to all persons in the country, citizen and noncitizen alike. And everyone must be secure that they will not be jailed because of their race or religion.

As long as terrorism is seen as a problem to be addressed through national security and law enforcement means, rather than political ones, policy makers will consistently undervalue the benefits to be derived from respecting civil liberties and human rights in the fight against terrorism. But promoting democracy, justice, and human rights will, in the long run, prove to be powerful weapons against terrorism. Secret arbitrary detentions—as many dictatorships have learned—can only make us more vulnerable.

5. RACIAL PROFILING POST–9/11:
OLD STORY, NEW DEBATE

TANYA E. COKE[1]

As with so many other issues of civil liberties, the events of September 11 radically recast the national debate around racial profiling. For a few years before 9/11, commentators, police, and politicians began for the first time to acknowledge the existence of criminal profiling based on race, and to condemn the practice. The Civil Rights Division of the Department of Justice had begun assert its powers to sue police departments where it found an egregious pattern and practice of racial profiling. By early 2000, some 80 percent of Americans said they had heard of racial profiling and felt it should be stopped.[2] September 11 changed all that. Within a month of the attacks, the converse became true, with a similar majority endorsing extra scrutiny, and even special identification cards, for Arab Americans.[3]

Of course, even "old school" racial profiling is nothing new. Long before the Drug Enforcement Administration (DEA) instructed state highway patrols to stop black and Hispanic drivers on suspicion of narcotics trafficking, racial profiling has been a timeworn tactic of law enforcement. Whatever the criminal plague of the moment, there has usually been at work the assumption that the poorest, darkest, or most recently arrived among us are at the center of vice. Native Americans, blacks, and a parade of immigrant groups have all, in their own time, been the targets of regular roundups. White vigilantes kept peremptory watch over black communities in the post–Reconstruction South through the enforcement of Black Codes and later, vagrancy laws.[4] So heavily targeted were the Irish by urban police in the mid-nineteenth and early twentieth centuries that "paddy wagon" became the favored term for the police vehicle used to conduct en masse sweeps.[5]

The historical precedents to the immediate issue of Arab profiling are, unfortunately, equally easy to find. In past crises of national security, our government has similarly singled out immigrant groups as the source of threat. In the infamous Palmer raids following the outbreak of World War I, the United States rounded up and deported hundreds of immigrants, often without a scintilla of evidence of anti-American activity. During the World War II, the federal government interned over 100,000 Japanese men, women, and children—without regard to citizenship or length of residence in the U.S.—in remote camps, confiscating their property in the process. To its shame, in cases like *Korematsu v. United States,*[6] the Supreme Court upheld these roundups as legitimate given the wartime threat to American security.

Viewed historically, the ethnic profile has a depressing inevitability about it. Indeed, race and immigrant status are what tend to distinguish trivial misdeeds from official crimes, and bad crimes from truly intolerable ones. The American experience with drug prohibition provides especially stark examples of this phenomenon. In the nineteenth century, opium was a popularly prescribed drug for middle-class American women suffering anxiety and other maladies. Its use did not become subject to criminal penalties until large numbers of Chinese began arriving on the West Coast of the United States, where authorities quickly moved to outlaw and close down their opium dens.[7] Legal authorities banned marijuana only when fear arose in 1930s that Chicanos—by then a visible and underemployed minority—would be incited to violence while smoking it.[8] Cocaine use, although illegal, had been almost normalized as the drug of choice among the white upper and middle classes in the late 1970s and 1980s. It took the drug's adoption by inner-city blacks in the form of crack a decade later to launch a "war on drugs" worthy of a new cabinet post, billions of dollars in law enforcement,[9] and penalties 100 times more severe than for powder cocaine.[10] Although relatively few Americans were actually using crack cocaine, it was the profile of the users—young, urban, poor, and black—that fueled a national media hysteria powerful enough to generate fifty separate pieces of legislation in Congress during a one-month period in 1986.[11] In each of these instances, the demand for a swift and severe response by law enforcement was stoked by racial fears that a minority underclass would, under the influence of mind-altering drugs, be unleashed as a rampaging criminal force. In short, race is the ingredient that lends criminal dimension to activities that, when engaged in by the majority, are considered within the realm of private conduct—behavior appropriate for the moral authorities of the church, not the State, to police.

Perhaps the most remarkable thing about racial profiling is not its tenacity, but the fact that so ingrained a practice actually became, for a time, a subject of heated controversy. Sometime around 1995, profiling acquired a name and began to attract public debate. The contemporary understanding of profiling arises from a description of drug couriers developed by the DEA and used to train state highway patrols as part of Operation Pipeline, a federal-state initiative to crack down on interstate drug trafficking nationwide. Among other things, the profile urged police to look out for black and Latino males traveling together, or in rental cars, especially those driving carefully within the speed limit.[12] Troopers were urged to find some pretext on which to stop and search such drivers for drugs.

Some, although far from all, police chiefs acknowledged that race played a sometimes significant role in deciding whom to stop and search. This revelation was hardly news within black communities, whose men had suffered harassment by police on local streets and highways for years. But "Driving While Black" (or DWB), an ironic phrase coined by black Americans, now entered the popular lexicon. Two major lawsuits subsequently produced empirical data indicating that race was a predominant factor in highway traffic stops. In *Wilkins v. Maryland State Police,* Robert Wilkins, a black Harvard Law School graduate and public defender from the District of Columbia, sued the Maryland highway patrol when he and three family members were subjected to a protracted and unwarranted search as they returned from a family funeral.[13] In *Wilkins,* a Temple University researcher hired by the plaintiffs conducted a "violator survey" that showed that, while 74.7 percent of speeders on that stretch of I-95 were white, while 17.5 percent were black, 79.2 percent of all drivers stopped and searched by the highway patrol were black.[14] The highway patrol's own records showed that half of the force stopped 80 percent African Americans, and two officers stopped *only* African Americans.[15] In a second case, public defenders in Gloucester County, New Jersey, used state police data to challenge the arrest of nineteen defendants arrested on the New Jersey Turnpike. That data showed that while blacks were no more than 13.5 percent of highway drivers, and 15 percent of speeders, they represented fully 35 percent of those stopped on the turnpike, and 73.2 percent of those arrested.[16]

Public scrutiny increased further after white state troopers shot four unarmed black college students during a stop on the highway. When a subsequent Department of Justice investigation confirmed a widespread practice of racial profiling, Governor Christine Todd Whitman fired the chief of the highway patrol after he defended the profile as "common-sense" policing.[17] In 1999, Bill Clinton called profiling "morally indefensible" and ordered federal law enforcement agencies to begin collecting racial data on all stops and searches.[18] Even cities like New York that had inaugurated, to great public acclaim, aggressive "quality of life policing" began to feel the backlash against profiling. When an African immigrant named Amadou Diallo died on a Bronx street corner in a hail of forty-one bullets, New York's famously tough-on-crime mayor, Rudolph Giuliani, disbanded the Street Crimes Unit, a narcotics and gun squad notorious among black and Hispanic residents for aggressive profiling. By 2000, polls showed that over 59 percent of Americans believed that racial profiling by police was widespread, with 81 percent saying they disapproved of the practice.[19] Across the nation politicians scrambled to decry the practice, and police chiefs mostly to deny it. George W. Bush was even heard to say that racial profiling "is wrong in America, and we've got to get rid of it."[20] In the wake of widespread and newly credible accusations of profiling, between January 1999 and September 2001 some thirteen states had passed legislation either requiring police departments to collect data on racial profiling, or simply banning the practice.

All this constituted rather headspinning change from just a few years earlier, when most Americans would have told you that if the police tracking criminal suspects by race, they certainly ought to be. For the first time in modern history, worries about racial disparity were galvanizing change in criminal justice—an arena particularly resistant to civil rights arguments.[21] September 11 changed all that.

FROM DRIVING WHILE BLACK TO FLYING WHILE BROWN

The terrorist attacks of September 11—or, more precisely, the fact that all nineteen of the hijackers were Arabic men—quickly recast the national consensus around profiling.

Within a month of the attack, surveys showed that a majority of Americans favored more intensive security checks for Arab and Middle Eastern people.[22] Perhaps most startling was the finding that African Americans, the most frequent targets and most vocal critics of racial profiling, were even more supportive of profiling Arabs than other groups. A Gallup Poll found that 71 percent of black respondents favored profiling of Arabs at airports, compared with 63 percent of other nonwhites and 57 percent of whites.[23] Sixty-four percent of blacks and 56 percent of other nonwhites favored requiring Arabs—including U.S. citizens—to carry special identification cards as a means of preventing terrorist attacks. "It's better to be safe than sorry," said one black man interviewed by the *Boston Globe*. "I know it's wrong, but we'll apologize later."[24] Perhaps most revealing, majorities of Arab Americans themselves agreed that extra scrutiny of their communities was justified.[25]

In the initial weeks after the attacks, President Bush and Attorney General John Ashcroft received high marks for their vocal expressions of concern for the safety of Arab Americans, hundreds of whom were victimized by hate crimes in the aftermath of the attacks. Within days, senior Bush administration officials met with Arab-American leaders. The Department of Justice signaled that it would prosecute perpetrators of hate crimes to the fullest extent of the law. President Bush gave a televised speech from a Washington, D.C., mosque in which he assured the nation's Muslim communities that terrorism, not Islam, would be the government's target.

If there is one thing President Bush gets credit for, it is mastering the new public relations of race. One need only recall the rainbow of humanity on display at the Republican National Convention to understand that George Bush is keenly aware of the shifting racial demographics of the country and its implications for American politics.[26] More skillfully and assiduously than Democrats, who have tended to take the immigrant vote for granted, President Bush has courted Hispanics with considerable success.[27] His Cabinet boasts two African Americans, one Japanese-American, an Asian woman, and a Hispanic man. As with other matters of race, it is also becoming clear that Bush is master of the empty gesture. Contrary to its assurances in the weeks after the attacks, the Bush administration's antiterrorism policy looks very much like "all Arabs, all the time":

• September 20, 2001. The Department of Justice (DOJ) publishes an interim regulation allowing detention without charges for forty-eight hours or "an additional reasonable period of time" in the event of "extraordinary circumstances." Federal authorities then proceed to detain some 1,200 immigrants, most of them immigrants from Arabic or Muslim countries, without formal charges.

• November 9, 2001. The attorney general orders state and local law enforcement to assist the FBI in conducting interviews of 5,000 men, ages eighteen to thirty-three, who entered the United States since January 2000 and come from nations where Al Qaeda is known to be active.[28] The interviews are to be "voluntary," but the government announces it will reserve the right to file the names of those who do not respond. Several days later, the Immigration and Naturalization Service (INS) directs its agents to respond to information gathered from state and local officers about immigration violations among the interviewees.

• November 19, 2001. The Bush Administration imposes new security checks on visa applications from "men from certain countries, aged 16 to 45." Although DOJ declines to specify to which countries the new procedure applies, the checks are enforced only against citizens from majority Muslim nations.

• February 26, 2002. The Department of Justice issues a final report on the interviews of 5,000 Arab and Muslim men. The report states that approximately half those on the list were interviewed; that fewer than twenty were taken into custody, most on immigration charges. Three criminal charges were filed, but none of these were connected to terrorist activity. The DOJ admits that most of those interviewed had no information about the 9/11 attacks; only two identified acquaintances who'd had flight training.[29]

• March 19, 2002. The DOJ announces another round of interviews of 3,000 additional Arab and Muslim men.[30]

• April 10, 2002. News is leaked of a new DOJ legal opinion stating that local law enforcement personnel have "inherent" power to enforce civil violations of immigration laws. If implemented, this policy would enlist thousands of local police officers in the service of the INS, empowering them to stop, question, and arrest visa violators and undocumented immigrants.

• June 11, 2002. The DOJ orders special scrutiny of all Yemeni citizens seeking to enter or leave the United States, including thorough inspections of their baggage.

• November 6, 2002. The DOJ orders young men with visas from Iran, Iraq, Libya, Sudan, or Syria to appear by December 16, 2002 in person before the INS for questioning, fingerprinting, and photographing. All such men are ordered thereafter to report annually to the INS for questioning, and to report all changes of addresses with ten days under penalty of prosecution.

• December 18, 2002. Two days after the above deadline for registration passes, the INS arrests and detains hundreds of Iranian, Iraqi, and other Middle Eastern men in Southern California who appeared for registration. The INS refuses to release details as to how many are arrested, but claims the detentions are based on visa status irregularities or criminal warrants.

But for outcry from a few Arab-American organizations and the ACLU, there has been remarkably little soul searching by the public or the media about the roundups.[31] Most commentators tend to pose the tradeoff as one of momentary inconvenience to a few versus the personal safety and security of the rest of us.[32] This complacency extends even to extreme cases of detention and mistake. The news coverage of the ultimately baseless stop and detention of three Muslim medical students traveling by car from Chicago to Florida to begin residency training in September 2002 was revealing in this regard. Police, acting on a tip from a woman who reported overhearing suspicious conversation among the men in a Georgia restaurant, stopped them as they traveled south, closing a twenty-mile stretch of I-75 while they searched the car. Investigators detained and interrogated the students for seventeen hours before they concluded the men posed no threat and released them. The stop proved costly: After the hospital sponsoring the mens' residency was deluged by hate e-mails, administrators there withdrew the offer of admission. Despite the fact that accusations proved groundless, Governor Jeb Bush and Senator Bob Graham effusively praised law enforcement officials and the tipster in Georgia as good patriots. For days afterward, news radio shows could be heard eliciting similar comments from callers and citizen passersby, frequently neglecting to mention the fact that the suspects in question were ultimately found to be innocent.

The most striking exception to these race-based policies has been the place one would most expect to find them in force: our nation's airports. There, Secretary of Transportation Norman Mineta has vociferously resisted race-based profiling. Mineta's antiprofiling stance has been widely accredited to his own experience of profiling as a child, when he and his family were interned during World War II. In the days after 9/11, the Department of Transportation (DOT) took pains to recirculate its policies of nondiscrimination toward passengers to airport security and other personnel. Complaints, say watchdog groups, have centered less on the actions of security screeners than on the behavior of airline passengers and pilots, who have in at least sixty instances ejected Arab-looking men from their flights.[33] In response to past complaints, especially from Arab and South Asian travelers, in 1998 the Federal Aviation Administration (FAA) instituted a system called the Computer Assisted Passenger Screening System (CAPS). CAPS combines purely random screens with twenty other behavioral identifiers—for example, travel destination or origin, past travel patterns, and the manner of ticket purchase. Race and ethnicity are not among the legitimate criteria. The DOT keeps the specifics of its profile a well-guarded secret, but experts who follow department policy say it was revamped in light of 9/11. Mineta insists, however, that CAPS II still does not include race as a suspect identifier. Arab and immigrant groups seem to agree that this is in fact the case. Anyone who has passed through airport security since 9/11 would probably concur: for every swarthy-skinned young man stopped, there are also white men in business suits and middle-aged women who can be seen removing their shoes and emptying their pockets for security officers.

For this race-blind policy, Mineta has been roundly criticized.[34] There are rumors that the secretary continues to confront serious opposition to the policy from within his department as well as from White House officials. Late in 2001, CBS journalist Mike Wallace interviewed Mineta for a *60 Minutes* story on profiling. The piece portrayed Mineta as a hopeless patsy, naively clinging to vague principles of civil rights in face of palpable threats of terrorism. When asked if the sight of three young Arab men kneeling in prayer before a flight would provide reason for airport personnel to conduct a stop-and-question, Mineta answered with an implacable, "No reason."[35] Of course, Mike Wallace is hardly alone in his impatience with traditional equal protection arguments in this context. Thomas Ambrose, a retired analyst on Middle Eastern terrorism for the State Department, articulated a commonly held view that "it is perfectly obvious that young Muslim males from the Middle East are far more likely to hijack planes than Aunt Molly, and any reasonable and effective security system must take this into consideration."[36] John Farmer, the attorney general of New Jersey who, before 9/11, won praise from civil rights leaders for his no-nonsense handling of the New Jersey Highway Patrol profiling scandal, put it in rather starker terms: "Let's be blunt," he said. "How can law enforcement *not* consider ethnicity in investigating these crimes when that identifier is an essential characteristic of the hijackers and their supposed confederates and sponsors?"[37]

The Aunt Molly question poses an interesting conundrum, one that has quietly divided civil rights groups accustomed to speaking in one voice about the impropriety of racially biased policing. Arab-American groups, before 9/11 a fairly marginal presence within civil rights coalitions, have sought out their colleagues for support in opposing the Justice Department's policies. The response has been positive, but not as quick or as vocal from some quarters as some Arab organizations might like. (Japanese-American groups have been extremely supportive, they say, for obvious reasons of history, as have been pan-Asian organizations, whose Sikh and Southeast Asian Muslim members have suffered discrimination when mistaken for Middle Easterners.) The implicit worry here is that, by equating "Flying While Brown" with Driving While Black, civil libertarians may be undermining the longer-term case against racial profiling. For now, all admit that 9/11 has all but extinguished the federal conversation about racial profiling. A federal bill to mandate racial data on traffic stops, sponsored by Representative John Conyers, was gaining momentum before September 11 but is now widely agreed to be dead on arrival.

BUT ISN'T THIS DIFFERENT FROM DWB?

So what about Aunt Molly? Is racial profiling in the antiterrorist context really as "morally indefensible" as garden variety criminal profiling? Or is the case of Arab terrorism a distinct case? The answer to this question requires some equivocation. Disagreements have simmered for years between civil rights and policing communities over how precisely to define racial profiling. Police officials prefer a definition that would proscribe using race as the *sole* basis for conducting stops and searches, while civil libertarians argue for the exclusion of *any* use of race, even in combination with other factors, except when a suspect is known to be of a certain race. Under either definition, on the face of it, Arab profiling and Driving While Black *are* the same thing: both use ethnicity as part of a profile to predict criminal behavior, in the absence of specific evidence that a crime has been committed by that individual (what lawyers and cops call "probable cause"). Yet several differences would seem to distinguish the case of antiterrorist profiling from drug war or other types of criminal profiling:

1. *This may not be selective enforcement.* One of the chief reasons why drug-war profiling is illegitimate is the fact that it trades on the myth that blacks and Hispanics are the principal perpetrators of drug crimes. While it is unquestionably true that some drugs find greater favor with one ethnic group over another (e.g., metamphetamines are favored by whites in the northern Midwest and Heartland states, while crack cocaine first predominated among poor blacks in the inner cities), research by various federal agencies consistently shows that drug use is an equal opportunity activity. Whites, blacks, and Latinos tend to use and abuse drugs in roughly equal numbers, with whites—the largest proportion of Americans—constituting the greatest number of users.[38] Drug sales, like most other things in American society, tend toward racial segregation, with drug users generally buying from sellers of the same race.[39] Thus, while blacks make up only 13 percent of the country's illicit drug users, it is selective enforcement by police—

perpetrated through racial profiling—that accounts for their higher arrest rates: 35 percent of those arrested for drug possession, and fully 74 percent of people sentenced to prison.[40]

There is no comparably strong case to be made about selective enforcement of terrorist laws. Like drug crimes, terrorist methods certainly admit zealots of all political stripes, races, and nationalities. We have Timothy McVeigh and the Aryan Nation to attest to that. Yet the violence and death inherent in acts of terrorism will tend to demand attention and prosecution whatever their source (though here too unevenly and in racial degrees: many African Americans complained that the federal and local governments did little to respond to a spate of black church burnings across the South in the mid-1990s, an echo of the thirty-eight years it took authorities to win final convictions in the 1963 firebombing deaths of four black girls in a Birmingham church). Still, if the government is defining Al Qaeda as the preeminent threat to American security and principal target of our counterterrorism campaign—and it is difficult to argue that it oughtn't—why, then, shouldn't nationality become a relevant aspect of the terrorist profile? The majority of the men on the FBI's Most Wanted Terrorists list were born in Saudi Arabia or Egypt.[41] All of twenty-two of those on the list as of this writing are from Arabic-speaking nations in the Middle East.

2. *Nationality profiling may not be the same as racial profiling.* Indeed, the terrorism threat faced by the United States is not so much associated with any particular race as with particular countries from which Al Qaeda and its satellites are believed to operate. Although the distinctions are easy to elide, profiling by nationality and profiling by race are not necessarily the same thing, either legally or in fact. As a factual matter, there is no perfect congruence between nationality and race or ethnicity. A passport holder from Cuba or the Sudan—or from the United States, for that matter—can just as easily look Middle Eastern, European, or black African. Many countries, particularly those with a history of immigration, slavery, or in which colonial powers drew arbitrary boundaries, encompass a diversity of ethnicities and language groups.

Legally, too, U.S. courts have long upheld discrimination on the basis of national origin in immigration matters. Until the mid-1960s, the United States subscribed to strict immigration quotas, and it still treats tourists and immigrants from certain countries (for example, Europeans and Cubans) with greater favor than others. This fact has allowed Bush officials to issue indignant statements forswearing racial or ethnic profiling, and to insist that they are not targeting Arabs but merely "people from countries where Al Qaeda operates." As outrageous as it is, the Bush administration is probably well within the bounds of constitutional law in hauling in noncitizen immigrants from Middle Eastern countries for fingerprinting and questioning.

Of course, the nationality distinctions we've made in immigration practices, whether 100 years ago or today, are generally little more than a screen for ethnic and racial discrimination. With few exceptions, U.S. border policies are designed to admit white immigrants from wealthy countries and screen out dark people from poor ones. In fact and in perception, the foreign nationals being targeted by the U.S. antiterrorist campaign are Middle Easterners from major Muslim countries. The now scores of detentions and deportations of Arab residents—as far as we can tell, all of them for petty immigration or minor criminal violations unrelated to terrorism—can, on the one hand, be read as a logical prioritization of INS enforcement resources. A more sinister, but historically consistent, view would be to interpret the registration program as a modern-day purge. The government rounds up people for fingerprinting, identifies grounds on which it might deport some of them, and then requires the rest to register at frequent intervals, thereby creating new grounds for deportation should they fail to do so. Those Arab nationals who remain do so knowing they are subject to secret surveillance methods approved under the USA PATRIOT Act. Those who might consider changing jobs or residences will think twice before doing so, knowing they risk incarceration or deportation should they or the INS fail to register properly the change of address. Much like the invisible electronic fences being used nowadays by pet owners, the government's registration program delivers the same fear-inducing, movement-confining benefits of internment without the unsightly look of barbed wire.

3. *The threat posed by terrorism is arguably greater.* It is a safe bet that drug abuse will wreak more havoc on the lives of more people than will ever be directly affected by a terrorist attack. Yet the catastrophic violence promised by another act of terrorism makes drug trafficking look like petty crime in comparison. The randomness of terrorism, too, heightens our collective fear in a way that makes us countenance extreme measures that we might not otherwise contemplate. Of course, it is John Ashcroft who has driven home this point most forcefully, reminding the public at every opportunity that extraordinary threats require extraordinary measures. In this climate of fear, complaints about the moral inde-

fensibility of racial profiling begin sounding like solipsistic whining. James J. Zogby, president of the Arab American Institute, agrees. "To complain about racial profiling on unfairness grounds tends to elicit more backlash than had people remained silent," he says.

If there is a case to be made against antiterrorist profiling, it will clearly have to be made on the grounds of its ineffectiveness as a law enforcement tool. Racial profiling may make us *feel* safer, but does it actually work to predict criminal behavior?

"OBSERVING" VERSUS "PREDICTING" BEHAVIOR

Experts on both sides of the issue agree that, in some instances, relying on race to catch suspects is permissible. To use race to describe and identify a known or witnessed individual—e.g., suspect six feet two inches tall, 150 pounds, black male, leather jacket—is perfectly legitimate. Indeed, in this context, race can be a more helpful identifier than other, changeable features, like facial hair or clothing. But, says David Harris, author of *Profiles of Injustice: Why Racial Profiling Cannot Work,* "While race can describe a person well, it predicts abysmally."[42] In the United States alone, there are 3.5 million Arabs and millions more Muslims. A substantial percentage of these Arabs are not Muslim, but Christian. Hundreds of thousands of "Middle-Eastern looking" visitors can be expected to pass through the nation's airports and transportations hubs each year. Because only an infinitesimal percentage of Arabs or Muslims are involved in terrorist organizations, race will do a particularly poor job of identifying the *particular* Arabs or Muslims in whom police should be interested. More significant, says Harris, is that "when you make race a principal determinant of who you are going to stop and track, police are misdirected from the first principle of policing, which is about observing suspicious behavior."[43]

The manhunt for the sniper who terrorized the suburbs of Washington, D.C., in the fall of 2002 underscores the fallibility of suspect profiles. Before the arrests of John Muhammad and John Lee Malvo, prognostications issued daily from "professional" crime profilers that the perpetrator was a disaffected white male in his thirties, acting alone—the standard profile of serial killers. Police did in fact stop Muhammad and Malvo on several occasions during the course of the investigation, but the two black men never aroused enough suspicion to warrant close questioning. Authorities concede that they were probably—and perhaps fatally—misdirected by the conventional wisdom that the sniper was a white man. In the end, it was an incriminating message, linked to Malvo through forensic evidence, that led to the arrests.

What, then, about using race plus other behavioral factors, like purchasing a last-minute airplane ticket, or driving a car preferred by drug dealers? Harris points to the fact that the Operation Pipeline profile devised by the DEA and implemented aggressively in New Jersey and Maryland included nonracial as well as racial factors, and still produced poor success rates to show for it. Among police departments that focused on profiling blacks and Latinos in drug and gun enforcement, the "hit rate"—or rate at which searches produced contraband—was actually *lower* for minorities than it was for whites.[44]

Harris ascribes this counterintuition in part to human nature. Race, along with gender and age, is such a culturally and visually powerful identifier that it tends to overwhelm the judgment of security personnel who could more usefully be scrutinizing behavioral clues. Harris describes a profile in which six behavioral characteristics are used to identify smugglers at airports: "If we let race become one of those factors, it is likely that someone who meets two of the six criteria would be acceptable to stop, whereas without race we would probably demand that four or five or six be present."[45]

Profiling casts so wide a net that it spreads finite law enforcement resources over more people than law enforcement would otherwise be interested in. Secretary Norman Mineta agrees. "Such an operation," he said in an April 2002 speech, "would generate so many 'false positives' that it would seriously hamper screeners in making the behavioral observations they need to make."[46] There is direct evidence from the airport security context to suggest this is smart policing.

In the mid-1990s, the Customs Department abandoned its practice of using race as part of its profile for deciding whom to stop and search on suspicion of smuggling. It found that when personnel focused solely on behavior and other race-neutral factors, the number of searches conducted dropped by 70 percent, but the "hit rate" for contraband improved dramatically—from just 5 percent to over 15 percent. Stated differently, Customs was able to reduce its manpower commitment to search operations by nearly three-quarters, while improving the number of productive seizures by 300 percent.[47] There is no reason to believe that the same principle wouldn't also apply to counterterrorism.

PROFILING AS A "HEADS UP"

Another reason why profiling on the basis of appearance or national origin may be counterproductive from a security standpoint is that it gives a heads up to would-be perpetrators of crime. Despite the fact that the hijackers were all young Arab men, it is false comfort to imagine that this will always be the case. Given the virtual certainty that Al Qaeda terrorists are closely watching the patterns of the counterterrorist screenings, it becomes critical to conduct random security checks, even of Aunt Molly. Indeed, to exempt from scrutiny any class of persons—grandmothers, priests, or those traveling with children—is likely to ensure terrorists will use that information to their advantage, by recruiting people who do not fit the profile, or using them to smuggle an explosive on board unwittingly. "Some kind of profiling is inevitable; that's just the world we live in," says Daniel Benjamin, a former director of counterterrorism with the National Security Council and co-author of *The Age of Sacred Terror,* a critique of America's terrorism defenses. "But it will still be insufficient because Al Qaeda is seeking to recruit Westerners—people who are disaffected, who are found in prison or otherwise attracted to a violent ideology. . . . There were thousands of people trained in Al Qaeda camps, and we know that many of them were South Asian or from other than Arab countries."[48] Indeed, consider some of the early arrests in the government's antiterror investigation—Jose Padilla, alleged shoe bomber Richard Colvin Reid, and John Walker Lindh. A Mexican-American, a British West Indian, and a Virginia WASP—none of these men fit either the ethnic or nationality profile.

There is also the fact that an Arab-based profile will do little or nothing to uncover destructive plans laid by terrorist organizations that originate in other countries. The more recent terrorist attacks in Indonesia in October 2002 make clear that the West has many enemies, not all of them Arabic speakers from the Middle East.

In short, profiling is both overinclusive and underinclusive. Profiling by "Middle Eastern" appearance to look for a relatively miniscule number of Al Qaeda operatives will ensnare thousands of innocents from Arabic and non-Arabic countries. At the same time, it will deflect attention from "less suspicious"–looking persons our enemies are more and more likely to recruit. Profiling the citizens of only Arabic speaking countries is clearly underinclusive, as it may fail to scrutinize operatives in further-flung regions of the world. The price of expanding the list to include people from more countries, or all Muslim countries, of course, just spreads law enforcement resources—and international goodwill—that much thinner.

UNDERMINING INTELLIGENCE GATHERING

Both street cops and security experts understand that good intelligence is the bedrock of effective crime prevention. If there are in fact sleeper cells of Arab terrorists in this country, waiting to commit more mayhem, then surely the best way to detect them is to gather intelligence from the inside. A number of antiterrorism experts have criticized the Bush administration's tactics as ineffective in this regard. Of the FBI interviews of Middle Eastern men, Kenneth P. Walton, a former FBI assistant director who established the first joint terrorism task force in New York City, says, "It's the Perry Mason School of Law Enforcement, where you get them in there and they confess. Well, it just doesn't work that way." [49] Ashcroft has sworn fealty to a policy of arresting suspects for "spitting on the sidewalk" on the grounds that jailing first, and investigating later, will protect against further attacks. "Th[is] policy of preemptive arrests and detentions carries a lot of risk with it," says former FBI Director William H. Webster. "You may interrupt something, but you may not be able to bring it down." [50] By contrast, former FBI officials say that effective counterterrorism employs informants, undercover agents, and surveillance—as well as the patience to let investigations play out for months or longer so that the full extent of planned activities and participants can be identified. The dragnets and preventive detentions ordered by Ashcroft, they say, will likely compromise the ability to infiltrate cells by forcing investigators to close terrorism investigations prematurely. [51]

If anything, September 11 made painfully clear the absence of adequate intelligence networks within Arab and Muslim communities in the United States, where many of the hijackers lived while planning the attack. Regular beat cops know how hard it is to build relationships with immigrants. Beyond the usual language barriers, many immigrants come from countries where police are an abusive force to be feared. Although more than 80 percent of Arabs in this country are U.S. born, the more recently arrived immigrants are the most insular, tending to keep one foot in America and one foot in the homeland. It is this community that has borne the brunt of hate crimes and blunderbuss investigatory tactics since 9/11. Yet these are the very residents law enforcement authorities need to cultivate. To build relationships with Arabs at home and abroad, to gather the kind of intelligence needed to fight the new threat, will require consistent and patient outreach.

The Justice Department's behavior, by contrast, reads like a primer on how to *undermine* trust with an immigrant community: round up 8,000 young Arab men for questioning; require thousands more to register with the INS; arrest and jail hundreds of them on minor immigration violations; describe them as "suspected terrorists," holding some for months without formal charges; and then deport them. Hussan Jaber, associate director of the Arab Community Center for Economic and Social Services in Dearborn, Michigan, says the Bush administration's policies have chilled the willingness of community members to cooperate. Dearborn's is one of the largest Arab-American communities in the country. "I honestly believe there was a high sense of anger about the events in New York, Pennsylvania, and Washington [among Arab Americans]," he says. "A huge number of people came to our agency to offer to assist the FBI. When the FBI made the call for interpreters, we were flooded with volunteers. Since that time, I hardly hear of anyone coming to us saying, 'What is it I can do?' " [52]

The sentiment about the United States among Arabs abroad, of course, is far more bitter. The roundups and mass registration of young Arab men have been heavily reported in the Middle Eastern media, with devastating consequences for foreign relations in the region, says James J. Zogby, president of the Arab American Institute. "The State Department has budgeted $16 million for advertisements in the Muslim world that emphasize how Arabs are living peacefully in America. Yet the almost weekly announcements of new initiatives out of the Justice Department have created a sustained wave of negative perceptions of how Arabs and Muslims are actually being treated. When you add to that the stories Arab students, many of them questioned in the investigation, are carrying back home, plus those who can no longer get visas for study, the picture being painted to the Middle East is quite bleak." [53]

Many local police departments have learned this same lesson in the DWB context. Casting the net widely over every Arab national, or even just young Arab men, is sure to ensnare many thousands of innocent people. Just as profiling has victimized black Americans, the government's dragnet of Arabs will humiliate hundreds of law-abiding people in their homes, at their schools, and on their jobs. The registration and interview program is branding entire communities as presumptive criminals, sending a message to employers and police that Arab origin is a factor worth our discrimination—and evidently the single most important factor in discerning terrorists among us. Notwithstanding the admonitions of the U.S. Civil Rights Division and other Bush administration officials that employment discrimination and hate crimes against Arabs are not to be tolerated, the government's own program of ethnic profiling only reinforces and encourages such behavior by private individuals.

These are the very policies that cost police departments dearly in their relations with black communities. For this reason, police chiefs resisted participating in the FBI interviews of young Arab men in early 2002. Chief Mark Kroeker of the Portland, Oregon, police department, along with several other police chiefs, refused to let his officers participate on the grounds that it would jeopardize relations his department had painstakingly worked to improve between police and local immigrants. Even more contentious has been a proposal by the INS that local police arrest and detain immigrants for civil violations of immigration law—i.e., for having entered the country illegally or overstayed a visa. When the Department of Justice issued a draft opinion in April 2002 advising that local police be deputized to enforce INS violations, it unleashed a firestorm of criticism from police chiefs across the nation.[54] Chief Arturo Venegas of the Sacramento Police Department articulated a frequently echoed complaint: "We've made tremendous inroads into a lot of our immigrant communities. To get into the enforcement of immigration laws would build wedges and walls that have taken a long time to break down."[55] Police also recognize that focusing investigations or arrests on immigrants undermines their ability to fight crime and protect victims. "Two immigrants recently helped us solve a crime," says Lieutenant Tomas Padilla of the Hackensack, New Jersey, police department. "Maybe they were undocumented, we didn't ask. But maybe that cooperation would not have occurred if we were forced to ask them for their immigration documents. When immigrants fear they might be deported, they are not going to report the crime."[56]

PROSPECTS FOR CHANGE

In other respects, of course, the broad public support for profiling Middle Easterners on national security grounds is bound to let local police off the larger hook of rooting out profiling within their departments. Even before 9/11, whatever commitment existed among police departments to stem racial profiling was limited to upper management. Many rank and file officers, who regarded the brouhaha over DWB as so much empty political correctness, will read the public endorsement of Arab profiling as vindicating the position that profiling is commonsense crime fighting. Police organizations and civil rights groups concede that racial profiling is not getting the attention today that it would have, absent the events of September 11.[57] Police groups acknowledge that 9/11 gave law enforcement a nice public relations boost at a time when their departments were taking a pounding over allegations of profiling and misuse of deadly force.[58] All this naturally weakens the incentive to get proactive on profiling. The passage of antiprofiling legislation on the state level has clearly slowed, too, since 9/11: as many as thirteen bills were passed within a two-year period between 1999 and 2000, while only two passed in 2002.

In other respects, though, 9/11 has not shut down the concern over racial profiling on the state level. It is difficult to say whether the slowdown in antiprofiling legislation would have happened, anyway, as profiling receded from the headlines. The arguments raised in state legislatures and city councils against requiring police to collect racial data on stops and searches of motorists or pedestrians are essentially the same ones heard before: too expensive, too burdensome, too insulting, not necessary here, etc. There is evidence to suggest that, even in departments that never admitted to the practice, the public outcry that developed against DWB profiling has made police executives more thoughtful about the need for training, for early warning systems to identify officers with troubling patterns of behavior, and for managerial accountability for the conduct of cops on the street.[59]

To a large degree, outside the Beltway, local law enforcement authorities continue to be consumed with the same priorities they had before 9/11: fighting everyday crimes in increasingly diverse local communities. At the October 2002 semiannual meeting of the Police Executive Research Forum, a national membership organization of chiefs and managers, the conference theme was race and policing. September 11 was not discussed, say the conference organizers.[60] Police seem instinctively to understand that to become conscripts in the Bush administration's rousts within immigrant communities is to undermine their own efforts at home. Says Hubert Williams, president of the Police Foundation, a research group that promotes innovations in policing, ". . . the trust and confidence of people living in a community . . . is a vital link for police for information. Where would this [the policing of immigration violations] fit in the context of priorities? Would it go ahead of robbery, homicide, drug offenses, any of those things?"[61]

Unfortunately, it is hard to imagine that the kind of political and public criticism that arose against drug war racial profiling will develop in the antiterrorist context anytime soon. There is first the fact that profiling is, to a certain degree, as inevitable and immutable as racism itself. As long as there is racism, there will be racial profiling. This is doubly true so long as the overwhelming majority of our law enforcement officers are whites who live outside the minority communities they are assigned to police. Moreover, the galvanizing of public opinion against DWB arose from two distinct conditions, neither of them currently present in the antiterrorism context. First, there was the flummoxing data showing that the "hit rates" for drugs were no better among blacks stopped and searched than among whites. The second was the realization that racial profiling was ensnaring—indeed oppressing—thousands of innocent people, and more specifically, a lot of black and Hispanic elites. Perhaps more than anything, it was highly publicized reports of black businessmen, athletes, judges, and actors—even black policemen—jacked up on the highway or while commuting to work, that convinced many whites there was more to complaints of racial profiling than "poor me" whining. By the late 1990s, many white people could name a black co-worker or acquaintance who could describe the indignity of being trailed and worse while driving, shopping, or jogging in the "wrong" neighborhood. The fact that many noncriminal, respectable citizens were being caught up in profiling also galvanized civil rights leaders—previously reluctant to make criminal justice a priority—to organize against it. Notwithstanding our tough on crime rhetoric, the notion of innocence still seems to have some currency in a nation that views (whether accurately or not) fairness as a bedrock of its legal system.

Antiterrorist profiling will affect thousands of Arabs, and equal numbers of people mistaken for them, without regard to class or social status, just as it has blacks and Hispanics in the drug war context. But much of the more egregious profiling is taking place not against longtime residents or citizens with fancy jobs, but against the more recent immigrant communities who are least politically connected and, given their often provisional legal status, least able to complain about it. Nor are there going to be hard numbers disproving the efficacy of profiling as became possible with DWB. Terrorism is so much rarer than drug trafficking that it becomes impossible to show low "hit rates." Moreover, there is the all important reality that terrorism is so deadly, many people will continue to argue that averting even one disastrous event is worth the price of stopping and questioning thousands of innocents.

FALSE COMFORT

This is bad news for the millions of upstanding Arabs living peaceably in this country. Criminal stereotypes have a disturbing self-fulfilling quality to them, as we learned with the drug war profile. Because everyone took as "common knowledge" that blacks were at the center of the drug trade, police willfully blinded themselves to the reality that profiling was actually wasting their resources. From their standpoint, profiling worked: they were stopping blacks, and often enough finding drugs. The artificially high arrest rates of blacks and Hispanics that profiling produced seemed to prove the efficacy—indeed, the necessity—of continuing to target them. Even though the empirical data showed that police were just as likely to find drugs in similar percentages among other racial groups, why discontinue a practice that appears to be working, and—comfortingly—confirms our deepest instincts? So deeply ingrained were these assumptions that police departments didn't even bother to analyze their own search and hit rates until sued by defense lawyers and civil libertarians. In many respects, police are no different from the rest of Americans who regard neighborhoods and schools that are populated by low-income, nonwhite minorities as commensurate with crime and disorder, and act accordingly. It is perhaps unsurprising that, faced with the impossible charge of clearing the streets of drugs and eradicating terrorism, police officers resort to means that on the surface appear most expeditious to those ends.

Moreover, on some level police recognize that in the war against crime, the battlegrounds are not equally pitched. They know that if they stop and search, say, every fifth passing white student on the campus of the local university, a lot of whites are likely to be caught and arrested with contraband, but their parents and the public would hardly stand for it. Or that if they spreadeagled every white motorist stopped for a traffic violation in Simi Valley, as they routinely do blacks in South Central, they would quickly have a band of private lawyers barking at their door. By the same token, the idea that, following Timothy McVeigh's arrest, the FBI would have issued an all points bulletin for every white male with a crew cut and a known affinity for far-right politics is as unthinkable as it is preposterous on the merits. Yet the investigatory methods now being undertaken by federal authorities in immigrant communities are little different. As David Cole argues in his book *No Equal Justice*, Americans tend to enforce the protections of the Constitution only to the degree that the majority will tolerate. In the case of both the antidrug war and the war on terrorism, it is simply easier to position the big guns and wide nets in poor or immigrant communities where the legal and political costs of enforcement will be lower.

One wishes, vainly, that concern about our civil freedoms would be sufficient to make us reject knee-jerk and ultimately misguided policies of profiling in the antiterrorism campaign. Or that our shameful history of needlessly interning and deporting thousands of immigrants in World Wars I and II would guide us in a different direction. Regrettably, all indications are that our government is stumbling down the same blind alleys it has traveled before.

6. LIVING IN FEAR: HOW THE U.S. GOVERNMENT'S WAR ON TERROR IMPACTS AMERICAN LIVES

ANTHONY D. ROMERO[1]

Most Americans believe they have nothing to fear from President Bush's war on terror if they're not doing anything wrong. The expanded spy powers they hear about seem unlikely to affect them or their neighbors as they go about their daily lives. Even when policies are enacted and actions taken in clear violation of the most fundamental liberties, Americans tend to assume they are a threat only to certain immigrant groups.

The full impact of the Bush administration's war on terror may not be understood even by members of Congress, since much of the government's actions since September 11, 2001, have been shrouded in secrecy. But sharp changes in policy have profoundly affected law-abiding individuals and communities throughout the United States. Thousands of Americans who have done nothing more than attend a particular church service or peace rally have come under surveillance or been placed on "no-fly" lists. Innocent people of Arabic and South Asian origin have been targeted by law enforcement officials and attacked by their neighbors; several have been killed. College students and retirees have been interrogated by Secret Service or FBI agents because of anonymous tips about their anti-Bush statements or the posters on their walls. People have lost jobs or been denied credit because their names wound up on unchecked but widely circulated lists of suspected terrorists—often because of mistaken identity or misspellings.

To drive home the extent of these intrusions into American lives, the ACLU has been collecting stories of law-abiding individuals caught up in the war on terror, and of policies shaped since 9/11 in states, cities, and counties beyond the Beltway—some of which are recounted in this chapter.

LIFE GETS TOUGHER FOR IMMIGRANTS

Changes in federal policy had an immediate impact on localities throughout the country, but immigrant communities were the first to feel their effect. Even as President Bush urged Americans to refrain from attacks on Muslims, FBI agents were combing cities and college campuses for people of Arabic or South Asian ethnic backgrounds or with Arabic names. They detained more than 1,200 within days of the attacks—leaving spouses, children, classmates, and employers to wonder where they had been taken, and who would be next. Information about them was scarce. The Justice Department refused to identify them, arguing that to do so might jeopardize national security and tip its hand to terrorists (though, ironically, it has consistently identified others taken into custody on suspicion of terrorism, including Yasser Esam Hamdi, Jose Padilla, James Ujaama, and Zacarias Moussaoui). The secrecy alarmed civil liberties and human rights groups, including the ACLU, which joined in a lawsuit on October 29, 2001, in U.S. District Court for the District of Columbia, seeking their names under the Freedom of Information Act.[2]

Then, in a further effort to deny information to the public and press following the September 11, 2001, terrorist attacks, the Justice Department closed all deportation hearings. Twice more, the ACLU went to court—with lawsuits arguing that transparency and accountability are essential to the workings of American democracy. In a precedent-setting August 26, 2002, decision, the U.S. Court of Appeals for the Sixth Circuit in Cincinnati declared that secret deportation hearings were unlawful because they were based solely on the government's assertion that the people involved may have links to terrorism. Judge Damon Keith rejected the Justice Department's claim that immigration hearings (conducted within the executive branch, with no jury and frequently without counsel) should be treated differently from in the judicial branch, where due process is required. "A government operating in the shadow of secrecy stands in complete opposition to the society envisioned by the framers of our Constitution," he wrote.[3] Immigration proceedings, he ruled, can be held in closed session only in those specific cases where the government can demonstrate a compelling interest in preventing terrorism. In the second lawsuit, the federal appeals court in the Third Circuit ruled against the ACLU, affirming the government's efforts to close deportation hearings and limit public understanding of the impact of the war on terror on immigrants' lives.[4]

The lack of information about the detainees was troubling for another reason: it would prove increasingly daunting over time to document the denials of rights and liberties that were taking place. Other moments in U.S. history had been fully documented by historians and civil libertarians, in comparison with the veil of secrecy that had been drawn around the post–September 11 sweeps. Compounding the challenge to civil libertarians, the government subsequently deported, or granted "voluntary departure" to, most of the detainees without disclosing who they were.

To ensure that a historical record would be created, the ACLU initiated an effort to identify them and chronicle the civil liberties abuses against them. We sent letters to the consulates or embassies of ten countries offering legal assistance to innocent people caught up in the government's crackdown on terrorism.

Foreign officials were at first hesitant to accept our help, not knowing who we were—and were surprised that an American organization was offering to challenge its own government. But they did eventually provide us with names, and in some cases U.S. government file numbers, of detainees—information that had likely come from the Justice Department itself. (The irony of the situation did not escape us; the department had apparently given the governments of suspected terrorists the very information it had refused to give the ACLU.) A documentary filmmaker hired by the ACLU used this information to contact family members or attorneys of detainees, and used her ACLU credentials to gain entrance to two detention centers in New Jersey, where she managed to interview several detainees.

Our inquiries did not stop there. In the spring of 2002, the ACLU extended its investigations abroad, collaborating with the Human Rights Commission of Pakistan (HRCP) to locate detainees who had been forcibly removed to that country, or who had been allowed to leave the United States voluntarily to avoid lengthy detentions possible resulting in the same outcome. Based in Lahore, the nonpolitical, nonprofit HRCP has been promoting human rights and democratic development throughout Pakistan since 1986. With the names, U.S. government file numbers, and contact addresses we provided (after obtaining them from the Pakistani Consulate), the HRCP set out to locate deportees in their own country.

Through dedication and perseverance, that organization was able to locate and interview twenty-one former detainees, now residing in Pakistan. Those interviews were illuminating. Before their detentions, according to information shared with the ACLU, their hopes and dreams were virtually indistinguishable from those of previous generations of immigrants who had come to our shores with high hopes and ambitions. They had been salesmen and housewives, and limousine, cab, and truck drivers, with children and homes in America, grateful to be in a country where they could make a better life for themselves.

That all changed as a result of their detention in the country that has prided itself on being a "nation of immigrants." Their testimonies detail anxiety-ridden days of detention and deprivation, which turned into weeks, which turned into months—typically culminating in deportation. Rounded up on "material witness" warrants but rarely charged with crimes, many had endured harsh living conditions and been deprived of counsel. These abuses are becoming widely known now that they have been detailed in a number of reports.[5]

In some cases, the U.S. government ignored the citizenship rights of children born in this country, shipping them off with their foreign-born parents. Field workers for the ACLU also found children flunking out of schools in Pakistan— unable to speak the local language, or to understand why they had been abandoned by the country in which they had grown up. The plight of such families has been captured in reports by Cable News Network (CNN), National Public Radio (NPR), and the *New York Times,* which accompanied ACLU staff on the field research.

FEAR YOUR NEIGHBOR

In the days after September 11, 2001, and the months that followed, it was dangerous to be an American of South Asian or Arabic descent—or even to have a superficial resemblance to one.

Two Sikh brothers were killed in separate incidents, almost 400 miles apart. Balibir Sing Sodhi, fifty-one, a Mesa, Arizona, gas station owner, was shot September 15, 2001, in front of his gas station. The man accused of shooting him stated that he had done it "because he was dark-skinned, bearded and wore a turban."[6] "I stand for America all the way! I'm an American. Go ahead. Arrest me and let those terrorists run wild!"[7] Sodhi's brother, Sukhpal Singh Sodhi a Los Angeles cab driver, was shot and killed the following August, while driving his taxi. No arrest has been made in that case.

According to a 2002 report, *Caught in the Backlash: Stories from Northern California,* the period after 9/11 saw dramatic rises in hate crimes (up 345.8 percent in 2001), as well as in the targeting of immigrants by law enforcement, racial, and ethnic profiling at airports, and a stifling of dissent.[8] That report, compiled by the ACLU of Northern California with other community and civil rights groups, told the stories of twenty people who were placed under suspicion in the September 11 fallout, and who were barred from flying or had had their loyalty questioned. Most were Muslims, South Asians, or political activists opposed to U.S. policy.[9] For example:

Charlotte Wu, a twenty-two-year-old sophomore at the University of California at Berkeley, learned how easily distrust can be induced among friends and neighbors after unwittingly arousing the suspicion of a classmate. In the fall of 2001 she was discussing a video game with a friend over the phone. Her friend asked, "How do you find the secret entrance?" Charlotte told him, "You have to press this button and that button. If you lay a bomb icon against the wall, it should help." Shortly afterward, three police officers came to her dorm door and questioned her about her conversation. UC police Captain Bill Cooper said Wu's suitemate had called police saying she had overheard Wu talking in a low voice about planting bombs and grenades. "It seemed to me we had to check it out," Cooper said. "When someone says my neighbor is planning to plant bombs, it would be irresponsible to ignore it." Wu now censors her own conversations.

Sugako Green, the granddaughter of a man who had spent part of World War II in a Japanese-American internment camp, was harassed and publicly humiliated by the security guard at a neighborhood store who tried to bar her from entering after 9/11 because of her appearance and the way she was dressed. Green, who is of mixed Palestinian and Japanese ancestry, wears the Muslim *hijab* (head covering) and *niqab* (veil). When she tried to enter an Oakland, California, Walgreens store on June 25, 2002, with her seven-year-old daughter, Alycia, and the daughter's four-year-old friend, she was blocked by the security guard, who called her "the bride of bin Laden," among other insults. They weren't permitted to enter the store until after the guard, turning to the girls, said, "I can't be having kids coming in our stores that might be strapped with bombs."

It also became more difficult for American Muslims to seek political office in 2002: Syed Mahmood, a Republican running for Congress in California's Thirteenth Congressional District, which includes Fremont, Union City, and Newark, was a case in point. His campaign signs were defaced as fast as he could put them up, and he received threatening calls and e-mails at his place of work: "We don't want any turbanheads running for government in this country," they said. "Take your signs down. You raghead!" And, "No camel jockeys in the government of the United States." In a year when other Republican candidates did well, Mahmood, who was born in India and grew up in Pakistan, was trounced more than three to one by Democrat Fortney "Pete" Stark. And only seventy Muslims ran for office at any level of government nationwide in 2002, according to American Muslim Alliance, down from 700 two years earlier—a 90 percent drop.

The terrifying impact of the 9/11 attacks on Arab and Muslim communities in the United States has been documented by Human Rights Watch in its report *We Are Not the Enemy: Hate Crimes Against Arabs, Muslims, and Those Perceived to be Arab or Muslim after September 11.* That report attributes seven murders, seven assaults, six attacks on places of worship, and two arsons to the xenophobia that swept the country after the attacks on the World Trade Center and the Pentagon.

Also of great concern are citizens who have come under federal scrutiny or have had their loyalty questioned while exercising their constitutionally protected rights of free speech or assembly. All Americans should be worried about government attempts to stifle political activism and opposition through assaults on First Amendment freedoms. For example:

Sister Virgine Lawinger, a seventy-four-year-old Catholic nun from Wisconsin who was barred from boarding a Milwaukee-to-Washington, D.C., flight in April, 2002, with nineteen others who opposed U.S. aid for Colombia and preemptive action against Iraq. Sister Virgine and her colleagues were questioned for two hours—missing their flight and a full day of activities in Washington, as a result. All were relatively inexperienced representatives of Peace for Action, a Wisconsin-based Catholic group, who had been headed for Washington to be coached by others in the art of lobbying. Seventeen members of Peace for Action's thirteen-member contingent were permitted to board their flight, but twenty, including Sister Virgine, were not. She may have been on an FBI "no-fly" list—developed and circulated in the aftermath of 9/11, which has prevented many others from flying—but she has been unable to find out the reason she and her colleagues were singled out.

Also barred from flying after 9/11 were Jan Adams and Rebecca Gordon, publishers of the periodical *War Times,* who had been critical of the government's Afghanistan policy, the erosion of civil liberties in the wake of the attacks, and the looming invasion of Iraq. They were taken from the boarding area of a San Francisco-to-Boston flight on August 7, 2002, by airline employees who warned them that if their names appeared on a so-called master list, the FBI would be called in. The police came and eventually permitted them to fly, but their boarding passes were marked with a big, red "S," singling them out for searches at every stop.

A Freedom of Information Act (FOIA) request, filed by the ACLU on behalf of Sister Virgine and others, and still pending as this book went to press, seeks to learn the reasons why they were barred from flying. It also asks how many individuals were placed on "no-fly" lists in error, how a person can get his or her name removed from such a list, and whether individuals are targeted based on First Amendment activity.

Danny Muller of Chicago had been employed for three years by Voices in the Wilderness, a Chicago-based campaign to end economic sanctions against the people of Iraq, when a routine trip to the post office brought him to the attention of Big Brother. Muller, a native of New York, had been a member of three delegations to Iraq, most recently in September 2002, with Representatives Jim McDermott (D-Washington) and David Bonior (D-Michigan). In November 2002, he and a colleague attempted to purchase 4,000 stamps for a bulk mailing. They requested stamps without the American flag, and the postal clerk called the police, who prevented them from purchasing stamps that day and questioned them about their patriotism. The following day, Muller's colleague returned to the post office and was asked to meet with the postal inspector, who quizzed him at length about his organization, its goals, and its (nonviolent) methods. The inspector told him that, in the future, they would have to provide advance notification of such mailings. The official later contacted the group to say that an investigation had determined that they were not "dangerous," and that advance notice was no longer required.

A. J. Brown was a freshman at Durham Technical Community College in Durham, North Carolina, when the Secret Service came calling on October 27, 2001. Someone had anonymously reported that she had a poster on her apartment wall critical of President Bush. Brown, who opposes the death penalty, did indeed, though it preceded the Bush presidency. The poster, citing the large number of people executed in Texas while Bush was governor, depicted him holding a rope, against a backdrop of lynching victims. "We hang on your every word," it said. And: "George Bush: Wanted, 152 Dead." The agents interrogated her for about forty-five minutes, and even after concluding that she posed no threat to anybody, wanted to know whether she had any maps of Afghanistan or "pro-Taliban stuff" in her apartment. (She did not.) They also asked her to fill out a form they insisted was "mandatory," requesting her name, race, address, phone number, and other identifying information. They said they had to investigate every reported threat to the president.

It is important to understand that these interrogations, detentions, invasions of privacy, and attempts at intimidation were not isolated incidents. These were just a few of the intrusions into the lives of ordinary people, going about their constitutionally protected business, that became commonplace after the government called on citizens to report "suspicious" people and behavior in their communities. As Dorothy Ehrlich, executive director of the ACLU of Northern California, told reporters after the November 2002, release of *Caught in the Backlash:* "We know these twenty stories are only the tip of the iceberg. Many more people were afraid to come forward and tell their stories."

And the police-state paranoia that brought Ms. Brown's poster, Mr. Muller's choice of postage stamps, and Sister Virgine's activism to the attention of authorities was of the government's own making. The Justice Department had set the tone, early in 2001, with its announcement of a plan to recruit ordinary, untrained Americans to spy on their neighbors.

The Terrorism Information and Prevention System (Operation TIPS), spelled out in the Homeland Security bill sent to Congress by the White House, was stunning in its audacity. Under this program, the Justice Department planned to recruit postal workers, phone and cable installers, and others with access to private workplaces and homes to report "suspicious," supposedly terrorist-related, activity to the government. Had lawyers for the ACLU, perusing the bill, not sounded the alarm to national media outlets and ACLU members, the Justice Department would have swiftly extended its reach into places even the police cannot go without suspicion of a crime—deep into the private lives and private business of ordinary, law-abiding Americans.

Operation TIPS was set in motion even before the bill establishing it was put to a vote in Congress. Volunteer tipsters were directed to a Web site where they could sign up as amateur spies. Incredibly, as a reporter for the Internet-based periodical Salon.com disclosed on August 6, 2002, a TV network was even recruited to play a role in the domestic spying effort. Salon.com's Dave Lindorff wrote[10] that the Justice Department was referring incoming calls from TIPS volunteers to the Fox Network's *America's Most Wanted* television show. Liberals and conservatives were horrified. Former House Majority Leader Richard Armey, one of the most powerful and conservative members of Congress, struck federal funding for TIPS from the Homeland Security bill, saying he objected to "citizens spying on one another." In the end, the administration backed down, and Operation TIPS was ultimately removed from the bill.

This is not to suggest that gathering reliable information on terrorist threats isn't part of the challenge. But the Justice Department, having tried to railroad a measure that never should have been proposed in the first place, showed its hand. It was shamelessly overreaching for terrifying new powers that could conceivably be used to spy on political opponents and stifle dissent. Even under fire from some of the president's staunchest conservative supporters, Attorney General Ashcroft refused to rule out the use of tipsters who spy on their neighbors of their own accord—one more indication that personal privacy wasn't high among the Constitutional rights and protections he had sworn to protect. It was a harbinger of things to come.

The FBI tried to extend its reach with a post–9/11 program called "Project Lookout," in which it compiled and then circulated the names of people it wanted to question in connection with the attacks on New York City and Washington. Like most of the government's post–9/11 efforts to combat terrorism, the agency refused to discuss it publicly—at least until late 2002, when innocent victims of the government's flawed strategy began to surface. In November 2002, the *Wall Street Journal* reported that, in a departure from its usual practice of closely guarding such things, the FBI had circulated unchecked, error-filled lists of names to hundreds of banks, car rental companies, travel reservation systems, casino operators, and other businesses and organizations throughout the United States—which in turn shared them with their branches, clients, and affiliates around the world. Many innocent Americans were wrongly fingered as "potential terrorists" because of mistaken identity or typographical errors, and were later cleared—but not before some lost their jobs, were denied credit, or were otherwise harmed. And by that time, the FBI had by its own admission "lost control" of the flawed list, which continues to circulate worldwide, via the Internet. People who have appealed to the agency for help in permanently clearing their names from all versions of the list have been advised to request removal from the Web site of each participating bank, credit agency, organization, or business for "each instance" of continued use—if they can find them. It is a tale of law enforcement and technology run amok.[11]

And as if that weren't enough to make us wary of further intrusions, in the autumn of 2002 the Bush administration had proposed the most intrusive domestic surveillance program of all. The new Total Information Awareness program would use the technology known as data-mining, untested in the national security arena, to track the daily activities of all Americans. It would sift through financial, educational, medical, travel, housing, and communications data, looking for "patterns that suggest" terrorist activity, in every aspect of our everyday lives. To direct it, President Bush recruited John Poindexter, the highest Reagan administration official to have been implicated in the Iran-Contra illegal arms-for-hostages scandal in the 1980s.

Under this program, as *New York Times* columnist William Safire wrote on November 14, 2002:

> Every purchase you make with a credit card, every magazine subscription you buy and medical prescription you fill, every Web site you visit and e-mail you send or receive, every academic grade you receive, every bank deposit you make, every trip you book and every event you attend—all these transactions and communications will go into what the Defense Department describes as "a virtual, centralized grand database."

> To this computerized dossier on your private life from commercial sources, add every piece of information that government has about you—passport application, driver's license and bridge toll records, judicial and divorce records, complaints from nosy neighbors to the FBI, your lifetime paper trail plus the latest hidden camera surveillance— and you have the supersnoop's dream: a "Total Information Awareness" about every U.S. citizen.

Because of its concerns over the intrusiveness of TIA, Congress temporarily froze funding for it in February 2002, mandating that the Pentagon prepare a report on the system's viability, cost, and impact to civil liberties and privacy. Even so, transportation officials subsequently announced the Computer Assisted Passenger Pre-Screening System (CAPPS II) for screening of airline passengers, which would utilize the very same data mining techniques that were proposed in TIA.

BEYOND THE BELTWAY: PANIC-DRIVEN POLICY

The war on terror has also led to many poorly thought out policy and procedural changes at the state and local levels. Taking their lead from the federal government, jurisdictions across America have sought to combat terrorism with far-reaching, panic-driven expansions of law enforcement powers that infringe on civil liberties. Many were unwarranted or ineffective, raising fundamental questions about the American values our elected officials have sworn to preserve and protect. These measures have included the adoption of harsh penalties for ill-defined crimes, restrictions on free speech or assembly, and dramatically increased surveillance of ordinary Americans.

As one might expect, penalties for acts of "terrorism" were increased in many states after 9/11. What is surprising, and troubling, is the nature of the punishment—and the grounds on which it applies. Thirteen states added terrorist acts to their list of crimes deserving of capital punishment either by referencing the death penalty directly or by referencing first-degree aggravated murder in a state where that establishes the death penalty as the punishment.[12] While the death penalty is inherently odious from a civil liberties perspective, it is also patently obvious that the death penalty would not have acted as a deterrent to the September 11 hijackers, as they were already prepared to meet their death in the pursuit of their horrible objective.

Equally disturbing is that under the new legislation in several states, severe penalties up to and including execution may be applied to crimes that fall under an extremely broad definition of terrorism. New York's new law defines terrorism as any act that aims to "intimidate or coerce a civilian population, influence the policy of a unit of government, or affect the conduct of a unit of government by murder, assassination or kidnapping."[13] It is easy to see that any number of events or actions could be said to influence the policy of a unit of government, including such innocuous activities as lobbying or peacefully protesting. Some states such as Connecticut have included brief descriptions of crimes that would incur the new penalties, but even these descriptions (for example, "computer crime in furtherance of a terrorist purpose" or "hindering the prosecution of an act of terrorism"[14]) are much too vague.

In their overly broad definitions of terrorism, state laws mimic the overwrought federal law. The USA PATRIOT Act's definition of terrorism includes "acts dangerous to human life that are a violation of the criminal laws" if they "appear to be intended . . . to influence the policy of a government by intimidation or coercion," and if they "occur primarily within the territorial jurisdiction of the United States."[15]

Another phenomenon of the post-9/11 period has been the squelching of dissent through restrictions on speech and assembly. The Bush administration has made many attempts to chill free speech through intimidation. Attorney General John Ashcroft set the tone in his testimony before the Senate Judiciary Committee on December 6, 2001, calling into question the patriotism of any who would dare to challenge his utterances or the actions of his Justice Department: "To those who scare peace-loving people with phantoms of lost liberty, my message is this: Your tactics only aid terrorists, for they erode our national unity and diminish our resolve. They give ammunition to America's enemies and pause to America's friends."[16] When the nation's top law enforcement official categorizes any American who exercises his or her First Amendment right to voice concerns over the way the administration is fighting the war on terror as "aid[ing] terrorists," it is cause for alarm.

Such McCarthyist attempts to prey on people's fears by branding opposing viewpoints as unpatriotic have already led to repressive actions in some localities. Groups seeking to stage peaceful protests from Pleasantville, New Jersey, to Columbus, Georgia, have had to argue for their constitutionally guaranteed freedom of expression in court. Even on college campuses, where historically dissent has been protected, Ashcroft's remarks have so poisoned the climate that tenured professors with contacts in the Arab world stand to lose their jobs, and speakers who try to defend the Constitution are booed and heckled.

In Pleasantville, an organization called the Coalition for Peace and Justice sought a permit for an antiwar rally in October 2001. Authorities gave the group the runaround, first telling them they needed an appointment with the chief of police, and eventually, after much stalling, telling them they would have to apply for an appointment by mail and wait up to two weeks for a response. The penalties for conducting a protest without a permit were severe: up to $1,000 in fines and 90 days in jail. Not until the ACLU intervened did the city back down—entering into negotiations with the coalition, agreeing not to enforce the ordinance, and ultimately promising to revise it.

Then, in November 2001, the City of Columbus sought an injunction against four School of the Americas (SOA) Watch leaders who were planning a protest march to the main entrance of the local military base, Fort Benning. SOA Watch had long opposed the School of the Americas' training of Latin American dictators and soldiers responsible for murders and human rights violations, and its annual protest march had become a local tradition. This time, however, the city tried to establish a buffer zone at least fifty yards from Fort Benning's main gate, citing post–9/11 security concerns. The ACLU defended SOA Watch in court, and the judge ruled against the city, saying, "We are all here to protect the American way of life and to protect it with the Bill of Rights and the U.S. Constitution. If we can do that, we will leave a legacy to our children's children." [17]

Protesters even had trouble exercising their rights of free speech and expression in the relatively progressive atmosphere of Cambridge, Massachusetts, the home of Harvard University. City Manager Robert W. Healy denied a protest permit to the Living Wage Campaign at Harvard on the grounds that a moratorium on permits, in effect since September 11, would remain in effect "until they [city officials] saw what was happening." [18] The city backed down at a February 7, 2002, meeting with local residents and the ACLU of Massachusetts, lifting the moratorium and agreeing to allow protests. The Harvard Living Wage Campaign seeks higher wages for employees who clean up after, cook for, and protect the students of Harvard.

Other states took steps to limit access to public information. New Jersey shut down its public-access Web site, while New York's director of the Office of Public Security issued a confidential memorandum to agency heads to remove "all sensitive information" from public view. Much like the ambiguous definitions of terrorism that could be used to justify persecuting individuals with no connection to actual terrorism, New York's definition of "sensitive information" included the catchall provision: "subjects and areas of relevant concern as determined by the agency."

Unfortunately, but not unexpectedly, this repressive atmosphere has trickled down from the government to the public and to educational institutions, normally the havens of intellectual exploration and debate. Tolerance was certainly lacking when Janis Heaphy, publisher of the *Sacramento Bee* newspaper, delivered a graduation speech at Cal State–Sacramento. "No one argues the validity and need for both retaliation and security," she began. "But to what lengths are we willing to go to achieve them? Specifically, to what degree are we willing to compromise our civil liberties in the name of security?" [19] She went on to urge the audience to protect their rights to free speech and to guard against unlawful detention—and was loudly booed. When she asked her audience how they would feel if racial profiling became routine, they applauded and hooted their approval. Eventually she was heckled off the stage.

Reminiscent of the FBI's persecution of Dr. Martin Luther King, Jr., and other political dissenters during the 1950s and 1960s, governmental invasions of privacy have been another troubling attribute of the post–9/11 period. The earlier abuses had led to congressional investigations, and eventually the Justice Department limited FBI surveillance and infiltration of religious and political organizations. Since September 11, 2001, however, the department has eased those restrictions on the FBI, setting the stage for abuse.

In Denver, Colorado, the local police department so aggressively monitored and recorded peaceful protest activities, compiling "intelligence files" on local residents and law-abiding advocacy groups, that the mayor himself declared it had gone too far. The ACLU filed a class-action lawsuit,[20] challenging practices that had targeted a Nobel Peace Prize–winning Quaker organization, the American Friends Service Committee, and a seventy-three-year-old Franciscan nun, Sister Antonia Anthony, a teacher of indigent Indians in the United States and Mexico, as "criminal extremists." The press has reported that targets of Denver's surveillance also included such notables as former South Dakota Senator James Abourezk, who headed the Senate Committee on Indian Affairs; entertainer George Carlin; Wilma Mankiller, who was awarded the Medal of Freedom, the nation's highest civilian honor, in 1998 for her work as principal chief of the Cherokee Nation of Oklahoma; and historian Vine Deloria, who wrote *Custer Died for Your Sins*. The suit, on behalf of 3,200 closely watched individuals and 208 infiltrated organizations, led to a city council resolution reaffirming existing (but overlooked) limits on intelligence gathering. Denver police may not gather information on individuals' First Amendment activities, the Council decreed, unless those activities relate to criminal acts and the subject is suspected of a crime.[21]

A three-judge panel appointed by Denver's mayor to review the spy files recommended such restrictions as "The retained information must be in writing and must be specific, containing articulable facts to give a trained law enforcement officer a basis to believe that there is a reasonable possibility that an individual or organization is involved in a definable criminal activity or enterprise."[22] These guidelines, which have been adopted, are similar to ones that the New York City Police Department recently removed. One member of the panel, former Colorado Supreme Court Justice Jean Dubofsky, told the *New York Times*, "I don't think they had a clue what the capacity of this was and what they were doing with it, honestly."[23]

While the Denver Police Department's disregard for civil liberties is the most egregious known example of such abuses to date, other states have moved in that direction. Virginia, Florida, Louisiana, and Maryland passed bills in 2002 that expanded electronic surveillance powers, and New York City attempted to join Chicago in rolling back checks on domestic spying. In fact, the *New York Times* reports that the New York Police Department has contracted with Orion, the computer company that sold the Denver police the software to run its spy files, and that 200 people in its intelligence division are being trained in its use.[24]

In New York City, limitations set down in what is known as the "Handschu agreement" (named for one of the plaintiffs in a precedent-setting, 1985 New York City ruling) simply assured that police will not gather information on ordinary citizens when there was no evidence of a crime, and that they would request permission to infiltrate a group from a three-person panel consisting of two police officers and a civilian. Like the restrictions placed on the FBI decades earlier, the Handschu agreement was a response to repeated intrusions on individual's privacy and civil rights. In the 1950s, the New York Police Department routinely compiled files on student leaders and others, and then passed the information on to the CIA. Then, in the 1960s, the NYPD engaged in covert and illegal "black bag operations" to monitor campus and civil rights leaders. These came to light in the trial of a group of Black Panthers, at which the defense was able to provide evidence of entrapment: a police officer posing as a Panther had provided the Panthers with a car and map with which to commit an armed robbery.

In a related case, Detective Oswaldo Alvarez in 1975 spied on Robert Collier, a Black Panther, with no criminal evidence to begin surveillance. Finding nothing incriminating, Alvarez's superiors went so far as to manufacture evidence to get a search warrant that led to Collier's arrest.

The judge in the Handschu agreement cited New York Supreme Court Judge Peter McQuillan's ruling in the Collier case, which stated in part: "Unwarranted police surveillance . . . intimidates, demoralizes, and frightens the community into silence. Arbitrary and protracted police surveillance of community groups is the hallmark of every closed society. . . . A good faith claim by a police agency to control crime in an efficient and effective manner does not justify every infiltration effort. . . . You need not be an overheated civil libertarian to fear limitless police surveillance and infiltration." [25]

In 2002, New York City sued to end the consent decree which established the Handschu agreement, invoking the recent terrorist attacks. It termed the Handschu provisions "daunting obstacles" to its counterterrorism operations. This argument was belied, however, by Police Commissioner Ray Kelly's inability to cite even one instance in which the agreement had hampered an investigation. In a further demonstration of arrogance, David Cohen, the New York City Police Department's deputy commissioner for intelligence and a thirty-five-year veteran of the CIA, asked that his own testimony be kept secret not only from the public but also from opposing counsel.

Several other cities had reported no problems with restrictions on surveillance. Chicago police said in December 2002 that in the two years since a similar consent decree was repealed in their city, they have not yet used their new powers.

As this book went to press, Los Angeles had not even attempted to challenge a similar consent decree; and speaking to the *New York Times,* Joe Gunn, executive director of the Los Angeles Police Commission, said, "I have not heard complaints that the antiterrorist division had been inhibited in its work."[26]

It was clear that revoking the Handschu agreement in New York would chill free speech by allowing the government to investigate any political group without suspicion of a crime, and to videotape or photograph demonstrations. "Who said you have to destroy a village in order to save it?" Jethro Einstein, one of the lawyers in the 1985 case, asked the *New York Times.* "We're protecting freedom and democracy, but unfortunately," he quipped in a burst of sarcasm, "freedom and democracy have to be sacrificed."[27]

In February 2003, a U.S. district court ruled on the city's request to void the Handschu agreement. The ruling did modify the agreement by permitting the NYPD to adopt the new Ashcroft-era guidelines, which abandon procedural protections such as the requirement that police provide a paper trail on their surveillance activities and their reasons for conducting surveillance. The door to abuse has been reopened.

Additional attempts to monitor all individuals, not just those who are suspected of a crime, can be seen in the administration's efforts to standardize identification cards. Federal initiatives to standardize state driver's licenses and link them to a central computer database would create a de facto national I.D. card. And such computer databases would almost certainly become the repositories of extensive personal information, which could be easily accessed and abused.

State governments have pushed the creation of identification cards even more strenuously than federal officials. In Iowa and Florida, rigid new regulations governing the issuance of driver's licenses require immigrants to show Immigration and Naturalization Service documents, and licenses are valid only as long as the individual's visa remains valid. In Iowa, the Department of Transportation also placed the statement "Non-Renewable/ Documentation Required" on the driver's licenses of all immigrants in red letters, blatantly discriminating against them and virtually branding them as aliens. This practice ceased after the ACLU complained. St. Paul, Minnesota, has gone even further, putting visa expiration dates on the face of immigrants' driver's licenses. The ACLU is challenging this rule in court[28] because of the negative repercussions it could have on immigrants who could then be easily identified and singled out for harassment.

STIRRINGS OF PATRIOTISM

In contrast to these grim developments in Denver, New York, and elsewhere, there have also been instances throughout the country of individuals and groups taking a stand against infractions of their civil liberties. Though Americans regardless of party affiliation tend to trust their government to do the right thing, and to rely on organizations such as the ACLU to act as watchdogs, many have shown remarkable courage in the face of Attorney General Ashcroft's attempts at intimidation. Patriots have risen in big cities as well as in rural villages to defend the Bill of Rights, displaying a better understanding of the core values that define them as Americans than some of their leaders.

Perhaps most encouraging are the numerous police departments that have come out against requirements that they assist in the enforcement of federal immigration laws. Jurisdictions in Detroit, Michigan; in Portland, Hillsboro, and Corvallis, Oregon; in Richardson and Austin, Texas; and in San Francisco and San Jose, California, have all raised objections. The California Police Chiefs Association, representing municipal law enforcement agencies throughout that state, took a strong stand against the involvement of local police in immigration enforcement. In a letter to Attorney General Ashcroft, the association wrote: "In order for local and state law enforcement organizations to continue to be effective partners with their communities, it is imperative that they not be placed in the role of detaining and arresting individuals based solely on a change in their immigration status." [29] In other words, anything that erodes the trust that police officers have struggled to earn in their communities will only make law enforcement harder.

Police realize that such requirements cause particular alarm in immigrant communities. Members of those communities can provide information that the police rely on, and would be less forthcoming if they had to worry about being charged with an immigration violation each time. Even "voluntary" responses to police interrogation—by people from countries where police regularly abuse their powers—is problematic, as such people may not know that they have a right to refuse to answer.

These objections are surprising, given state law enforcement agencies' dependence on the federal government for funding. The Bush administration is expected to provide $1.5 billion in aid to local law enforcement agencies for antiterrorism efforts; yet these dedicated officers feel strongly enough not only to stand up for what they know is right, but also to risk the loss of significant funding.[30]

However, similar warnings have been sounded by former federal law enforcement officials. Oliver Revell, former FBI executive assistant director, told the *Washington Post* that the Justice Department's strategy of using local police to search for illegal immigrants is not effective and "really guts the values of our society, which you cannot allow the terrorists to do."[31] Joining Revell, former FBI assistant director Kenneth P. Walton said, "It's the Perry Mason School of Law Enforcement, where you get them in there and they confess. Well it just doesn't work that way. It is ridiculous."[32]

University officials in several locations have also refused to become complicit in the FBI's efforts targeting foreign students. At the end of 2002, for instance, agents with the Louisville, Kentucky, FBI field office requested detailed information on foreign students and faculty from local college officials. They requested the "names, addresses, telephone numbers, citizenship information, places of birth, dates of birth and any foreign contact information available." The FBI was rebutted, however, by several college officials—including Jane Fitzpatrick, general counsel for Morehead State University, and another university official of Eastern Kentucky University who stated that she would not reply to the FBI request without a court order.[33]

Many town and city bodies have passed ordinances reaffirming their protection of civil liberties in response to federal excesses—with ringing criticisms of the Bush administration's strategy of infringement. At the signing of the Takoma Park, Maryland, City Council's resolution,[34] drafted with the help of the ACLU, the mayor stated, "The terrible terrorist attacks were not the cause, but the opportunity [for the federal government] to enact these [anti-liberty] changes."[35]

Some communities have put their opposition to the administration's erosion of civil liberties into pronouncements which seem much more in the spirit of the framers of our Constitution than do recent federal decrees. The people of Berkeley, California, for instance, vehemently opposed the reduction of access to public information, declaring in an April 22, 2002, letter to President Bush: "Since September 11, the federal government has taken steps to choke off sources of information, impose voluntary censorship agreements with the media, and pollute the information pool with disinformation."[36]

The people of Ann Arbor, Michigan, wrote, "It is an important matter that our country seek a balance between national security and the prevention of discrimination based on race, religion or nationality in the constitutional rights afforded all individuals."[37]

These communities also provide explicit instructions for moving forward. In direct rebuttals to the Bush administration and its actions, the people of Cambridge, Massachusetts, and Carrboro, North Carolina, adopted identical resolutions calling on law enforcement "to preserve residents' freedom of speech, religion, assembly, and privacy; rights to counsel and due process in judicial proceedings; and protection from unreasonable searches and seizures even if requested or authorized to infringe upon these rights by federal law enforcement acting under new powers granted by the USA PATRIOT Act or orders of the [federal] Executive Branch."[38]

In yet another stirring example of patriotism, the people of Amherst, Massachusetts, expressed concern "that actions of the Attorney General of the United States and the U.S. Justice Department since the September 11, 2001 attacks pose significant threats to Constitutional protections in the name of fighting terrorism."[39] They decreed that, "to the extent legally possible, no Town employee or department shall officially assist or voluntarily cooperate with investigations, interrogations, or arrest procedures, public or clandestine, that are judged to be in violation of individuals' civil rights or civil liberties."[40]

As this book went to press, seventy-one communities had passed similar resolutions and according to the *New York Times,* similar measures are underway in more than sixty others from Chicago, to Los Angeles, to Tampa, indicating that people at the state level are ready and willing to fight improper federal measures.[41] Indeed, states and localities may be the greatest hope for preserving the ideals of a nation built on liberty.

THINK LIBERTY, ACT LOCALLY

What is needed now is precisely the kind of debate, discussion, and action we have begun to see in communities like Takoma Park, Carrboro, and Ann Arbor. Interestingly enough, such debate and local action would bring us back to the very beginnings of the American Revolution. Although many Americans were taught in grade school that the Declaration of Independence was the work of Thomas Jefferson, who wrote under the influence of a British philosophy of natural rights, the historian Pauline Maier of the Massachusetts Institute of Technology tells a different story.[42] The colonists had been busy publishing local declarations of independence for some time, Maier discovered, debunking the popular myth. These local declarations were well known throughout the colonies, and they shared a common goal: to explain, advocate, and justify independence to as broad an audience as possible.

As a result, the final and most famous Declaration was a homegrown expression of colonial discontent and popular political beliefs. It did not spring whole from the head of one man, but rather was the result of widespread popular debate and discussion that ultimately led to consensus on the nature of the problem and what needed to be done.

This is precisely the kind of intelligent public debate that we need right now on important issues affecting the quality and content of our democracy. It falls to all individuals—living in local communities—to be the progenitors of that change and the protectors of our most cherished freedoms.

7. THE WAR ON TERRORISM: THE GUANTÁNAMO PRISONERS, MILITARY COMMISSIONS, AND TORTURE

MICHAEL RATNER[1]

Imagine the following scenario. Somewhere in the world, the United States fights a war and captures and detains enemy soldiers; somewhere in the world, the United States captures and detains people it claims are terrorists. Those detained may have been arrested because of an informant's tip or because of someone receiving money for information regarding alleged terrorists; the tip and the information may or may not be reliable. Consequently, those arrested may be completely innocent. These people are flown to the United States Naval Base, Guantánamo Bay, Cuba, and are imprisoned for years.[2] The captured soldiers are not accorded the rights of prisoners of war. The alleged terrorists are not charged with a crime. They do not have access to their families or attorneys.

Maybe, years later,[3] a few will be released, others may remain in Guantánamo indefinitely, and others, possibly, will be tried by a special military commission.[4] That trial may occur at Guantánamo, or wherever the United States chooses, even on an aircraft carrier.[5] The trial may be entirely in secret. If they are found guilty, they may be executed and their bodies disposed of, possibly at sea.[6] They might be found not guilty by the tribunal. However, even then, Secretary of Defense Rumsfeld has said that they may not be released.[7] He has announced that the United States is engaged in a long war against terrorism; it may be a fifty-year war, and until that war is over, if it ever ends, some will remain imprisoned at Guantánamo.[8] This scenario is not farfetched. Some of this is already occurring, and if the Bush administration is to be believed, the remainder may unfold.

One might think such governmental actions, so seemingly at odds with notions of fairness and liberty, could be challenged in the courts. One might believe that a court in the United States would make, at least, a determination as to the legality of the detentions and trials of those imprisoned. However, one would be wrong. In March 2002 a petition for a writ of habeas corpus was filed on behalf of the detainees in Guantánamo, but the petitioners lost.[9] They lost not because the federal district court decided that what the government was doing was right, but because the court decided it could not even hear the case and determine whether the detentions were legal. Even though the detainees are imprisoned by the United States, the district court refused to look into their detentions. The federal court has ruled that it will not and cannot hear cases on behalf of noncitizens imprisoned at Guantánamo.[10] It is as if Guantánamo is on another planet, a permanent United States penal colony floating in another world.

The above described scenario illustrates three of the most worrisome aspects of the United States' war on terrorism: the indefinite detentions at the United States Naval Base, Guantánamo Bay, Cuba; the lack of any judicial review of those detentions; and the plan to employ military commissions to try some of those detained. As of November 2002, approximately 625 persons from 44 countries have been jailed at Guantánamo, many of them since January 2002;[11] this number was unchanged as of January 2003.[12] Their names are kept secret, and the government has refused to permit visits by attorneys or family. No charges have been filed against them. Although many were captured on the battlefield,[13] they are not being treated with the rights the Geneva Conventions accords to prisoners of war (POWs) and may be held indefinitely. The United States has vigorously opposed court review of these detentions.[14] The serious threat the detentions raise is not just to the rights of those detained at Guantánamo, but to all of us. They raise the specter of executive detentions not subject to review by any court and without any basis in law. It is fundamental to freedom that detentions must be pursuant to law and that courts are to act as a check on unbridled executive power. The right to be free from executive detention is in serious jeopardy.

Attorney General Ashcroft has stated: "Foreign terrorists who engage in war crimes against the United States do not deserve constitutional rights."[15] Apparently, the attorney general has determined that the people he calls "suspected terrorists" are guilty before they are tried. Their guilt can then be confirmed by trials in front of military commissions that are more likely to convict because they do not fully protect constitutional rights. It's reminiscent of the famous trial scene in *Alice in Wonderland*—"No, no!" said the Queen. "Sentence first—verdict afterwards."

It is fundamental to freedom that those accused of crimes are tried before regularly constituted courts that are impartial, guarantee a defendant's rights, are public, and allow appeal to a higher court. Yet, some of those detained at Guantánamo will apparently be tried before military commissions that will not fully guarantee these rights.[16] These special courts are ad hoc commissions in which the president designates the defendants for trial, the secretary of defense chooses judges (who are the jury as well), the trials can be closed, and no court appeal is permitted, even from a sentence of death. The employment of military courts could be widely expanded beyond those imprisoned at Guantánamo. The administration has already spoken of employing them against alleged terrorists in the United States.[17] The last time military commissions were employed was almost sixty years ago, and those precedents have been widely criticized.[18] Until recently, the United States itself was highly critical of countries such as Peru that employed such military commissions. Trial before such commissions represents not justice, but a threat to liberty.

Many in the United States do not seem concerned by this scenario.[19] This is, in part, because the detentions are occurring outside of the United States with little or no press access to inform us of what is transpiring. Many people are unconcerned because it is not happening to them, but to noncitizen Muslims picked up from around the world. Many also believe those at Guantánamo must be guilty of something. In addition, in an environment in which we are all frightened of the next act of terrorism, many are willing to give the government more leeway, believing that its actions will make us safer.

This turning a blind eye to lawless action flowing from the government is dangerous, and not only for those imprisoned at Guantánamo. The government also has applied its detention policies to citizens, holding them without charges. Currently, citizens Jose Padilla, a suspected terrorist, and Yaser Hamdi, a suspected enemy combatant, are being held in military brigs in South Carolina and Virginia and have not yet had access to attorneys or family.[20] Under the government's rationale, it can treat citizens it imprisons in the United States the same way as it treats noncitizens at Guantánamo. It need simply label them as enemy combatants, whether citizens or not, as it has done with Hamdi and Padilla. That designation, according to the government, allows them to be held with the same lack of legal rights as are noncitizens on Guantánamo. The only difference is that Hamdi and Padilla, unlike the noncitizens detained at Guantánamo, can obtain minimal court review of their designation as enemy combatants.[21] This minimal review may not be the result of their citizenship, but rather their presence in the United States. Were Hamdi and Padilla held in Guantánamo, they might not even be permitted that limited court review.

WHO WAS CAPTURED AND TAKEN TO GUANTÁNAMO?

On October 7, 2001, the United States and its allies began their war against the Taliban rulers of Afghanistan and Al Qaeda members who were present in that country. The United States allied itself with the Northern Alliance forces that had been opposing the Taliban for many years. The war was over relatively quickly. On December 17, the last Al Qaeda stronghold fell, and on December 21, the interim government of Hamid Karzai was sworn in. During that brief war, thousands of Taliban and Al Qaeda fighters were captured, primarily by the Northern Alliance. Many of these were detained in Mazar-e Sharif prison and in Shibarghan prison under appalling conditions.[22] CIA and other United States officials carried out extensive interrogations of the prisoners. The Northern Alliance later freed some of them; others remain in prison in Afghanistan.[23] Six hundred were killed in a major prison riot.[24]

On January 11, 2002, the United States military began transporting some of these prisoners captured in Afghanistan to Camp X-Ray[25] at the United States Naval Base, Guantánamo Bay, Cuba. There were allegations of ill treatment of some prisoners both in transit and at Guantánamo, including reports that they were shackled, hooded, and sedated during the twenty-five-hour flight from Afghanistan, and that their beards and heads were forcibly shaved.

I have had some personal experience with the living conditions in Guantánamo. In the early 1990s, I represented Haitian refugees who were held there, and I visited the base a number of times. Its land is bleak and hardscrabble; little grows there except cacti; the heat is intense, and scorpions, mosquitoes, and banana rats are abundant.[26] When this new group of prisoners arrived at Guantánamo, the environment was much the same, but the conditions were harsher. They were housed in makeshift, small (8 feet by 8 feet), open-air, wire cages that failed to protect against the elements.[27] The cages were surrounded with fences topped by razor barbed wire, and the compound was encircled with watchtowers. In this early period, the detainees remained shackled when using the portable toilets or showers, and temperatures frequently went above 95 degrees Fahrenheit. Halogen floodlights blazed all night so that they could be continuously monitored. The pictures released in January 2002 of the prisoners at Guantánamo show them kneeling in the blazing Cuban sun, wearing blackened goggles, masks, ear covers, and shackles. These photos caused a public outcry, as did the conditions under which the prisoners were being held.

Over the next months, more prisoners were taken to Guantánamo. It is assumed that most of these were associated with the Taliban or Al Qaeda and taken from Afghanistan or Pakistan.[28] However, prisoners from other places have been imprisoned in Guantánamo, including five Algerians and a Yemeni from Bosnia.[29] This later group was obviously not composed of combatants captured in the theater of war. They were suspected of planning attacks on the U.S. embassy in Sarajevo. These detentions indicate that Guantánamo will be used to hold not only those picked up in Afghanistan and Pakistan, but also others that United States officials suspect are dangerous, might have information, are allegedly involved in terrorism, or with Al Qaeda. At the end of 2002, while preparing for war with Iraq, United States officials suggested that some of those captured in any new war would also be sent to Guantánamo.

In late April, the United States transferred the prisoners to Camp Delta, a new longer-term prison camp within the Guantánamo complex that is designed to house as many as 2,000 prisoners.[30] The cells are small (8 feet by 6 feet, 8 inches), but they have running water and apparently better protect the prisoners from sun and rain. Judging from the few photographs that have been released, the prison looks like rows of one-story, self-storage facilities. Little is known about this new prison, because reporters are not allowed into it; in fact, the press cannot now see the building, as a green screen has been erected to block any view. However, in September 2002, it was reported that there was trouble between the guards and the inmates concerning the treatment of the prisoners and claims by detainees of their innocence. This resulted in solitary confinement for eighty of the prisoners and suicide attempts by others, according to reliable press reports.[31]

WHAT WE KNOW ABOUT THE DETAINEES

Not much is known about those imprisoned in Guantánamo; certainly, nothing is known publicly as to whether particular detainees have allegedly committed crimes, are affiliated with the Taliban or Al Qaeda, or are there by mistake. No attorneys, family, or press are allowed to visit, but the International Committee of the Red Cross has a regular presence in Guantánamo and presumably has visited the prison and the detainees. As is standard with the Red Cross, it has said nothing regarding particular detainees.

The Bush administration has made general statements regarding the alleged character of those detained, without allowing any of the detainees access to attorneys and without bringing anyone before any kind of trial proceeding that could determine their status or their involvement with terrorism. At the time of the transfers to Guantánamo, Secretary of Defense Donald Rumsfeld called the detainees "hardened criminals willing to kill themselves and others for their cause."[32] He emphasized their dangerousness: "Every time people have messed with these folks, they've gotten in trouble. And they are very well trained. They're willing to give up their lives, in many instances."[33] The United States military officials in charge of the prison said they were told to expect "the worst of the worst."[34] "These are the worst of a very bad lot," said Vice President Cheney. "They are very dangerous."[35]

There may well be a number of terrorists among those imprisoned. However, the Bush administration has refused to bring them before any kind of tribunal or court that can determine whether some are terrorists, POWs, or innocent. The October 2002 release of three Afghani men, after almost a year at Guantánamo, suggests that the administration's sweeping rhetoric has been overblown. It should not have taken eleven months to determine that these men were not terrorists. One of the men released said that he was 105 years old. David Rhode, a *New York Times* reporter, described him: "Babbling at times like a child, the partially deaf, shriveled old man was unable to answer the simplest questions."[36] When asked if he was angry with American soldiers he said that he did not mind, because they "took my old clothes and gave me new clothes." A second Afghani man, released at that time, said that he was 90 years old and was described as a "wizened old man with a cane" who had been arrested in a raid on his village.[37]

A third younger man said that he had been cut off from the outside world for eleven months and had only received a letter from his family three days before he was to leave Guantánamo. He said he was kept in his cell twenty-four hours a day with only two fifteen-minute breaks for exercise a week. This third man admitted that he had fought with the Taliban, but said that he had been forced to do so. After he surrendered, he said, soldiers of the warlord Abdul Rashid Dostum falsely told the United States that he and nine others were officials of the Taliban. His release appears to confirm the essential elements of his story. These men are hardly the "worst of the worst." Here were men, particularly the two aged detainees, who should have never been taken to Guantánamo, and yet they were imprisoned. Here were men who, had there been a hearing before some form of a tribunal, would have been freed long before.

Information about a few of the other detainees is also known from their relatives and from delegations of officials from various countries. Some of the prisoners have been able to send short, censored letters through the Red Cross to their families.[38] These letters appear to be few and far between. A few families that received letters have contacted lawyers, and lawsuits have been filed from which some information is known about the detainees.

For example, according to his family, Mamdouh Habib, an Australian citizen, traveled to Pakistan in August 2001 to look for work and a school for his two teenage sons. On October 5, 2002, just before he was about to return to Australia and two days prior to the war, Pakistani officials detained him. He was transported to Egypt, where Egyptian authorities detained him. Eventually he was turned over to the United States and taken to Guantánamo. Obviously, he was nowhere near the fighting in Afghanistan. A delegation from Pakistan that visited its citizens on Guantánamo for purposes of interrogation has also questioned the continued detention of many of the Pakistanis. The delegation concluded that almost all of the fifty-eight Pakistanis detained were low-level foot soldiers and had no link to Al Qaeda.[39] Some of these may have been imprisoned because of United States reward money given to the members of the Northern Alliance in exchange for alleged member of Al Qaeda.[40] On the basis of that visit, Pakistan requested the release of nearly all the Pakistani prisoners.[41]

These stories of the innocent, of some detainees not involved in any fighting, of detainees who were no more then lowly foot soldiers, demonstrate the importance of a legal process for determining the status of those imprisoned on Guantánamo. It demonstrates the wisdom of those who insist that the rule of law requires treating people fairly.

LEGAL OBSTACLES TO THE RIGHTS OF PRISONERS ON GUANTÁNAMO

The United States Naval base at Guantánamo Bay occupies approximately thirty-one square miles of land in southeast Cuba, an area larger then Manhattan. The U.S. has occupied Guantánamo Bay since 1903, shortly after the end of the Spanish-American War, under a treaty that gives it "complete jurisdiction and control" over the area. The lease continues in perpetuity unless mutually abrogated.[42] Despite claims of national sovereignty made by Cuba over the area, the United States insists its occupation is legal and that it will remain in Guantánamo in perpetuity or until the United States decides otherwise.

The naval base is a self-sufficient and essentially permanent city with approximately 7,000 military and civilian residents—an American enclave with all the residential, commercial, and recreational trappings of a small U.S. city. It has its own schools, generates its own power, provides its own internal transportation, supplies its own water, and has an airfield. Crimes committed by both civilians and foreign nationals living on the base are brought before courts in the mainland United States. Cuba and its courts have no authority over the base in any respect. The United States naval Web site accurately describes Guantánamo Bay as "a Naval reservation, which for all practical purposes is American territory." [43] This is unlike any other base the United States has in a foreign country. The United States is essentially sovereign over Guantánamo.

From the government's point of view, imprisoning the detainees at Guantánamo has a number of advantages. It is close enough to the United States to be conveniently accessible to military and intelligence agencies. Yet, it is only accessible with the permission of the United States, which prevents news reporters from scrutinizing the treatment of the detainees except under the eyes of the government. No reporter has been in the prison, and no reporter has interviewed any prisoner in Guantánamo. The base also offers security advantages, which reflect a legitimate concern. To the extent that outsiders might attempt to either attack the base or free prisoners, that is almost impossible. It is far more secure, for example, than bases in Saudi Arabia or the Philippines.

A major advantage to the administration of jailing the detainees at Guantánamo is the government's view that no court in the United States—or in the world, for that matter—has jurisdiction to review the legality of the detentions or the government's treatment of the prisoners. Additionally, the Bush administration's position is that noncitizens held outside the United States—and it considers Guantánamo outside the United States—have no constitutional rights. [44] These arguments stem from cases decided during World War II [45] and from court decisions concerning Haitian refugees interned at Guantánamo during the early 1990s.

In the Haitian cases, the government asserted that no court in the world could review its treatment of the refugees. The cases in United States federal courts were divided on this question. To the extent those courts concluded that the naval base at Guantánamo was more akin to United States sovereign territory, they permitted review and determined that the refugees had some constitutional protection. [46] However, to the extent courts deemed Guantánamo more akin to a foreign country, review was denied and the refugees were found to have no constitutional rights.[47] It should make no difference that those cases concerned refugees, and the current situation concerns alleged terrorists and combatants; the issue is still whether U.S. courts can hear cases concerning the rights of persons in U.S. custody at Guantánamo.

Considering the status of Guantánamo, which for all intents and purposes is United States–controlled territory, it is difficult to accept an argument that what occurs there should be exempt from United States court review. It is also difficult to accept the view that the United States can imprison people anywhere in the world and be free from judicial oversight. Yet, so far, as is discussed below, the courts have accepted the United States' claim.

THE DETAINEES' LEGAL STATUS AND THE RIGHT TO "COMPETENT TRIBUNALS"

The situation of the prisoners at Guantánamo needs to be examined under two bodies of international law. First is the law that applies in times of armed conflict, which is called humanitarian law. The primary sources for that law are the Geneva Conventions of 1949, treaties ratified by the United States and most of the countries of the world. The Geneva Conventions concern, among other topics, the treatment of people captured on the battlefield or in the theater of war. This body of law is applicable initially to those persons captured in the war with Afghanistan. This would include primarily the Taliban soldiers and militia fighting alongside them.[48]

As to detainees from outside the theater of war, such as those Guantánamo detainees arrested in Bosnia-Herzegovina, the Geneva Conventions do not apply. International human rights law determines their rights. They must be formally charged, given access to counsel, and tried. This would include alleged international terrorists.

The key principle is that some body of law applies to every person detained and gives him or her a legal status and certain rights under international law. The international prohibition on arbitrary detention prohibits detentions in violation of existing law. No one can be treated in whatever manner a country decides.

The Geneva Conventions apply whenever there is an armed conflict between two or more parties to the conventions, even if one of the parties—here, the Taliban—was not diplomatically recognized by the United States. The conventions establish that captured combatants, as POWs, have the "combatant's privilege." That privilege gives a soldier the right to shoot at soldiers of the enemy forces; without that privilege, a soldier could be tried for murder. POWs can be interned, but not imprisoned, unless it is demonstrated, on an individual basis, that there are security risks. They have significant rights to humane treatment as well as communication by letter with their families. POWs can still be questioned and they can be prosecuted for war crimes, but they retain their POW status. Importantly, POWs cannot be tried by military commissions for war crimes; they must be tried by the same courts as American soldiers would be tried. That would mean trial by courts-martial, which grant substantially more rights then military commissions.

Although resistant at first, the Bush administration finally grudgingly acknowledged that the conventions applied to those captured on the battlefield in Afghanistan, but with caveats that eviscerated the application of the conventions. The White House announced that although the United States would apply the Geneva Conventions to soldiers that it decided were from the Taliban, it would not extend the protections to prisoners it believed were members of Al Qaeda.[49] However, in reality, the Bush administration would not apply the terms of the conventions to any of the Guantánamo prisoners. Specifically, the United States refused to apply Article IV of the Third Geneva Convention that requires that all regular members of a government's army be granted POW status; and that members of a militia fighting alongside those armed forces would receive such status. This might well include members of Al Qaeda captured on the battlefield. So by refusing to apply this key provision, the Bush administration was in fact refusing to apply the Geneva Conventions in a meaningful way.

The United States' decision that neither the Taliban fighters nor the militia fighting alongside them were POWs was made without following the procedures specified in Article V of the Third Geneva Convention. That article requires the convening of a "competent tribunal" to determine the status of each individual captured "should any doubt arise" as to his status. (Such "competent tribunals" are not the military commissions that the United States is establishing to try war crimes.) The United States never held such "competent tribunals," but made a blanket determination that no one captured on the battlefield was a POW. The Third Geneva Convention also requires that all such prisoners be treated as

POWs pending such hearings. The United States has repeatedly refused the entreaties of the international community to treat all the detainees under the Article IV and Article V procedures established under the Third Conventions.[50]

Nor was there any reason for the United States not to employ such tribunals. Prior to the war in Afghanistan, the United States military had adopted regulations for these tribunals, which are staffed entirely by its military personnel. Such tribunals were used in Vietnam, and over a thousand such tribunal hearings were held during the 1991 war against Iraq. Had such tribunals been held, it could have been determined that some of those imprisoned on Guantánamo were wrongly detained. As to the others, it would have been determined that they were POWs with rights and protections afforded them under the Geneva Conventions.

The United States has tried to justify its position legally, but in a manner that is inconsistent with international law. It has labeled those detained as enemy combatants, and claims that the military's authority to capture and detain enemy combatants is well settled. But, enemy combatants are a general category, not a status under the Geneva Conventions. Under the Geneva Conventions, enemy combatants are either prisoners of war with all of the rights that attach to that status, or they are not, in which case they come under the protections of the Fourth Geneva Convention.

The Fourth Convention treats such non-POWs as civilians, but if the person is suspected of activities hostile to the state, he can be detained and denied certain rights, such as the right to communicate (write letters). In addition, anyone captured, POW or otherwise, can still be criminally prosecuted. This means that members of Al Qaeda and any other person captured in the theater of war and found not to be a POW can still be detained. However, these determinations must be made individually.

By deciding unilaterally that it would not apply the actual terms of the Geneva Conventions to those captured in the theater of war, the U.S. has violated international humanitarian law. Its position raises serious questions as to the legal authority under which the Guantánamo detainees are being held. If, as the United States claims, the detainees have no status under the Geneva Conventions, then the rules of international human rights law apply. However, those rules require that they be arrested, charged, represented by attorneys, and tried. Obviously this is not occuring, since, as explained above, U.S. domestic criminal law is not being applied. The United States is holding these people outside both international and domestic law.

The Geneva Conventions were created to provide, among other things, humane conditions and limits on the duration of confinement. POWs, which is what many of those in Guantánamo appear to be, may only be detained until the "cessation of active hostilities." That circumstance has occurred with regard to the war in Afghanistan. As to non-POWs, they may be held until the "general close of military operations," which arguably has also occurred in Afghanistan.

The United States contends, however, that it was fighting not just a war against Afghanistan but also an international war against Al Qaeda that may not end for many years.[51] This argument does not address the rights of former Taliban combatants now in custody. Furthermore, there is a serious question as to whether the efforts to disable and destroy Al Qaeda constitute a war under international law. A war, other than a civil war, is between states. It is not defined as between a state and a terrorist organization. That type of activity is an international law enforcement effort, akin to tracking down drug dealers, and is subject to international human rights law that requires charges and trials.

Detainees at Guantánamo who were captured outside the theater of the Afghanistan war are examples of the legal twilight surrounding the "war" on Al Qaeda. There is very little information available regarding these people, except for six prisoners who were arrested in Bosnia-Herzegovina and taken to Guantánamo. Five Algerians and one Yemeni were taken from a prison in Sarajevo in January 2002, despite a local court order releasing them for lack of evidence. The United States claims "their activity posed a credible security threat to U.S. personnel and facilities and demonstrated involvement in international terrorism."[52] The Geneva Conventions do not apply to these six men, but their rights should remain protected under international human rights law.

The United States is trying to avoid treating these and others as human rights law requires by calling them all "battlefield detainees."[53] This is obviously incorrect. The fact that the United States is or was fighting a war in one part of the world, Afghanistan, does not permit it to capture people anywhere in the world and label them combatants without showing they were involved in the armed conflict. These and others have been captured because of their alleged role in international terrorism. They are suspects. Their capture should be treated as a matter of criminal law.

There is one exception under which the United States could hold alleged international terrorists, including members of Al Qaeda, for some period without charges and trial. Article IV of the International Covenant on Civil and Political

Rights permits such detentions in a very narrow class of cases: during a public state of declared emergency threatening the life of the country. To avail itself of this exception, the United States must notify, through the U.N. secretary-general, the other countries that are parties to the treaty. The United States has neither declared such an emergency nor has it notified the secretary-general.

The administration has yet to announce charges or trials for any of the Guantánamo detainees, Taliban or otherwise, and has stated that some of these people may be held indefinitely.[54] According to Secretary of Defense Rumsfeld, this means until the war against terrorism is over, which could be many years, that is, until "we feel that there are not effective global terrorist networks functioning in the world . . ."[55] Military commissions may eventually try some of those at Guantánamo, but Rumsfeld has said that even if such commissions acquitted certain captives, the government planned to keep some at the base. In other words, the administration considers itself entitled to capture, arrest, and detain people from anywhere in the world, interrogate them, refuse them access to lawyers and family, not charge them or bring them before any courts, not release them even if tried and acquitted, and imprison them indefinitely.

LEGAL CHALLENGES

There have been three U.S. court challenges to the detentions at Guantánamo,[56] one in the United Kingdom,[57] and one before the Inter-American Commission of the Organization of American States.[58] As of January 2003, the request to the commission by various human rights groups was the most successful. Although the commission is not a court, its mission is to enforce the principal regional human rights treaty, the American Declaration of the Rights and Duties of Man, the provisions of which protect the right to life, fair trial, due process, and freedom from arbitrary detention. In its decision of March 13, 2002, the commission called upon the United States to "take the urgent measures necessary to have the legal status of the detainees at Guantánamo Bay determined by a competent tribunal."[59] The commission explained that everyone who is captured by a state must have a legal status, and that it is for a tribunal and not a government to determine that status. In strong language, the commission found that the

> detainees remain entirely at the unfettered discretion of the United States government. Absent clarification of the legal status of the detainees, the Commission considers that the rights and protections to which they might be entitled under international

or domestic law cannot be said to be the subject of effective legal protection by the state.[60]

Although the commission has ruled that member states of the OAS are under an "international legal obligation" to comply with its decisions, the United States has refused to comply. The commission reiterated its order mandating commissions in July 2002 and held a hearing on the United States' failure to implement this ruling. As of April 2003, the United States has still not complied, and there is no power in the commission to compel compliance.

The challenge to the detentions filed in the courts of the United Kingdom was on behalf of one of the detainees, Ali Abbasi, a citizen of England. Although the British Court could not order a remedy for the detentions because the United States government was not a party to the lawsuit, it described the detention situation in stark terms: "[I]n apparent contravention of fundamental principles recognized in both jurisdictions [U.S. and U.K.] and by international law, Mr. Abbasi is at present arbitrarily detained in a 'legal black hole.' "[61] The court was especially critical of the U.S. government's claim that there was no court in the United States that could review the indefinite detentions in a territory over which the United States had exclusive control:

> We have made clear our deep concern that, in apparent contravention of fundamental principles of law, Mr Abassi may be subject to indefinite detention in territory over which the United States has exclusive control with no opportunity to challenge the legitimacy of his detention before any court or tribunal.[62]

The U.K. Court hoped the "anxiety that we have expressed [regarding the legal situation of the detainees]" will be "drawn to the attention of the appellate courts in the United States."[63] The Court took pains to say that it believed this "anxiety" was also felt by the federal district court in the United States that had ruled against the detainees and that it "believe[d] the United States courts have the same respect for human rights as our own."[64] As of January 2003, there has been no ruling by the U.S. appellate court.

The two cases filed in federal court in Washington, D.C., on behalf of Australian, English, and Kuwaiti citizens detained in Guantánamo are the critical cases, for the United States government must adhere to any final court rulings. As of this writing, the federal court decisions have been favorable to the U.S. government, but the appeals, which may ultimately be heard by the Supreme Court, have not been completed. In ruling on these cases, the federal judge accepted the government's argument that her court had no jurisdiction to hear the cases and therefore could not rule on the legality of the detentions. She found that American courts could not hear cases brought on behalf of aliens held by the United States outside the territory of the United States—thus determining that, despite the U.S. government's "complete jurisdiction and control" of Guantánamo Bay, the naval base was outside the U.S. courts' authority.[65] The cases are on appeal. Without any court review of the legality of the detentions, there is no check on the actions of the government.

TRIALS BY MILITARY COMMISSIONS

On November 13, 2001, President Bush signed a military order establishing military commissions to try members of Al Qaeda and suspected international terrorists.[66] Under this order, noncitizens, whether from the United States or elsewhere, who are accused of membership in Al Qaeda or of aiding international terrorism, can be tried before one of these commissions at the discretion of the president. The Bush administration has said that it will try some of those held on Guantánamo by these military commissions. As of December 2002, the Department of Defense was working on final preparations for the commissions.

Although military commissions were employed during and in the aftermath of World War II, their use was always restricted to defendants associated with the armed forces of a state who were alleged to have violated the laws of war. The military commissions established by the Bush administration include defendants who are not combatants on behalf of a state and who, therefore, as a matter of law, cannot commit violations of the laws of war. Violations of the laws of war, in general, can only be committed by state actors. If a nonstate actor, such as a member of Al Qaeda, or an alleged international terrorist murders people, it is a crime, but it is not a war crime. Such alleged criminals, terrorists or otherwise, should be tried by regular criminal courts and under U.S. criminal statutes of which the United States has abundance. To the extent the Bush administration plans to try alleged international terrorists by military commissions, whether they are members of Al Qaeda or not, it is proceeding contrary to law. No U.S. Supreme Court case and no rule of international law permits military commissions to try crimes that do not constitute war crimes.

A second major problem with the commissions is the procedures to be employed at the trials. The proposed commissions are not courts-martial, which provide far more protections for the accused—although less than those required in civilian trials. Courts-martial require that arrests be made upon probable cause and mandate an investigation and hearing before a trial can occur. The accused can request a specific military counsel and can choose his civilian counsel. Hearsay evidence and involuntary confessions are not permitted. A unanimous verdict is required for offenses in which the death penalty is mandatory. Trials are public, and there are two levels of appeal, including an appeal to the U.S. Court of Appeals for the Armed Forces, which is composed of civilian judges. The defendant can request the Supreme Court of the United States to hear an appeal.[67]

Although the Bush administration has said why it prefers military commissions rather then civil courts for trials of alleged enemy belligerents and alleged international terrorists, it has not fully explained why trial by courts-martial would not allay most of its concerns.[68] Courts-martial, like commissions, do not require civilian jurors, judges, or courts, and can dispense justice relatively rapidly. Unlike military commissions, courts-martial are established courts and would not be subject to the criticism that they are ad hoc commissions set up as a means of obtaining convictions more easily.

By contrast to even the limited rights of courts-martial, the military commissions alter or eliminate many of these rights. This remains so even after the Department of Defense issued a set of procedures, in March 2002, that modified some of the more egregious aspects of the commissions as set forth in the president's original order.[69] Under the new procedures, the president still designates the suspects who are to be tried; there is no preliminary hearing or indictment. The secretary of defense appoints the judges, most likely military officers, who act as judges and jury deciding both questions of law and fact. Unlike federal judges who are appointed for life, these officers have little independence. Normal rules of evidence, which provide some assurance of reliability, do not apply Hearsay and even evidence obtained from involuntary confessions is admissible. Defendants can be found guilty of a crime carrying a potential death penalty by a two-thirds vote of the judges, although unanimity is required to impose the death penalty. If a defendant can afford a civilian counsel (he is entitled to military counsel), that attorney must be determined by military authorities to be eligible for access to classified information. The only appeal from a conviction is to the president or the secretary of defense, although that appeal goes first to a three-person military review panel that then gives a "recommendation" to the secretary of defense or the president. Thus, there is no review by a civilian court, and the final decision remains in the hands of the president or secretary of defense.

Incredibly, the entire process, including the carrying out of the death penalty, can occur in secret. Although the procedures for the military commissions state that the proceedings will be open unless the presiding officer determines otherwise, the circumstances under which trials can be closed are broad and open to abuse. Trials can be closed in the interests of "national security" and other similar reasons. The trials can be held anywhere the secretary of defense decides, presumably even onboard an aircraft carrier. Access by the press is not guaranteed; the procedures state that the judge "may also allow attendance by the public and press."[70]

These new commissions represent such a departure from fair and impartial courts that there has been a broad outcry against their use both in the United States and Europe.[71] Even an important conservative American columnist, William Safire, was highly critical.[72] This outcry was probably a factor in the government's decision to have the so-called twentieth hijacker, Zacarias Moussaoui, tried in a regular federal court in the United States.

While military commissions were used during and immediately after World War II, their use now would not comply with important international treaties. The International Covenant on Civil and Political Rights requires that persons be tried before regularly constituted courts established in accordance with preexisting laws. Further, the Third Geneva Convention requires that POWs be tried under the same procedures as United States soldiers for similar crimes, and United States soldiers are tried by courts-martial or civilian courts, not by military commissions. This may be one important reason the United States is refusing to classify the Guantánamo detainees as POWs: if they were considered POWs, the government would not be free to use military commissions.

Surprisingly, some law professors have argued in favor of these commissions, saying that secrecy is necessary for security.[73] The primary argument is that it might be necessary to disclose classified information in order to obtain convictions. But, in fact, procedures for safely handling classified information in federal courts have been successfully used, as in the trial of those convicted in the 1993 bombing of the World Trade Center. The 1993 trials also demonstrate that trials of suspected terrorists do not require military commissions, but can safely be held in federal courts.

Trials before military commissions will not be trusted in either the Muslim world or in Europe, where previous terrorism trials have not required the total suspension of the most basic principles of justice. It would be much better to demonstrate to the world that the guilty have been apprehended and fairly convicted in front of impartial and regularly constituted courts.

A NOTE ON THE USE OF TORTURE

In some way, those sent to Guantánamo may be the lucky ones: as far as we know, torture is not used on Guantánamo during interrogations. Since September 11, dozens of prisoners have been sent to third countries, including Egypt, Jordan, and Morocco, whose intelligence agencies maintain close ties to the CIA.[74] As has been reported in the *Washington Post,* these people have been transported without going through normal extradition procedures, a process akin to kidnapping. Intelligence agencies in these countries use interrogation tactics such as torture and threats to families that are illegal in the United States and violate international human rights law.[75] As one American official said of this practice of sending captives to foreign countries for interrogation: "We don't kick the [expletive] out of them. We send them to other countries so they can kick the [expletive] out of them."[76] In addition, thousands of others have reportedly been arrested with U.S. assistance and detained in foreign countries known for their brutal treatment of prisoners.[77]

Even if U.S. officials are not themselves involved in the torture of detainees, they may be complicit in torture and guilty of a crime. The Convention Against Torture prohibits torture carried out at the "instigation of or with the consent or acquiescence" of officials.[78] Handing someone over to a foreign intelligence service with the knowledge that the person will be tortured would fit within the prohibitions of the convention. One U.S. official who is involved with sending detainees to foreign countries admitted he knew they were likely to be tortured: "I . . . do it with my eyes open."[79] Torture is also a violation of U.S. criminal law and is punishable, in the United States, by death or life in prison.[80]

According to press reports, it also appears that U.S. officials engage in treatment of detainees that may constitute torture. Witnesses have reported that captives are "softened up" by the U.S. military.[81] The detainees are "blindfolded and thrown into walls, bound in painful positions, subjected to loud noises and deprived of sleep."[82] Although the Bush administration may regard this type of treatment as indispensable, there is resistance to the use of torture from some law enforcement officials. One former FBI chief of counterterrorism said in an October 2002 interview: "Torture goes against every grain in my body. Chances are you are going to get the wrong person and risk damage or killing them."[83]

CONCLUSION

With regard to the Guantánamo detainees, the Bush administration is openly disregarding a legal framework that is fundamental not only to defendants' rights but to the rights of all people. Its assertion of the power to imprison people indefinitely, without charges and court review, is the very conduct the United States has forcefully condemned in other countries. The prohibition against executive detentions is the key to human liberty. It is no small matter to see an administration ignore that prohibition. The Bush administration's plan to try some of the Guantánamo detainees and others by ad hoc military commissions undercuts a system of justice and procedures that is necessary to insure that only the guilty are punished. Finally, any use of torture or methods of interrogation akin to torture should be anathema to all societies that call themselves civilized. Without respect for the international and U.S. legal framework, the violations of the rights of Guantánamo detainees will continue, and will continue to threaten the rights of others who depend on the fair application of the law.

8. BREAKING THE CODE: OR, CAN THE PRESS BE SAVED FROM ITSELF?

MICHAEL TOMASKY[1]

For a post–9/11 parable about the extent to which the contemporary, high-tech state will go to control information and yet be able to appear as if it is not really doing so, the story of the Ikonos satellite pictures would be difficult to top. The Ikonos is a civilian satellite launched in 1999 by a Colorado-based company called Space Imaging. It is capable of taking photos at a one-meter resolution—that is, from its station roughly 423 miles up in the sky, it can focus on something as small as one square meter. The photos are, or originally were, intended for non-military clients and uses. The Department of Defense has never needed to rely on private-sector satellite technology: As you might imagine, it has its own satellite snaps, taken by seven different satellites positioned strategically in the heavens, and the pictures produced by them are, as you might again imagine, reliable to an even sharper resolution.

But on October 10, 2001, the third day of the Afghan war, the Ikonos entered the Pentagon's consciousness in the following way. U.S. forces that day had bombed Al Qaeda training camps near Darunta, northwest of Jalalabad. There were initial reports of heavy civilian casualties. The Pentagon would have its own pictures that would show whether this had in fact happened—pictures that, naturally, it would never release if such casualties had occurred. But what about Ikonos? It occurred to some sharp cookie in the Pentagon that Ikonos could photograph evidence of such casualties, and that potential purchasers of such photographs would quite possibly include the news media.

What to do? The laws governing the use of images produced by satellite photography give the Defense Department the power to exercise something called "shutter control" over such images—to seize them, that is, claiming a potential breach to national security. This option was rejected, according to the British newspaper *The Guardian,* which broke the story on October 17, 2001,[2] because Pentagon officials felt it may have invited a legal challenge from the Fourth Estate on prior restraint grounds. So a clever Plan B was pursued: The Pentagon entered into a contract with Space Imaging that gave the department commercial control over all images produced by Ikonos. The contract, handled by the Pentagon's National Imagery and Mapping Agency (NIMA), cost taxpayers more than $2 million a month. The "shutter control" issue was avoided, and we all had a happy war.

Several aspects of this vignette offer mordant amusement to the twenty-first-century media/government consumer: the accidental exposure of a world most of us know nothing about (information that leads any thinking person to the inevitable, logical conclusion that such a picture can be snapped, anytime, of any one of us); the Bondian impulse to take ownership of a fancy new technology (can't you picture Roger Moore talking about something called Ikonos with M over a rare armagnac before jetting off to meet our man in Istanbul?); and, most disturbingly, the use of commercial means to circumvent a constitutional principle ("We didn't do it primarily to censor," an unnamed NIMA official told *Satellite Week*, "[but] we get that as an additional benefit").[3]

But the Ikonos story is most revealing for its punch line, which is this: how likely was it, really, in the first week of a war that set out to avenge the most shocking attack on American soil in the country's history, that U.S. news organizations were going to sue the Pentagon over such images? Maybe the knees of a few media organizations would have jerked upon hearing the phrase "prior restraint," and a small number would have signed on to some sort of legal action. But honestly, what U.S. news organization at that time was showing the remotest interest in the subject of civilian Afghani deaths? Not a single one. I should note here that I was a supporter of that war and that if someone had said to me then that Afghani civilian deaths were maybe priority number five or six at best, I would not necessarily have disagreed. Even so, it's a subject that deserved a good deal more coverage than it got, and one that a free press should consider an obligation. The *New York Times* finally wrote a major story about it well after the war had wound down. The following July. On a Saturday.

It's only natural, too, and another mordant amusement, that it was a British newspaper that broke this story; the U.S. press wasn't interested in such topics in the slightest, and still isn't—indeed, the story was not pursued by the mainstream American press. And all the while, of course, the Ikonos affair was just a relatively small manifestation of a much larger crusade taking place abroad and at home. The Pentagon was restricting access to hot spots as never before, keeping most journalists trying to cover the war hundreds of miles away from the action. Colin Powell was calling his excellency the emir of Qatar, where the Al Jazeera network is based, to try to force that government to take some action against the network.

At home, John Ashcroft was doing his thing, detaining suspicious creatures under the auspices of a new law, the PATRIOT Act, which was written in such a breathlessly calamitous hurry that few members of the House Judiciary Committee even had time to read what they were voting on, and which, saliently, no major American newspaper's editorial page opposed before its passage (look it up). The *Washington Post* did run an editorial raising some civil liberties concerns after the bill became law.[4] The *New York Times,* that supposed redoubt of closet Socialism, stayed silent. Later, of all people, John Poindexter, a convicted felon who once lied to Congress about laws being broken inside the White House, was resuscitated to oversee a Department of Justice program designed to give the government "Total Information Awareness" on the activities of persons suspicious and unsuspicious. In these and many other such cases, a familiar media pattern asserted itself: the administration proposed; the media, however notionally, lived up to its responsibility by reporting the story and gathering a few quotes from this critic or that; in a day or two, the story died; and everyone went on his merry way, eager for the next leak about Saddam Hussein's perfidiousness.

For all intents and purposes, the government already has shutter control.

Future historians of the late twentieth-century and early twenty-first-century conservative movement will note several signal victories it has achieved. But I'm willing to wager they will agree that no propaganda victory has been more colossal than the way the movement seems to have persuaded the country that it gasps under the jackboot of this thing called the liberal media. This ceaseless chatter started as a matter of strategy back in the mid-1970s, when a man named Reed Irvine formed a group called Accuracy In Media (AIM, see?) to monitor the press and point out examples of liberal bias. Back then there really was a liberal media: Such chat shows that existed at the time—*Agronsky & Co.,* say—would typically feature a couple of liberal commentators, an "objective" reporter or two who wasn't supposed to give opinions but who more often than not swam with the tide, and one conservative. Often it was the curmudgeonly James J. Kilpatrick, and his job was clear: to be the official crank. Defend the position that no one really took seriously. I used to watch these shows with my father. When Kilpatrick fulminated, Dad never got angry, as I'd expected. He just shook his head and laughed.

In September 2002, I went on CNN's *Reliable Sources* to talk about former New Jersey Senator Robert Torricelli, who had just folded up his campaign for reelection in the wake of a damaging Senate ethics report. I was there to defend the "liberal" point of view on Torricelli, which was not that he was a magnificent human being who was the victim of a McCarthyesque smear campaign, but that, while he surely had himself to blame for his distress, there *was* something excessive about the way some of the New York media twisted the knife once it was lodged in his back. (For example: One local New York station, WNBC, aired a segment attacking Torricelli that ran to nearly forty minutes—unheard of in this age of six-second sound bites, and not something the station did when even one of its home-state senators, Alfonse D'Amato, faced similar ethics scrutiny.) I'd appeared with two reporters, from the *New York Post* and the *Philadelphia Inquirer,* who dispatched the senator with the usual epithets and against whose grenades my small-arms fire was little match. As I left the studio it dawned on me: things had come full circle since the seventies, and now *I* was the crank! The show was designed around the idea that there was only one way to think about this question, but for the sake of "balance" there was this alternate view that had to be given its due, which meant, of course, that it would be simultaneously presented and mocked. Some teenager was watching somewhere, noting the way his father shook his head and laughed whenever I spoke.

The media's great power is to tell us all how to think about a topic. By what gets reported or ignored, put in or left out, which experts are interviewed, which adjectives are used, and the manner in which the anchor's brow is furrowed, the media presents the news through the use of a code with which any skilled media consumer is familiar enough. The code is the essence of today's media. Its language is not reason or rational debate; it is chiefly about consumers' emotional responses to images, sound bites, anecdotes. It creates feelings. The code always existed, to some extent, but not in the way it exists now, in the twenty-four-hour, instantaneous news cycle, when things get repeated so fast and so often that they achieve plausability and verisimilitude whether they deserve to or not. The code has a special fondness for the small things, the little factoids or anecdotes that are supposedly telling, and amplifies them into definitive statements about a person's, or an organization's, fundamental character. The code then takes these anecdotes and offers prompts, pointing consumers toward the desired conclusion: For example, Democratic Senator John Kerry gets $200 haircuts, so he's an elitist, and therefore incapable of being president and certainly not someone you could imagine having a beer with, this last hypothetical having somehow become a pivotal measure of a person's fitness for the presidency.

Such anecdotes are, of course, part of the process of politics, part of the game. And this, fundamentally, is the instant news cycle's obsession: The game. Who's up, who's down, who looks better, who frames the issue, who "seems" more "genuine." Cable shows and Web sites don't want to traffic too much in substance; who's going to watch a ten-minute segment on the dry particulars of the Bush tax cuts or the Kyoto Protocol? But a historic segment on the politics of these matters, on their language and symbolism—that will get ratings.

The game is what the media are mainly interested in. And conservatives are much better at this game than liberals. Conservatives understand how to use the code. Fox invented and has trademarked it ("fair and balanced," Fox's motto, is insanely duplicitous and cynical, and at the same time a stroke of utter genius). Right-wing editorial pages get it. Conservative politicians and pressure groups understand its uses—pushing their agenda, making sure they say things over and over and over until they dominate the coverage—in a way their liberal counterparts comically do not. Calling CNN the liberal equivalent of Fox—or the "Communist News Network," as House majority leader Tom DeLay once put it—is preposterous, as even the DeLays of the world must know deep down. But they have to keep doing it, because incessant carping about the liberal media is itself a part of the code: maintaining the posture of the embattled minority has always been an indispensable part of the armature of movements that really run things but don't want anyone to know it.

The last but most vitally important thing about the code is getting the mainstream media to play along with it. Which, by and large, they do. A quarter century of warning liberals in the media—and, admittedly, most elite-media professionals are personally liberal, at least on cultural and social questions—that their every move is being watched has produced exactly the desired effect: as a general rule, they now bend over backward to demonstrate that they can be "tough" on liberals and "fair" to conservatives. This has been true for several years now—it began with the Republicans' efforts to delegitimize the Clintons in every way possible, which were zestfully picked up by the *New York Times* and the *Washington Post* and that good old Bolshie News Network.

But September 11 intensified this state of affairs into something qualitatively new. Now, we had an authentic crisis on our hands, as opposed to an oral-sex crisis; and soon, we had a real, live military engagement, of broader scale and longer duration than any since Vietnam. Now, the media had a good excuse to be fair to Republicans—the party was leading us through a war, after all, avenging a dagger that had struck at our civilization's very heart. Now, the code could be brought out a little more into the open, made slightly more apparent to the news consumer—because the point now, for Fox and the *Wall Street Journal* and Rush Limbaugh and the Heritage Foundation, was to convince the American public that George W. Bush was the right man for this job, the GOP the right party, and anyone who dared to think otherwise was either just not a serious person or, if the dissenter happened to be someone of stature who couldn't be quite so easily dismissed, was being unpatriotic.

Since that time, during the Al Qaeda war and on into the stoking of war against Iraq and the midterm elections, the code has had two chief manifestations that are new. The first I alluded to above: the idea that we'd all better thank our lucky stars that the Republicans were in the White House when September 11 happened, because the pusillanimous Democrats just aren't man enough to have handled it. I have heard even Democrats say something like, "Can you imagine if Al Gore had been president when this happened?" Well, as a matter of fact, I can. Al Gore enlisted in the U.S. Army after getting a Harvard degree (how many young men did *that* in 1969?), volunteered to go to Vietnam, made himself one of Congress's leading experts on arms control issues, gained a broad familiarity with the world and its leaders as vice president, and chaired a commission on domestic antiterrorism and aviation security that recommended a $1 billion package of preemptive measures, many of which were not funded by the Republican-controlled Congress. In each of these particulars he is the clear moral and/or intellectual superior of the current presidential incumbent. The only things that would have prevented a President Gore from running a successful war against terror would have been (a) a conservative opposition that would have questioned every decision he made and almost certainly sponsored congressional hearings into the Clinton/Gore "failures" to "prevent" September 11 from happening, and (b) a media that, intent on its ability to prove it could be "fair" to the right, would have eaten all of it up.

Actually, the Clinton administration's record on fighting terrorism ranges from decent to surprisingly farsighted, again the evident superior of the pre–9/11 Bush administration's—more money and manpower were devoted to fighting terrorism in the defense, treasury, and justice departments under Clinton than Bush (early in the Bush term, for example, John Ashcroft moved dozens of agents from the antiterror beat to child pornography).[5] These are facts. But the code isn't about facts, so the Clinton record, like the Gore résumé—and, by the way, like

John Kerry's $200 haircuts, which apparently never happened, either—can be shunted aside. Clinton *looked* wishy-washy. Bush looks tougher. He talks about good and evil, and black and white. *That's* what matters.

The second new manifestation flows from the first: Since the Republicans are "better" at flexing U.S. muscle, it follows that their assertions—about Al Qaeda, about Iraq—instantly have more credibility; and so an important aspect of the movement toward war (especially with regard to Iraq) is the media's receptivity to repeating what the administration says. There have been occasional and notable exceptions to this trend, but by and large, the U.S. press has followed the government's agenda since 9/11 in a way that hasn't been the case for decades. And, it should be noted, news organizations have sometimes lowered their standards in doing so. *Buffalo News* columnist Douglas Turner—and one has been more likely to find analyses of this sort in regional papers like the *Buffalo News* than in the big, national papers, precisely because regional papers aren't really in on the code—wrote a fascinating column about how the Associated Press was going with stories on aspects of war on the basis of very thin sourcing in a way the AP would not have dared a generation or two ago.[6] On October 2, 2002, a month before the midterm elections, the AP's Washington bureau moved a piece asserting that a top Al Qaeda operative "was in Baghdad about two months ago, and U.S. officials suspect his presence was known to the government" of Saddam Hussein. A potentially explosive story that played right into the administration's game plan; ever since 9/11 happened, the administration has been desperate to prove an Al Qaeda–Iraq link, the better to justify its planned Iraqi invasion. This revelation, if true, would be awfully handy for the administration (and a month out from the elections, no less!). On whose word did the AP hang this major story? It cited "a defense official."

Things weren't always this way. Turner notes that the AP's original August 2, 1964, story on the Gulf of Tonkin attacks used named sources (of course, we now know that these sources must have been lying, but at least their names were in the paper and they were thus subject to some form of accountability for their words). But now, "a defense official" will do just fine, particularly if the story supports the administration's view of things.

Like I said, the government already has shutter control.

Large chunks of the media have been transformed, about three-quarters of the time, into an arm of the conservative movement. This is *the* political story of our age. Official censorship is, of course, something to be vigilant about, something that must be monitored at all times. But no political movement or presidential administration will ever get very far in this country with official censorship. The First Amendment is too deeply ingrained in the culture; it's something that any news outfit, from *The Nation* to the Fox News Channel, will defend.

But if the center-point of the national discourse is pushed further and further to the right, if the chummy echo-chamber of the national media becomes less able (or willing) to withstand the brickbats of the conservative pressure groups . . . well, at that point, who even *needs* censorship? The press will be—in important ways, already is—censoring itself. What happened in microcosm with the Ikonos photographs will have happened on the larger stage: The government— that is, a conservative government—through commercial means (its friendly broadcasters and newspaper editorialists), will have subverted what was once a constitutional principle, that the Fourth Estate should question, probe, doubt, discomfort, expose. That is a far more likely scenario for choking off dissent in this day and age than official censorship.

There are signs, as I write these words, that some Democrats, who have long understood this to be the case, are finally starting to talk about it openly. Gore told the *New York Observer* that "there are some major institutional voices that are, truthfully speaking, part and parcel of the Republican Party." Clinton, speaking in New York City on December 3, 2002, said the Republicans "have an increasingly right-wing and bellicose conservative press," while "we have an increasingly docile establishment press." Maybe, at long last, the code is being broken. But doing so will need more than one press interview from a politician who appears to be retired, at least for the time being, and one speech from another who certainly is. Democrats and liberals need to figure out how to play this game. Then they need to build institutions to counter what the right has won. This will take time, money, savvy, and courage; all things contemporary liberalism doesn't have much of. But you have to start somewhere.

PART III

PRIVACY, SECRECY, AND PUBLIC HEALTH

9. BALANCING IN A CRISIS? BIOTERRORISM, PUBLIC HEALTH, AND PRIVACY

JANLORI GOLDMAN[1]

Since the terrorist attacks of September 11, 2001, the subsequent anthrax cases, and the rising fear of smallpox being intentionally spread, both the states and the federal government have been moving quickly to enact new laws and appropriate billions of dollars to anticipate, prevent, and respond to potential bioterrorist attacks. Dedicating new resources to improve and expand our nation's public health infrastructure serves the goal of "preparedness" and also advances a more sweeping agenda that public health advocates have been clamoring for over many years.[2] But, in the rush to act on bioterror as a potential public health emergency, policy makers are leaving privacy and civil liberties behind, perpetuating a common and persistent misperception that to vigorously preserve public health, core values of individual privacy and autonomy must be sacrificed.

In fact, just the opposite is true—a public health agenda that ignores privacy and civil liberties will undermine public trust and confidence in the very system that is striving to safeguard its health and safety. Such a trade-off is unnecessary and dangerous. If people fear that actions taken in the name of public health are unjustifiably coercive or put them at risk for adverse health effects, or that their sensitive medical information is being collected and shared outside the public health system for purposes unrelated to antibioterrorism goals, they will not fully and honestly participate in critical public health activities. We are far more likely to succeed in preventing and responding to a potential act of bioterrorism if our nation embraces the principle that advancing public health and preserving individual liberties are symbiotic and inextricable. To ensure that public health goals are not undercut by lack of public trust and participation, privacy must be built into the framework of our nation's laws, policies, and practices related to public health emergencies.

Concern about the inadequacy of our public health system to identify and respond to a potential bioterrorist attack is not new.[3] Similarly, the lack of privacy rules and safeguards in the public health system has also been well documented.[4]

Instead of moving hastily and in a lopsided fashion to address our fears to the exclusion of preserving and advancing other values, we can seize this unique opportunity to focus on securing far-reaching, vital expansions both to our public health systems and to our privacy.

Many public health experts assert that the United States Constitution vests in the government broad authority to safeguard the community's health and welfare.[5] As early as colonial times, public health has been regulated through a series of local and state regulations to control illnesses and diseases, and to impose sanitary restrictions on water, food and living conditions. It was not until President Roosevelt's New Deal programs that a federal public health role emerged and eased the way for advances in medicine and science to become part of the national regulatory scheme. The federal Communicable Disease Center was established in 1946, and later expanded into the Centers for Disease Control (CDC), under the authority of the Department of Health and Human Services. The CDC's stated mission is to "promote health and quality of life by preventing and controlling disease, injury, and disability . . . by working . . . to monitor health, detect and investigate health problems, conduct research to enhance prevention, develop and advocate sound public health policies, implement prevention strategies, promote healthy behaviors, foster safe and healthful environments, and provide leadership and training."[6] However, the states have long maintained control over public health, and local public health officials have often resisted federal interference.

Post-September 11, the public health world is undergoing a seismic shift to federalize, harmonize, and consolidate much of the states' individual authority. The fear of bioterrorism—real and perceived—is creating a rollback of well-established medical privacy laws, including provisions of the medical privacy regulation issued pursuant to the 1996 Health Insurance Portability and Accountability Act. New laws and policies that are being put in place to protect public health and national security fail to acknowledge the damage that will occur to the public health enterprise if we do not safeguard individual privacy from the outset. The demands on public health officials today are straining the seams, but we must let out more room to accommodate the development of strong privacy rules and policies. Public health officials cannot afford to do otherwise if the goals of bioterrorism preparedness are to be achieved with broad public trust and participation.

PRIVACY AND PUBLIC HEALTH AT RISK

Individual rights—and privacy in particular—need not be posited against protecting the community weal.[7] No right is absolute, and I do not argue here that individual privacy rights are equal to or should trump all other interests. But the Bush adminstration's current approach, which pits privacy against competing interests, ignores the vital role that privacy plays as a positive factor in enhancing individual as well as community health. As the Hippocratic oath taken by doctors for thousands of years recognizes, protecting privacy is central to improving quality of care, access to health services, and advancing public health.[8] Without trust that their most sensitive health information will be safeguarded, patients are reticient to fully and honestly disclose personal information to their doctors and other clinicians. Research data documents that one in five people believes that his or her personal health information has been used inappropriately, without his or her knowledge or consent.[9] Translated into action, this means a significant percentage of people withdraw from full participation in their own health care for fear that their medical records will be used against them—to deny them jobs, benefits, social standing, or the ability to avoid unwanted exposure.

Nearly 20 percent of people in this country engage in some form of privacy-protective behavior to shield themselves from unwanted disclosure of health information. These behaviors include giving a health care provider inaccurate or incomplete information, paying out-of-pocket for care that is covered by insurance, doctor-hopping to avoid a consolidated record, or, in the most egregious cases, avoiding care altogether.[10] The percentage of people afraid to fully participate in his or her own care, or who take steps to avoid disclosure, greatly increases when a sensitive, stigmatizing illness or condition is at issue, such as multiple sclerosis, or a genetic predisposition to develop a certain disease.[11]

The empirical data come to life through the hundreds of front-page stories depicting harm caused by the misuse of medical information outside the health care arena. To highlight just a few:[12]

• A North Carolina woman was fired from her job after her employer discovered from her health plan that she had been diagnosed with an incurable—and very costly—genetic condition.[13]
• A Tampa, Florida, public health worker walked away with a computer disk

containing the names of over 4,000 people who had tested positive for AIDS, and sent the disk to two newspapers.[14]
• Boston University created a private company to sell medical records and genetic material on over 12,000 people collected for more than fifty years as part of its well-known Framingham Heart Study. People were persuaded to participate in the study as an altruistic act intended to benefit the community, and were assured the information would be kept confidential.[15] Following the furor over the plans to commercialize the research records, the company disbanded, but the university is continuing to consider the plan.[16]
• Just as the Defense Department has begun computerizing the medical records of all military personnel and their families, over 500,000 patient records containing sensitive health information, claims data, and Social Security numbers, were stolen from a Pentagon health care contractor.[17]

The magnitude of harm increases exponentially with the advent of electronic medical records. Security breaches at a number of large hospitals and universities in recent years have caused thousands of peoples' medical records to be widely available online.[18]

When people do not trust the health care system to protect their privacy and to safeguard their information, they put themselves at risk for undiagnosed and untreated conditions. Consequently, the community suffers as well, since the data available for public health and research is incomplete and unreliable.[19] If, in a public health emergency such as a smallpox outbreak, even a small percentage of people refuse to step forward to be vaccinated or treated, or are afraid to fully trust that the public health system will protect them and not hurt them, an epidemic will be harder to contain and more people are likely to die or become seriously ill. Our nation risks failing in its public health mission, and needlessly sacrificing individual liberties, if the equation is not altered—first, to add privacy to the public health benefits side as a means of encouraging trust and participation, and second, to factor in the costs to public health of people withdrawing from full participation in seeking and receiving care.

Since the September 11 terrorist attacks, the 2001 anthrax cases, and the persistent alerts from President Bush and Attorney General Ashcroft that another attack may be imminent, federal and state policy makers have pressed ahead to enact a number of hastily drafted, ill-considered laws that impact public health and undercut decades of privacy and civil liberties laws.[20] A new set of laws and systems are being developed along two overlapping tracks—one focused on responding to a public health emergency (meant to include an intentional bioterrorist attack as well as a "natural" epidemic), and the second aimed at the daily, ongoing collection, analysis, and storage of data on peoples' routine encounters with the health care system (over-the-counter and prescription drug purchases, admissions to hospitals and emergency rooms, lab results, etc.). The CDC is urging the states to adopt a Model Public Health Emergency Act that would ensure that the ubiquitous collection and monitoring of routine health encounters would not be hampered by existing state and federal privacy laws.

The overarching policy assumption in this post–September 11 climate is that any early warning, surveillance, and response system for bioterrorism requires more information in more hands. There has been a dangerous absence of public debate over how much information is needed, by whom, and for what purpose, in order to achieve public health preparedness goals. To continue to bypass this debate, however, threatens the effectiveness—and fairness—of the entire enterprise.

Formulating policies and plans in the throes of a crisis, while the public is panicked, makes it more likely—if not inevitable—that privacy and civil liberties will be given little weight when balanced against the government's interest in protecting public health and safety.[21] A crisis is a risky time in which to consider both the intrinsic value of safeguarding individual privacy, as well as the benefits to individual and community health that result from public health policies that value privacy, confidentiality, and autonomy.

HEALTH PRIVACY LAWS PRE–SEPTEMBER 11

To guard against a potential bioterrorist attack, state and federal policy makers are moving aggressively to put new laws and policies in place, billions of dollars are being appropriated, the public health information infrastructure is being drastically expanded, and a massive smallpox vaccination plan has been announced. The CDC's power as the nation's chief public health watchdog has expanded, while at the same time, the new Department of Homeland Security is absorbing much of CDC's authority to prevent and respond to a potential boterrorist attack. Unfortunately, current federal and state health privacy laws are being theatened as antibioterrorism initiatives supercede them.

Recent precedent does exist for requiring privacy protections as part of overhauling health information systems. In recognition of the magnified risk to privacy that comes with computerizing and centralizing sensitive data, the federal Health Insurance Portability and Accountability Act (HIPAA) of 1996 mandated that privacy and security rules be designed hand-in-hand with the development of a common language and uniform transaction codes for health information collected and shared by health care providers and plans.[22] Therefore, HIPAA can be used as a model for crafting a coherent health information policy with privacy and security built in at the front end.

Prior to the recent enactment of state and federal laws related to bioterrorism and public health, a legal framework did exist both for the collection and privacy protection of personal health information for public health purposes and, more generally, for the privacy protection of personal health information collected by the government and the private sector. The courts and Congress have established a privacy right for medical records, and that right—not being absolute—also provides for information to be collected and used for public health and national security purposes. Before enacting sweeping new laws that overturn and undercut existing safeguards, we should consider the privacy laws that were enacted prior to September 11 to address long-standing concerns about public health emergencies and terrorist threats.

In 1977, the Supreme Court ruled that a constitutional right of privacy exists for medical records gathered and used by the government. In *Whalen v. Roe*,[23] which involved a challenge to a New York State statute requiring doctors to report to the state information about the prescribing of a certain class of drugs, the Court found that individuals have a right of privacy in their own health information. At the same time, the Court recognized that important public health activities required the collection and storage of such information "which is personal in character and potentially embarassing or harmful if disclosed." No constitutional violation was found because the law in question was deemed to mandate strong standards for safeguarding privacy. These seem quaint by modern standards, but included limits on which government officials could access the records, the computer system was run "off-line" to prevent unauthorized access, and the computer tapes were stored in locked file cabinets.[24] *Whalen* and its progeny stand for the constitutional principle that public health and surveillance activities involving personal health information may be conducted only if the activities are justified, and strong privacy and security rules are built in at the outset.[25]

Following on this principle, during the 1980s and 1990s there was intense public debate over how to craft a federal statute that created a privacy right in peoples' medical records, while at the same time allowed for the sharing of medical information within and outside of the health care arena. After nearly a decade of legislative handwringing, Congress passed the Health Insurance Portability and Accountability Act in 1996, and included a provision mandating that if Congress failed to to enact a medical privacy law by 1999, then the executive branch would be required to promulgate regulations. Congress bundled the privacy mandate into HIPAA's "administrative simplification" provision, which is aimed at streamlining the nation's health information infrastructure by requiring health providers and plans to shift toward standardized, electronic formats for sharing medical information.[26] Congress missed its deadline, and in 2000 the Clinton administration issued landmark rules for protecting the privacy of peoples' medical information.

In enacting HIPAA, Congress was clear that privacy and security should be addressed as part of the advancement of a national health information policy. As both the Congress and the executive branch have acknowledged, the potential for privacy intrusions increases as health information is collected and shared electronically, using a common language. Also, it is more efficient to build in privacy and security at the same time health information systems and practices are being revamped. Finally, bundling together the implementation of privacy, security, and transaction standards is much cheaper than trying to incorporate safeguards at a later date. Studies by the Office of Management and Budget (OMB) and the Congressional Budget Office (CBO) found that the cost of complying with the new privacy regulation is significantly offset by the savings that will be achieved by the move to standardized transactions.[27]

The landmark medical privacy rules grants people the right to see and copy their own medical records; limits the collection and use of medical information by health care providers, plans, and others; limits employers' and law enforcement access to medical records; and provides for the imposition of civil and criminal penalties for violation. The regulation's general principle is to bar the use and release of "protected health information" (PHI)[28] unless allowed or required by the rule. The regulation permits exceptions—uses and disclosures without patient authorization are permissible for a range of public health, national security, and emergency purposes. Further, the law does not preempt state laws that are more stringent and not in conflict with the federal rule, thereby leaving the states free to enact and maintain laws specifically geared to a state's public health concerns.

As former White House Privacy Counselor Peter Swire and his then-deputy Lauren Steinfeld concluded in a 2002 article, the medical privacy rule "stands up well to concerns of the post–September 11 era. Concerns about public safety are met by existing provisions that permit disclosures to protect national security, to react to emergency circumstances, and to respond to law enforcement inquiries. Concerns about public health . . . are also met by the current rule. We are not aware of any needed disclosures for public health purposes that are prohibited by the medical privacy rule."[29]

Again, HIPAA leaves intact state public health reporting and surveillance laws, some of which were enacted with strong confidentiality provisions attached to reassure the public that sensitive health information would be collected and used for public health purposes only. State laws in this area are usually condition and circumstance specific, such as for HIV/AIDS, mental health, adoption, domestic violence, communicable diseases, and registries.[30]

BIOTERRORISM INITIATIVES POST–SEPTEMBER 11

In January 2002, Congress appropriated $1.1 billion in block grants for bioterrorism preparedness, to be spread over all the states and a number of major cities to strengthen local capacity to address public health emergencies related to terrorism.[31] To qualify for grants, the Department of Health and Human Services (HHS) requires states to submit a comprehensive plan for improving the local public health system and preparing for a bioterror attack. Many states not only drew up plans but also rushed to introduce—and often enact—legislation aimed at giving them broader authority to anticipate and respond to public health emergencies. By June 2002, HHS had approved plans and released funds to nearly half the states and had partially approved plans for the other half. Also in June 2002, Congress enacted the Public Health Security and Bioterrorism Preparedness and Response Act,[32] which authorized additional bioterrorism-related funding to increase vaccine stockpiles and to bolster the communications systems connecting private sector health care providers with local and national public health departments.

Many state officials have said that in order to qualify for the federal funds, they are pushing their legislatures to enact the CDC's Model State Emergency Health Powers Act,[33] which has been sharply criticized by some public health experts and civil liberties groups. Significant shortcomings of the model act are that it fails to incorporate privacy and civil liberties safeguards, grants too much power to law enforcement officials in public health matters, and mandates the routine collection of sensitive and identifiable health information.[34]

Overall, at least $3 billion has been earmarked by Congress and the executive branch for spending on bioterrorism programs. The money has been spread among twenty federal departments and a range of programs. Who receives this money and for what purposes is likely to have significant implications for individual privacy and civil liberties. As of January 2003, none of the new budget allocations or laws required that privacy and civil liberties safeguards be included as part of creating a national public health information infrastructure, enacting state public health emergency laws, or developing early detection and surveillance systems that rely on extensive reporting of personal health information by doctors, hospitals, health plans, and pharmacies to public health officials.

HOMELAND SECURITY ACT

A case in point is the Department of Homeland Security, created by Congress in November 2002.[35] One of its chief missions is to consolidate and coordinate a wide range of antiterrorist activities within one federal agency. Although the general purpose of the bill was widely supported by Congress, specific concerns with the bill delayed its passage.[36] Although not a central issue holding up action, some members of Congress, as well as public health officials and civil liberties advocates, expressed fear that the new department would wrest public health authority and decision making away from the CDC, the National Institutes of Health (NIH), and state officials.[37] In response to these concerns, the American Public Health Association adopted a resolution at its November 2002 annual meeting to "oppose the subordination of public health to national defense and antiterrorism." The resolution, passed with 95 percent support, recognizes "the limited effectiveness of proposed secondary prevention strategies for defending against chemical and biological attacks, as well as the hypothetical nature of the risks such attacks might pose to public health, as compared to existing and inadequately controlled problems, such as contaminated food and water and breakdown in immunization rates," and notes that instead of actually improving funding for general public health activities, new monies are only going to biodefense and combating terrorism, while state funding for core public health initiatives is being cut.[38]

Also, in bringing under one roof law enforcement, intelligence gathering, public health, and national security, the Department of Homeland Security is positioned to conduct sweeping surveillance and data-mining activities, with scant attention paid to preserving individual privacy. As the Homeland Security bill was being considered, a number of members of Congress and privacy advocates called for the creation of a high-level privacy office within the new department, which Congress did incorporate in the final bill. However, substantial issues remain about the extent to which privacy rules will be developed and enforced, and whether Congress and the executive branch will play a vigorous oversight role.[39] For the Bush administration is making clear that, in the name of combating terrorism, privacy laws and policies must give way to surveillance and information collection.

This policy thrust is further underscored by the Pentagon's Total Information Awareness program, conceived and run by John Poindexter with the goal of monitoring peoples' daily movements and interactions.[40] The Pentagon's own Web site has featured a chart describing the new data-mining program under the logo "Knowledge Is Power" and declaring its intention to cull through a boggling array of information systems, including medical, credit, education—and even veterinary.[41] The danger here is that the HIPAA privacy regulation's limits on the use and disclosure of personal health information will be overcome by the national security and public health emergency authority built into the Homeland Security Act, the Total Information Awareness program, and new state laws based on the CDC's Model Act.

THE CDC'S MODEL STATE EMERGENCY HEALTH POWERS ACT

Prior to September 11, the CDC began developing a model law to be enacted by state legislatures with the goal of updating, strengthening, and harmonizing the state laws by putting in place a uniform national policy to address emergency health threats caused by bioterrorism and epidemics. The drafting process for the Model State Emergency Health Powers Act (the Model Act) was put on the fast track after the attacks, and released in the fall of 2001.

The Model Act grants the state governors authority to declare a public health emergency, which then triggers a wide range of powers to test, treat, vaccinate, isolate, quarantine, and seize property. The act broadly defines a public health emergency as "an occurrence or imminent threat of an illness or health condition that is believed to be caused by any of the following: bioterrorism, the appearance of a novel or previously controlled or eradicated infectious agent or biological toxin; a natural disaster; a chemical attack or accidental release; and poses a high probability of . . . a large number of deaths . . . [or] serious or long-term disabilities; or widespread exposure to an infectious or toxic agent that poses a significant risk of substantial future harm to a large number of people . . ."[42] The concern here is that the act gives the governors overly broad authority to declare a public health emergency and impose coercive measures, without clear limits, and with no legal requirement that less restrictive means be imposed where appropriate.

The Model Act further mandates that health care providers, including pharmacists, report "all cases of persons who harbor any illness or health condition that may be potential causes of a public health emergency" and report any "unusual or increased prescription rates, unusual types of prescriptions, or unusual trends in pharmacy visits that may be potential causes of a public health emergency." A provider or pharmacist's report shall include the illness or condition, the patient's name, date of brith, sex, race, occupation, work and home addresses, doctor's name, and "any other information needed to locate the patient for follow-up."[43] The question is, what is unusual? The danger is that existing privacy laws will be preempted to allow the private and public sector to collect, analyze, and store all routine health encounter data so as to be able to detect any unusual pattern or case. The Model Act also empowers state public health officials to detect, track, and interview people who are the subject of a reported condition or illness. Taken together, the act's implications for privacy are significant, giving broad, unfettered authority to government officials to surveil routine health encounters, and impose coercive measures with few limits or checks.

Although the Model Act does imposes some limits on access to and disclosure of the personal health information collected to persons having a "legitimate need to acquire and use the information" to treat the individual, conduct epidemiological research, investigate causes of transmission, and to "appropriate federal agencies or authorities pursuant to federal law," the standard is so vague and open-ended, it is not difficult to imagine, for instance, a federal official (law enforcement, public health, national security, or otherwise) invoking new legal authority under the Homeland Security Act or the Total Information Awareness program, claiming to have a "legitimate" interest in the information.

The act has been sharply criticized by an array of public health experts, consumer groups, and civil liberties advocates, who believe that it fails to incorporate privacy safeguards on the collection and sharing of patient medical information; vests too much unfettered power in law enforcement and the governors' offices (while reducing the involvement of public health officials); too broadly defines "public health emergency," which then becomes a trigger to justify coercive measures such as quarantine, isolation, treatment, and testing; and includes no penalties for misuse of information or overreaching authority.[44] When the Model Act was first made public, the New England Coalition for Law and Public Health sent a letter to HHS Secretary Tommy Thompson signed by professors of public health and law stating that the Model Act was dangerous and unnecessary because it focused only on public health's coercive authority and not on requiring less drastic measures if there is are such alternatives. The coalition letter concludes, "We firmly believe that there is no need for model legislation enhancing public health's emergency powers."[45] Another analysis of the Model Act by law professors at the University of Missouri reached the same conclusion, stating that the act "will not improve public practice or our response to bioterrorism. In fact, it may make such responses more difficult by undermining confidence in public health agencies and disrupting the complex web of existing state public health laws."[46]

In addition, the Health Privacy Project urged that the Model Act should be redrafted to narrow the definition of public health emergency; to clarify that state officials should use the least restrictive means possible, and resort to quarantine, isolation, and forced treatment only as a last resort; should incorporate privacy safeguards on the collection and redisclosure of personal medical information; and add penalties for violations.[47] At a January 2002 meeting sponsored by the Open Society Institute's Program on Medicine as a Profession, and co-convened by the Health Privacy Project and the Johns Hopkins Bloomberg School of Public Health, public health experts and officials, health care professionals, researchers, AIDS activists, the ACLU, and the National Conference of State Legislatures (NCSL) achieved unanimity on the inadequacy of current proposals.[48] This broad spectrum of participants also agreed on the need for resources and expertise on privacy, so that policy makers can develop alternative, more targeted plans to prevent and respond to bioterrorism without being driven by law enforcement priorities and without sacrificing broader public health goals.

The Model Act's authors have stated that they intended it to be a resource and a checklist for states to use in drafting their own law.[49] But given the limited time, the pressure from the federal government to take action, and scant state resources to address both the privacy gaps in the Model Act as well as the interplay of the Model Act with a state's existing public health law, many states have merely adopted a version of the CDC's model. As of August 2002, eighteen states had passed public health emergency powers legislation based on the Model Act, and many other states have introduced similar legislation to be considered in the next legislative session.

State public health emergency laws may be outdated and, if so, should be strengthened and updated. But state legislatures should take action in a deliberative, informed manner that incorporates privacy and other civil liberties. One of the Model Act's chief authors, Georgetown University Law Professor Larry Gostin, concluded in a 1999 law review article that state public health laws are inadequate to protect privacy and should be strengthened to incorporate privacy safeguards, enforcement, and oversight.[50] Yet, the Model Act provides the states with no mandate to treat privacy as integral to the success of such a massive public health endeavor. In the absence of more balanced and comprehensive resources, states are likely to continue enacting laws that are too extreme and lopsided,[51] giving too much discretion to the state's executive branch, subverting the authority of public health officials, and setting no limits or guidance as to whether and how privacy should be addressed.

Again, a chief reason that state legislatures are rushing forward to take action is because the federal government has explicitly tied the release of block grant money to the states developing and beginning to implement their own bioterrorism response plans.[52] To satisfy the CDC and HHS that they are taking concrete bioterrorist preparedness steps, state legislatures are enacting variations on the Model Act, often over objections of legislators with privacy concerns, public health experts, and civil liberties groups.[53]

CREATION AND LINKING OF HEALTH INFORMATION NETWORKS

A major focus of federal and state antibioterrorism efforts has been the creation, improvement, and linking of information networks to connect health care providers, hospitals, and pharmacies, with local, state, and federal public health officials.[54] Prior to September 11, the reporting, collection, and monitoring of specific diseases (e.g., AIDS, tuberculosis), medical conditions (e.g., brain tumors), and events (e.g., gunshot wounds) were all core public health activities that provided public health officials with information needed to anticipate, prevent, and respond to diseases and epidemics. Mandatory reporting requirements are mainly governed by state law, and require reporting to state public health departments. In some cases in which the CDC has determined that national coordination is needed, the states will report to the CDC certain nonidentifiable data that is then published in aggregate form in the *Morbidity and Mortality Weekly Report.*[55]

Following September 11, public health funding and initiatives have expanded—and some would argue have shifted—to focus on potential bioterrorist attacks. HHS Secretary Thompson stated in February 2002 that the nation's hospitals must draw up plans to "track suspicious diseases, . . . and increase communication among the health industry, local health officials and federal agencies."[56] But an HHS press statement added, "while bioterrorism preparedness is the impetus behind these grants and plans, Secretary Thompson said the ultimate benefit will be a stronger, more unified public health system that is better able to care for the public—whether during the routine of winter flu season or the stress of a terrorism attack."[57]

A number of state initiatives are moving forward quickly to link hospitals, labs, and emergency rooms to public health officials, often using private, unregulated networks. The CDC funds many of these efforts, partly through initiatives (predating September 11) that are aimed at building the states' public health infrastructure. But the massive infusion of resources post–September 11 has fueled the rapid creation of networks that vary from state-run information-sharing systems to state/academic collaborations, to efforts initiated solely by the private sector.

Typical of these new initiatives is the CDC–funded Texas Health Alert Network (HAN), which is intended to link all state public health offices, health care centers, and even law enforcement agencies[58] with the stated goal of disseminating data on disease outbreaks and buttressing surveillance capabilities.[59]

Also emblematic of the heightened focus on linked networks is the privately run Biomedical Security Institute, operated by Carnegie Mellon University and the University of Pittsburgh, which is developing a system to "track, in real time, unusual increases in illnesses, flu-like symptoms and other outbreaks of disease at emergency rooms in Western Pennsylvania."[60] Known as Real-Time Outbreak and Disease Surveillance (RODS), the system receives all routine encounter data on patients from twenty hospitals in western Pennsylvania over a private computer network, including the main reason a person went to the emergency room and the patient's age, gender, and zip code. RODS was also test-run at the 2002 Winter Olympics in Utah, where it functioned as a bioterrorism and disease outbreak monitoring system, receiving and analyzing data on all hospital admissions in the area.

Before RODS could be put in place, its developers asserted that certain safeguards were developed to overcome privacy limits in state law that would otherwise have prohibited patient records to be disclosed by the facilities where they were treated.[61] At this point, the Institute states that most identifiable information, such as a patient's name, address, and Social Security number, is maintained separately within RODS to safeguard privacy,[62] although it is unclear what physical and procedural hurdles prevent the re-linking of records to identify individual patients. But where does the information collected by RODS go? What are the legally enforceable rules governing the collection, storage, security, and reuse of identifiable patient data by RODS? None exist at this time.[63]

Private companies are also seizing on the bioterrorism threat to develop new products and activities. For instance, Cerner Corporation has a division dedicated to the collection and reporting of laboratory data and is advertising that its reporting system would "act as a constant monitor and alert health officials when necessary."[64] But who decides when an alert is necessary? What personal health information is collected, how is it stored, and who has access to it for what purposes? Again, this use of laboratory data takes it far out of the hands of patients and the clinicians who treat them, magnifying the risk that medical information may be used for purposes not intended—or expected—by most people.

An overarching concern here is that large, networked databases that contain peoples' medical information will not be used solely for the limited public health purpose of monitoring for a potential bioterror event. The easy availability of such sensitive and valuable data makes access by those not directly charged with public health activities virtually inevitable. The health information network initiatives, taken together with the new authority of the Department of Homeland Security,[65] the planned Total Information Awareness program,[66] and new state public health emergency laws, give the government the legal and technical capacity to cull through and gather a vast array of sensitive health information and other personal data.[67] This is not to argue that the motivations of the public health officials pressing for these expansions are anything but well intentioned. Nevertheless, once these networks are created and are used to collect, store, and analyze sensitive personal information on nearly everyone who has routine bloodwork, enters an emergency room, or is prescribed medication, the temptation to use—and misuse—this vast and valuable resource will be irresistible to employers, researchers, law enforcement, marketers, and hackers.[68]

FEAR OF SMALLPOX'S RETURN:
COERCIVE TREATMENT, TESTING, AND QUARANTINE?

The lesson of the anthrax cases in the fall 2001 is that a bioterrorist attack is possible. They have engendered widespread fear of a more sweeping and destructive attack from any number of biological agents, being spread intentionally—by either a criminal in our midst or through an international terrorist attack. And they have sparked the massive infusion of government and private sector support for plans to prevent and respond to such attacks, but with smallpox rather than anthrax as the main focus.

On December 13, 2002, the Bush administration announced a nationwide smallpox vaccination plan to immunize 500,000 military personnel, and 500,000 health care and emergency personnel most likely to be exposed to the disease in the event of an outbreak. The plan envisions the eventual vaccination of over 10 million people in such "first responder" positions, and the vaccine is to be offered on a voluntary basis to the general public possibly as early as 2004. The administration's plan also includes guidelines for the quarantine and isolation of certain infected, contagious, or vulnerable individuals.[69]

The smallpox plan has raised a number of privacy and autonomy concerns—as well as fundamental questions about risk—that the administration and the CDC have yet to answer as of early 2003. For example, in December 2002, at least two hospitals were refusing to vaccinate workers, citing concern about the risk of dangerous side effects and the inadvertant transmission to patients that "outweigh the remote threat of an attack."[70]

An October 2002 poll sponsored by The Robert Wood Johnson Foundation found that 65 percent of people would be willing to be vaccinated against smallpox,[71] but doctors, emergency personnel, and the public were quoted in press stories following the announcement of the plan as saying they were confused and concerned about the risks of contagion from the vaccination site and serious side effects, including death. The chief doctor at an emergency room in New York City stated that he would not be vaccinated because he had a fourteen-month-old child at home.[72] A nursing supervisor in Los Angeles said, "There is a period after vaccination where a person is infectious and should not be at work or caring for patients. That's two to three weeks. I can't have my staff at home that long."[73]

Routine vaccination against smallpox ended in the United States in 1972. At the end of that decade, the disease was eradicated worldwide. If smallpox were to recur, the consequences could be grave. The virus is contagious, and 30 percent of those infected die. But the Bush administration's plan to reinstitute the vaccine and immunize health care and emergency workers, as well as military personnel, augments the concern that serious privacy and civil liberties issues are not being adequately addressed in post–September 11 bioterrorism plans. As greater numbers of people now have compromised immune systems and other medical conditions that make them more vulnerable to serious side effects or even death from the vaccine, our public health system must be prepared to justify the need for renewing vaccinations and must develop a clear, defensible plan for medical screening and testing of potential vaccinees. There must also be a set of rules in place upfront as to how information will be gathered and stored, how data regarding who is and is not vaccinated will be handled, and the safeguards for the results of any prescreening and testing. Failure to develop a detailed, enforceable plan to protect the privacy of this sensitive information will make people fearful of participating in a vaccination plan, and may subject them and their communities to contagion in the event of an attack.

Prior to the September 11 attacks and subsequent anthrax cases, public health officials were growing increasingly concerned about the threat of a bioterrorist attack. In June 2000, government officials conducted an exercise that simulated a smallpox attack on Oklahoma City. Dubbed "Dark Winter," the test projected that in three months, 1 million people would die in twenty-five states.[74] "Dark Winter" pointed to massive deficiencies in the nation's vaccine supply, as well as to the absence of a plan to vaccinate, test, quarantine, and handle mass casualties. The terrorist attacks and anthrax cases pressed public health officials to confront these weaknesses.

But anticipating a smallpox outbreak raises significant medical privacy and autonomy issues. Many more people are at risk for serious side effects—and death—from the smallpox vaccine than they were thirty years ago, given that the percentage of people with risk factors has risen tremendously. People with immune disorders or compromised immune systems caused by cancer treatment, HIV or AIDS; anyone with a skin condition or who had eczema as a child; pregnant women; and children under the age of one are the major groups at risk for a severe adverse reaction to the vaccine. Add to these numbers the people living with those at higher risk. Vulnerable people can be infected by contact with someone who was vaccinated, "because the live virus is shed from the sore at the vaccination site for two to three weeks."[75] If we only count those Americans who have suffered from eczema and the people who live with them, 30 million people might be ineligible or at unreasonably high risk for taking the vaccine.[76]

Further, there is dispute about whether a serious risk of a smallpox attack exists; in other words, we do not have proof that the smallpox virus is in the hands of international terrorists or potential criminals in the United States. Dr. D. A. Henderson, credited with eradicating smallpox and recently a senior adviser to HHS Secretary Thompson, testified in May 2002 that there was no information to suggest that a smallpox attack was likely, "yet there is a tremendous demand for smallpox vaccine from every quarter."[77] Also, public health experts disagree on the speed of transmission, with some infectious disease specialists stating that "smallpox is a barely contagious and very slow-spreading infection," and suggesting that while even a single case would be an emergency, in many instances it could be contained easily.[78]

Privacy and autonomy questions that must be answered include:

• How will the government and health professionals determine if a person is at risk for adverse effects? Prior to being vaccinated, will all people receive a battery of diagnostic tests and fill out a detailed medical history to determine if they are HIV positive, had eczema as a child, are pregnant, or have a yet-undiagnosed immune deficiency? Who will perform the testing, and under what conditions will the information be collected, stored, and re-disclosed? Will the patient have access to the medical records, and who else will have access? What penalties will be in place if the information is misused?

• If a person is deemed to be at risk, and a decision is made not to vaccinate, will that person be isolated or quarantined to shield her from the live virus carried by her vaccinated family members, co-workers, and neighbors? Or will those at risk be forced to be vaccinated if the government determines that the risk of adverse effects is outweighed by the greater risk of death if infected (30 percent)?

• In the event of a mass vaccination program, how will the government compel people to come forward? How will the government identify people who have not been vaccinated?

Many people are anxious about entering the health care system for fear that their medical information will be used to harm them (for instance, to deny them a job or benefits, or deport them). Moreover, given that over 40 million people lack health insurance in this country, many people cannot afford health care and are reluctant to seek treatment.[79] A vaccination, treatment, and quarantine plan that addresses these issues of privacy and inequity would go a long way towards buttressing compliance and fostering trust in the public health system, if indeed the plan is warranted and employs the least restrictive means necessary to accomplish its goals.

THE NEED FOR SAFEGUARDS: HISTORICAL LESSONS

As we develop a public health approach to bioterrorism and other threats, historical lessons must caution us about the dangers of overreaching, of prejudice, stigma, and fear. As Professor Lawrence Gostin points out in his treatise on public health law:

> . . . personal control measures have been applied in ways that may be better explained by animus than by science. Several campaigns of restraint in nineteenth- and twentieth-century America demonstrate the influence of prejudice: isolation of persons with yellow fever, despite its mode of transmission by mosquitoes; arrests of alcoholics, especially poor Irishmen, in the false belief that cholera arose in part from intemperance; mass confinement of prostitutes "suspected" of having syphilis in state-run "reformatories"; and house-to-house searches and forced removal of children thought to have poliomyelitis.[80]

The campaigns against tuberculosis and typhoid were characterized by animus against the poor and the immigrant minorities of their times,[81] and the handling of HIV/AIDS in the late 1980s, as well as the anthrax cases in the fall of 2001, illustrate how perilous a situation can become when there is a dearth of clear medical evidence on how to treat a condition, combined with confusion and fear in the community about who might be infected, whether they are contagious, and what is the best course of treatment. As more personal health information is swept into a nationwide surveillance system, the risk of discrimination, stigma, and misuse increases tremendously. Even if certain medical information related to diagnosis and treatment is treated as confidential within the health care system (to limit disclosure to employers, co-workers, neighbors, and even family members where appropriate), certain kinds of treatment may in and of themselves result in public disclosure. Consider the inadvertent disclosure that would result if one is forced to undergo quarantine, isolation, or civil confinement for care and treatment.

The early treatment of people with HIV and AIDS by policy makers, the health care system, the general public, and public health officials was characterized by misinformation, prejudice, and fear. Taken together, these factors were incendiary, and resulted in widespread discrimination and stigma against infected individuals, mainly gay men. The history of the AIDS epidemic and the unnecessary and unjustifiable damage caused has been exhaustively documented.[82]

As Laurie Garrett chronicles in *Betrayal of Trust: The Collapse of Global Public Health,* "Bigotry against homosexuals and injecting drug users . . . blinded the general public, politicians, the medical community, and sadly, many public health leaders to the urgency of responding to AIDS when effective action might have had a profound impact."[83] A 1988 poll found that more than 75 percent of respondents had "no sympathy for homosexuals suffering from AIDS." "Popular indignation was evident in proposals for punitive measures, such as branding with a tattoo, isolating, and establishing special institutions."[84] Eventually the public health response to this level of societal hostility was often to build privacy and security into the testing, treatment, and counseling for HIV and AIDS to ensure that people could step forward without fear of reprisals. "All disease surveillance and identification of infected individuals was made confidential or anonymous, thus protecting individuals from societal discrimination. And HIV infections were never reported; only full-blown AIDS cases were tracked, amid clearly justifiable concerns about protecting the civil liberties of outwardly well, HIV-positive individuals."[85] To some extent, public health policy with respect to HIV and AIDS developed with a recognition that barriers to testing and treatment needed to be addressed with privacy and antidiscrimination protections, to benefit not only the individual but also the larger community.

In the months following the September 11, 2001, attacks, deadly anthrax spores killed five people and infected at least thirteen others, most of whom inhaled the spores contained in letters sent through the U.S. Postal Service. Government officials initially alerted the public that the anthrax cases (occurring in Florida, the Washington, D.C., area, New York City, New Jersey, and Connecticut) bore the marks of a bioterrorist attack. At this writing, no one has yet been charged in the cases, and it is debatable whether the anthrax came from sources outside the United States or was obtained within this country by someone who may have had authorized access to the bacteria. In any case, the anthrax cases caught public health officials by surprise, and early statements from the CDC, HHS, and local public health officials were conflicting, confusing, and sometimes inaccurate.

In this context of confusion, public health officials at the state and federal levels offered conflicting advice and treatment, and at times appeared to provide care that disproportionately favored one group over another—Capitol Hill congressional staff (predominantly white) over postal workers (predominantly black) in the southeast D.C. facility that processed the mail sent to Senate and House offices. After Senate staff opened mail addressed to Senators Tom Daschle and Patrick Leahy containing anthrax spores, health officials quickly advised all staff working in the Capitol Hill buildings to receive nasal swab testing for spores (which took days to confirm), and, to be on the safe side, immediately begin taking a course of Cipro, the antibiotic known to be most effective in treating anthrax. Conversely, the postal workers who had processed the contaminated mail were advised that nasal swab testing and precautionary doses of Cipro were unnecessary. Subsequently, a number of postal workers became seriously ill from anthrax exposure, and one died. Capitol Hill staff were later advised by government doctors to get the anthrax vaccine (38 percent chose to do so), but while the vaccine was offered to postal workers, only about 3 percent chose to participate (152 out of over 5,000 exposed). As the D.C. health director lamented at the time, "The absence of a clear recommendation from the CDC about who should take the vaccine, coupled with the absence of any follow-up care, makes it difficult for the postal workers to say 'we'll take it.'" [86]

The postal workers' reluctance to receive the vaccine may have been due in part to the distrust and resentment that had developed over the previous months as government officials focused their treatment resources on congressional staff, mistakenly believing that anthrax could not be transmitted through unopened envelopes. Public perception of how the government handled the anthrax cases is important to understand, given that the public's willingness to participate in future public health actions is critical to the success of any new program. As a reliable barometer of strong currents in public sentiment, *Saturday Night Live* ran a skit in November 2001 at the height of the anthrax scare in which an actor played CDC head Dr. Anthony Fauci being interviewed by reporters. The Fauci character asserted, "I'd like to reassure the American public by saying this: we have cleaned the State Department, the White House, the Supreme Court and the Capitol Building with state-of-the-art decontamination instruments, and have installed dozens of $20 million irradiation lasers to keep all dangerous substances away from the U.S. government." A reporter follows up, "What about the post office?" Fauci replies, "We've given each post office some Baby Wipes and a Dustbuster."[87]

LOOKING AHEAD

To ensure that an invigorated public health system succeeds in its mission to anticipate, respond to, and prevent potential bioterrorist attacks and other public health emergencies, we must seize this opportunity to build up the public health infastructure through renewed community and clinical awareness of its importance—while incorporating privacy and security safeguards. To this end:

• Congress and the executive branch must insist that the Homeland Security Act, and other federal legislation and policies related to bioterrorism, be amended to include clear privacy rules, vigorous oversight mechanisms, and enforceable penalties for breaches;

• the CDC and its parent, the Department of Health and Human Services, should require that privacy protections be developed as an integral component of any public health initiative that involves the collection of personal health information, or the potential for intrusive, coercive action such as mandatory treatment, isolation, or quarantine;

• the Pentagon's Total Information Awareness program should be abolished, and Congress should prohibit the executive branch from spending any resources on any such program in the future that would so broadly override existing medical privacy law; and

• state legislatures should revisit already enacted laws modeled on the CDC's State Emergency Health Powers Act to incorporate comprehensive privacy safeguards for the collection, use, and storage of personal health information by public health departments and private organizations involved in a public health mission. States that have not yet passed new public health emergency legislation should build privacy rules in at the outset.

The continued absence of such safeguards, and the codification of vague promises that power will not be abused and good judgment will be employed, ignore the historical lessons we've learned: during a crisis, privacy and other civil liberties are given little weight in the balancing of competing law enforcement, national security, and commercial interests. Preserving public health and protecting privacy can—and must—go hand in hand.

10. THE PUBLIC HEALTH FALLOUT FROM SEPTEMBER 11: OFFICIAL DECEPTION AND LONG-TERM DAMAGE

JOEL R. KUPFERMAN[1]

The environmental and public health nightmare that began in New York City on September 11, 2001, was unprecedented in nature, and its scope is still being discovered—mainly without the help of the Bush administration's environmental agencies. The persistent "WTC cough," hundreds of new cases of asthma, the broad, wind-borne dissemination of toxic elements, a by-now unmanageable spread of toxic dust initially carried out of the World Trade Center and debris-collection sites by rescue workers and since spread by former rescue vehicles like city buses and fire trucks—these are some of the reasons why, at this writing, more than 500 firefighters have sustained permanent disabilities that have forced them to retire,[2] why 25 percent of nurses examined at a downtown hospital in March 2002 had serious respiratory disorders,[3] and why these cases are the tip of a very large iceberg.

The way the Environmental Protection Agency (EPA) responded in the crisis was, sadly, an opportunity to glimpse the Bush administration's larger attitude toward environmental policy and toward public access to key environmental information. The EPA, which misled the public about the health impact of asbestos found in the ambient air and also failed to investigate or respond thoroughly on a range of crucial issues, led other federal, state, and local authorities to rest easily with their own misdirected policies, affecting the long-term health of no one knows how many New Yorkers. In the context of the Bush administration's broader hostility to civil liberties, and its particular, determined retreat from environmental protections and engagement, the environmental/public health story of the World Trade Center collapse is a chilling reminder of the damage that unaccountable government can do—damage that in this case will linger for generations.

To protect an environment, including its inhabitants, requires that people have a say about the issues that affect their lives, and that the press and citizen groups hold the government to account for its stewardship of air, soil, and water. This public participation should not be hindered by political differences or undue pressure for a particular form of patriotism. At the cornerstone of urban environmentalism are the principles of self-determination and equal protection, a free-flowing exchange of information and ideas at all levels of governance. This is not merely the wish list of the neighborhood activist. The Freedom of Information Act (FOIA) was enacted for just this purpose. The comparable New York State regulation provides a compelling preamble:

> The people's right to know the process of government decision and the documents and statistics leading to determinations is basic to our society. Access to such information should not be thwarted by shrouding it with the cloak of secrecy or confidentiality. . . . Any conflicts among laws governing public access to records shall be construed in favor of the widest possible availability of public records.

These principles are all the more essential in a public emergency.

Another underlying precept of environmentalism is the interrelatedness of seemingly disparate ecosystems. As researchers document PCBs migrating from urban hazardous waste sites to Arctic Sea ice algae and making their way into the breast milk of Inuit women, so we must apply this concept to our cities. Toxins leaching into the groundwater at the Ground Zero excavation must be assumed to have a relationship with the Hudson River, just two blocks away. As the U.S. Geologic Survey researches winds transporting Saharan red sand to the Caribbean islands and eventually Texas, so may we assume that the steady, black plume rising for weeks from the former World Trade Center had an impact on the millions of people living in its path—certainly in Brooklyn, Manhattan, Queens, Staten Island, and Long Island, and probably beyond.

Policy makers at the EPA, and the manufacturers of literally thousands of common office and building fixtures in lower Manhattan, could not have predicted the wholesale and cataclysmic demolition of some 15 million square feet of office space. But it would be overly simplistic to attribute the actions of public health and environmental officials to confusion under pressure, at least after the first few days. It has become evident that federal, state, and city agency actions and decisions were closely tied to economic and political motivations that placed other goals ahead of public health, and that these decisions led agencies to withhold critical health information from even the communities most at risk. The principles of environmental justice—the right to clean air, water, and other resources—were sacrificed early, and then over and over, to the interests of political recovery and the bottom line.

The risks of wholesale liability loomed large. Much of the World Trade Center complex was demolished into a fine powder that spread as far as wind and water might take it; the reach of possible public health consequences, with their requirements for government response and compensation, was initially incalculable. Firefighters and police officers, iron workers and operating engineers, medical personnel and many others, were originally thought to be limited by law to consideration under workers' compensation and similar programs—that is, they could collect based on the limited liability of their employers in exchange for "no-fault" determinations. But those surrounding the disaster—survivors and residents—had no such limitations. In the larger affected area, beyond Ground Zero, as dictated by the principle of interrelatedness, millions of potential victims were placed at risk and could conceivably make demands for public aid or compensation.

Through its air-quality testing choices and its management of information to the public, the EPA sought to limit the government's responsibility, and liability, even at the cost of exposing people to health risks they had a right to know about and the option to avoid. This was made possible, in part, by the laziness of the local press, which should have investigated inconsistencies and demanded transparency. But the principal fault lies with those charged with carrying out environmental law and protecting the public.

FIRE AND ASH

As the twin towers collapsed, thousands of fleeing workers and area residents were coated with a thick, white dust that quickly began to irritate their skin and lungs. Gray clouds of highly corrosive material containing concrete particles, asbestos, finely crushed windows, and fiberglass and heavy metals choked the streets. Gasping survivors gulped down the toxin-laden dust as the entire area— buildings, streets, and ground, interiors and exteriors—was blanketed with fallout. Once the rescue effort could be organized, an arbitrary dividing line, first at Fourteenth Street in Manhattan, was then moved quickly southward to Canal Street and finally to Chambers Street, only five blocks from the northern perimeter of Ground Zero. The luxury developments of Battery Park City were evacuated, and residents fled much of the area below Canal Street as large parts of lower Manhattan were without power, water, and telephone service.

Immediately, landlords lost rental income; the retail, entertainment, and tourism economics of the city shut down; the real estate market took a nosedive.

Schools, the financial markets, government agencies, and all but the most necessary places of business closed. Roads, subways, bridges, and tunnels connected to this area would remain closed, or with limited access, for months. Layoffs began, and what had been worrisome signs of recession before September 11 intensified. At the same time, the nation began an outpouring of affection for the city that had perhaps not been seen since the Giants won the pennant in '51. Whatever our grief was locally—and it was great—we in New York sensed that we were not alone.

It became somebody's job to make sure the secondary economic and political tragedy did not eclipse the WTC fire and collapse itself. A "clean" environmental bill of health for what was left of lower Manhattan was the way to get the city and the country back to work. The push was on to shift the public's understandable shock to an uneasy restoration of order, including the difficult task of trying to keep decimated financial markets from fleeing what was now deemed a major target of our enemies, and attracting back tourists. While the world mourned, the clock began ticking to reopen the New York Stock Exchange, a block away from the disaster site.

At the site itself, an inferno burned on, despite continuous streams of water from several directions and the government's continuous reassurances that the fire would soon die out. With the exception of a single day, when the wind turned north, the huge plume of black smoke emerging from Ground Zero drifted southeast, day after day, over much of lower Manhattan, Brooklyn, and southern Queens.

As the EPA and its colleague state and city agencies like to insist, precisely what was in that plume will never be known; capturing the smoke for testing presented obvious hazards. But common materials of modern offices—synthetic fabrics, plastics, laminates, and building supplies containing formaldehyde; fluorescent lamps containing mercury; the di-electric fluids that encase electrical cables; approximately four pounds of lead from each computer; PCBs from capacitors, electrical cable insulation, and transformers—were clearly elements in highly toxic fires and dust storms. The plume contained, at the very least, toxic lead, asbestos, volatile organic compounds, dioxins, mercury, nickel, vandium, sulfur, PAHs, PCBs, and furans.

And there was more. The World Trade Center had housed many facilities specific to the tenant government agencies, including a Secret Service shooting range that kept millions of rounds of lead ammunition on hand. An array of hazardous chemicals was stored in a U.S. Customs lab, including thousands of pounds of arsenic, lead, mercury, and chromium, among other toxic substances.[4] The City of New York maintained an emergency generator at its command center located at 7 WTC, with a large, aboveground fuel storage tank that had been exempted from violation of local building codes. And more still: some 130,000 gallons of PCB-contaminated transformer oil at an electrical substation at 7 WTC likely contributed to its collapse and to the toxic residue later found in the area.

On September 13, against a backdrop of mounting patriotism, EPA Chief Christine Todd Whitman helicoptered into the city to deliver to television cameras the most uplifting news New Yorkers could hope for in those terrible days. As governor of New Jersey, Whitman had amassed a track record of effectively subordinating environmental concerns to those of industry, but in this extraordinary situation, her message was reassuring. Whitman reported that the EPA was "greatly relieved to have learned that there appear to be no significant levels of asbestos dust in the air in New York City."[5] The news came as welcome contrast to the grim reports of the thousands of body bags that Mayor Giuliani had ordered in. "We are working closely with rescue crews to ensure that all appropriate precautions are taken," said Whitman. "We will continue to monitor closely."[6]

That monitoring appeared to produce even better news, as Whitman reported on September 21, after the financial markets had reopened. She was relieved, she said, to be able to say "that a host of potential contaminants are either not detectable or are below the Agency's concern levels. . . . Results we have just received on drinking water quality show that not only is asbestos not detectable, but also we cannot detect any bacterial contamination, PCBs or pesticides."[7] This appeared to be enough for most news outlets in the city and nationally. With a few notable exceptions, warning of possible respiratory exacerbation for individuals with already compromised systems, the news media latched on to the good news with servile uniformity.

In the meantime, hundreds upon hundreds of rescue workers—firefighters, police, iron workers, operating engineers, and others—entered and left what became known as Ground Zero, aiding in the rescue effort. They were surrounded by concentric rings of aid workers who provided food, clothing, and support, many of them volunteers from all over the country. As the fire raged on for weeks, a self-contained city sprang up below Canal Street: makeshift command centers and relief stations were set up in Stuyvesant High School and other local schools, in firehouses and local hotels and any other public spaces that could be commandeered. A dismal order gradually replaced the initial, impassioned chaos.

The Ground Zero workers were surrounded by a foul, corrosive, and irritating odor that permeated lower Manhattan, provoking the widely reported "WTC cough." The hacking cough, which plagued many New Yorkers well beyond the immediate area for months, was just one sign that residents' long-term health was being compromised. According to Dr. Stephen M. Levin, medical director of a major center on environmental and occupational medicine, "Some of the asthma contracted by New Yorkers will persist for the rest of their lives."[8]

After the search for survivors waned and workers at the site shifted into a recovery mode, the priority established by the EPA, the Occupational Safety and Health Administration (OSHA), and the Federal Emergency and Management Agency (FEMA) in deference to commercial downtown interests became the cleanup of the streets' exterior areas. John L. Henshaw, assistant secretary of labor for OSHA—in an understated comment that would characterize the agencies' disinformation all down the line—advised, "Keeping the streets clean and being careful not to track dust into buildings will help protect workers from remaining debris."[9]

But in the meantime, the most rudimentary elements of proper handling of a toxic disaster were being ignored. In one instance, which would have been laughable in other circumstances, the EPA publicized sending in vacuum trucks, but the trucks were sent without the HEPA filters necessary to suck up the dust.[10] Further, the EPA did not carry out serious testing of the dust, as described below, and did only minimal and spotty testing of ambient air much beyond Ground Zero, despite the evident dispersal of dust in the wind; there was, in other words, only the most limited attempt to determine the nature and scope of the health risk to the city's population before cleanup advisories were issued. And EPA, OSHA, and the city's Department of Health did not provide much in the way of personal protective gear and respirators to the workers at Ground Zero and debris-removal areas; a study by the National Institute of Environmental Health Sciences determined that, to the extent that workers got protection, it was mainly due to the activism of the operating engineers' union, not the appropriate—and much wealthier—government agencies.[11]

At this critical juncture—in a move that has since been criticized soundly by such diverse observers as the City Council,[12] accountability advocate Congressman Jerrold Nadler,[13] and the *Wall Street Journal*—the EPA determined that it was only responsible for cleaning and decontaminating the outsides of buildings in lower Manhattan, not for the cleanup of building interiors where people worked and lived. The EPA delegated the interiors of buildings to the overwhelmed and beleaguered NYC Department of Environmental Protection (DEP); the DEP was supposed to help residents ensure the safety of their homes with trained cleaning personnel, proper decontamination equipment, and the like. The EPA's position in this case contradicted both its own recent experience and the law that governs it. Just days before September 11, in the town of Libby, Montana, the EPA had taken complete responsibility to clean all the homes of that former asbestos mining center—where, as it happened, asbestos levels, while patently unsafe, were lower than those found by independent sampling in lower Manhattan.[14] The EPA had taken total responsibility for the Libby cleanup because, under the Clean Air Act's NESHAP standards, the federal government is required to ensure that people are not exposed to asbestos at dangerous levels, especially in airborned or friable (readily convertible to airborne) forms. The EPA also fast-tracked Libby to a place on the National Priorities List as a Superfund site, because the governor of Montana requested it; as a result, Libby does not have to wait years for EPA to assess its hazards and make comparative cost-benefit judgments. But the World Trade Center collapse did not get this kind of treatment; Governor Pataki did not request it, and the EPA did not undertake it voluntarily.

As the *Wall Street Journal* would report eight months later, the DEP, in turn, also passed the buck, allowing landlords to determine if their own buildings were clean without the DEP testing to check.[15] In a memo to New York City landlords dated May 11, 2002—two days after the *WSJ* article—the DEP tried to back-pedal by demanding that landlords provide "copies of the environmental hazards assessments including bulk sample [samples of tests on dust] results and air monitoring results and a summary of clean-up activities" for their buildings.[16] As of January 2003, only ninety landlords had responded to the DEP's demand,[17] and the DEP had not stepped up pressure on them to comply. The Clean Air Act and New York City asbestos laws require a certain quality of clean-up effort where asbestos is discovered, but with the EPA saying the air was clean, as discussed below, and with the DEP taking no action to test buildings, landlords were allowed to superficially assuage the cleanup issue with improper cleaning methods and, in the process, destroyed easily accessible evidence of toxins. New Yorkers were left at the mercy of their landlords to determine whether their homes or workplaces were safe.

The city's health department (DOH) did as badly or worse. When the department surveyed downtown residents for a January 2002 study, 59 percent of respondents indicated that they had received information about how to clean their apartments of the WTC dust, under protocols issued by the health department itself. The DOH protocols, issued on September 17, 2001, advised residents facing reentry into their apartments around Ground Zero, "The best way to remove dust is to use a wet rag or wet mop. . . . Where dust is thick, directly wet the dust with water and remove it in layers with wet rag and mops." [18] Nowhere in the advisory did the health department inform that the "dust" inside these homes might well contain asbestos and myriad other toxic substances; nor did the protocols suggest that professional testing and decontamination (otherwise known as abatement) should be sought, for residents' protection and as required by law if the dust contained more than 1 percent asbestos. [19] It was this advisory that the EPA repeatedly cited in referring concerned residents to local authorities for guidance on cleaning building interiors.

The remains of the WTC complex were removed along various routes to the closed Fresh Kills landfill on Staten Island: truck convoys passed through the Brooklyn Battery Tunnel through Red Hook (with wind blowing dust off the tops of the trucks' contents), and barges moved on the Hudson River. In Fresh Kills, New York City detectives and FBI personnel sifted through the debris. A report produced by an industrial hygienist for the NYC Detectives' Endowment Association, and passed to my organization, found that while respirators were available to these workers from OSHA upon request, the agency had not provided training and fitting as necessary in their use, nor had the detectives received "quality information . . . on what the health and safety hazards might be and what controls are being implemented to reduce these hazards." [20] Several of the detectives were felled by the noxious fumes that rose off the landfill.

Firefighters' and detectives' associations, since immediately after the disaster, had been approaching the organization that I direct, the New York Environmental Law and Justice Project, to ask for advice and share information. We were receiving a stream of statements from rescue workers and their unions, who were increasingly worried about exposures. At the same time, office workers and neighborhood residents near Ground Zero were complaining of eyes tearing and skin itching. They spoke of the dust that covered their furnishings and floors, of being denied the right to wear a mask indoors at their city jobs for fear of creating "panic," of clogged air filters in newly bought home-filtering machines, and awakening at night in spasms of coughing. They talked about needing asthma inhalers and nebulizers for the first time, and reported that nonunion contractors were being hired by landlords to "clean up" in a haphazard fashion. These people were finding it very hard to get precise, practical information from city and federal agencies. Meanwhile, residents were tracking whatever dust was on their clothes around to their jobs, schools, and other locations. And what incensed rescue and cleanup workers most was that they were not given even basic advice on how to limit their own and their families' exposure. Thousands of workers—who displayed bravery beyond measure—were exposed to a surfeit of toxic substances, while very few were encouraged to wear the scant personal protective gear available, and even fewer were advised of the potential hazards they were unknowingly tracking home to their families on their clothes and effects.

In late November 2001, Dr. Stephen Levin, of the prestigious Mount Sinai–I. J. Selikoff Center for Occupational and Environmental Medicine, testified before the New York State Assembly's Standing Committees on Environmental Conservation, Health, and Labor. He noted then that conditions "seen in adults who have been at *or near*" (emphasis added) the WTC site "for as little as twenty-four to thirty-six hours" included "reactive airways disease, new onset or exacerbation of pre-existing asthma, RADS [reactive airway dysfunction syndrome], sinusitis, irritant rhinitis, persistent cough, and diffuse irritation of nasal mucosal surfaces." Particularly among first-responders "or individuals who were hit by the cloud of dust and debris" following the collapse, Dr. Levin found "a dramatic increase in GERD [gastro-esophageal reflux] symptoms," which in some people are life-threatening.[21] As of late January 2003, Dr. Levin had examined some 3,500 rescue workers and volunteers, starting immediately after the WTC collapse, and found that half suffered from either serious respiratory disorders and/or psychological distress.[22]

The obvious questions should have been: What was in this dust and smoke? What is causing the present ailments? and What long-term health effects might result? But the EPA, in an abdication of its responsibility, did at most insufficient testing of the area, and very limited—and unpublicized—testing of interiors. The agency began testing the ambient air within a few days of the attack, and continued for several weeks. But it circumscribed the range of its monitoring arbitrarily—with almost no air sampling in Brooklyn, for example, though that borough got the full impact of windborne fallout from the burning plume. Paul Bartlett, Queens College environmental scientist and an international expert in the dispersion of toxic substances, found EPA and other agencies' monitoring inadequate to determine the degree and extent of exposure. According to Bartlett, their "detection limits are aimed at threshold levels for occupational exposure. They aren't treating this as a disaster, so they're not asking to what extent and how far are people being exposed or who is possibly being affected by the release of chemicals. They're just checking what emissions are exceeding regulations."[23]

What testing the EPA did do was initially withheld from the scientists and medical community, labor unions with men on-site, and local leadership. When pressed to back up assertions that all was well, the EPA tended to point, for support, to the New York City Department of Environmental Protection, the local agency with responsibility for hazardous waste cleanup and disposal. But the DEP—ill equipped for a disaster of these dimensions but unwilling to admit it—refused to release its data in timely fashion, even to a joint committee of the state legislature. Moreover, when that data was finally obtained and made public by the Environmental Law and Justice Project, in November 2001, through a state Freedom of Information Law request, it revealed that the DEP had conducted testing without using the highest-quality equipment available, such that its results were always less refined and informative than they should have been about the true risks and potential impact.

To be fair, on September 11, no one could comprehend the full severity and repercussions of what had happened. But as the weeks passed, the agencies' evasions became policy. Medical experts were seeing health effects but could not properly diagnose or help patients because they did not have adequate information. Environmental scientists were expecting to learn the components of the fallout in order to make immediate decisions that would affect cleanup, recovery, and future systemic planning. And meanwhile, the EPA and OSHA kept saying there was no problem.

THE EPA'S TESTING AND REPORTING

It was not until three weeks after September 11 that the EPA Web site began posting a "representative sampling" of air-monitoring results, from various places in lower Manhattan. In those three weeks, the agency was testing the ambient air but not releasing the results, and it was not testing settled dust with the highest-scrutiny techniques available but was choosing, instead, cheaper and nonaggressive techniques that, predictably, yielded lower results. Nor was it testing air inside offices or apartments near Ground Zero, where people were told it was safe to return within three days of the disaster.

One thing the EPA did report, in the days just after September 11, was that its own headquarters at 290 Broadway—a few blocks from Ground Zero—had been tested and found safe for asbestos. The tests had reportedly shown the presence of airborne asbestos but at "less than one-tenth of the maximum level allowed in workplaces by the Occupational Safety and Health Administration."[24] Bonnie Bellow, regional spokeswoman for the EPA, would announce on Friday, September 14, that, according to tests the previous day, "There's nothing at this point that indicates that business can't resume in the Wall Street area on Monday as well."[25] The agency also noted, however, that parts of its building had later undergone thorough asbestos cleaning. The logical question arose: If all is well, why was 290 Broadway undergoing an asbestos abatement? This question was not posed by the press, though, and EPA did not clarify the contradiction on its own.

Neither did EPA reveal a key fact about its headquarters cleanup: it had hired an industrial hygienist to use a particular type of high-sensitivity sampling method, called micro-vaccuum, which sucks out even the tiniest particles and subjects them to highest-scrutiny analysis.[26] This seems only responsible, and indeed it was. But the EPA, in failing to reveal the facts, was then able to take a position that micro-vac testing was unnecessary for schools and residences in lower Manhattan. Not only did EPA fail to *require* the use of the most thorough tests to seek evidence of asbestos and other toxic substances in lower Manhattan; it actively discounted results obtained when the micro-vac was used independently in the neighborhood. At 105 Duane Street, residents hired a certified industrial hygienist who used micro-vac on December 3 and found 555,000 asbestos structures per square centimeter in samples from the air-supply vent (at least fifty times the recommended safe level). The EPA criticized the testing method and contended the finding was an aberration. The landlord then failed to do a proper abatement on the building, based on EPA and DEP assurances that the test results could be ignored. Actions like this prompted an EPA scientist, Cate Jenkins, to criticize the agency in a series of memos that circulated in the scientific community and became well known to organized downtown residents.[27]

The EPA was not the only agency withholding relevant health-affecting information, putting out positive spin, and giving residents instructions and guidance that fell short of what was legally required. A U.S. Department of Health and Human Services "fact" sheet on dust and debris issued September 16 advised: "The most immediate hazards to health and well-being are from unstable buildings, broken glass, jagged metal and other harmful things." In response to the question, "What is in the dust?" the flyer advised, "We expect that materials that would be present would be at concentrations lower than those normally associated with health hazards," and made no mention whatsoever of asbestos, lead, concrete, fiberglass, or any of the other known toxic substances contained in WTC building components and contents, defining dust only as "fine particles that originally made up materials of the WTC and the aircraft that struck it."

Given the official agencies' determination to be upbeat, and the evidence of people's endangerment, it became important to take some independent samples, which I did for the Environmental Law and Justice Project on September 19, at Vesey and Liberty Streets, on the outer perimeter of Ground Zero.[28] ATC Associates, a laboratory that had been used by New York City and its Board of Education, analyzed the samples. Four samples indicated content of between 1 percent and 5 percent chrysotile asbestos—that is, up to five times the level at which the law requires immediate decontamination—and a very high level of fiberglass, which the National Toxicology Program defines as a "likely carcinogen." (Soon after the Law Project's results became public, the New York State Department of Health threatened local labs with loss of their licenses if they processed any more "independent sampling," according to a lab director who received such a warning.[29]

On September 24, the Law Project hand-distributed these findings to the local area's residents and emergency workers, in a fact sheet produced with the help of Monona Rossol, an experienced industrial hygienist. Although the EPA, Mayor Giuliani, and the city's health department called the Law Project's warnings alarmist, some members of the media began to call. One in particular, Juan Gonzalez of the *New York Daily News,* began to follow the environmental story closely and to publish what he could.

When EPA began posting a "representative sampling" of air-quality monitoring data on its Web site, on October 3, the postings involved three grades of filtering of information. First, the EPA had tested narrowly as to location and as to matter tested, as noted above; given that the samples posted were selective and so few, and taken mostly outdoors rather than indoors, they did not give an accurate picture of what people were exposed to. Second, the postings were a selection from the total pool of EPA data available—all of which should have been made available for scientific, health-agency, journalistic and public-health communities to examine. Third, the EPA's explication of the selective data it posted was disingenuous and scientifically misleading, and as with the other filtering this minimized the findings of dangerous toxins. For example, the Web site featured a significant number (27 out of 442) of ambient air samples taken in September that registered above the current AHERA (Asbestos Hazard Emergency Response Act) standard for permissible exposure levels, which is 70 structures per millimeter squared. The agency explained these as "spikes" in toxicity, momentary aberrations, even though its own testing was too spotty to establish whether such results would have been aberrations or not. And it argued that they should be averaged into the rest of the data, such that the results would not exceed AHERA or other regulatory limits, even though that is not how toxicity works: beyond certain levels, even short-term exposure to certain toxics is alarmingly dangerous.

The accompanying EPA press release on October 3 also contained some troubling inconsistencies. The agency continued to argue that the public's health was not at risk, advising yet again that testing "found no evidence of any significant public health hazard to residents or visitors to the New York metropolitan area." The agency further recommended, "There is no need for concern among the general public, but residents and business owners should follow recommended procedures for cleaning up homes and businesses if dust has entered."

In that press release the EPA advised the public that it had "been evaluating samples of air against an extremely stringent standard, the AHERA standard." The statement went on to stress that "levels of asbestos above the AHERA standard do not imply that there is an immediate health threat to the public." Indeed, it said, "asbestos exposure becomes a health concern when high concentrations of asbestos fibers are inhaled over a long period." Quite apart from misrepresenting the asbestos threat, as explained further below, the EPA misused the AHERA standard, which is intended for evaluating *after* a cleanup has taken place.

The results of the bulk sampling data, as posted on the Web site, were also worrisome. Forty-eight of 177 bulk samples collected by EPA contained more than 1 percent asbestos, but on the Web site the EPA did not report how much more. And the press release glossed this over, stating blandly, "The existence of dust that contains more than 1 percent of asbestos does not in itself constitute a significant health hazard—ambient air samples are more accurate measures of actual exposure potential, and asbestos is primarily considered hazardous after long-term exposure—but dust samples do provide important information about potential exposure."

These statements directly contradict scientific knowledge and the EPA's own rules, established in 1986 pursuant to the Toxic Substances Control Act. Those rules state, first of all, "Available evidence supports the conclusion that there is no safe level of exposure to asbestos. This conclusion is consistent with present theory of cancer etiology and is further supported by the many documented cases where low or short-term exposure has been shown to cause asbestos-related disease." [30]

The rules go on to state:

> Most occupational studies have been conducted on populations exposed to high airborne concentrations of asbestos for long periods of time. However, short-term exposures have also been shown to increase the risk of lung cancer and mesothelioma. In addition, there are many documented cases of mesothelioma linked to extremely brief exposures to high concentrations. . . . [31]

In sum, according to the EPA's own rules, there are no safe levels of exposure to asbestos, but in its press releases, the agency advised that the asbestos-laden samples posed no danger. The public was being told that only long-term, high levels of exposure were dangerous, while EPA rules make clear that even short-term and low levels of asbestos exposure cannot be classified as safe.

News outlets like the *New York Times* and *New York Post* fell into line with confirmations of the EPA story. As later reported in *The American Prospect* by media reporter Alyssa Katz, the *Times* ran no fewer than thirteen stories emphasizing the safety of the site between September 12 and February 24, 2002.[32] The Environmental Law and Justice Project wrote a letter to the *Times*, which was published in mid October 2001, describing the results of our samples, including the presence of up to 5 percent asbestos in the dust. But there were no follow-up calls from the press.

Where were the media? As *Daily News* reporter Juan Gonzalez details in his compelling book *Fallout: The Environmental Consequences of the World Trade Center Collapse,* there was substantial pressure on the press to self-censor in the aftermath of September 11. He writes, for example, of the demotion of a *Daily News* editor who had attempted to assemble a team to report on the environmental hazards around Ground Zero. Gonzalez told *The American Prospect*'s Katz, "In 25 years as a reporter, I've never faced as much scrutiny or as much difficulty getting stories in the paper as I have had around this issue." [33]

The media's portrait of a scientific public-health consensus was, actually, way off the mark, and it would not have been difficult to find inconsistencies if reporters had been encouraged to investigate. In November 2001, OSHA made a presentation for the Standing Committees on Environmental Conservation, Health and Labor of New York's State Assembly, where it reported that, based on its sampling results at the WTC site, the agency was "confident that asbestos does not pose an airborne hazard to workers."[34] Yet the National Institute of Environmental Health Sciences, though its Worker Education and Training Program, had already issued a report in October that cited "significant risks that have been and continue to be faced by these on-site and recovery workers." The NIEHS report stated: ". . . the exposure data, as well as the potential for serious exposure to toxic materials (including asbestos) among the construction response workers, raises significant concerns" and found Ground Zero "to be a very dangerous working environment where many workers lack the hazard-specific training required under current OSHA standards."[35] Among that study's sources was a city Department of Health "WTC Disaster Site Worker Injury and Illness Surveillance Update"; that is, the city's own surveys were showing hazards. Because of reports like this one, the information was circulating at some levels, but it was not being provided to rescue workers and city residents who needed to protect themselves.

Speaking of this period, Bruce Lippy, an industrial hygienist with the operating engineers' union's National Hazmat Program, later stated that "60 percent of our samples were greater than the EPA clearance level . . ."[36] And the city's health department reported in January 2002 that 50 percent of residents in lower Manhattan continued to experience symptoms likely related to the World Trade Center disaster, such as nose, throat, and eye irritation.[37] As of January 2003, over 1,000 claims have been filed against the City of New York by firefighters who sustained respiratory damage and/or were exposed to dangerous toxic substances as a result of the city's failure to provide them with respirators during rescue and recovery efforts at the WTC.[38]

FOIA: WHAT FEDERAL, STATE, AND CITY AGENCIES KNEW

On September 21, 2001, the Environmental Law and Justice Project requested, under the Freedom of Information Act, all monitoring data studies and reports of air, dust, and bulk, including but not limited to hazardous materials and water samples taken in lower Manhattan and Staten Island landfills in response to the WTC collapse. On October 19, the project picked up more than 600 pages of testing results from EPA monitoring points and stations, primarily located at or near Ground Zero. What the documents revealed was that, in spite of their assurances to the contrary, EPA, OSHA, and the various other health and environmental agencies—which met weekly throughout the crisis—knew of the dangers present at Ground Zero and beyond, on the ground and in the air. EPA's own data listed findings above regulated levels—information not posted on its Web site. (Later, the agency would claim this was an oversight.)

The documents also revealed that analyses prepared for the EPA by scientists were held back from publication, though their findings were highly relevant to health care providers trying to diagnose and treat those with acute symptoms, to say nothing of the public at large, which deserved to know its own risks. Among the reports that were withheld or delayed was one by Paul J. Lioy, which was based on testing done within a week of the WTC collapse but which was not released until April 2002. The testing was conducted at EPA's own labs in Kansas City and involved bulk samples of settled dust and smoke gathered on September 16 and 17. The labs found metals, radionuclides, ionic species, asbestos (in concentrations ranging from 0.8 percent to 3 percent), PAHs, PCBs, and a host of other toxic substances that can cause cancer and/or respiratory and/or debilitating illnesses.[39]

The documents also revealed how high the concentration of dangerous contaminants remained even three weeks after the WTC towers' collapse. After people were back in the area at the EPA's urging, living and working full-time, the documents show that the following results were coming from the agency's downtown stations.

EPA Daily Summary, September 21: "Dust Samples: Twenty-four dust samples were analyzed between September 19 and 20, which included samples from the general area of Stuyvesant High School and Battery Park. Twelve of the 24 samples showed asbestos levels slightly above the EPA levels of concern."

EPA Daily Summary, September 26: "AIR: Non-FIXED Samples in New York City Dioxin-Analysis of four air samples showed all samples were at or above EPA's removal action guidelines, which is [sic] based on a 30-year, 24-hour exposure risk scenario. However, there is no short-term exposure problem. These samples were captured at the plume still emanating from fires within the World Trade Centers debris pile. We expect that these levels measured will only persist for a few weeks until the fires are extinguished."

EPA Daily Summary, October 4: "Ambient Air Sampling: Metals—10 samples were taken on October 2 within the vicinity of the emergency response operations. Of these chromium results for 4 samples exceeded EPA's removal guideline . . ."

EPA Daily Summary, October 14: "Dioxin—Ten samples were collected on October 2 and analyzed for dioxin/furans. Four of the samples showed results above the guideline level at which EPA would take some type of action to reduce people's exposure."

EPA Daily Summary, October 14: "Carbon monoxide—A direct reading of carbon monoxide was detected at 19 parts per million (ppm) at one location (Greenwich and Liberty). This is above the National Ambient Air Quality Standard (NAAQS) 8-hour average of 9 ppm, but is below the NAASQ 1-hour average of 35 ppm and the OSHA permissible level of 50 ppm."

EPA Daily Summary, Ambient Air Sampling: "VOCs [volatile organic compounds]— . . . Benzene was detected at three locations above the OSHA limit in the plume on the debris pile. Benzene was not detected at three parameter locations."

EPA Daily Summary, Ambient Air Sampling, October 15: "VOCs—Sampling for volatile organic compounds (VOCs) was conducted on Oct. 13 and Oct. 14 in the smoke plume within the debris pile at ground zero. Benzene exceeded the OSHA time-weighted average permissible level at two locations, on both days. Benzene was not detected in the breathing zone (approx. 5–6 feet above ground) at 3 locations several blocks from ground zero."

We forwarded the information to the *Daily News*'s Juan Gonzalez, whose reporting reached the front page the next day.[40] This data was also immediately placed on the Law Project's Web site, which was visited by hundreds of government agencies, scientific groups, and medical institutions over the next several months.

Additional requests for documents were filed, under New York State's Freedom of Information Law (FOIL), with both the state's Department of Environmental Conservation (DEC) and the city's Department of Health (DOH). Among information requested of the DEC was air-monitoring data from stations in the city and mobile units near the WTC, for asbestos, fiberglass, cellulose, particulates, and other toxic and hazardous materials. DEC initially declined to provide any information, stating, "Your FOIL request . . . is at this time being denied due to on-going criminal investigation."[41] Only after an appeal and repeated demands did the Environmental Law and Justice Project obtain the relevant documents on November 13, 2001. They indicated, among other things, that during spot testing, the DEC's monitors became clogged with dust; the monitors should have been replaced or reset, but they were not. This was the agency to which the EPA had delegated oversight of interiors of buildings.

The city health department's testing results, when finally released after appeals, were even more disturbing. The DOH documents showed that when the offices of City Hall workers—the mayor's deputy chief of staff, for example—and others in downtown Manhattan were tested, an "overload" of dust was found. Normal procedure requires that the testing machines be recalibrated and the tests be redone so that the overload material can be analyzed for asbestos and other toxics, but the DOH did not conduct further tests. And it did not tell the public about the overload dust finding. On its Web site, such results were merely listed as "n.a."

DECONTAMINATION AND DOWNTOWN HEALTH

During 2002, as the WTC site was cleared and the city returned to some version of normalcy, environmental and health concerns seemed limited to the people living near Ground Zero and the rescue workers who remained ill, like the hundreds of firefighters who either took medical leave or continued working with new respiratory problems. The rest of the city went on with life, but downtown, long-term concerns developed into a long-term, unhappy dialogue with city, state, and federal agencies. This is not to say that New Yorkers in general were sanguine: a poll taken in March 2002 found that 70 percent did not believe the EPA's assurances about Ground Zero air safety.[42] But downtown New Yorkers—most of whom had returned to their homes well before the end of 2001—were even more skeptical and, increasingly organized, were pressing hard for both information and remedial action.

Parents of children enrolled in lower Manhattan schools such as P.S. 58, Stuyvesant High School, and the Borough of Manhattan Community College, for example, had serious concerns about the safety of the buildings where the young people spent their days. The buildings had been commandeered as emergency quarters from September 11 onwards, and required decontamination. Such corporate giants as Shearson Lehman, in abating their own affected property at the World Financial Center, had opted to completely dispose of all fibrous materials, from couches to carpets to rugs. By contrast, despite threatened lawsuits and protests from lower Manhattan citizen groups, the city's Department of Education throughout 2002 opted not to take the same thorough measures in area schools. When parents at Stuyvesant High School hired an environmental engineer to use the ultrasonication method—an EPA–approved,[43] low-cost, sophisticated test for carpets and other woven fabrics, which are reservoirs for asbestos and a source of continued release of asbestos particles—they found 60,000 to 2.5

million structures of asbestos per square centimeter in school carpets, an extraordinarily high concentration.[44] This was *after* the school had undergone an EPA–backed abatement. The Department of Education called the parents' test results "inconclusive," [45] choosing instead to dicker about what "background levels" of asbestos were acceptable for exposing young people.

The EPA's refusal to handle abatements on the insides of residential buildings became a focus of community activism. In April 2002, in part to keep pressure on EPA to meet its responsibilities, my organization tested a residential loft building—just north of the Chambers Street cleanup boundary set by EPA—which happened to house a day care center, and found asbestos. Initially the EPA's response was "Not our department." But when an EPA official relented and agreed to cooperate with DEP in taking samples from the building, it found asbestos in concentrations up to 5 percent—five times the cut-off level for immediate abatement. (By contrast, the DEP found zero asbestos at the same site—utilizing the same technology that it, and private companies, had utilized since September 11—which suggests that all along its testing methodology must have been seriously inadequate and its results therefore wildly optimistic.) In a victory for downtown residents, the EPA announced ten days later that it would undertake the substantial cleanup of all requested apartments south of Canal Street, thus expanding its zone of responsibility northward by ten blocks and finally acknowledging its responsibility for interiors. This was a $5 to $10 million obligation it had tried to shirk for nine months.

The efficacy of the EPA–funded cleanup remained controversial, however, challenged by tenant organizations such as 9/11 Environmental Action, as well as by Congressman Nadler and State Senator David Patterson, EPA scientist Cate Jenkins, Joel Shufro of the New York Committee on Occupational Safety and Health (NYCOSH), former Councilwoman Katherine Freed, Dr. Marjorie Clark of Lehman College, attorney Barbara Olshansky with the Center for Constitutional Rights, and others. Many felt it was too little and very much too late. And it did not include office buildings and their tenants. Meanwhile, the DEP, as noted above, was embarrassed into demanding reports on cleanups from landlords, in May 2002,[46] but neither enforced its demand nor checked on building conditions itself.

Then there was the management of contaminated city vehicles: faced with a devastating loss of personnel and equipment, the city quickly reclaimed any trucks, fire engines, and buses that had initially been used to respond to the disaster. In April 2002, the Uniformed Firefighters Association, concerned about members' exposure, asked the Environmental Law and Justice Project to conduct testing on fire engines; our testing showed up to 5 percent chrysotile asbestos on vehicles that had *already* been "decontaminated" by a city contractor. In our capacity as environmental counsel to the firefighters, the Law Project obtained an internal FDNY memo that in August 2002—nearly a year after the disaster, plenty of time for agencies to share basic public-health information—informed fire department tour commanders city-wide that caked WTC debris on respirators and apparatus (this includes trucks) "does not constitute an immediate health hazard. Asbestos is only a hazard when it becomes friable and airborne." [47] This statement is extremely misleading. The asbestos found on the trucks (and respirators) is already WTC dust and can easily become broken up into breathable particles when disturbed by firefighting activity.

The memo continued: "OSHA does not have any exposure limits for this time type of exposure, as it is not a hazard." [48] Unfortunately for those who have to wear these supposedly nonhazardous respirators, the Law Project—in random testing of oxygen tanks and masks that are stored on fire trucks and worn by firefighters to enter burning buildings—found dust containing asbestos. Why is this not being remedied?

City buses used to transport rescue workers to and from Ground Zero are another area of concern, as they do not appear to have undergone proper abatement. Officials of the Transit Workers Union have reported to the Environmental Law and Justice Project that, so far as they have been able to discover, the city has not conducted a thorough abatement on these vehicles, which were returned to service transporting city residents and reportedly continue in use at this writing. Further, a spokesman for the Army Corps of Engineers informed us that other government vehicles used in the rescue effort do not appear to have undergone proper abatement. [49] Why not, now that the immediate emergency is over and a long-term view of the consequences should be the top priority for the responsible agencies?

It is not alarmist to ask such questions, but merely sensible. And policy makers should be pursuing solutions to these problems, even if it means admitting that mistakes were made, because that is how to improve response for any future emergency, and it is the only way to retrieve the public's confidence.

THE BIGGER PICTURE

Accompanying the environmental and public health disaster in New York City is an erosion of civil liberties nationwide since September 11. The USA PATRIOT Act permits the government to shroud itself in secrecy and restrict civil liberties in the war on terrorism. Undercutting the right of citizens to obtain crucial information and to be partners in this complicated process, volumes of information critical to environmental activism and policy are being "scrubbed" from government Web sites in the name of deterring terrorism, including EPA Web site postings of key guidelines and databases.[50] For example, the National Advisory Committee for Acute Exposure Guidelines Levels (AEGLs) for Hazardous Substances, managed by the EPA, will no longer post exposure guidelines for short-term emergency exposure levels. In March 2002, the EPA announced that it would limit public access to—and data posted on—the Envirofacts databases, a directory of toxic sites nationwide and the toxicity of the substances found there.

Freedom of Information Act requests, meanwhile, have been presented as competing with our security, such that we may lose our capacity to learn what we are breathing. Attorney General Ashcroft, in a department of justice memorandum on FOIA issued just weeks after September 11, contrasted "full compliance" with the FOIA with the "fundamental values that are held by our society"—defined as "safeguarding our national security, enhancing the effectiveness of our law enforcement agencies, protecting sensitive business information, and not least, preserving personal privacy."[51] The public's right to know cannot compete.

At the same time, the EPA's inaction around September 11 set a dangerous precedent by undermining the authority of all environmental statutes. In the midst of a disaster that necessitated extensive action, the EPA, New York State's DEC, and the city's DEP enforced the law less aggressively than in periods of normalcy. As of this writing, the DEP has issued only three asbestos violations for lower Manhattan since September 11.[52]

Among the environmental laws that are at risk, in this climate, are the Comprehensive Environmental Response, Compensation, and Liability Act (CERCLA);[53] the Resource Conservation Recovery Act (RCRA); the Community Right-to-Know Act;[54] and the National Contingency Plan, which gives the EPA powers, in an emergency, that the agency failed to make use of in responding to September 11.[55] Under the National Contingency Plan, the president is authorized to act whenever a hazardous substance is released into the environment that may present an imminent danger to the public health or welfare. The administration, under law, could have pulled out all the stops to test, analyze, and remediate the toxic results of the WTC collapse—and could have required state and local agencies to do the same—but, although the appropriate technology was available and although billions of dollars had already been set aside for the New York recovery effort, it chose not to do so.

Further, in a new use of an old office, the White House has attacked independent scientific inquiry within the federal purview, by subjecting any agency regulation or collection of information to a review process by the Office of Information and Regulatory Affairs, within the Office of Management and Budget. For example, in December 2002, after the EPA's cleanup of Libby, Montana, the OMB thwarted the EPA's plan to alert Americans nationwide about the dangers of Zonolite insulation—manufactured in Libby—which contains highly cancerous fibers and is present in 15 to 35 million American homes. The OMB cited cost reasons for not alerting the public to this hazard.[56]

In another bureaucratic maneuver with large implications, the EPA administrator is now authorized—by an executive order dated May 6, 2002—to classify information as "secret."[57] This new power threatens the release of such information as was obtained on the toxic fallout of the WTC collapse. And within the EPA, dissent and self-evaluation have become a lot harder: the Office of the Ombudsman, charged with the agency's internal oversight and for many years quite independent, has had its wings clipped. After publicly questioning the agency's decisions around the World Trade Center disaster, exposing the inaction of the EPA, and cooperating with the inquiry of officials like Congressman Jerrold Nadler, in late November 2001, Ombudsman Robert Martin and his chief investigator, Hugh Kaufman, were told that the office was to be placed under the direct control of the EPA inspector general. This would effectively end the ombudsman's autonomy, as he or she now must clear all public statements before they are issued.[58] Martin resigned.

These setbacks for transparency are part of a wider political agenda in which the weakening of EPA's role in protecting the environment and enforcing protective laws is a foregone conclusion. In February 2002, the director of the agency's Office of Regulatory Enforcement, Eric V. Schaeffer, resigned in protest, charging that the EPA was "fighting a White House that seems determined to weaken the rules we are trying to enforce."[59] A week later, he testified before the Senate Governmental Affairs Committee that the EPA was weakening air pollution standards to appease the energy industry, in violation of the Clean Air Act. Energy companies, he pointed out, release one-fourth of the 5 million tons of sulfur dioxide emitted annually, and 2 million tons of nitrogen oxide—producing acid rain and choking smog that each year lead to 10,600 deaths; 5,400 cases of chronic bronchitis; childhood asthma; and over 1.5 million lost work days.[60] EPA used to penalize these companies. But as Schaeffer predicted in his testimony, in November 2002, the EPA announced changes in pollution standards for power plants, changes that weaken emission controls. A nongovernmental study published in 2002 found a "steep decline" in environmental enforcement and fines under the Bush administration.[61]

Important as environmental rules, standards, and enforcement are to public health, access to complete and accurate information is even more essential because it is the guarantee of official accountability. In this regard, it is especially worrisome that so-called whistle-blower provisions will become vestigial law—leaving little room for dissent and challenge in the face of improper action. As the *Washington Post* reported in October 2002, "President Bush's interpretation of the new corporate accountability law that deals with whistle-blower disclosures to Congress" was used by the U.S. Labor Department's solicitor to deny protected status to a government lawyer who sought to pass reports on toxic materials on federally owned land to a U.S. congressman.[62]

For private workers—and virtually all the WTC cleanup work has now been privatized—there are no protections whatsoever if they wish to publicize inadequate cleanup methods or inadequate protective measures. Not only does New York State have an extremely weak whistle-blower law, but these private sources of information are not covered by it; they are at the mercy of employers.

It is only in a climate of open government that responsibilities for public health and environmental protection can be taken up with the vigor and dedication that were needed to face the tragedy of September 11, 2001. Demands for transparency from independent activists, journalists, and the public at large are not only protected by the Constitution, they are a requirement of mature citizenship. The health fallout from the World Trade Center disaster will be with us for many years to come, and the fallout in terms of mistrust of the environmental authorities represents a challenge that should motivate us all.

PART IV

GLOBAL THREAT, GLOBAL CITIZEN

11. AXIS OF ANTAGONISM: U.S.–EUROPEAN RELATIONS IN THE WAR ON TERRORISM

GARY YOUNGE[1]

When President George W. Bush arrived in Germany in May 2002, he cut a rather bemused figure not unlike Ernest Harrowden in *The Picture of Dorian Gray.* Oscar Wilde described Harrowden as "one of those middle-aged mediocrities, who have no enemies, but are thoroughly disliked by their friends." And so it was that Bush landed on a continent nominally full of allies to face a swathe of angry protest that would follow him to France and Italy.

Bush can be forgiven for being somewhat baffled. The outpouring of sympathy from Europe following the terror attacks on September 11 had been widespread and genuine. The day after the Twin Towers collapsed, a signed editorial in the French daily *Le Monde,* neither a paper nor a country renowned for pro-American sympathies, declared, "We are all Americans." [2] In the months that followed, support for the bombing of Afghanistan had been virtually unanimous, from both national leaders on the continent and the European Union.

And yet Bush touched down in Berlin to a 20,000-strong demonstration with banners condemning his "imperialist crusade" and lambasting him as an "unwanted warmonger." Even as German Chancellor Gerhard Schroder pronounced Bush "extremely welcome," his police force reported the second attack in six days on an American commercial target in Berlin. Protesters had broken into the garage of an American advertising agency, slashed the tires of two cars, and daubed "Stop War" on one of them. [3]

Since September 11, relations between the United States and Europe have wavered between acrimony and sycophancy with all too rare moments of constructive, progressive engagement. On the one hand, European governments have expressed concern at the Bush administration's unilateralist instincts, disregard for human rights, and determination to engage in military conflict where diplomatic solutions have not been exhausted. On the other, they are eager to maintain good relations and meaningful influence with the world's sole superpower, fearing isolation and retribution if they should break ranks. "Europeans are, in fact, wary of the consequences and even the motives of an American attack on Iraq,"

Jim Hoagland wrote in the *Washington Post*. "But their governments know that an American disaster in which they stood aside would also be a disaster for them. They must equally worry that Washington will succeed without them."[4] Their own experiences of fighting terrorism, domestic political pressure, and more liberal political cultures steer them away from the foreign policy course mapped out by the United States. Their post-colonial nostalgia and relative economic and military weakness draw them toward it.

At one end of the spectrum stands Germany, whose relations with America plunged to a postwar low during the election campaign of September 2002. Lagging behind in an exceptionally close race, Schroder, a Social Democrat, drew on the widespread opposition to war against Iraq (which stood at 80 percent[5]) to boost his fortunes. In a scarcely veiled riposte to America's military pretensions, he told a rally at the University of Münster, just a week before the election, "Germany has no reason to allow itself to be lectured by others. On the existential questions that decide general politics the decisions are made in Berlin—in Berlin and nowhere else."[6]

Within Germany, the strategy worked. A late swing to Schroder's party gave him a narrow majority, thanks in no small part to the increase in vote for the staunchly antiwar Greens. But the rhetoric that put him in power in Berlin put him out of favor in Washington. There was not an olive branch big enough to assuage the aggrieved mood in the White House. "I have no comment on the German election's outcome," said Defense Secretary Donald Rumsfeld. "But I would have to say that the way it was conducted was notably unhelpful and, as the White House indicated, has had the effect of poisoning the relationship [with the U.S.]."[7]

On the other end of the spectrum is Britain, where Prime Minister Tony Blair has resolved to stand shoulder to shoulder with Bush, acting as a conduit between America and the rest of the world, thereby softening American rhetoric and stiffening European backbone. As the Labour leader, whose party's traditions and support base are similar to Schroder's, one might have expected Blair, a former member of the Campaign for Nuclear Disarmament, to have been more circumspect. But despite expressions of concern from many Labour members of Parliament and mounting public opposition to the war on Iraq without United Nations approval—in September 2002 it stood at above 70 percent[8]—Blair has remained steadfast. Nine days after the World Trade Center attacks, Bush singled out Britain for special mention in his address to a joint session of Congress, saying, "America has no truer friend than Great Britain. Once again, we are joined together in a great cause—so honored the British Prime Minister has crossed an ocean to show his unity of purpose with America. Thank you for coming, friend."

Blair's close relationship with Bush earned him widespread criticism in Britain. "Fairly or unfairly, Blair is now firmly cast as America's poodle," wrote Adrian Hamilton in *The Independent*. "Where it matters, in the court of public opinion, the British Prime Minister is seen as surrendering his country's independence for a mythical influence." [9]

A MULTILATERAL EUROPE AND UNILATERAL UNITED STATES

To make sense of these inconsistencies—both actual and apparent—we must first take a step beyond the immediate. For while the incongruous urban void that occupies the site where the World Trade Center once stood may be labeled Ground Zero, the time at which the first planes flew out of a clear blue sky and into a fresh new hell was not year zero. "The world itself was not transformed by the terrorist attacks on the Pentagon and the World Trade Center," wrote Quentin Peel in the *Financial Times*. "But changes that were already under way were dramatically accelerated by those events." [10]

From late in 2000 the divergences of political cultures and national interests in Europe and America, which had existed for some time, were clearly evident. While a question mark hung over the validity of the result of the U.S. presidential elections, there seemed little doubt American foreign policy was going to take an abrupt shift in tone and direction, if Bush were to win. During his presidential campaign Bush had expressed little interest in foreign policy and announced his reluctance to engage in nation building. "There may be some moments when we use our troops as peacekeepers, but not often," [11] he said in the final presidential debate.

The Republicans, wrote *The Guardian's* chief foreign affairs columnist, Martin Woollacott, "embody the contradictions of American society—the sense of entitlement to world power allied to the sense that they are being asked to take too much responsibility for others, the worship of military strength allied to a deep disinclination to use it and the desire to be in charge allied to the desire to be left alone. That is what could make the next four years a dangerous time in the life of the world." [12] Within the first 100 days of Bush's presidency he had reneged on the Kyoto Accord controlling greenhouse gases and shown his determination to push ahead with the Star Wars weapons program, despite much international opposition.

Meanwhile, most of Europe was moving in a very different direction. At the time of Bush's inauguration, Britain, Germany, and France all had Social Democratic governments, with traditions of international solidarity linking them to liberation movements ranging from the Sandinistas in Nicaragua to the African National Congress in South Africa. All these parties had shifted to the right during the nineties, but nonetheless remain way to the left of the Republican Party under Bush. And the process of economic, monetary, and political integration of the European Union (EU) was continuing apace, forcing an unprecedented level of cooperation between participating nations.

In 2002, individual currencies would disappear and the euro would take their place. With the euro's impending arrival came the inevitable reality that the authority of the nation-state would be forever submitted to a greater whole. The various countries signed up not only to a currency but to keep their budget deficits, inflation targets, and public debts within certain agreed boundaries or else face penalties. In so doing they had to pool their sovereignty. This had a thoroughgoing impact on European views regarding the future shape of international relations. "Europe's own great experiment in multilateralism, in creating the European Union to overcome the bitter rivalry between France and Germany, has convinced them that diplomacy works better than war," argued Peel.[13]

At this stage, the political and economic makeup of Europe is extremely fluid—more akin to the United States during the late eighteenth to mid-nineteenth centuries, acquiring new states and negotiating the power balance between the center and the periphery. At the time of this writing, the EU has fifteen members (twelve of which have adopted the euro) and is about to incorporate another ten countries in May 2004. Yet, each nation has its own very particular political culture, economic profile, and history, which makes formulating a common foreign policy difficult. Germany has the legacy of Nazism and Cold War division; France of twice being invaded in the last century; Spain, Portugal, and Greece of relatively recent, postwar dictatorships. British governments, meanwhile, assert their "special relationship" with America courtesy of shared histories and language. "Attitudes to the use of military force and to the United States still vary widely across the EU," claims *The Economist*. "In normal times those differences can be papered over. In a crisis, when countries have to make hard choices, differences are more likely to be exposed."[14]

Nonetheless, some on the left in Europe regard the deeper and broader integration of the EU primarily as a means to challenge American political and economic hegemony by creating a bloc large and strong enough to confront the excesses of U.S. leadership. "A unipolar world is a dangerous place," argued a former British minister and Labour member of Parliament, Peter Kilfoyle. "It is like standing on one leg—one is far more liable to lose balance than when one is standing on two, or even four legs. Increasingly, it is clear that there needs to be an effective counterbalance to this overpowering American hegemony. The time has surely come for the UK government, along with its European partners, to have the courage, within the restraints of realpolitik, to reassess its foreign policy priorities in line with our national interests and these new realities." [15]

The problem with this project, to date, is that it lacks democratic legitimacy. The real flaw in the staggering pace of European integration over the past ten years—which has seen the continent go from a free trade area like the North American Free Trade Association to a region where millions share the same-color passports, currency, and a court of human rights—is the lack of democratic accountability that has gone with it. Neither the president of the European commission nor any of the commissioners, who wield most power in the EU, are elected. At the time of this writing, only one country, Denmark, has had the opportunity to vote specifically on whether they should join the euro or not—and they voted no. And while a European parliament does exist, it has few powers, and turnout for elections has reached record lows.[16]

The desire to create a more progressive counterbalance to American power is a sound one, but it cannot be built without the consent of those in whose name it has been created. This lack of democracy leads, ineluctably, to a lack of legitimacy. Where foreign policy is concerned, this means that even when representatives of the EU say important and useful things, their views can be dismissed because, in reality, they do not represent anyone at all. The EU may yet both cohere and democratize its structures sufficiently to one day act as a counterweight to U.S. hegemony. In the meantime, the fundamental contradictions in the paths that Europe and the United States were taking before September 11 were clear. When Bush took the oath of office he stood at the head of a more reactionary U.S. administration that was keen to assert its national independence and military might and reluctant to take engage in the international arena. Meanwhile, the nations of a more liberal but fragmented Europe were abandoning key areas of their sovereignty as their military spending continued to fall. "Europe emphasizes norms, treaties and institutions, partly because they don't have an alternative," wrote Ivo Daalder of the Brookings Institution. "The U.S. emphasizes power." [17]

SYMBOLS AND SUBSTANCE

In many respects, those issues relating to foreign and domestic policy that were of most interest to Europeans at the time of Bush's inauguration—namely, capital punishment and respect for international law, the difference between the Bush administration and the one which preceded it—were symbolic rather than substantial.

The difference in approach to international law was already clear under President Clinton's administration. When the former British foreign secretary Robin Cook told then-Secretary of State Madeleine Albright that he had "problems with our lawyers" over using force against Yugoslavia without Security Council approval, Albright responded, "Get new lawyers." Clinton, unlike Bush, had signed up for Kyoto. But he had not honored it. The United States had promised to cut carbon-dioxide emissions by 7 percent from 1990 levels by 2012. Instead, emissions rose by more than 10 percent on 1990 levels by 2000.

A major issue for Europeans with Bush in the White House was Texas's record on capital punishment and his connection to it as the former governer there. A reasonable grievance, but not one that had hindered their attraction to Clinton, who, during his presidential campaign, had returned home to order the execution of Ricky Rector—the murderer with severe learning difficulties, who saved a piece of pecan pie from his last meal to "eat later." [18] But while symbols should not be mistaken for substance, they should not be dismissed as insubstantial, either. Bush's outright rejection of Kyoto sent a message to many Europeans that he had no desire to even look like a team player. While Clinton's arrival in Europe always attracted throngs of cheers, reaction to Bush, from the outset, was hostile. "Europeans generally get on better with Democrats than Republicans," wrote *The Economist*. "Mr. Bush does not seem as clever as Bill Clinton; his folksy manners come over as simple-minded." [19]

On his very first presidential visit in June 2001, three months before the terrorist attacks in New York and Washington, he touched down in Spain, one of the few countries in Europe at the time with a right-wing government. Demonstrators were waiting. "Thousands of Spaniards gave the welcome expected for President Bush in Madrid," wrote Pedro Calvo Hernando in the Spanish paper *Diario 16*, "in a demonstration in which they condemned almost all the decisions and attitudes of a person who is unpleasant and dangerous to humanity. This man bears the standard of everything we repudiate the most."[20] *Le Monde*'s tone was only marginally less shrill: "Europeans have found, rightly, in their rejection of the death penalty, a providential cause; this allows them to assert their moral and legal superiority over American power."[21]

As a child of the Empire—my parents arrived in Britain from Barbados in the early sixties, although I was born near London—I find the level of sanctimony in some of these and other commentaries from Europe difficult to stomach. While their criticisms of U.S. foreign policy are sound, the haughtiness of the tone in which they are delivered is not. Given their record as colonizers and belligerent dictatorships over recent centuries, it is difficult to find any European nation—neither the French, British, Portuguese, Belgians, Dutch, Spaniards, Germans, Austrians, nor the Italians—that has any claim on the moral high ground.

Former British Prime Minister Winston Churchill, for example, was "a robust champion of the use of poison gas in warfare and could not understand the 'squeamishness' of those who objected to it,"[22] reported the *Times,* following the 1997 release of a memo from the British Air Staff dated May 22, 1919. "I am strongly in favor of using poisonous gas against uncivilised tribes,"[23] Churchill wrote in that memo. At the beginning of the last century, German colonizers virtually extinguished an entire ethnic group in what is now Namibia: "In 1904 in Southwest Africa the German general, Lothar von Trotha, issued an 'extermination order' for the Herero people. Men were to be shot on sight, and women and children were to be shot or driven from the land," writes Clinton Cox, in the London-based quarterly *Race and Class.*[24]

The legacy of these colonial escapades lives on in the racism currently infecting European political culture, with openly racist parties winning seats in local and national government in Britain, Belgium, Italy, Denmark, Norway, Austria, and the Netherlands in the past three years. Not to mention France, where the leader of the far-right Front National, Jean-Marie Le Pen, beat the incumbent Socialist prime minister in the first round of the presidential elections in April 2002.

So when their governments or citizens slam America for its brutality and imperialist pretensions, they must do so with sufficient self-awareness to see what most of the rest of the world has seen: that their nations have acted in similar and even more pernicious ways whenever they have had the opportunity. Without that humility in tone and historical perspective, they open the door to the American Right, who point to Europe's colonial record and dismiss accusations of American wrongdoing as little more than sour grapes. Before long they are arguing not about democracy and human rights but about which empire has been more benign.

This kind of bickering between the powerful has little interest to most of humanity. The difference between Europe and America is significant and has grown, but to the vast majority of the developing world, American domination represents a qualitative and material plot development in the narrative of European empire, rather than a break from it. And if there was an amnesiac quality to some of the critical commentaries of Bush, there was a nostalgic strand to those who welcomed him. From some came a desire not to forget the brutality of Empire but to return to its mythology and share in its privileges under the cloak of Captain America. "Many Europeans view Mr. Bush as a self-satisfied, execution-supporting president of a world power so intoxicated with itself that its pays little or no heed to the concerns and interests of others," wrote Klaus-Dieter Frankenberger in the German daily *Frankfurter Allgemeine Zeitung*. "Europe should understand the U.S. challenge as an appeal to become a partner that can assume a greater share of the burden and not an impudent rival."[25]

DIFFERENT RESPONSES TO TERRORISM

When the Twin Towers collapsed a few months after Bush first arrived on the Continent, Europe's emotional response was much the same as the rest of the world's—a mixture of shock, grief, and sympathy. But a serious rift between Europe and America soon emerged over an appropriate intellectual response. Those in Europe who believed there was a causal relationship between U.S. foreign policy and the attacks were relatively few in all but a handful of countries. But a consensus did quickly emerge that there was a contextual relationship between what America had done around the globe and what had now been done to it. Few European commentators of any repute drew direct links between the political manipulations and military incursions into Central and South America, world trade agreements that are punitive toward poorer nations, and the situation in the Middle East. But few serious analysts in Europe felt they could ignore them, either. "September 11th confirmed the world view of this administration," said Daalder. "They believed it was a dangerous world and that proved it. Europe thinks the threats are more diffuse, and complicated."[26]

The fact that few in America were in a frame of mind, in the aftermath of the attacks, to engage with such questioning was more surprising to many Europeans than it ought to have been. The country was in pain and shock. Military conflicts polarize opinion and marginalize dissent. The American response to September 11 was culturally specific—the flag waving, emotional outpouring, and twenty-four-hour nonstop news coverage would not have happened anywhere else in the world—but it was not politically anomalous. Generally speaking, people affected by political violence are less willing to see complexity and nuance in the face of the very real and immediate threat of war.

During the height of the conflict in Northern Ireland, many people in Britain could not comprehend America's apparent leniency toward and sympathy for the Irish Republican Army. What many Americans saw as the political and military response to a colonial legacy stretching back centuries was regarded by most Britons as the cowardly tyranny of a criminal cell. The closer you are to political violence and its consequences, the less likely you are to brook discussion about the historical, economic, or political context that might have contributed to it.

Europe has been no stranger to the political violence associated with terrorism. There have been groups like the Baader Meinhof Gang in Germany during the seventies, which have more in common with U.S. militias—small, isolated cells with no popular base and drawing on no coherent legitimate grievance. In the Basque country in Spain, Northern Ireland in the United Kingdom, and Chechnya in Russia, moreover, there are organizations that are or have been committed to violence that have drawn broad support, at various times, from the communities they claim to represent. On the whole, it has been political engagement with those more rooted movements that has proved the most successful antidote to political violence. What has been truly puzzling about Blair's support for the war on terror, as conceived and executed by the Bush administration, is that the British know its failings only too well because they abandoned virtually the same strategy after several decades of bloodshed in Northern Ireland.

For more than twenty years the British state attempted to quell unrest among the predominantly Catholic nationalist community in Northern Ireland through a mixture of military and judicial means that denied any political roots to the conflict. In the late seventies the authorities changed the status of those who were incarcerated for their involvement in illegal republican activities from political prisoners to common criminals, sparking the 1981 hunger strikes. As well as stationing thousands of troops in the province, the British government implemented increasingly repressive laws, such as the draconian Prevention of Terrorism Act and a broadcasting ban. Among other things, the act denied the right to trial by jury and gave the security services the right to detain individuals for seventy-two hours without charging them. The broadcasting ban produced one of the most bizarre sights to behold in a modern democracy. Representatives of Sinn Fein, the political wing of the IRA, which had an elected representative in the British Parliament, were not allowed to have their voices heard on television or radio. The logic was that to allow them air time would give them "the oxygen of publicity." So whenever they were interviewed, their words would be dubbed by an actor.

The consequence of these measures was that large numbers of the nationalist community were alienated, and Britain's civil rights record was decried around the world. Given that during the same period we saw significant loss of life in the IRA bombing of Harrods, Enniskillen, and the Grand Hotel in Brighton, we can safely say that what the antiterrorism laws did not do was stop, stem, or in any way effectively combat terrorism. Nor did they help much to catch terrorists: according to Home Office statistics, 97 percent of those arrested under the Prevention of Terrorism Act between 1974 and 1988 were released without charge. Only 1 percent were convicted and imprisoned.

The act was used instead as an information-gathering exercise for the British security forces. "It was a measure of social control," says Penny Green, a professor of law and criminology at Westminster University. "It was used to repress political activity. A fishing expedition used for scanning information on a whole community."[27]

Only once the British state and a significant portion of the nationalist community had conceded that there could be no military solution to the dispute could they move forward. The political settlement that they devised, with considerable help from President Clinton, was not without its problems, and it has suffered from intermittent crises.[28] But by acknowledging the political roots of the conflict they were able to demilitarize the dispute, and a number of those formerly branded as "terrorists" became engaged within the political process.

So there is a weary familiarity, for many in Europe, to Bush's antiterrorist rhetoric. We have seen it fail in Northern Ireland. And we are seeing it fail in Chechnya, where Russia's use of force as the sole means of dealing with the issue does not extinguish conflict but inflames it. We have witnessed how the judicial regimes that seek to regulate these militarized disputes move like arsenic in the water supply of civil society, contaminating the political culture and infecting the very notion of civil rights.

AXIS OF ANTAGONISM

So the deep and genuine cleavage between the way Europeans and Americans viewed the world soon became even deeper. The Bush White House turned from unilateralism in isolation to unilateralism in intervention, which proved far more popular in America, where his approval ratings soared, than it did in Europe, where they plummetted. Only 20 percent of Germans viewed Bush in a good light[29] compared with around 80 percent in America.[30] His State of the Union address in January 2002—when he first mentioned the "axis of evil"—his uncritical support for the policies of Israeli Premier Ariel Sharon, and the treatment of prisoners at Camp X-Ray in Cuba's Guantánamo Bay, all gave Europeans the sense that the Bush administration did not really care what the rest of the world thought of what he said or what he did.

The following month, February 2002, was tense. Several leaders in Europe expressed their dismay at the path the Bush administration was taking. France's former foreign minister, Hubert Vedrine, branded the "axis of evil" speech "simplism" from a U.S. now acting as a "hyperpower." Germany's Green foreign minister Joschka Fischer said, "For all the differences in size and weight, alliance partnerships between free democracies cannot be reduced to obedience. Alliance partners aren't satellites."[31] British politicians preferred to characterize their difference of perspective with the United States as a blip. "Iraq policy is in process at the moment," one British diplomat told *The Guardian* in February 2002. "And during the process there are always arguments. What matters is that we agree on the end product. And there is every sign that we will."[32] The Bush administration, on the other hand, was more candid in its language and less conciliatory in its approach.

The *New York Times* reported that the president was fuming about "weak-kneed European elites"[33] and even Secretary of State Colin Powell said Vedrine had had a "fit of the vapours."[34] The approach of the Bush administration reflected a new reality that European leaders were reluctant, at first, to acknowledge. There were real and important differences between the United States and Europe on foreign policy that no amount of diplomatic language could disguise.

But while many European leaders were in denial, by May, polls revealed a growing disquiet among their electorates. There was a depressing symbiosis in this insensitivity, as views on both sides of the Atlantic hardened. One-third of Italians felt the attacks on the Twin Towers had been "somewhat justified."[35] In Greece, where resentment dates back to U.S. support for the military dictatorship from 1967 to 1974 and 90 percent had opposed the NATO bombing of Serbia, 30 percent believed the attacks were "justified."[36] In France, a book *L'effroyable Imposture,* which suggests that September 11 was staged by a wing of the U.S. military to justify taking over Afghanistan, became a bestseller. These were the crudest and most unpleasant manifestations of the fact that the White House was losing the ability to persuade Europe that the agenda it was pursuing was in anyone's interests apart from its own. But it was the imminent threat that the U.S. course would draw them into war with Iraq that finally forced European leaders to assert their diplomatic clout.

IRAQ: A TURNING POINT?

As of early March 2003, French, German, and to a lesser extent Russian opposition to military action against Iraq had provided some space for smaller nations on the U.N. Security Council to resist American pressure to give the U.N.'s imprimatur for war. After months of weapons inspections began to produce results, with Iraq finally complying and destroying some of its missiles, the French pledged to veto any American- and British-sponsored action authorizing war so long as the inspections were bearing fruit. France's refusal to endorse an attack forced a more cautious approach on the White House and nudged it to the negotiating table in the Security Council.

It was not Britain saying yes but the rest of the world saying no that brought about negotiation. One retired, senior U.S. officer told *The Guardian,* "Generally speaking, Blair's support has allowed this to go the way that it has. Had the UK taken the position of the French and the Germans, there would be much greater solidarity against military action."[37]

The fact that America went to the U.N. was not a victory; it slowed the United States down, but it did not alter its course. The Bush administration's backing for multilateralism appeared to hold good only so long as multilateralism backed the U.S. Even as the negotiations over a new U.N. resolution on Iraq intensified in October 2002, Powell insisted: "The U.S. does not need any additional authority even now, if we thought it was necessary to take action to defend ourselves."[38]

But the return of the weapons inspectors at least restored a principle the Bush administration had tried to bury alive: that before there can be prosecution there must first be proof. Moreover, this period of European resistance to America pressure suggested that there were other options for transatlantic relationships beyond sycophancy and acrimony—namely, negotiation, diplomacy, and even the rule of international law. And by moderating the pace at which the White House headed for war, it provided the political space for many in America to mount domestic resistance to the administration's foreign policy. Given Europe's inconsistent record in challenging the Bush administration thus far, it will always be a moot point how long this resistance will last, how effective it will be, and how and when it may assert itself. But having established that such resistance is possible, Europeans have already revealed its potential.

12. THE "WAR ON TERROR" AND WOMEN'S RIGHTS: A PAKISTAN-AFGHAN PERSPECTIVE

FARIDA SHAHEED[1]

These are difficult and worrying times for women's rights activists in Pakistan. As an activist in a nongovernmental women's group working to strengthen rights and political engagement at the grass roots and to promote women's rights at the policy level in Pakistan, I am deeply concerned at the fallout of the U.S.–led "war on terror." I am equally concerned as someone consciously engaged in the international women's movement. I believe many women in the region, and beyond, share this concern for reasons I explain in this article.

The post–September 11, 2001, scenario of a unipolar world dominated by a U.S.A. bent upon carrying out its new self-proclaimed global mission to separate the good guys from the "evildoers," with the U.S. as the sole adjudicator of who is whom, does not bode well. The almost immediate U.S. decision to respond to violence with more violence, the complete dismissal of pleas to bring those responsible for September 11 to justice through a due process of law, the disregard for international human rights standards as well as law in the pursuit of the "war against terror"—all implied that the establishment and upholding of the rule of law, pivotal to human rights, were no longer valid or relevant. The subsequent U.S. decision to act "collectively when it can and unilaterally when it has to" encourages others to follow suit, undermining the U.N. as a forum for collective decision making and standard setting.[2] Likewise, the paring down of civil liberties within the United States provides a handy precedent for those eager to curtail rights in their own countries. Finally, with respect to women, using the rallying cry of women's oppression in Afghanistan in the opening chapter of the "war against terror" hijacked the women's rights discourse and conscripted it in the service of military actions, making a mockery of genuine women's rights activism. The moment military action started, Afghan women—whose rights were made so much of in the prelude to war—found themselves marginalized, their pleas with the international community and the United States in particular to desist from war drowned out.

The instrumental use of the language of women's rights is problematic. Coupled with the "either you're with us or against us" logic of the "war on terror," it renders the already complex task of promoting women's rights even more complicated, especially if the U.N. is further sidelined. Numerous shortcomings notwithstanding, the U.N. system and processes have been important mechanisms for women's human rights, formulating a basic framework and setting minimum standards through international consensus building. That the U.N.'s processes can transcend cultural specificities is particularly significant, for culture and questions of identity—frequently intertwined with religion—are so often used to deny women rights.

In South Asia, the increasing use of religion to deny women their rights, to curtail their liberties, and to circumscribe their lives has gone hand in hand with the rise of violence and intolerance and the ascendancy of essentialist politics of identity or "fundamentalisms" across religions. But denying women rights by reference to religion is a global problem, and in the past two decades it has led to the creation of women's networks that transcend national and even regional divides, amongst them Women Living Under Muslim Laws (focused on Muslim countries and communities), Women Against Fundamentalisms (addressing Hinduism, Judaism, Christianity, and Islam), and Catholics for a Free Choice (concerned with reproductive rights and the Catholic Church). The main objective of the WLUML network, with which I work, is to unlock the restraining factors on women's self-expression and decision making in Muslim societies. Key amongst the restraining factors is the isolation in which women wage their battle; it makes them believe that the construction of womanhood prevalent in their specific village, community, or country (a) is the only one possible, and (b) has religious sanction. This emanates from a widespread ignorance of legal provisions in their states as well as ignorance of Islam itself, but it stems equally from the deliberately promoted myth of one homogenous Muslim world that is promoted by right-wing conservative political movements in their pursuit of political power.

Each of these transnational women's networks has consciously created and nurtured linkages across identities and with the global women's movement. Their work has just become more difficult, if more urgent. The "good vs. evil" discourse of the "war on terror" complements and confirms the discourse of the religious right and of extremists.

WOMEN'S RIGHTS AND THE "WAR ON TERROR"

There has probably never been a war in which the prelude to military action was so focused on women's oppression and lack of rights as in the opening, Afghanistan chapter of the U.S.–led "war on terror." Suddenly a veritable media blitz decried the appalling condition of Afghan women under the Taliban, so inhumane a condition that others needed to go to war to "liberate" these women. The proponents were unlikely supporters of women's rights in any country. George W. Bush—whose policies have seriously undercut women's reproductive rights inside and outside the U.S.—self-righteously informed the world that the "evildoers" were oppressing women; Newt Gingrich, a self-proclaimed hawk, said that to win the military war, the U.S. needed to first win the "moral argument" by showing "we are against the side who would oppress women." [3]

The oppression of women in Afghanistan was not news for those linked through the global women's movement, and certainly not for those living in Afghanistan and neighboring countries. It is inconceivable that the world's policy makers were unaware of the progressively deteriorating conditions of Afghan women, or the violations of the rights of men as well as women, long before September 11, 2001. The *mujahideen,* freedom fighters of yesteryear's war against the Soviets, ranged from conservatives to religious fanatics, and shared an anti-women perspective. They made no bones about their attitude or behavior. Between 1990 and 1996, the press had already brought to light their resurrection of the barbaric practice of treating "enemy" women as spoils of war (*mal-e-ghanimat*) and of prostitution slave camps set up in Jalalabad by these "freedom fighters." International elements of the *mujahideen* then took this horrific concept back to their home countries, such as Algeria, and more women in more places became the hapless victims of rape, torture, and murder. [4]

But in the 1990s, the United States saw in Afghanistan an access to the vast oil reserves of Turkmenistan, estimated to be capable of meeting U.S. domestic needs for the next thirty years and those of a poor country for centuries. [5] Consequently, when Taliban leaders visited the U.S. in 1997 and were entertained by both the Clinton administration in Washington and oil company executives of Unocal in Texas, there was no mention of the plight of Afghan women; no voice was raised against their oppression.

Clearly, as American feminist Nikki Craft warned on November 8, 2001, "In the propaganda carnival surrounding Mr. Bush's war, women [were] being used for a specific agenda, not defended in their own right and for their own sake."[6] Concern for Afghan women notably did not extend to listening to Afghan women themselves, who called upon the U.S. to desist from, subsequently to stop, the war on Afghanistan. Indeed, the Revolutionary Afghan Women's Association (RAWA), an outspokenly anti-Taliban women's organization, stated in October 2001:

> America, by forming an international coalition against Osama and his Taliban-collaborators and in retaliation for the September 11 terrorist attacks, has launched a vast aggression against our country. If until yesterday the U.S. and its allies, without paying the least attention to the fate of democracy in Afghanistan, were supporting the policy of Jihadis-fostering, Osama-fostering and Taliban-fostering, today they are sharpening the daggers of the Northern Alliance. And because of this policy they have plunged our people into a horrific concern and anxiety in fear of experiencing the dreadful happenings of the years of the Jihadis' "emirate."[7]

A similar plea came from groups linked through the Afghan Women's Network (AWN), a group that since 1993 has brought together scores of individuals and several dozen Afghan women's groups, largely based in Pakistan. The AWN stated:

> . . . in whatever name the war might be fought, jihad, justice, terrorism, etc., we ask you to stop it. . . . Stop this war in the name of the Afghan child, the Afghan mother, and a nation who have [sic] sacrificed more than enough. The continuation of war will . . . hinder the chances of a peaceful solution in the future. We call upon the international community and the countries and groups involved in this war to support us by listening to us and ensuring [that] our rights as citizens of this world are respected.[8]

As these activists predicted, the first round of the "war on terror" did very little to end women's oppression in Afghanistan. Many of the *mujahideen* factions returned to power and, though once again projected as heroes, the men who make up these forces have remained as brutal as before. As of January 2003, when this is written, human rights abuse is rampant outside Kabul. Once again, women are being raped and tortured and, according to Afghan women with whom my colleagues and I are in contact, abuses are spreading to areas hitherto spared.[9]

After all the media blitz, there are indeed a few women in the Afghan Interim Government, but there is little political or material support for a women's agenda. The Afghan Women's Council (AWC), a health-oriented group based in Peshawar (Pakistan), noted after several trips to Afghanistan in 2002 that the "poor gender policy" in government, the U.N., and nongovernmental initiatives has relegated Afghan women to "noninfluential positions," and reported that people's lack of access to human rights in parts of the country and the fear of a "breakdown of the fragile security arrangements" was making it difficult to mobilize or work with women.[10]

Even exceptionally prominent Afghan women face serious obstacles in their work. The Interim Government's first Minister for Women, who also served as Afghanistan's deputy prime minister, Dr. Sima Samar, was targeted soon after she assumed office and was accused of blasphemy, for which the punishment is death. Clearly she was too outspoken, too much a human rights and women's rights activist to be allowed to do the job. After the controversy, she was quickly shunted out of the Women's Ministry. It is improbable that she will face any less resistance, where women's rights and needs are concerned, in her new position as head of the Human Rights Commission. As it is, the government's ability to protect human rights is greatly impeded by its lack of influence beyond Kabul.

Instead of "the gunmen being replaced by penmen" as Afghan women hoped,[11] most parts of Afghanistan have been "entrusted to regional military commanders, many of whom have human rights records rivaling the worst commanders under the Taliban," as documented by Human Rights Watch (HRW).[12] While there is undoubtedly a need for a monitoring system to prevent such violations, as recommended by the AWC, HRW, and others, such measures seemed doomed to failure since, as HRW reported, the "American military forces have maintained relationships with local warlords that undercut efforts by U.S. diplomats and aid agencies to strengthen central authority and rule of law."[13]

PAKISTAN: SHIFTING TOWARD THE RIGHT

As is very obvious by now, Pakistan is experiencing its own fallout from the U.S.–led "war on terror." Some effects are just beginning to emerge. Others were almost instantaneous, like the way previous calls by the international community for a return to democracy in Pakistan were replaced by praise for General Musharraf as a key ally in the "war against terror." More ominously for rights discourse and activists, in some areas of Pakistan, nongovernmental organizations (NGOs) working on health, education, rehabilitation of land mine victims, and women's skill development and employment came under immediate attack.

With nightfall on October 7, 2001, the "war on terror" moved from rhetoric to U.S.–led military strikes and bombing in Afghanistan.[14] By noon the next day in Pakistan's northern areas abutting Afghanistan, eight NGOs had been razed to the ground one after the other, their equipment destroyed or stolen, the homes of at least three activists assaulted, two completely destroyed. The attack was carried out by mobs chanting slogans against the U.S. and accusing these civil society organizations of being U.S. agents—even though all but one of those attacked were local self-help groups and the exception was an NGO exclusively focused on rehabilitating land-mine victims.[15] The mobs were galvanized by politically engaged people for whom the start of bombings in Afghanistan was the signal to unleash their anger at the U.S.–led strikes and against the volte-face executed by Pakistan's government on its relations with the Taliban. Civil society groups made a suitably weak public target for elements clearly unwilling to risk a direct confrontation with Pakistan's military government, other than in media-driven public protests.

Attacks on civil society groups instigated by the religious right are not new in Pakistan—especially when the targets are groups promoting human rights and most particularly those promoting women's rights or development. It is not that rights activists pose any real threat to politico-religious parties. They are seen, however, as principal opponents in discursive contestations, the articulation of ideas and visions that accompany activism. Labeling rights activists "Western agents" is intended to undermine credibility and public support; harassment and physical attacks (including beatings and bombs) are intended to intimidate and silence them. Until recently, rights activists were reassured by the lack of public support for politico-religious parties, which were roundly rejected whenever sporadically held elections allowed people a say in who should rule the country. Also reassuring was that hitherto these parties were sharply divided amongst themselves. There is little room for reassurance today.

One year into the "war on terror," Pakistan's October 2002 parliamentary elections may have been a disturbing harbinger of the future. Unexpectedly, voters elected an unprecedented number of politico-religious party members whose stands and policies have been consistently antiwomen. This bodes ill for pluralism and human rights in general. Six political parties combined as the Mutahida Majlis Amal—United Action Front, or MMA—won 45 of the 272 general seats, vastly increasing their strength from a marginal six to seven seats in the last assembly. Joined by other non–MMA conservatives and women on special additional seats,[16] they present a formidable parliamentary force and may even dominate the upper house of the Senate.[17]

The rhetoric and game plan of the U.S.–led "war on terror" directly contributed to the electoral victory of the MMA. The initial use of the word "crusade" by Mr. Bush to describe the proposed "war against terror" in 2001 was more than unfortunate; it was a veritable godsend for those politico-religious parties who have long claimed that the West in general and the United States in particular is engaged in a war against Islam. The Bush administration's retraction, though rapid, was always going to be too late. It was ignored, and the term happily picked up by the politico-religious parties; it fed directly into their emotionally charged political mobilization, which presents the situations of Kashmiris in India, Palestinians in the Middle East, Chechens in Russia and, of course, Muslims in Bosnia as evidence of a global war on Muslims. In 2002, as further proof, these elements pointed to the U.S.'s aggressive preparations for a war on Iraq and the possible later targeting of Iran.

The MMA also capitalized on sensibilities outraged by the U.S. military strikes in Afghanistan and Pakistan's unquestioning compliance with U.S. dictates and demands, such as the presence of U.S. troops starting immediately before the action. Anger directed at the U.S. was fueled by the Bush administration's callous dismissal of Afghan civilian deaths as "collateral damage,"[18] denying human status to those killed, and by the further destruction of a country already devastated by twenty years of war and threatened with famine. It is not coincidental that the MMA's major success was in the two provinces that form the long border with Afghanistan (North West Frontier Province and Baluchistan).[19] Putting aside its political manifesto, the MMA's electoral campaign focused on opposition to the U.S. intelligence and armed forces presence in Pakistan, the U.S.–led war on Afghanistan, and the "war on terror." The MMA promised to remove American troops from Pakistan, to close air bases and other facilities to foreign personnel, and to replace externally driven agenda setting with policies premised on national interests and resisting external pressures, notably that of the United States (but also the World Bank and the IMF). The MMA's victory should therefore be understood less as an endorsement of its religious conservatism than as a measure of anti-American feeling.

Mr. Bush's incessant reiterations of the binary division of the world through his "either you're with us or against us" rhetoric do not help. The U.S. is not perceived as a champion of either justice or welfare in this region or elsewhere, e.g., Latin America. Its foreign policies have far too often bolstered and protected dictators and authoritarian regimes, governments that have treated their citizen-subjects with disdain and displayed a complete disregard for human rights. Consequently, if forced to choose, people may well elect to be counted amongst those against the U.S. irrespective of the character and qualities of those they therefore end up being associated with. Ominously, for example, the November 19, 2002, funeral prayers for Aimal Kasi, executed a week earlier in the U.S. for killing two CIA operatives, drew a mammoth crowd in the provincial capital of Baluchistan, with mourners condemning the U.S. as "an enemy of the Muslim world." Many probably shared the sentiments of a boy who, when asked why he was there, said, "I don't know who Kasi was, I only know that he was killed by the USA."[20]

As part of the "war on terror," the U.S. has been, if not instigating, then at least collaborating with domestic agencies in Pakistan as they curtail civil liberties and flout legal procedures. One example is the increased number of arbitrary detentions of "suspects." In a country where politically motivated detentions have been common under both civilian and military rule, the outcry was muted until a renowned orthopedic surgeon, Dr. Amir Aziz, was picked up on October 21, 2002, by U.S. and Pakistani intelligence operatives and held without charges and incommunicado for several weeks, leading to country-wide protests. Aziz's only "crime" seems to have been possibly possessing information on Osama bin Laden (and by extension Al Qaeda) by virtue of having run free medical camps regularly in Afghanistan for many years and the possibility that he personally treated bin Laden. Only when the Lahore High Court ordered that he be produced in court was Aziz mysteriously returned to his home in the early hours of November 19. No charges were framed, and although officials denied the involvement of U.S. personnel, "quoting Dr. Aziz, his brother said the FBI and CIA has interrogated him with the assistance of local military and intelligence agencies."[21] According to newpapers, two other doctors "were arrested . . . along with seven other family members on December 19 [2002] by FBI"; and again, after a raid in Karachi on January 9, 2003, newspapers reported the presence of "foreign 'guests' . . . in the official vehicles" and noted that those arrested had been "taken to undisclosed location[s]."[22]

We live in a world characterized by inequity and injustice, in which the U.S. is perceived to be the uncontested leader of the West, dominating world politics and the U.N. In the eyes of many people in this region, and in the Muslim world at least, the dual standards adopted by the U.S. with respect to rights and justice thus render suspect the entire edifice of an international community that has, and can enforce, universal standards of justice and rights for everyone. When extremists promise to address—sometimes by any means available—the blatant inequities and injustices at home and abroad, these goals resonate with many people, and this resonance produces recruits for extremist groups and the religious right. At the same time, this equation confronts and can impede rights activists trying to mobilize support for a more equitable and just world through the human rights discourse, due process of law, and nonviolent means.

CURRENT CONCERNS IN LIGHT OF THE PAST

The current concerns of activists in Pakistan and Afghanistan cannot be understood without stepping back to the 1980s, when Pakistan acted as a cat's paw in the U.S.'s proxy war with the USSR in Afghanistan—a war from which Afghan society has not recovered and that left Pakistani society beleaguered with the results of deep-rooted changes.

In Afghanistan, the opposition's mainstay was tribal lords and religious authorities earlier engaged in an armed struggle to overthrow Hafizullah Amin's "godless" (*la-deeni*) Marxist government and eager to eradicate the equally "godless" Soviets and their Afghan "puppets." Collectively referred to as the *mujahideen,* these groups were projected and promoted by those supporting them—not least the U.S. government—as "freedom fighters" and lauded as such in mainstream media. Their ideological stances were deliberately ignored, whether it was their utter disregard for democracy and its principles or their marginalization of women and opposition to women's rights. Their other abuses of human rights both on and off the battlefields were similarly ignored. The objective, of course, was to "draw the Soviets into the Afghan trap" [23] and weaken them, not to promote democracy in the region, just as today the objective of the "war on terror" is to defend and secure U.S. national interests—political, economic, and corporate.[24]

Under General Zia-ul-Haq (1977–1988), Pakistan was the main conduit of arms and ammunition for Afghan groups bankrolled by the U.S. and Saudi Arabia. Many of the arms never reached Afghanistan, and flooded Pakistan instead, giving rise to a "Kalashnikov culture," where verbal disagreements and disputes gave way to armed clashes in every arena, political or personal. Society was brutalized, intolerance became ascendant and, thanks to Zia's policies, there was a veritable mushrooming of politico-religious groups armed to the teeth.

Unlike previous dictators, Zia combined military might with religious bigotry and pursued an aggressive policy of so-called "Islamization" as a justification for continued martial law. Censure from the international community was minimal, allowing Zia to pursue his domestic policies without restraint. The military hanged a former democratically elected prime minister after a trial that made a mockery of justice; suspended fundamental rights, and introduced military courts and brutal punishments such as public floggings and hangings. In the name of a self-serving "Islamization," human rights in general and the rights of women and minorities in particular were rescinded or circumscribed or undermined; separate electorates and other measures established virtual apartheid for non-Muslims; constitutional and other legal amendments induced a shift in legal proceedings from the text of the law and case precedent to people's personal interpretations of religious injunctions. Democratic secular spaces evaporated, political parties were banned, the press muzzled.

Women—one of the least powerful groups in a deeply patriarchal society—became an easy and preferred target of the military's "Islamization" campaign, allowing the military to claim movement toward an "Islamic" model without antagonizing any powerful section of society. All women government servants and school and college students were directed to wear the *chador,* or veil;[25] women in the Foreign Office no longer received postings abroad; scholarships and promotions were denied to women in state institutions; jails filled up with women victimized through the 1979 Hudood Ordinances that made all extramarital sex a crime against the state. State-controlled electronic media extolled the virtues of "Islamic" (occasionally "Eastern") women, defined as those who stayed at home, veiled themselves, and adjusted to oppressive domestic conditions, and contrasted this with the "depravity" and "loose morals" of Western society. The resultant atmosphere seemed to give every man on the street the moral right to chastise any woman not meeting *his* definition of "propriety." Those defending women's rights and challenging the new policies and laws as unjust were labeled "Westernized" and/or "Western agents" whose concerns were to be dismissed.

In this oppressive environment, an outward adherence to an Islam defined by the military and its ally, the Jamaat-i-Islami (a conservative politico-religious party), became the sole criterion for political correctness and acceptability. Religiosity became the new and seemingly only currency for political power. Politico-religious parties proliferated and took up arms. With all political actors adhering to the new rules of the game, the scope for dissent and opposition articulated in terms other than a religious idiom virtually disappeared and, with it, pluralism.

In war-torn Afghanistan, civil society disintegrated, and by the mid-1990s human rights violations became the norm. The United Nations' Convention on the Elimination of All Forms of Discrimination Against Women (CEDAW), signed by Afghanistan under Soviet influence, was never ratified. The *mujahideen* adopted a religious idiom and retrogressive policies, especially with respect to women.[26] Amid the outcry (and hype) over the Taliban's mistreatment of women and the *burqa,* it is forgotten that banning Western clothes for women and ordering women to "cover themselves from head to toe in a veil made of a material that was neither soft nor rustled"[27] was first passed in 1990, as a *fatwa* (religious edict or opinion) by the *mujahideen* "government-in-exile" in Peshawar, years before the Taliban came to power. Further, "women were not to walk in the middle of the street or swing their hips; they were not to talk, laugh or joke with strangers or foreigner."[28]

Unconditional and massive U.S. support for the *mujahideen* and Zia legitimized and actively promoted the instrumental use—more accurately, the abuse—of religion in the political arena well beyond these two countries. As a leading Pakistani peace and human rights activist has noted:

> General Zia ul Haq brought a messianic zeal to redefine Pakistan as an Islamic state run by Sharia (Islamic Law) and Islamicize its institutions . . . "Islam, Pakistan, Jihad" became emblazoned on banners at Pakistani Army recruitment centers, beards proliferated, promotions went with piety, and few could be seen to miss Friday prayers. A new ethos was created; this was to be an army not just for Pakistan, but for the greater glory of Islam . . . [creating] a global *jihad* industry, financed by the U.S. and Saudi Arabia.[29]

True. For during this earlier war in Afghanistan, thousands of men, Afghans as well as non-Afghans, were recruited and trained to fight the Soviets. International linkages of right-wing political forces were created or strengthened. As recruits were armed beyond their wildest imagination, they were also legitimized, allowing battle-hardened combatants, especially Arabs who participated by the thousands, to return home—to Algeria for example—to brutalize their own societies with impunity.[30] The *mujahideen,* living and training in Pakistan, strengthened and encouraged like-minded Pakistani elements to impose their brand of Islam and morality regardless of state institutions and laws, just as later, Islamabad's support to the Taliban regime led to a "Talibanization" of Pakistani society, especially along the border areas.

The departure of the Soviets from Afghanistan in 1990 signaled the end of U.S. interest in the area (until oil refocused attention in the mid-1990s). But the forces set in motion continued apace, leaving Afghan and Pakistani societies reeling with the consequences, one being the entrenchment of a supposedly religious framework for any discourse on women's rights and women as symbols of an "Islamic" order. In Afghanistan, the first order passed by the *mujahideen* on assuming power in Kabul was that all women should wear the *burqa*. One reporter noted:

> . . . the most visible sign of change on the streets, apart from the guns, is the utter disappearance of women in western clothes. They used to be a common sight. Now women cover up from ankle to throat and hide their hair, or else use the burqa. Many women are frightened to leave their homes. At the telephone office, 80 percent of the male workers reported for duty on Saturday, and only 20 percent of the females.[31]

The subsequent battle for central control was so vicious and Afghan society so ravaged, that a battle-fatigued people hoping for an end to the fighting accepted (in some places, even welcomed) the Taliban in 1996.

In Pakistan, the hugely damaging legal and structural changes wrought by Zia were largely left untouched by subsequent governments that, learning from Zia, occasionally used the emotive "Islamization" ploy as a cover to appropriate more, and more arbitrary, power. A silver lining of the Zia era, however, was the emergence of a vibrant and vocal women's rights movement resisting reactionary policies. Though limited in numbers and confined to major urban centers, activists managed, paradoxically enough, to put women on the national agenda.[32] Building on this, civil society activists successfully reclaimed some space for a rights-based approach after Zia's death in 1988. One victory was Pakistan's ratification of CEDAW in 1996 without any of the reservations by reference to Islam and shari'a that had characterized ratification by Muslim-majority states for several years.[33] A rights-based approach informed Pakistan's National Report for the 1995 Beijing Conference and the subsequent 1998 National Plan of Action for Women.

In Afghanistan, the departure of the Soviets foreclosed any remaining space for women's overt activism in support of women's rights. The penalties for even minor transgressions of dictated norms progressively became so severe as to preclude any rights discourse. Resistance took other forms, such as teaching and providing medical care at great personal risk. The onus of systematically raising women's rights concerns thus fell exclusively on women refugees in different parts of the world, but their pleas for assistance fell largely on deaf ears until the Bush administration's instrumental use of women's oppression in the "war on terror." Had the concern truly been Afghan women, their voices, as articulated by numerous Afghan women's groups opposing the bombardment of their country, should have shaped action. But the compulsions for war lay elsewhere. And the outcome of U.S. military action, as foreseen by Afghan women, is neither conductive to women's rights nor supportive of their engagement in defining their society, except in a marginalized way.

Afghan women's groups like RAWA, AWN, and AWC fear a return to the conditions of the 1990s when warlords wreaked havoc. Moreover, the new government has stated, on more than one occasion, that it will strive for an "Islamic" society and will uphold "Islamic" laws and punishments. Clearly, the "war on terror" has done little to redefine the parameters within which women struggle for their rights, and women's rights remain contingent on someone's interpretation of Islam.

In Pakistan, the war has unquestionably given a boost to forces opposed to women's rights. Women's rights activists are experiencing a sense of déjà vu as the MMA issues calls for segregating all schools by gender, legislating laws according to the recommendations of the Council of Islamic Ideology (notorious for its antiwomen suggestions), and the participation of women "within the framework of Islam." MMA leaders have promised that they will not make veiling compulsory but will merely create an environment in which women will willingly veil themselves. This is hardly comforting, given that Iranian officials also claim that veiling in Iran is not compulsory.

A WINDOW ON THE FUTURE

Many people in Pakistan, but also in many Muslim countries and communities, perceive the U.S.–led "war on terror" as spreading rather than diminishing terror—both directly through the use of force and war instead of dialogue, and by fueling a sense of injustice at the double standards with respect to human rights and democracy. Because the "axis of evil" identified by the Bush administration is Muslim-majority countries (with North Korea thrown in for good measure), and because the reason forwarded by the Bush administration for the planned war on Iraq (which seems almost inevitable at the time of writing, in January 2003) is its weapons of mass destruction but there is world silence on the Israeli bomb, the sense of injustice is likely to be stronger in Muslim countries and communities. Hence, though there is probably little popular support for Saddam Hussein in the Arab world, Mai Yamani, a Saudi Arabian scholar, speaks for many who perceive the buildup to a U.S. war on Iraq as "converting Iraq along with Palestine into an Arab cause," fostering more fanatics and nurturing recruitment for the politico-religious right in authoritarian states.[34] (Meanwhile, signs that started appearing in Seoul store windows in December 2002 saying, "U.S. citizens not welcome here" warn of wider repercussions.)

Promoting women's rights is never an easy task. It is especially difficult in those parts of the world where the concepts and discourse of human rights are still fragile elements, peripheral to the dynamics of state and society, and where human rights advocates have barely managed to establish a foothold. The hold is particularly precarious where civil society is itself deeply divided. In many Muslim countries and communities, an apparent fault line separates those adopting a human rights perspective to promote the universality and indivisibility of rights in a democratic system, from those promoting reactionary religious revivalism now infused with the traditional Third World themes of anti-imperialism and nationalism or pan-nationalism[35] (the latter now recast in religious terminology as the Muslim *ummah*). Seemingly, the fault line also divides the supporters and opponents of women's rights.[36]

By lending itself to and fueling existing contestations over identity, by presenting dichotomous choices as absolutes, and by reducing the scope for pluralism in the world at large, the "war on terror" may lead people to withdraw from an engagement with a rights discourse and struggle, especially if the only seeming choice is either to be a willing or unwilling cog in the U.S. agenda or to be deemed in opposition to it. If the only strong visible opposition to U.S. policies is the one articulated by politico-religious elements condemning them as a "war on Islam," the impact on rights activists in Muslim communities and countries will be particularly damaging. The demonization of "Islam" in Western media and/or political discourse only alienates the average Muslim who, because of this sharpened polarization, starts to view local rights activists as abetting the attack on Islam. Under attack or suspicion from within their own community, rights activists may opt to maintain a low profile or silence on injustices at home.

There are several implications for women and rights activists. First, the high-profile, self-serving use of women's rights as a U.S. flagstaff may delegitimize indigenous women's movements and groups by association. Second, the present scenario may jeopardize the links painstakingly created between the global women's movement and rights activists in Muslim countries and communities and obstruct new linkages. In this, the lack of media coverage of the voice of opposition from within the United States is problematic because it implies that all Americans are squarely behind their government's policies. It is particularly unfortunate that a number of visible and vocal women in the U.S. as well as Europe, insensitive to the voices and concerns of Afghan women, saw fit to support the "war on terror" as a panacea for women in Afghanistan.[37] Equally, the almost obsessive focus on removing the *burqa* and veil by even well-intended women in the West belittles the struggle of Afghan women who will tell you time and again that women's rights depend on peace and security, not war; on women's greater decision making in their lives and society, and not on the reopening of beauty parlors in Kabul.[38]

To avoid fragmentation within the global women's movement it is essential that the agenda be set by indigenous women who are supported in their struggle. More broadly, it is critical that domestic opposition to U.S. policies become more visible and that the U.N. regain credibility as an international forum for consensus building and for the setting of universal standards of human rights for all.

Finally, apart from being inflammatory rhetoric, the Bush administration's binary logic of the "either you're with us or against us" echoes the false dichotomous choices forwarded by "fundamentalists" who, by engaging in essentialist politics of identity, are bent upon denying ordinary people the right to choice, to dissent, and to self-expression. These choices are central for the promotion of all human rights. They are critical at an even more personal and immediate level for women because of the burden so frequently placed on women to be the repositories of culture and identity. In this part of the world, a constant theme of our struggle for women's rights, as also for human rights in general, has been to reject—as actively and vociferously as possible—the attempts at an imposition of dichotomous choices and worldviews.

In the end, one can only agree with Eduardo Galeano when he writes, "In the struggle of Good against Evil, it's always the people who die,"[39] but also note that in many parts of the world, the other likely casualties of the "war on terror" will be pluralism, rights discourses, and women's rights.

13. HUMAN RIGHTS, THE BUSH ADMINISTRATION, AND THE FIGHT AGAINST TERRORISM: THE NEED FOR A POSITIVE VISION

KENNETH ROTH[1]

Leadership requires more than a big stick and a thick wallet. It also requires a positive vision shared by others and conduct consistent with that vision. The campaign against terrorism is no exception. The United States, as a major target, took the lead in combating terrorism. But the global outpouring of sympathy that followed the attacks of September 11, 2001, soon gave way to a growing reluctance to join the fight and even resentment toward the government leading it.[2]

How was this goodwill depleted so quickly? In part, the cause was traditional resentment of America and its role in the world—resentment that was softened only temporarily by the tragedy of September 11. In part it was opposition to U.S. policy in the Middle East. And in part it was growing disquiet that the means used to fight terrorism were often in conflict with the values of freedom and law that most people embrace and that President George W. Bush said the United States was defending.

Despite its declared policy of supporting human rights, the Bush administration in fighting terrorism refused to be bound by human rights standards. Despite a U.S. tradition at home of government under law, the administration rejected legal constraints, especially when acting abroad. Despite a constitutional order that is premised on the need to impose checks and balances, the U.S. government seemed to want an international order that placed no limits on a nation's use of power save its own avowed good intentions. As I write at the end of 2002, these attitudes are jeopardizing the campaign against terrorism. They are also putting at risk the human rights ideal.

This is hardly to say that the United States is among the worst human rights offenders. But because of America's extraordinary influence, the Bush administration's willingness to compromise human rights to fight terrorism set a dangerous precedent. Because of the leadership role that the U.S. government so often has played in promoting human rights, the weakening of its voice weighed heavily, particularly in some of the front-line countries in the war against terrorism, where the need for a vigorous defense of human rights was great.

HUMAN RIGHTS AND THE CHALLENGE OF TERRORISM

Terrorism is antithetical to human rights. Since targeting civilians for violent attack is repugnant to human rights values, those who believe in human rights have a direct interest in the success of the antiterrorism effort. Yet, the Bush administration's tendency to ignore human rights in fighting terrorism is not only disturbing on its own terms, it is dangerously counterproductive. The smoldering resentment it breeds risks generating terrorist recruits, puts off potential antiterrorism allies, and weakens efforts to curb terrorist atrocities.

Terrorism cannot be defeated from afar. Curbing terrorism requires the support of people in the countries where terrorists reside. They are the people who must cooperate with police inquiries rather than shield terrorist activity. They are the people who must take the lead in dissuading would-be terrorists. But if they see Washington embracing the governments that repress them, they will hardly feel inclined to help. Their reluctance only increases if their entire community is viewed as suspect, as many young male Middle Easterners and North Africans have felt since September 11.

Clearly the United States needs to take extra security measures. But the U.S. government must also pay attention to the pathology of terrorism—the set of beliefs that leads some people to join in attacking civilians, to believe that the ends justify the means. A strong human rights culture is an antidote to this pathology, yet in too many places the Bush administration saw human rights mainly as an obstacle to its goals. Human rights and security are mutually reinforcing, yet too often the administration treated them as a zero-sum game.

Even someone as unsympathetic to human rights as President Ronald Reagan at the height of the Cold War understood the need for a positive vision. He understood that the United States could not only be *against* Communism. It had to stand *for* democracy, even if at times his support was no more than rhetorical. Similarly, it will not work for the Bush administration today to be only against terrorism. It will have to stand for the values that explain what's wrong with attacking civilians—the values of human rights.

There were hints of such a positive vision in 2002—in prominent parts of a speech that President Bush gave at West Point in June; in part of his administration's National Security Strategy, released in September; and in the conditions for disbursing increased international assistance (the Millennium Challenge Account), announced in November. But this rhetorical embrace of human rights has translated only inconsistently into U.S. conduct and foreign policy.

The sad irony is that for much of the past half-century, the United States was often a driving force behind the strengthening of the human rights ideal. It took the lead in drafting the Universal Declaration of Human Rights, building the international human rights system, and lending its voice and influence on behalf of human rights in many parts of the world. Often this support for human rights was inconsistent—tempered by strategic concerns and a deep resistance to applying international law at home. Yet the U.S. government could still be found at the forefront of many human rights battles, and it contributed significantly to building a global consensus about the importance of human rights as a restraint on legitimate governmental conduct.

The Bush administration, too, tried to advance human rights in places where the war on terrorism was not implicated, such as Burma, Belarus, and Zimbabwe. The administration has publicly recognized the connection between repression and terrorism, and to a limited extent tried to promote human rights in some places that were more directly involved in the fight against terrorism, such as Egypt and Uzbekistan. Yet it compromised the long U.S. engagement on human rights in three important respects.

First, in several key countries involved in the campaign against terrorism, such as Pakistan and Saudi Arabia, even rhetorical U.S. support for human rights was rare—often nothing more than the State Department's once-a-year pronouncements in its global human rights report. The administration also showed little inclination to confront such influential governments as Russia, China, and Israel that used the fight against terrorism to cloak or intensify repression aimed at separatist, dissident, or nationalist movements that were themselves often abusive.

Second, even when the Bush administration did try to promote human rights, its authority was undermined by its refusal to be bound by the standards it preaches to others. From its rejection of the Geneva Conventions for prisoners from the war in Afghanistan to its misuse of the "enemy combatant" designation for criminal suspects at home, from its threatened use of substandard military commissions to its abuse of immigration laws to deny criminal suspects their rights, the administration fought terrorism as if human rights were not a constraint.

Third, the Bush administration intensely opposed the enforcement of international human rights law, from the International Criminal Court to more modest efforts to affirm or reinforce human rights norms. Similar exceptionalism could be seen in such actions as the administration's rejection of the Kyoto Protocol on global warming or its blocking of efforts to strengthen the Biological Weapons Convention. This opposition suggested a radical vision of world order—a view of the superpower as unconstrained by international law. Certain influential elements in the administration seemed to view international law as an unnecessary encroachment on U.S. latitude—a set of rules to be avoided because they might in the future restrict the United States in unforeseeable and inconvenient ways. Instead, they advocated determining the proper scope of governmental conduct, if not through unilateral assertions of power, then at least through case-by-case negotiations, where America's overwhelming economic and military strength was more likely to prevail.

But even American might has limits. Shared norms—of commerce, peace, or human rights—are needed so that most governments voluntarily abide by them. Pressure may still be needed to rein in recalcitrant governments, but an effective global order depends on most governments living voluntarily by agreed-upon rules. Even if the result is disappointing in a particular case, most governments recognize that a system of law is in their interest over the long run. But that logic breaks down if the superpower routinely exempts itself from the enforcement of international law. If shared norms give way to relations built on power alone, the world will revert to a premodern, Hobbesian order. That can hardly be in the long-term interest of the United States or anyone else.

The Bush administration's neglect of human rights in fighting terrorism was visible throughout 2002 in its own treatment of terrorist suspects, its bilateral relations with other governments, and its behavior in international fora.

TREATMENT OF TERRORIST SUSPECTS

Historically, the United States has been expansive in its compliance with the requirements of international humanitarian law (the laws of war) with regard to belligerents captured in the course of an armed conflict. For example, the United States afforded prisoner-of-war status to Chinese soldiers captured during the Korean War even though the People's Republic of China was not a party to the 1949 Geneva Conventions. It provided POW status to many captured guerrillas during the Vietnam War. During the 1991 Gulf War, the U.S. military convened special tribunals to determine the legal status of more than 1,000 captured Iraqis, as the Geneva Conventions require.

The United States upheld international standards in part out of recognition that they ultimately benefit U.S. soldiers. Needless to say, the reverse is also true: the failure to comply with the Geneva Conventions encourages noncompliance by others when U.S. servicemembers must depend on the conventions for their protection. Unfortunately, the Bush administration broke with this long U.S. tradition in its treatment of terrorist suspects and others detained in the war against terrorism.

A good illustration was the administration's treatment of the people detained at Guantánamo Bay, Cuba. The administration's unjustifiably narrow reading of the Geneva Conventions effectively placed these detainees in a legal black hole where they could be kept in long-term arbitrary detention despite international prohibitions. For instance, the Third Geneva Convention provides that captured combatants are to be treated as prisoners of war until a "competent tribunal" determines otherwise.[3] Under the standards set out in the convention, the detainees who were former Taliban soldiers would almost certainly qualify as POWs, while many of the detainees who were members of Al Qaeda probably would not.[4] But the administration refused to bring any of the detainees before a tribunal and unilaterally asserted that none qualified as POWs. This flouting of international humanitarian law could not be explained by the exigencies of fighting terrorism. Treating the detainees as POWs would not have precluded the United States from interrogating them or prosecuting them for committing terrorist acts or other atrocities. And POWs, like other detained combatants, can be held without charge or trial until the end of the relevant armed conflict.

The administration's refusal to apply the Geneva Conventions seemed to stem in part from its desire to minimize public scrutiny of its conduct. For instance, in the absence of criminal prosecutions, the Geneva Conventions require that all detainees, regardless of their status, be repatriated once "active hostilities" have ended.[5] In the case of at least the Taliban detainees, that would seem to have required repatriation as soon as the war with the Afghan government was over— that is, presumably, after a *loya jirga* (grand assembly) elected Hamid Karzai president of Afghanistan in June 2002. But by refusing to apply the Geneva Conventions, the administration avoided making such a determination.

The Bush administration also breached the rule of law to take custody of some detainees. In October 2001, it sought the surrender in Bosnia of six Algerian men who were suspected of planning attacks on Americans. After a three-month investigation, Bosnia's Supreme Court ordered the men's release from custody for lack of evidence. When rumors spread of U.S. efforts to seize the suspects, anyway, Bosnia's Human Rights Chamber—which was established under the U.S.–sponsored Dayton peace accord and includes six local and eight international members—issued an injunction against their removal. Yet in January 2002, under U.S. pressure, the Bosnian government ignored this legal ruling and delivered the men to U.S. forces, who whisked them out of the country, reportedly to Guantánamo.

The line between war and law enforcement gained importance as the U.S. government extended its military efforts against terrorism outside of Afghanistan and western Pakistan. In November, the U.S. Central Intelligence Agency used a drone-launched missile to kill Qaid Salim Sinan al-Harethi, an alleged senior Al Qaeda official, and five companions as they were driving in a remote and lawless area of Yemen controlled by tribal chiefs. The Bush administration accused al-Harethi of masterminding the October 2000 bombing of the U.S.S. *Cole*, which had killed seventeen sailors. Based on the limited information available, the attack on al-Harethi did not seem to be an extrajudicial execution, given that his alleged Al Qaeda role arguably made him a combatant, the Yemeni government apparently lacked control over the area in question, and there evidently was no reasonable law enforcement alternative. Indeed, eighteen Yemeni soldiers had reportedly been killed in a prior attempt to arrest al-Harethi.[6]

However, the U.S. government made no public effort to justify this use of its war powers or to articulate the legal limits to such powers.[7] Even someone who might be classified as an enemy combatant should not be subject to military attack when reasonable law enforcement means are available. The failure to respect this principle would risk creating a huge loophole in due process protections worldwide. It would leave everyone open to being summarily killed anyplace in the world upon the unilateral determination of the United States (or, as the approach is inevitably emulated, any other government) that he or she is an enemy combatant.

The appropriate line between war and law enforcement was crossed in the case of Jose Padilla, a U.S. citizen Attorney General John Ashcroft claimed had flown from Pakistan to the United States in May 2002 to investigate creating a radiological bomb. U.S. officials arrested him as he arrived at Chicago's O'Hare International Airport and briefly held him as a material witness. Then, instead of the Justice Department charging him with this serious criminal offense and bringing him to trial, President Bush declared him an "enemy combatant." That designation, the administration claimed, permitted it to hold him without access to counsel and without charge or trial until the end of the war against terrorism, which may never come. With no link to a discernible battlefield, that assertion of power, again, threatened to create a giant exception to the most basic criminal justice guarantees. Anyone could be picked up and detained forever as an "enemy combatant" upon the unverified assertions of the Bush administration or any other government. At the end of 2002, this radical claim was being litigated before U.S. District Judge Michael Mukasey in the Southern District of New York.

Due process shortcuts also plagued the Bush administration's detention of some 1,200 non–U.S. citizens whom the government sought to question regarding their links to or knowledge of the September 11 attacks. Of this group, whose number has never been fully disclosed, 752 were detained on immigration charges but treated like criminals. Rather than grant them the rights of criminal suspects, the administration used immigration law to detain and interrogate them secretly, without their usual right to be charged promptly with a criminal offense and (in case of economic need) to government-appointed counsel. Immigration detainees would ordinarily be deported, allowed to leave the country voluntarily, or released on bond pending a hearing on their case. But these "special interest" detainees were kept in jail until "cleared"—that is, until proven innocent of terrorist connections—often for many months. Through the end of 2002, none of them had been charged with a crime related to September 11.[8]

President Bush's November 2001 order authorizing the creation of military commissions to try non-American suspects lacked the most basic due process guarantees and raised the prospect of trials that would have been a travesty of justice. In March 2002, the Defense Department issued regulations for the commissions that corrected many of the due process problems of the original order. However, the regulations still allowed the commissions to operate without even the fair-trial standards applicable in U.S. courts-martial. Defendants in such courts-martial are entitled to appeal to the U.S. Court of Appeal for the Armed Forces—a civilian court outside the control of the executive branch—and ultimately to petition the U.S. Supreme Court. But the commission regulations permit appeal only to another military panel of people who must answer to the president. That makes the president, through his surrogates, prosecutor, trial judge, and appellate judge. Especially as applied away from the exigencies of the battlefield, these compromised commissions violate the minimum legal requirement of "an impartial and regularly constituted court respecting the generally recognized principles of regular judicial procedure."[9] If these commissions are used to try detainees who should be considered prisoners of war, and thus are entitled to the more protective procedures of a court-martial,[10] the Bush administration would open itself to war-crimes charges.[11]

This pattern of abuse in the Bush administration's own conduct sent a signal of contempt for basic human rights standards. It suggested that the administration saw international human rights standards as an inconvenient obstacle to fighting terrorism—one that was readily sidestepped—rather than as an integral part of the antiterrorism effort.

BILATERAL RELATIONS

In its bilateral relations, the U.S. government made some efforts to promote human rights while fighting terrorism. After September 11, for example, many assumed that Washington's limited promotion of human rights in the front-line states of Central Asia would end; in fact, in some ways it intensified, especially as the war in Afghanistan subsided. It is true that the larger U.S. military presence in Uzbekistan, Kyrgyzstan, and Tajikistan associated the United States with these countries' repressive policies—as did frequent presidential summits and enhanced aid packages. And the Bush administration consistently exaggerated these governments' progress toward reform to justify continued aid. But more often than in the past, administration officials pressed the region's leaders to release prisoners, respect media freedoms, and allow civil society to function, in part due to more frequent interaction at all levels between administration officials and governments in the region. The administration also took its first limited steps to use its leverage with these countries to promote human rights, canceling a high-level meeting with the Kazakh foreign minister with the aim of freeing a Turkmen dissident detained on Kazakh soil, and suspending a trade mission to Kyrgyzstan over its refusal to allow an independently operated printing press.[12]

In Colombia, linked by Secretary of State Colin Powell to the global war on terrorism, Washington also took several positive steps. In September 2002, Attorney General John Ashcroft announced the indictment on drug charges of Carlos Castaño, the head of the vicious and murderous paramilitary organization, the

United Self Defense Forces of Colombia. Other paramilitary and guerrilla leaders with abusive records were also charged with drug offenses. In November, the State Department suspended the U.S. visa of Colombian Admiral Rodrigo Quiñones, who had been repeatedly linked to serious abuses; that led to Quiñones's resignation as Colombia's military attaché to Israel. The same month, the State Department announced the suspension of military assistance to a Colombian air force unit that had been implicated in a deadly violation of the laws of war and a subsequent cover-up—the first time the United States had suspended assistance to Colombia on human rights grounds. These actions began to signal to Colombia that it must address at least the most extreme human rights abuses. Still, the U.S. government's dominant concern remained fighting the guerrillas and curbing drug trafficking. That led the State Department, in a May 2002 certification, to exaggerate Colombia's progress in meeting human rights conditions attached to massive U.S. military aid.

In countries that were critical to the fight against terrorism, the Bush administration's support for human rights was at best inconsistent and at worst completely absent. Afghanistan, the primary focus of antiterrorism efforts after September 11, illustrated the problem. The military overthrow of the highly abusive Taliban raised the prospect of greater freedom for the Afghan people. And if one judged by Kabul, the Afghan capital where international peacekeepers patrolled, life improved dramatically. But the Bush administration sought security for the rest of the country on the cheap. Throughout 2002, it offered at best lukewarm support to the deployment of international troops outside of Kabul (European governments were equally reluctant) and took few meaningful steps to demobilize factional forces or establish a professional Afghan army. Instead, it delegated security to resurgent warlords and provided them with money and arms.

In some parts of the country, the consequences looked much like life under the Taliban—a far cry from President Bush's vow to help Afghanistan "claim its democratic future." [13] For example, Ismail Khan, the Herat-based warlord in western Afghanistan, stamped out all dissent, muzzled the press, and bundled women back into their *burqas*. Those who resisted faced death threats, detention, and sometimes even torture. [14] Afghans who had taken refuge in Iran during Taliban rule complained to Human Rights Watch that they had been freer under the Iranian clerics than they were under Khan. Yet U.S. Defense Secretary Donald Rumsfeld, after a visit to Herat in April 2002, called Khan an "appealing person." [15] Under growing pressure to address the violence and insecurity outside of Kabul, the Bush administration announced in November 2002 that it would send a small number of soldiers and civil affairs officers to eight to ten Afghan provincial cities, mainly for development work. Their mere presence promised some modestly enhanced security, but it was far from the focused security effort needed to end warlord abuses.

In Pakistan, General Pervez Musharraf pushed through constitutional amendments that extended his presidential term by five years, arrogated to himself the power to dissolve the elected parliament, and created a military-dominated National Security Council to oversee civilian government. But when asked about this disturbing trend, President Bush said, "My reaction about President Musharraf, he's still tight with us on the war against terror, and that's what I appreciate." [16] Only as an afterthought did President Bush also mention the importance of democracy.[17] With Washington supporting Pakistan's military ruler and the repressive warlords next door in Afghanistan, it should have been no surprise that anti-American political parties in Pakistan were the big winners in October 2002 parliamentary elections. Their victory as well in simultaneous local elections in the two provinces bordering Afghanistan threatened to complicate U.S. efforts to apprehend any residual Taliban and Al Qaeda forces in the area.

In Indonesia, an abusive military and allied militia have been major factors in separatist and communal strife. The government's inability to hold abusive military figures accountable has been a major cause of popular discontent. Military-sponsored atrocities in East Timor in 1999 led the United States to cut off some military assistance. But with Indonesia seen as a major front in the battle against terrorism, the Bush administration tried to resume military training, even though little if any progress had been made in subjecting the military to the rule of law.

In a particularly egregious move, the administration sought dismissal of a lawsuit brought in U.S. court by victims of military atrocities in Indonesia who sought compensation from Exxon Mobil for its alleged complicity in the abuse. The suit, filed in June 2001 in Washington, alleged that the Indonesian military had provided "security services" for Exxon Mobil's joint venture in Indonesia's conflict-ridden Aceh province, and that the Indonesian military had committed "genocide, murder, torture, crimes against humanity, sexual violence and kidnapping" while providing security for the company from 1999 to 2001. The plaintiffs claimed that Exxon Mobil had been aware of widespread abuses committed by the military but had failed to take preventive action. In a July 2001 letter from

State Department Legal Adviser William H. Taft IV, the administration justified its opposition to this effort to enforce human rights standards in part out of its stated fear that Indonesia would retaliate by stopping its cooperation in the war on terrorism.[18]

A broad range of other U.S. allies in the war on terrorism received similarly soft treatment for their human rights abuses. For example, Russian President Vladimir Putin faced only mild criticism of his troops' continuing brutal behavior in Chechnya; their atrocities only intensified after Chechen militants took some 700 people hostage in a Moscow theater in October 2002. In China's western Xinjiang province, Beijing has long repressed the Turkic-speaking Uighur majority, China's largest Muslim population; despite the Bush administration's occasional criticism of Chinese conduct in Xinjiang, the administration's decision to designate as a terrorist organization the small East Turkistan Islamic Movement, which was said to be a Uighur movement from Xinjiang, provided new cover for Chinese repression of the Uighurs. The Israeli military in fighting armed Palestinian groups and their suicide bombings continued to employ such abusive practices as the use of excessive lethal force and the collective punishment of Palestinian civilians, yet Washington frequently shielded Israel from international pressure and continued to supply it unconditionally with weapons and military assistance. Because Malaysian Prime Minister Mahatir bin Mohamad was outspoken in support of the campaign against terrorism, the Bush administration also muted its criticism of his government, whether for its use of administrative detention or its continued imprisonment on trumped-up charges of former Deputy Prime Minister Anwar Ibrahim.

The overriding message sent by these U.S. bilateral actions was that human rights are dispensable in the name of fighting terrorism. That policy may have provided greater leeway for short-term security measures. But if an important aim was to build a culture of human rights in place of the pathology of terrorism, it sent a dangerous and counterproductive signal—one suggesting that it is acceptable to replace respect for the life of every person with the view that the ends justify the means.

INTERNATIONAL FORA

At the multilateral level, the Bush administration consistently opposed any effort to enforce human rights standards. This posture was not entirely new. Both Democratic and Republican administrations have always kept human rights treaties at arm's length. The U.S. government has never ratified three of the seven leading human rights treaties[19] or the leading treaty governing modern armed conflict.[20] Even when the U.S. government has ratified a human rights treaty, it has done so in a way that denies Americans the ability to enforce the treaty in any court, whether international or domestic.[21] This resistance to enforceable human rights standards only intensified after September 11.

The resistance was on display at the March–April 2002 session of the U.N. Commission on Human Rights, the leading U.N. human rights body. Mexico proposed a resolution that stressed the importance of fighting terrorism consistently with human rights. The resolution did not condemn any nation; it simply reaffirmed an essential principle. Yet the Bush administration opposed even this motherhood-and-apple-pie statement. It was joined by Algeria, India, Pakistan, and Saudi Arabia—hardly committed supporters of the international enforcement of human rights. Mexico withdrew the resolution. Not until eight months later, in December 2002, did the U.N. General Assembly eventually adopt a similar resolution, when the administration's opposition failed to derail it.

The administration also opposed efforts at the United Nations to strengthen the prohibition against torture. It objected to a proposed new Optional Protocol to the Convention Against Torture, which establishes a system for inspecting detention facilities where torture is suspected—an important preventive measure. The administration's position was at first puzzling, since the United States opposes torture as a matter of policy and has ratified the Torture Convention. If Washington wanted to avoid scrutiny under this new inspection procedure, it could simply not ratify the protocol, which, as its name suggests, is optional. The administration's decision, instead, to try to deprive other nations of this added human rights protection stemmed from an evident desire to avoid strengthening any international human rights law that might even remotely be used to criticize its own conduct—especially, one must assume, its interrogation of security suspects.[22] The optional protocol came to a vote before the U.N. General Assembly in December 2002; the United States was one of only four governments to oppose it, against 127 supporters.

At the U.N. General Assembly Special Session on Children, in May 2002, the Bush administration sought to prevent any reference in the final document to the Convention on the Rights of the Child. The United States is the only country in the world not to have ratified the treaty (other than Somalia, which has no national government). The special session—the highest-level U.N. summit on children in a decade—presented an important opportunity to reaffirm the rights contained in the convention. But the administration objected to any mention of the concrete rights of children, preferring vaguer reference to children's "well-being."

The administration was no better when it came to the rights of women. In December 2002, it launched an attack on the Cairo Programme of Action, a population control program endorsed by 179 countries, by seeking to remove the phrases "reproductive health services," "reproductive rights," and "consistent condom use" from a conference document for the U.N.–sponsored Fifth Asian and Pacific Population Conference. The document was adopted over U.S. objections. In addition, the administration withheld $34 million appropriated by Congress for the United Nations Population Fund (UNPF), claiming that the UNFPA supported coerced abortion and sterilization in China. A State Department investigation found no basis for that claim. The UNFPA said this amount could have prevented 2 million unwanted pregnancies, 800,000 induced abortions, 4,700 maternal deaths, and 77,000 infant and child deaths.

The administration's opposition to the enforcement of human rights standards was most extreme in the case of the International Criminal Court (ICC). The court has numerous safeguards to address legitimate U.S. concern about politicized prosecutions. Crimes are defined narrowly—more narrowly than even U.S. military manuals. Several independent panels of judges oversee prosecutorial decisions. A mere majority of the states party can impeach an abusive prosecutor (and most of the states party are democracies, given that ratification subjects a government's own conduct to the court's jurisdiction, and U.S. allies). Governments can avoid ICC prosecution altogether by conducting their own good-faith investigation and, if appropriate, prosecution. Moreover, the ICC does not purport to exert jurisdiction over a suspect unless the suspect's government has ratified the court's treaty or the suspect is alleged to have committed a crime on the territory of a government that has ratified the treaty—both long-accepted bases of jurisdiction.

Yet, the Bush administration declared a virtual war on the court. It repudiated former President Bill Clinton's signature on the ICC treaty. It threatened to shut down U.N. peacekeeping unless U.S. participants in U.N.–authorized operations were exempted from ICC jurisdiction. It threatened to cut off military aid to governments unless they agree never to deliver an American suspect to the court.

And President Bush signed legislation authorizing military intervention to free any American suspect held by the ICC—dubbed the "Hague Invasion Act." With occasional exceptions, the administration did not discourage governments from ratifying the ICC treaty for the sole purpose of addressing conduct by others, and by the end of 2002, eighty-seven governments had joined the court—well above the sixty needed for the treaty to take effect. But the Bush administration's efforts to exempt Americans from the court's investigations and prosecutions advanced a double standard that threatens to undermine the court's legitimacy.

By these multilateral interventions, across a wide range of issues, the Bush administration signaled that human rights standards are at best window-dressing. They are fine grand pronouncements, but their universal enforcement—enforcement that might affect the United States even indirectly—was to be avoided. Such hypocrisy only undermined these norms. It also undermined the credibility of the United States as a proponent of human rights, whether in fighting terrorism or in combating more traditional repression and abuse.

CONSEQUENCES FOR THE CAMPAIGN AGAINST TERRORISM

The Bush administration's willingness to sidestep human rights as it fought terrorism had potentially profound and dangerous consequences. At the very least, it meant that the United States was a party to serious abuse. If Washington provided assistance to abusive warlords in Afghanistan or a military dictatorship such as Pakistan's, it became complicit in the abuses that they foreseeably committed.

In addition, as noted, Washington's neglect of human rights threatened to impede its campaign against terrorism. As President Bush himself observed, repression fuels terrorism, by closing off avenues for peaceful dissent. Yet if the U.S. campaign against terrorism reinforces that repression, it risks breeding more terrorists as it alienates would-be allies in the fight against terrorism.

The administration's subordination of human rights to the campaign against terrorism also bred a copycat phenomenon. By waving the antiterrorism banner, governments such as Uzbekistan seemed to act as if they had greater license to persecute religious dissenters, while governments such as Russia, Israel, and China seemed to act with greater freedom as they intensified repression in Chechnya, the West Bank, and Xinjiang.[23] Tunisia stepped up trying civilians on terrorism charges before military courts that flagrantly disregarded due-process rights.[24]

Claiming that asylum seekers can be a "pipeline for terrorists" entering the country, Australia imposed some of the tightest restrictions on asylum in the industrialized world.[25] Facing forces on the right and left that had been designated terrorists, Colombia's new president, Álvaro Uribe, tried to permit warrantless searches and wiretaps and to restrict the movement of journalists (until the country's highest court ruled these measures unconstitutional).[26]

In sub-Saharan Africa, some of the mimicry took on absurd proportions. Ugandan President Yoweri Museveni shut down the leading independent newspaper for a week in October 2002 because it was allegedly promoting terrorism (it had reported a military defeat by the government in its battle against the Lord's Resistance Army rebel group).[27] In June, Liberian President Charles Taylor declared three of his critics—the editor of a local newspaper and two others—to be "illegal combatants" who would be tried for terrorism in a military court.[28] Eritrea justified its lengthy detention of the founder of the country's leading newspaper by citing the widespread U.S. detentions.[29] Zimbabwean President Robert Mugabe justified the November 2001 arrest of six journalists as terrorists because they wrote stories about political violence in the country.[30] Elsewhere, even former Yugoslav President Slobodan Milosevic defended himself against war-crimes charges by contending that abusive troops under his command had merely been combating terrorism.[31]

The inconsistency of the Bush administration's attention to human rights abroad also weakened an important voice for human rights when the United States did speak out. The most dramatic example was the case of Saadeddin Ibrahim, the Egyptian democracy activist who was sentenced in July 2002 to seven years in prison for his peaceful political activities. To its credit, the administration not only protested but also said it would withhold an incremental increase in aid that might have gone to Egypt. That was a dramatic step—the first time in the Middle East that the United States had conditioned aid on the positive resolution of a human rights case. But in light of Washington's long history of closing its eyes to human rights abuses in the Middle East, and its failure to protest Egypt's similar persecution of Islamists for nonviolent political activity, many Egyptians distrusted the administration's motives, and even some Egyptian human rights groups denounced the action. In December, Egypt's highest appeals court—with a long tradition of independence from the government—reversed Ibrahim's conviction and ordered a new trial. But Washington's voice was shown to have been compromised as a means to build broad public support for human rights.

POSSIBLE WAR IN IRAQ

As this chapter was written in late 2002, war in Iraq was threatening. Leaving aside the question of whether war should be launched, there was reason for considerable anxiety about how a war might proceed from the perspective of the lives of noncombatants in Iraq.

In human rights terms, Saddam Hussein is as bad as they come. In 1988, in the notorious *Anfal* campaign, he committed genocide against the Kurds. After using chemical weapons on at least forty occasions to drive Kurds from their highland villages, his forces rounded up and executed some 100,000, mostly men and boys. In suppressing the 1991 uprisings, his forces killed an estimated 30,000 Iraqis, mostly Kurds in the north and Shi'a in the south. In the following years, untold atrocities were committed against the Marsh Arabs. On a day-to-day basis, the Iraqi government used arbitrary detention, torture, and execution to maintain power.

But the threatened war on Iraq was not a humanitarian intervention in the sense that it would be waged primarily for the purpose of benefiting the Iraqi people. If Saddam Hussein had been overthrown in a palace coup and replaced by an equally repressive dictator who nonetheless was willing to cooperate in ridding the country of alleged weapons of mass destruction, there clearly would be no invasion. That said, it is important from a human rights perspective to stop the possible use of weapons of mass destruction when there is a credible threat of their use. However, any war to be fought in Iraq will be judged in significant part by the degree to which the attackers take into account the potential risks facing the Iraqi people, particularly in light of the atrocities that Saddam Hussein has shown himself capable of committing.

First, it will be important to examine whether the attackers did everything feasible to avoid civilian casualties by their own forces. That means, at minimum, avoiding such controversial practices as using cluster bombs near populated areas (as occurred during the Gulf War of 1991, the Yugoslav war of 1999, and the Afghan war of 2001–02). It means not using military force to target civilian morale or to attack political supporters of a regime who are not directly contributing to the military effort (as occurred in Yugoslavia). And it means taking all feasible precautions to avoid misidentifying targets, especially in the case of "targets of opportunity" when the review system is necessarily abbreviated (as occurred in all three above-noted wars but particularly in Afghanistan, where special operations forces in the field were used extensively to identify targets).

Second, it will be important to determine whether the United States and its allies took into account the history of abuse already suffered by the Iraqi people and made serious attempts to prevent its recurrence. As noted, on numerous occasions as part of the 1988 *Anfal* genocide, Saddam Hussein used chemical weapons against Iraqi Kurds. If upon a U.S. invasion the Iraqi president sees that the end of his rule is near, his history suggests that he might resume the slaughter by using any chemical or biological weapons in his possession to kill many of his own people, either in retaliation or in an effort to embarrass his attackers. During the 1991 uprising, Iraqi rebel forces, both Kurdish and Shi'a, demonstrated that they are capable of summarily executing government officials, Baath Party members, and their perceived supporters. Unless restrained during a new war, there is every reason to believe that they will pick up where they left off, but this time as perceived U.S. proxies. Also in 1991, some neighboring countries closed their borders to people fleeing the war in Iraq. Turkey, in particular, left Kurds to die of exposure to the winter cold on the mountains along its border. Facing the possibility of a renewed war, it publicly threatened to close its borders again.

The Bush administration took some steps in 2002 to prevent repetition of these abuses in anticipation of war. It warned Iraqi troops that they would be prosecuted if they used weapons of mass destruction. And it cautioned the relatively organized Kurdish forces against committing atrocities, although that message was more difficult to deliver to less organized Shi'a forces. But it remained an open question whether the administration could avoid repetition of the Kosovo tragedy, when unprepared U.S. troops were forced to watch from the sidelines as the forces of Slobodan Milosevic escalated their attacks on Kosovar Albanian civilians in response to the NATO bombing campaign. The stakes were particularly high because the possible availability of weapons of mass destruction in Iraq threatened killing on a much larger scale. The potential dangers that Iraqis faced heightened the importance of neighboring governments permitting them to flee and take refuge elsewhere.

One especially difficult issue concerned combatants taken prisoner. During the Afghan war, the United States took insufficient steps to prevent allied Northern Alliance forces from committing atrocities against prisoners. During the Gulf War, Iraq severely mistreated coalition prisoners of war. The urgency of preventing repetition of those abuses was complicated by the Bush administration's degrading of the Geneva Conventions at Guantánamo, since that made some arguments in defense of captured combatants more difficult to advance.

The Bush administration was also reticent about its postwar strategy. Having failed to repudiate its "warlord strategy" in Afghanistan, it left uncertainty about whether it would build the rule of law in Iraq. It spoke about bringing senior Iraqi officials to justice, but offered no guarantee of fair trials and independent tribunals. It remained vague about whether it would proceed against only a "dirty dozen" top officials or ensure at least some form of accountability for people farther down the chain of command. It made no offer to subject its own conduct and that of its allies to international scrutiny, leaving the impression that it might settle for victor's justice. The resolution of these issues would play an important part in determining whether, even with Saddam Hussein gone, possible war with Iraq would hold much promise of improving the plight of the Iraqi people.

CONCLUSION

The security threat posed by terrorism should not obscure the importance of human rights. Military or police action can be seductive. It leaves the impression that the problem is being addressed firmly, head-on. Concern with human rights, by contrast, may seem peripheral—of long-term utility, undoubtedly, but not a high immediate priority.

That view is profoundly mistaken. An antiterrorism policy that ignores human rights is a gift to the terrorists. It reaffirms the violent instrumentalism that breeds terrorism as it undermines the public support needed to defeat terrorism. A strong human rights policy cannot replace the actions of security forces, but it is an essential complement. A successful antiterrorism policy must endeavor to build strong international norms and institutions on human rights, not provide a new rationale for avoiding and undermining them.

NOTES

Introduction, *by Aryeh Neier*

1. *Laird v. Tatum*, 408 U.S. 1 (1972).

2. *United States v. United States District Court*, 407 U.S. 297 (1972).

3. *United States v. New York Times Co.*, 403 U.S. 713 (1971).

4. Timothy Egan, "In Sacramento, a Publisher's Questions Draw the Wrath of the Crowd," *New York Times*, December 21, 2001.

5. Michael Janofsky, "Cities Wary of Anti-terror Tactics Pass Civil Liberties Resolutions," *New York Times*, December 23, 2002.

6. Testimony, December 6, 2001.

7. Richard Hofstadter, *The Paranoid Style in American Politics and Other Essays* (New York: Vintage Books, 1967).

1. The Course of Least Resistance: Repeating History in the War on Terrorism, *by David Cole*

1. This chapter is adapted from "The New McCarthyism: Repeating History in the War on Terrorism," 38 Harvard Civil Rights and Civil Liberties Law Review 1 (2003). I am or was counsel in several of the cases discussed herein, including *Reno v. American-Arab Anti-Discrimination Committee*, 525 U.S. 471 (1998); *Turkmen v. Ashcroft*, CV-02-307 (E.D.N.Y. 2002); *Humanitarian Law Project, Inc. v. Reno*, 205 F.3d 1130 (9th Cir. 2000), *cert. denied*, 532 U.S. 904 (2001). Kate Didech provided excellent research assistance.

2. Ralph S. Brown, Jr., *Loyalty and Security: Employment Tests in the United States* (New Haven: Yale University Press, 1958), 14.

3. See e.g., Pam Belluck, "Hue and Murmur Over Curbed Rights," *New York Times*, November 17, 2001, B8; Jack Goldsmith and Cass R. Sunstein, "Military Tribunals and Legal Culture: What A Difference Sixty Years Makes" (University of Chicago Law School, Public Law and Legal Theory Working Paper No. 27, 2002), available at http://www.law.uchicago.edu/academics/publiclaw/resources/27.jg -cs.tribunals.pdf; Eric L. Muller, "12/7 and 9/11: War, Liberties, and the Lessons of History," *West Virginia Law Review* (2002); Marty Meehan, "More Tools Needed to Fight Terrorism," *Boston Herald*, October 3, 2001, 29; Jeffrey Rosen, "Liberty Wins—So Far; Bush Runs Into Checks and Balances in Demanding New Powers," *Washington Post*, September 15, 2002, B2; Jeffrey Rosen, "What Price Security? Testing the Resilience of American Values," *New York Times*, November 18, 2001, section 4, p. 1.

4. Brown, *supra* note 2 at 14–15.

5. Attorney General John Ashcroft, Prepared Remarks for the U.S. Mayors Conference, October 25, 2001, available at http://www.usdoj.gov/ag/speeches/2001/agcrisisremarks10_25.htm.

6. *United States v. Rahman,* 189 F.3d 88 (2d Cir. 1999).

7. Sedition Act of 1918, ch. 75, 40 Stat. 553 (repealed 1921).

8. Zechariah Chafee, Jr., *Free Speech in the United States* (Cambridge: Harvard University Press, 1948), 52.

9. *Gilbert v. Minnesota,* 254 U.S. 325 (1920); *Schenck v. United States,* 249 U.S. 47 (1919); *Frohwerk v. United States,* 249 U.S. 204 (1919); *Abrams v. United States,* 250 U.S. 616 (1920); *Debs v. United States,* 249 U.S. 211 (1919).

10. Peter Irons, "'Fighting Fair': Zechariah Chafee, Jr., the Department of Justice, and the 'Trial at the Harvard Club,'" 94 *Harvard Law Review* 1205 (1981).

11. I say "generally" because by its terms, the Smith Act punished speech—advocacy of the overthrow of the United States government by force or violence—and many Communists, including the national leadership of the party, were prosecuted for conspiracy to so advocate, and for conspiracy to organize a group to so advocate. See *United States v. Dennis,* 341 U.S. 494 (1951); Michael Belknap, *Cold War Political Justice: The Smith Act, the Communist Party, and American Civil Liberties* (Westport, CT: Greenwood Press, 1977); Arthur J. Sabin, *In Calmer Times: The Supreme Court and Red Monday* (Philadelphia: University of Pennsylvania Press, 1999); William M. Wiecek, "The Legal Foundations of Domestic Anticommunism: The Background of Dennis v. United States," 2001 *Supreme Court Review* 375 (2001).

12. Eleanor Bontecou, *The Federal Loyalty-Security Program* (Ithaca, NY: Cornell University Press, 1953), 171; see generally *id.* at 57–204 (on the makeup, evolution, and uses of the attorney general's lists).

13. *Yates v. United States,* 354 U.S. 298, 318 (1957). The *Yates* decision effectively ended prosecutions under the advocacy sections of the Smith Act. Sabin, *supra* note 11 at 10–11.

14. 444 U.S. 395 (1969).

15. *NAACP v. Claiborne Hardware,* 458 U.S. 886, 932 (1982).

16. 367 U.S. 203 (1961).

17. *Id.* at 224–25.

18. *Id.* at 224–25, 229–30.

19. 18 U.S.C.A. 2339B; 8 U.S.C. 1182(a)(3)(B)(iv)(VI) (West Supp. 2002); International Convention for the Suppression of the Financing of Terrorism (UN, 1999); see, e.g., Jeff Gerth and Judith Miller, "Report Says Saudis Fail to Crack Down on Charities That Finance Terrorists," *New York Times,* October 17, 2002, A20; Serge Schmemann, "U.N. Gets a Litany of Antiterror Plans," *New York Times,* January 12, 2002, A7; Kurt Eichenwalk, "Global Plan To Track Terror Funds," *New York Times,* December 19, 2001, B5.

20. John Walker Lindh, the so-called American Taliban, was charged with providing material support to two terrorist organizations by attending their training camps. *United States v. Lindh,* No. CR. 02-37-A (E.D. Va. October 4, 2002), available at http://news.findlaw.com/hdocs/docs/terrorism/uswlindh020502cmp.html. Lynne Stewart, the attorney for Sheikh Omar Abdel Rahman, has been charged with providing material support to an Egyptian terrorist organization by facilitating communications between the Sheikh and the group. *United States v. Sattar,* No. CR. 02-395 (S.D.N.Y. Apr. 4,

2002), available at http://news.findlaw.com/hdocs/docs/terrorism/ussattar040902ind.pdf. Five young men from Lackawanna, New York, have been charged under the material support statute for attending an Al Qaeda training camp. *United States v. Goba,* No. 02-M-107 (W.D.N.Y. October 21, 2002), available at http://news.findlaw.com/hdocs/docs/terrorism/usgoba102102ind.html. James Ujaama, a Seattle activist, has been charged with providing material support by planning to set up a training camp here for Al Qaeda. *United States v. Ujaama* (W.D. Wash. August 28, 2002), available at http://news.findlaw.com/hdocs/docs/terrorism/usujaama82802ind.pdf. A group in Portland has been charged under the material support statute for seeking to go fight in Afghanistan on behalf of Al Qaeda. *United States v. Battle,* CR-02-399-HA, available at http://news.findlaw.com/hdocs/docs/terrorism/usbattle100302ind.pdf. And a group of men in Detroit has been charged under the same statute for allegedly operating as an underground support unit for terrorists attacks and a "sleeper" operational combat cell. *United States v. Koubriti,* No. 01-80778 (E.D. Mich. August 28, 2002), available at http://news.findlaw.com/hdocs/docs/terrorism/uskoubriti82802ind.pdf.

21. John Mintz, "Muslim Charity Leader Indicted," *Washington Post,* October 10, 2002, A14; John Mintz, "U.S. Labels Muslim Charity as Terrorist Group," *Washington Post,* October 19, 2002, A2; John Mintz and Neely Tucker, "Judge Backs U.S. on Assets Seizure," *Washington Post,* August 10, 2002, A12.

22. 18 U.S.C.A. 2339B (West 2000 & Supp. 2002).

23. 8 U.S.C.A. §§ 1189(a)(1), (c)(2) (West 1999 & Supp. 2002) (setting forth criteria for designation of terrorist organizations).

24. The secretary of state's first designation under the law listed thirty organizations. 62 Fed. Reg. 52, 649–51 (October 8, 1997). The list has expanded since September 11, but still includes only thirty-five organizations. Fact Sheet, Office of Counterterrorism, U.S. Department of State, Foreign Terrorist Organizations (October 23, 2002), available at http://www.state.gov/s/ct/rls/fs/2002/12389.htm. Prominent terrorist groups like the Irish Republican Army (IRA) are notably not on the list.

25. *Peoples' Mojahedin Organization of Iran v. U.S. Sec. of State,* 182 F.3d 17, 23 (D.C. Circuit 1999)— Secretary of state's determination that an organization's activities undermine our foreign policy for purposes of designating terrorist groups is a judicially unreviewable political question—*cert. denied,* 529 U.S. 1104 (2000).

26. *Humanitarian Law Project v. Reno,* 205 F.3d 1130 (9th Circuit 2000), *cert. denied,* 532 U.S. 904 (2001).

27. *Buckley v. Valeo,* 424 U.S. 1, 65–66 (1976), quoting *NAACP v. Alabama,* 357 U.S. 449, 460 (1958). Monetary contributions to political organizations are a protected form of association and expression. *Id.* at 16–17, 24–25; *Roberts v. United States Jaycees,* 468 U.S. 609 (1984)—The First Amendment protects a nonprofit group's right to solicit funds; *Citizens Against Rent Control v. Berkeley,* 454 U.S. 290, 295–96 (1981)—monetary contributions to a group are a form of "collective expression" protected by the right of association; *Service Employees International Union v. Fair Political Practices Commission,* 955 F.2d 1312, 1316 (9th Cir)—"contributing money is an act of political association that is protected by the First Amendment," *cert. denied,* 505 U.S. 1230 (1992); *In re Asbestos Litigation,* 46 F.3d 1284, 1290 (3d Cir. 1994)—contributions to political organization are constitutionally protected absent specific intent to further the group's illegal ends.

28. *Humanitarian Law Project v. Reno,* 205 F.3d at 1134; Gerald Neuman, "Terrorism, Selective Deportation and the First Amendment after Reno v. AADC," 14 *Georgetown Immigration Law Journal* 313, 330 (2000).

29. Brief for the United States on Reargument at 8, *Scales v. United States,* 367 U.S. 203 (arguing that "specific intent" showing is unnecessary "on the principle that knowingly joining an organization

with illegal objectives contributes to the attainment of those objectives because of the support given by membership itself").

30. See 18 U.S.C.A. § 2339A (West Supp. 2002) (criminalizing material support of terrorist activity); Racketeer Influenced and Corrupt Organizations Act (RICO), 18 U.S.C.A. §§1961–68 (West 2000 & Supp. 2002); Money Laundering Control Act of 1986, 18 U.S.C.A. §§1956–57 (West 2000 & Supp. 2002) (forfeiture of property is authorized by 18 U.S.C.A. §§ 981–82) (West 2000 & Supp. 2002).

31. *Humanitarian Law Project v. Reno,* 205 F.3d at 1133.

32. *United States v. Goba,* No. 02-M-107 (W.D.N.Y. October 21, 2002), available at http://news.find law.com/hdocs/docs/terrorism/usgoba102102ind.html.

33. 50 U.S.C. §§ 21–24 (2000).

34. See generally Gregory Sidak, "War, Liberty, and Enemy Aliens," 67 *N.Y.U. Law Rev* 1402 (1992).

35. See David Cole, "Enemy Aliens," 54 *Stanford Law Rev* 953, 989–94 (2002).

36. See generally Robert K. Murray, *Red Scare: A Study in National Hysteria, 1919–1920* (Minneapolis: University of Minnesota Press, 1955); William Preston, Jr., *Aliens and Dissenters: Federal Suppression of Radicals, 1903–1933* (Cambridge: Harvard University Press, 1963), 208–37; Louis F. Post, *The Deportations Delirium of Nineteen Twenty: A Personal Narrative of a Historic Official Experience* (New York: Da Capo Press, 1923).

37. Post, *supra* note 36 at 307.

38. See Preston, *supra* note 36 at 221 (estimating 10,000 arrests); Post, *supra* note 36 at 167 (estimating about 6,000 arrest warrants issued, and about 4,000 warrants executed). Many aliens were arrested without warrants. Preston, *supra* note 36 at 221; Post, *supra* note 36 at 96, 111.

39. Preston, *supra* note 36 at 214–18; Murray, *supra* note 36 at 211. Prior to December 31, 1919, Rule 22, which governed immigration hearings, provided that:

> At the beginning of the hearing under the warrant of arrest the alien shall be allowed to inspect the warrant of arrest and all evidence on which it was issued, and shall be apprised that he may be represented by counsel.

As amended that day, the rule read:

> Preferably at the beginning of the hearing under the warrant of arrest *or at any rate as soon as such hearing has proceeded sufficiently in the development of the facts to protect the Government's interests,* the alien shall be allowed to inspect the warrant of arrest and all the evidence on which it was issued and shall be apprised that thereafter he may be represented by counsel.

Constantine Panunzio, *The Deportation Cases of 1919–1920* (New York: Da Capo Press, 1921), 37 (emphasis added).

40. Post, *supra* note 36 at 167.

41. *Id.* at 192.

42. Robert D. Warth, "The Palmer Raids," 48 *S. Atlantic Q.* 1, 18 (1949).

43. *Fong Yue Ting v. United States,* 149 U.S. 698 (1893)—holding that deportation is not punishment, and does not require protections of criminal process.

44. *Aguilera-Enriquez v. INS,* 516 F.2d 565 (6th Circuit 1975), *cert. denied,* 423 U.S. 1050 (1976)—no constitutional right to counsel for indigent in deportation hearings; 8 U.S.C. 1229a(b)(4)(A) (2000)—statutory right to counsel "at no expense to the Government." Congress has forbidden legal

services attorneys from representing foreign nationals who are here in violation of their visas. See Omnibus Consolidated Rescissions and Appropriations Act of 1996, Pub. L. No. 104–134, § 504(a) (11), 110 Stat. 1321, prohibiting the use of Legal Service Corporation funding for unlawful aliens.

45. The Japanese Immigrant Case (*Yamataya v. Fisher*), 189 U.S. 86 (1903)—holding that aliens are entitled to due process in proceedings to expel them.

46. See generally, David Cole, "Secrecy, Guilt by Association, and the Terrorist Profile," 15 *Journal of Law and Religion* 267 (2001–02), which discusses the use of secret evidence in immigration proceedings.

47. *Supplementary Detailed Staff Reports on Intelligence Activities and the Rights of Americans, Book III, Final Report of the Select Committee to Study Governmental Operations with Respect to Intelligence Activities,* S. Rep. No. 94-755, 94th Cong., 2d Sess. 438–39 (1976), hereinafter Church Committee Staff Report. For an excellent summary of the detention program, see Robert Justin Goldstein, "An American Gulag? Summary Arrest and Emergency Detention of Political Dissidents in the United States," 10 *Columbia Human Rights Law Review* 541, 558–61 (1978).

48. Church Committee Staff Report, *supra* note 47 at 438–41; Hearings Before the Senate Select Committee to Study Governmental Operations with Respect to Intelligence Activities, 94th Cong. 1st Sess., Vol. 6 at 416–26, 657–65.

49. Act of September 25, 1971, P.L. 92–128, §2, 85 Stat. 347.

50. Richard Longaker, "Emergency Detention: The Generation Gap 1950–71," 27 *Western Politics Quarterly* 395 (1974).

51. Wiecek, *supra* note 11 at 427.

52. Church Committee Staff Report, *supra* note 47 at 441, 445–46.

53. Robert Goldstein, *Political Repression in Modern America from 1870 to the Present* (Boston: G. K. Hall, 1978), 419.

54. Church Committee Staff Report, *supra* note 47 at 87, 509–18.

55. 18 U.S.C. § 4001(a)(2000).

56. Robert Justin Goldstein, "An American Gulag?"; *supra* note 47, at 572 (1978).

57. Ralph Brown, *supra* note 2 at 5–7; Eleanor Bontecou, *The Federal Loyalty-Security Program* (Ithaca, NY: Cornell University Press, 1953), 106–10.

58. *Bailey v. Richardson*, 182 F.2d 46, 57–58 (D.C. Cir. 1950), *aff'd by an equally divided Court,* 341 U.S. 918 (1951); see generally, Alan Barth, *The Loyalty of Free Men* (New York: Viking Press, 1951), 111–14.

59. 182 F.2d at 66.

60. *Id.* at 58.

61. Laura Kalman, *Abe Fortas: A Biography* (New Haven: Yale University Press, 1990), 137–41.

62. Brown, *supra* note 2 at 181–82.

63. Michael Linfield, *Freedom Under Fire: U.S. Civil Liberties in Times of War* (Boston: South End Press, 1990), 86–87.

64. Barth, *supra* note 58 at 62.

65. Ellen Schrecker, *Many Are the Crimes: McCarthyism in America* (Boston: Little, Brown, 1998), xiv–xv; Barth, *supra* note 58 at 64–66 (on Hollywood's blacklisting of individuals who refused to testify before HUAC).

66. Zechariah, Chafee, Jr., *To the American People: A Report upon the Illegal Practices of the United States Department of Justice* (Washington, D.C.: National Popular Government League, 1920).

67. At a recent American Bar Association panel on which I appeared, a Justice Department official objected to the characterization of the enemy combatants' detention as "incommunicado," pointing out that the detainees are allowed visits from the International Red Cross. But that's about it. Those held as enemy combatants are not permitted phone calls, visits, or contact with anyone outside the military other than the International Red Cross and, on occasion, a diplomatic mission. They are permitted to send and receive only highly censored personal mail. They are kept in their cells for all but thirty minutes a week, unless taken out for interrogation. And they cannot consult a lawyer. Joseph Lelyveld, "In Guantánamo," *New York Review of Books,* November 7, 2002, 62.

68. *Id.*

69. Attorney General John Ashcroft. Prepared Remarks for the U.S. Mayors Conference, October 25, 2001, available at http://www.usdoj.gov/ag/speeches/2001/agcrisisremarks1025.htm ("Taking suspected terrorists in violation of the law off the streets and keeping them locked up is our clear strategy to prevent terrorism within our borders."); see also Department of Justice, "Attorney General Ashcroft Outlines Foreign Terrorist Tracking Task Force," October 31, 2001, available at http://www.usdoj.gov/ag/speeches/2001/agcrisisremarks1031.htm.

70. The Justice Department reported that 1,182 individuals had been detained in the first seven weeks of the post–September 11 investigation. Dan Eggen and Susan Schmidt, "Count of Released Detainees Is Hard to Pin Down," *Washington Post,* November 6, 2001, A10 (reporting 1,182 detained); Todd S. Purdum, "A Nation Challenged: The Attorney General; Ashcroft's About-Face on the Detainees," *New York Times,* November 28, 2001, B7 (reporting over 1,100 detained); Matthew Brzezinski, "Hady Hassan Omar's Detention," *New York Times,* October 27, 2002, sec. 6, p. 50 (reporting 1,147 detainees at last count in November 2001). After November 5, 2001, facing criticism that it had arrested so many people but had charged no one with any terrorist crimes, the Justice Department simply stopped issuing a running tally of its detentions. Amy Goldstein and Dan Eggen, "U.S. to Stop Issuing Detention Tallies," *Washington Post,* November 9, 2001, A16.

It seems clear that the pace of detentions dropped after the first several months, although it is also clear that the preventive detention campaign continues to this day. If detentions had continued at the initial rate of 1,182 in seven weeks, or approximately 600 a month, there would be more than 8,000 arrests after fourteen months. Even assuming that the rate of arrests dropped off substantially after the first few weeks, it is likely that they would now number in the range of 2,000. The Justice Department admitted in May 2002, for example, that it had detained nearly 600 persons in its "Absconder Apprehension Initiative," which selectively targets aliens with deportation orders who come from Arab countries. Dan Eggen, "U.S. Search Finds 585 Deportee Absconders," *Washington Post,* May 30, 2002, A7. See also "Guidance for Absconder Apprehension Initiative," Memorandum from the Deputy Attorney General, January 25, 2002. Several hundred more have been arrested in connection with the INS's Special Registration program, which requires nationals of twenty-five predominantly Arab and Muslim countries to report, register, and be photographed and fingerprinted. Thus, the government's own figures from early November 2001, plus its reported detentions under the Absconder Apprehension Initiative and Special Registration Program, exceed 2,000 persons, not counting others detained on immigration, criminal, and material witness charges since November 2001.

71. See generally Cole, *supra* note 35 at 960–65; Human Rights Watch, *Presumption of Guilt: Human Rights Abuses of Post–September 11 Detainees* (August 15, 2002), available at http://www.hrw.org/reports/2002/us911/Index.htm#TopOfPage.

72. Danny Hakim, "Four Are Charged with Belonging to a Terror Cell," *New York Times,* August 29, 2002, A1 (reporting that three of the four men charged as part of a Detroit terror cell were initially arrested during post–9/11 preventive detention sweeps, and also reporting on indictment of James Ujaama); Desmond Butler with Alan Cowell, "Swedish Police Rush to Trace the Trail of Hijacking Suspect," *New York Times,* September 2, 2002, A4 (reporting that Ujaama had been detained since July).

73. Remarks of Attorney General John Ashcroft, U.S. Attorneys Conference, New York City, October 1, 2002, available at http://www.justice.gov/ag/speeches/2002/100102agremarkstousattorneysconfer ence.htm; Lawyers' Committee for Human Rights, *A Year of Loss: Reexamining Civil Liberties Since September 11* (September 5, 2002), p. 15, citing Letter from Assistant Attorney General Daniel J. Bryant, U.S. Department of Justice, to Senator Carl Levin, Chairman of Permanent Subcommittee on Investigations, Senate Commission on Governmental Affairs (July 3, 2002).

74. 50 U.S.C. § 1701(a) (2000).

75. Exec. Order No. 12,947, 3 C.F.R. 319 (1995), reprinted in 50 U.S.C. § 1701 (2000).

76. *Id.* at § 1(a)(iii).

77. Exec. Order No. 13,224 § 1(d), 3 C.F.R. 786, (2001), reprinted in 50 U.S.C.A § 1701, (West Supp. 2002).

78. Uniting and Strengthening America by Providing Appropriate Tools Required to Intercept and Obstruct Terrorism (USA PATRIOT) Act of 2001, Pub. L. 107–56, 115 Stat. 272, § 106 (amending 50 U.S.C. §§ 1702(a)(1)(B) and adding 1702(c)).

79. *Global Relief Foundation, Inc. v. O'Neill,* 207 F.Supp.2d 779 (N.D. Ill. 2002).

80. *Holy Land Foundation for Relief and Development v. Ashcroft,* 219 F.Supp.2d 57 (D.D.C. 2002).

81. I develop this theme at much greater length in David Cole, "Enemy Aliens," *supra* note 35, and in a book of the same name, to be published by The New Press in September 2003.

82. Oren Gross, "Cutting Down Trees: Law-Making Under the Shadow of Great Calamities," in *The Security of Freedom: Essays on Canada's Anti-Terrorism Bill,* ed. Ronald Daniels, Patrick Macklem, and Kent Roach (Toronto: University of Toronto Press, 2001), 39.

83. *Id.* at 40–42.

84. See, e.g., Zbigniew Brzezinski, "Confronting Anti-American Grievances," *New York Times,* September 1, 2002, sec. 4, p. 9; Thomas Friedman, "Tone It Down a Notch," *New York Times,* October 2, 2002, A27; Frank Bruni, "Europe Pauses and Grieves, But Takes Issue With U.S.," *New York Times,* September 12, 2002, B1; Neil MacFarquhar, "Threats and Responses: Security; For Americans in Mideast, Daily Balance of Risk," *New York Times,* October 31, 2002, A12; Raymond Bonner, "Southeast Asia Remains Fertile For Al Qaeda," *New York Times,* October 28, 2002, A1; Craig A. Smith, "Saved by U.S., Kuwait Now Shows Mixed Feelings," *New York Times,* October 12, 2002, A11.

2. How Democracy Dies: The War on Our Civil Liberties, *by Nancy Chang*

1. Nancy Chang is the Senior Litigation Attorney at the Center for Constitutional Rights, a progressive nonprofit legal and educational organization located in New York City. She is currently working on several lawsuits that challenge antiterrorism measures discussed in this article. She is the author of *Silencing Political Dissent: How Post–September 11 Anti-Terrorism Measures Threaten Our Civil Liberties* (New York: Seven Stories Press, 2002).

2. Uniting and Strengthening America by Providing Appropriate Tools Required to Intercept and Obstruct Terrorism Act of 2001, Pub. L. No. 107–56.

3. The Homeland Security Act of 2002, Pub. L. No. 107–296.

4. See Adam Clymer, "Antiterrorism Bill Passes; U.S. Gets Expanded Powers," *New York Times,* October 26, 2001, A1; Robin Toner and Neil A. Lewis, "House Passes Terrorism Bill Much Like Senate's, but With 5-Year Limit," *New York Times,* October 13, 2001, B6; Mary Leonard, "Civil Liberties," *Boston Globe,* September 21, 2001, A13; Jonathan Krim, "Anti-Terror Push Stirs Fears for Liberties; Rights Groups Unite to Seek Safeguards," *Washington Post,* September 18, 2001, A17.

5. See Nat Hentoff, "Terrorizing the Bill of Rights," *Village Voice,* November 20, 2001, 32 (quoting Barney Frank as stating, "This was the least democratic process for debating questions fundamental to democracy I have ever seen. A bill drafted by a handful of people in secret, subject to no committee process, comes before us immune from amendment."); Jill Zuckerman, "Bill Ok'd to Expand Antiterror Powers," *Chicago Tribune,* October 31, 2001, 1.

6. See Jesse Walker, "No More Surprises; Government Doesn't Need More Power," *Milwaukee Journal Sentinel,* May 26 2002, 01J.

7. Statement of U.S. Senator Russell Feingold, "On the Anti-Terrorism Bill," October 25, 2001.

8. See Dan Balz, "Gore: Bush Loses Terror Focus," *Washington Post,* November 21, 2002, A16.

9. See Timothy Burger, "Senate OK's Homeland Security Bill," *Daily News,* November 20, 2002, 30.

10. See Homeland Security Act § 214(a)(1)(A); Sabrina Eaton, "Liberals, Conservatives Upset about the Secrecy Provision," *Plain Dealer,* November 25, 2002, A4; David Firestone and Elisabeth Bumiller, "Stalemate Ends in Bush Victory on Terror Bill," *New York Times,* November 13, 2002, A18. The term "critical infrastructure" is defined at 42 U.S.C. § 5195c(e) as "systems and assets, whether physical or virtual, so vital to the United States that the incapacity or destruction of such systems and assets would have a debilitating impact on security, national economic security, national public health or safety, or any combination of those matters."

11. See Homeland Security Act § 232(b)(2). The Federal Advisory Committee Act is codified at 5 U.S.C. App.

12. See, e.g., Homeland Security Act § 891 *et seq.;* William Safire, "You Are a Suspect," *New York Times,* November 14, 2002, A35.

13. The Homeland Security Act has been described as "interest-laced" because it includes measures "protecting such special interests as pharmaceutical firms and former airport screening companies, [as well as] measures that let companies hide environmental or public health threats behind a department-provided security mantle." Editorial, "Homeland Security; New Department Offers Efficiency, But Also Poses Risks," *Buffalo News,* November 27, 2002, B10.

14. This article does not discuss the myriad antiterrorism laws that have been passed by state and local legislatures across the United States following the September 11 attacks. Like their federal counterparts, these laws threaten to criminalize speech and protest activities, limit the availability of public records, and expand government surveillance powers. See Eve Pell, "Homeland Security x 50," *The Nation,* June 3, 2002.

15. See Human Rights Watch, *World Report 2002* (Human Rights Watch, New York, 2002), 487–489 (section on United States), available at www.hrw.org/wr2k2; Amnesty International, "Amnesty International's Concerns Regarding post-September 11 Detentions in the USA" (Amnesty International,

London, 2002), available at <http://web.amnesty.org/ai.nsf/Index/AMR510442002?OpenDocument &of=COUNTRIES%5CUSA>.

16. See *Hamdi v. Rumsfeld*, 316F.3d450 (4th Circuit 2003); *Padilla v. Bush*, 233 F. Supp. 2'd 564 (S.D.N.Y. 2002).

17. See USA PATRIOT Act § 224(b).

18. See James Madison, *The Federalist No. 47*, p. 304, Isaac Krammick, ed., 1987.

19. See e.g., Adam Clymer, "Government Openness at Issue at Bush Holds Onto Records," *New York Times*, January 3, 2003, A1.

20. The Freedom of Information Act is codified at 5 U.S.C. § 552.

21. "Memorandum for Heads of All Federal Departments and Agencies," from John Ashcroft, Attorney General, October 12, 2001. See also Ruth Rosen, "The Day Ashcroft Foiled FOIA," *San Francisco Chronicle*, January 7, 2002, D4.

22. *Center for National Security Studies v. U.S. Department of Justice*, 215 F. Supp. 2d 94, 103 (D.D.C. 2002).

23. *Id.* at 96 (citation omitted).

24. *Center for National Security Studies v. U.S. Department of Justice*, No. 01-2500 (D.C.Cir.).

25. *Detroit Free Press v. Ashcroft*, 303 F.3d 681, 683 (6th Circuit 2002).

26. *North Jersey Media Group v. Ashcroft*, 308 F.3d 198, 219 (3rd Circuit 2002). The author is one of the attorneys representing the plaintiffs in this suit.

27. *Id.*

28. See Jim Vandehei, "Bush Directive Limiting Classified Data to Congress after Leak Angers Leaders," *Wall Street Journal*, October 10, 2001, A6.

29. See "ACLU Demands DOJ Unveil Surveillance Data," *United Press International*, August 21, 2002.

30. "Special Administrative Measure for the Prevention of Acts of Violence and Terrorism," 66 Fed. Reg. 55062 (October 31, 2001), amending 28 C.F.R. §501.3(d).

31. USA PATRIOT Act § 223(c)(1)(e), amending 18 U.S.C. § 2712.

32. James Madison, Speech in the Virginia Constitutional Convention (December 2, 1829).

33. *In re All Matters Submitted to the Foreign Intelligence Surveillance Court*, 218 F. Supp. 2nd 611 (Foreign Intelligence Surveillance Court 2002), *abrogated on other grounds, sub. nom In re: Sealed Case No. 02-001*, 310 F.3rd 717 (Foreign Intelligence Surveillance Court Rev. 2002). The Foreign Intelligence Surveillance Act is codified at 50 U.S.C. § 1801 *et seq.*

34. *Id.* at 620.

35. See Ted Bridis, "FBI Memo Cites Agents' Blunders; Lapses in Terror, Spy Probes Listed," *Chicago Tribune*, October 10, 2002, 18.

36. Since 1983, the United States government has defined the term "terrorism," "for statistical and analytical purposes," as the "premeditated, politically motivated violence perpetrated against noncombatant targets by subnational groups or clandestine agents, usually intended to influence an audience." See *Patterns of Global Terrorism 2001*, U.S. Department of State (May 2002), xvi.

37. See USA PATRIOT Act § 802, amending 18 U.S.C. § 2331. The definition of "terrorism" in the Homeland Security Act subsumes and expands the definition of "domestic terrorism" in the USA PA-

TRIOT Act. For the purposes of the Homeland Security Act, "terrorism" includes "any activity that involves an act that is dangerous to human life or potentially destructive of critical infrastructure or key resources, and is a violation of the criminal laws of the United States or of any State or other subdivision of the United States, and appears to be intended to intimidate or coerce a civilian population, to influence the policy of a government by intimidation or coercion, or to affect the conduct of a government by mass destruction, assassination, or kidnapping." Homeland Security Act § 2(15).

38. *The Attorney General's Guidelines on General Crimes, Racketeering Enterprise and Terrorism Enterprise Investigations* (2002) ("Ashcroft Guidelines"). See also Adam Liptak, "Changing the Standard: Despite Civil Liberties Fears, F.B.I. Faces No Legal Obstacles on Domestic Spying" *New York Times,* May 31, 2002, A1.

39. Ashcroft Guidelines at 16.

40. *Id.* at 4–5; *Brandenburg v. Ohio,* 395 U.S. 444, 447–48 (1969).

41. Ashcroft Guidelines at 9 and 17.

42. *Id.* at 21–22.

43. See 18 U.S.C. § 2339A(b).

44. See Safire, *supra* note 12.

45. See, e.g., USA PATRIOT Act §§ 314, 351, 355, 356, 358, 365, 366, 505, and 507. The Supreme Court long ago established that searches and seizures of personal records maintained by a third party are not covered by the Fourth Amendment because the subject of the records, having shared the information in the records with the third party, cannot claim a reasonable expectation of privacy in the records. See, e.g., *United States v. Miller,* 425 U.S. 435, 443 (1976).

46. Dan Eggen, "Justice Made Limited Use of New Powers, Panel Told," *Washington Post,* October 18, 2002, A11.

47. See Ted Bridis, "Number of U.S. Wiretaps Down Last Year," *Associated Press,* April 30, 2002.

48. *Id.*

49. See Miles Bensor, "Tech Firms Feel Heat as U.S. Snoops on Citizens," *Times Picayune,* April 28, 2002, 1.

50. *Id.,* quoting Professor Peter Swire, Ohio State University.

51. The probable cause requirement of the Fourth Amendment requires that law enforcement officers have reasonably trustworthy knowledge of facts and circumstances that are sufficient to warrant a prudent person to believe that an offense has been or is being committed. See, e.g., *Brinegar v. United States,* 338 U.S. 160, 175–76 (1949). This requirement is not met by a mere hunch or guess. *Id.*

52. 50 U.S.C. §§ 1804(a)(7)(B) and 1823(a)(7)(B).

53. USA PATRIOT Act § 218, amending 50 U.S.C. §§ 1804(a)(7)(B) and 1823(a)(7)(B).

54. *In re Sealed Case No. 02–001,* 310 F.3d 717.

55. *In re All Matters Submitted to the Foreign Intelligence Surveillance Court,* 218 F. Supp. 2nd 611.

56. *In re Sealed Case No. 02–001,* 310 F.3rd at 735.

57. See Adam Liptak, "In the Name of Security, Privacy for Me, Not Thee," *New York Times,* November 24, 2002, § 4, 1.

58. See Eric Lichtblau, "Justice Department Seeks to Use New Power in Terror Inquiries," *New York Times,* November 24, 2002, A1.

59. USA PATRIOT Act § 215, amending 50 U.S.C. §§ 1862 and 1863.

60. USA PATRIOT Act § 215, amending 50 U.S.C. § 1862(a)(1).

61. USA PATRIOT Act § 215, amending 50 U.S.C. § 1862(c)(1).

62. See 50 U.S.C. § 1862(b)(2)(B), prior to its amendment by USA PATRIOT Act § 215.

63. USA PATRIOT Act § 215, amending 50 U.S.C. § 1862(a)(1).

64. See 50 U.S.C. § 1862(a), prior to its amendment by USA PATRIOT Act § 215.

65. USA PATRIOT Act § 215, amending 50 U.S.C. § 1862.

66. See Julia Scheeres, "Librarians Split on Sharing Info," *Wired News,* January 16, 2003, at www.wired.com/news/privacy/0,1848,57256,00.html. See also Bill Marvel, "Is the FBI Watching What You're Reading?" *Bergen Record,* August 25, 2002, O-1.

67. See Library Research Center, Graduate School of Library and Information Science, University of Illinois, *Public Libraries and Civil Liberties Questionnaire; Public Libaries' Response to the Events of 9/11/2001; One Year Later,* at Question 15(a), available at http://www.lis.uiuc.edu/gslis/research/final results.pdf.

68. *Id.,* at Question 13(a).

69. USA PATRIOT Act § 213, amending 18 U.S.C. § 3103a. The definition of the term "adverse result" in Section 213 of the USA PATRIOT Act is borrowed from a statute establishing the standards under which the government may provide delayed notice when it searches stored e-mail and other wire and electronic communications—searches that are not nearly as intrusive as physical searches of one's home or office. The term is defined in 18 U.S.C. § 2705(a)(2) as: "(A) endangering the life or physical safety of an individual; (B) flight from prosecution; (C) destruction of or tampering with evidence; (D) intimidation of potential witnesses; or (E) otherwise seriously jeopardizing an investigation or unduly delaying a trial."

70. *Wilson v. Arkansas,* 514 U.S. 927, 929 (1995).

71. See David Johnston, "FBI Director Rejects Agency for Intelligence in the United States," *New York Times,* December 20, 2002, A22; Laura Sullivan, "Domestic Intelligence Agency Gains Support; FBI Struggles to Prevent New Office That Could Take Its Counterintelligence Role," *Baltimore Sun,* December 10, 2002, 3A.

72. Homeland Security Act §§ 201 and 202.

73. *Id.* § 201 (d)(14).

74. *Id.* §§ 221 and 222.

75. *Id.* §§ 891 and 892.

76. *Id.* § 201 (e)(2).

77. See Ann Davis, "FBI's Post-September 11 'Watch List' Mutates, Acquires Life of Its Own," *Wall Street Journal,* November 19, 2002, A1.

78. *Id.*

79. *Id.*

80. Attorney General John Ashcroft, "Prepared Remarks for the U.S. Mayors Conference," October 25, 2001. See also Dan Eggen, "Tough Anti-Terror Campaign Pledged," *Washington Post,* October 26, 2001, at A1; Karen Gullo, "Ashcroft Discusses New Powers," *Associated Press,* October 25, 2001.

81. See Todd S. Purdum, "Ashcroft's About-Face on the Detainees," *New York Times*, November 28, 2001, B7; Amy Goldstein and Dan Eggen, "U.S. to Stop Issuing Detention Tallies," *Washington Post*, November 9, 2001.

82. Tamar Lewin, "The Domestic Roundup: As Authorities Keep Up Immigration Arrests, Detainees Ask Why They Are Targets," *New York Times*, February 3, 2002, Section 1, 14.

83. See Susan Sachs, "U.S. Defends the Withholding of Jailed Immigrants' Names," *New York Times*, May 21, 2002, A17; David Firestone and Christopher Drew, "Al Qaeda Link Seen in Only a Handful of 1,200 Detainees," *New York Times*, November 29, 2001, A1.

84. See 66 Fed. Reg. 48334 (September 20, 2001) (amending 8 C.F.R. § 287.3(d)).

85. USA PATRIOT Act § 412(a), adding 8 U.S.C. § 1226A(a).

86. See *Zadvydas v. Davis*, 533 U.S. 678 (2001).

87. See *County of Riverside v. McLaughlin*, 500 U.S. 44 (1991).

88. See Christopher Drew and Judith Miller, "Though Not Linked to Terrorism, Many Detainees Cannot Go Home," *New York Times*, February 18, 2002.

89. See *Turkmen, et al., v. Ashcroft, et al.*, CV 02-2307 (E.D.N.Y.). The author is one of the attorneys representing the plaintiffs in this suit.

90. See USA PATRIOT Act § 414, amending 8 U.S.C. § 1365a; USA PATRIOT Act § 415, amending Pub. L. 106–215, § 3; 67 Fed. Reg. 67765–68 (November 6, 2002); 67 Fed. Reg. 70525–28 (November 22, 2002); 67 Fed. Reg. 77642–44 (December 18, 2002). See also Reuters, "Arab, Muslim Groups Sue INS, Ashcroft Over Detentions," *Washington Post*, December 25, 2002, A13.

91. See Steve Fainaru and Margot Williams, "Material Witness Law Has Many in Limbo," *New York Times*, November 24, 2002, A01 (reporting that at least forty-four individuals have been detained as material witnesses).

92. See 18 U.S.C. § 3144.

93. *U.S. v. Awadallah*, 202 F. Supp. 2nd 55, 58 (S.D.N.Y. 2002).

94. *Id.*

95. *In re the Application of the United States for a Material Witness Warrant, Pursuant to 18 U.S.C. § 3144, for John Doe*, 213 F. Supp. 2nd 287, 299 (S.D.N.Y. 2002).

96. *U.S. v. Awadallah*, No. 02–1269 (2nd Circuit).

97. See *Hamdi v. Rumsfeld*, 2003 U.S. App. LEXIS 198 (4th Circuit January 8, 2003); *Padilla v. Rumsfeld*, 2002 U.S. Dist. LEXIS 23086 (S.D.N.Y. 2002).

98. *Id.*

99. See Benjamin Weiser, "U.S. Asks Judge to Deny Terror Suspect Access to Lawyer, Saying It Could Harm Interrogation" *New York Times*, January 10, 2003, A11.

100. See, e.g., *Detroit Free Press v. Ashcroft*, 303 F.3d 681 (6th Circuit 2002); but see, e.g., *North Jersey Media Group*, 308 F.3d 219 (3d Circuit 2002).

101. See Alison Mitchell, "The 2002 Elections: Victorious Republicans Preparing a Drive for Bush Agenda and Judgeship Nominees," *New York Times*, November 7, 2002, A1.

102. Homeland Security Act §§ 880 and 1514.

103. Michael Janofsky, "Cities Wary of Antiterror Tactics Pass Civil Liberties Resolutions," *New York Times*, December 23, 2002, A1.

3. After 9/11: A Surveillance State?, *by Reg Whitaker*

1. Reg Whitaker, *The End of Privacy: How Total Surveillance Is Becoming a Reality* (New York: The New Press, 1999).

2. United States Department of the Treasury, Financial Crimes Enforcement Network, *Strategic Plan 2000–2005*, http://www.fineen.gov/finstrategicplan2000.paf.

3. Simon Davies, "Spies like US," *Daily Telegraph*, December 16, 1997.

4. P.L. 107–56, 115 Stat. 272 (2001), Uniting and Strengthening America by Providing Appropriate Tools Required to Intercept and Obstruct Terrorism (USA PATRIOT Act).

5. A relatively objective analysis is provided through the Congressional Research Service: Charles Doyle, CRS Report for Congress, *The USA PATRIOT Act: A Legal Analysis*, April 15, 2002. The Justice Department's own appreciation of the act can be found in Department of Justice, *Justice Department Accomplishments in the War on Terrorism: The Shift from Investigation to Prevention*, no date, pp. 18–29.

6. Electronic Privacy Information Center, *The USA PATRIOT Act.* http://www.epic.org/privacy/terrorism/usapatriot/; Electronic Frontier Foundation, *EFF Analysis of the Provisions of the USA PATRIOT Act That Relate to Online Activities*, October 31, 2001. http://www.eff.org/Privacy/Surveillance/Terrorism_militias/20011031_eff_usa_patriot_analysis.html; Timothy Lynch, "Breaking the Vicious Cycle: Preserving Our Liberties While Fighting Terrorism," Cato Institute, *Policy Analysis* 443, June 26, 2002.

7. Orin Kerr, "Internet Surveillance Law after the USA PATRIOT Act: The Big Brother That Isn't," George Washington University Law School, Public Law Research Paper No. 46; 97 *Northwestern University Law Review* (forthcoming, 2003). See Patricia Cohen, "9/11 Law Means More Snooping? Or Maybe Less?," *New York Times*, September 7, 2002.

8. An internal FBI e-mail message dated April 5, 2000 recounts how a pre–9/11 investigation of terrorists linked to Osama bin Laden went awry when CARNIVORE captured not only the communications of the court-authorized target, but also picked up e-mails of noncovered individuals, in violation of federal wiretap law: "FBI Docs Obtained by EPIC: Carnivore Hampered Terror Probe," *EPIC Alert 9/11*, June 5, 2002.

9. Declan McCullagh, "Anti-Attack Feds Push Carnivore," *Wired News*, September 12, 2001, reported that "Just hours after three airplanes smashed into the buildings . . . FBI agents began to visit Web-based, e-mail firms and network providers, according to engineers at those companies who spoke on condition of anonymity. . . . An administrator at one major network service provider said that FBI agents showed up at his workplace on Tuesday "with a couple of Carnivores, requesting permission to place them in our core, along with offers to actually pay for circuits and costs."

10. *U.S. Foreign Intelligence Surveillance Court*, Memorandum Opinion, May 17, 2002, available at: http://www.washingtonpost.com/wp-srv/onpolitics/transcripts/fisa_opinion.pdf. Philip Shenon, "Secret Court Says F.B.I. Aides Misled Judges in 75 Cases," *New York Times*, August 23, 2002; Dan Eggen and Susan Schmidt, "Secret Court Rebuffs Ashcroft: Justice Dept. Chided on Misinformation," *Washington Post*, August 23, 2002.

11. Philip Shenon, "Justice Dept. Denounces Secret Court on Wiretaps," *New York Times*, September 28, 2002.

12. United States Foreign Intelligence Surveillance Court of Review: In re: Sealed Case No. 02–001, consolidated with 02–002, on Motions for Review of Orders of the United States Foreign Intelligence

Surveillance Court (Nos. 02–662 and 02–968). Argued September 9, 2002, Decided November 18, 2002.

13. David G. Savage and Henry Weinstein, "Court Widens Wiretapping in Terror Cases," *Los Angeles Times,* November 19, 2002.

14. "A Green Light to Spy," *New York Times* editorial, November 19, 2002.

15. Dan Eggen, "Broad U.S. Wiretap Powers Upheld," *Washington Post,* November 19, 2002, A01.

16. Electronic Privacy Information Center (EPIC), *Alert* 9:23, November 19, 2002.

17. *Ibid,* 26–28.

18. Mary Minow, "The USA PATRIOT Act and Patron Privacy on Library Internet Terminals." LLRX.Com, February 15, 2002, http://www.llrx.com/features/usapatriotact.htm; Nat Hentoff, "Has the Attorney General Been Reading Franz Kafka?," *Village Voice,* February 9, 2002; Martin Kasindorf, "FBI's Reading List Worries Librarians," *USA Today,* December 17, 2002.

19. Herbert N. Foerstel, *Surveillance in the Stacks: The FBI's Library Awareness Program* (Westport, CT: Greenwood Press, 1991).

20. Statement by the president, "President signs Justice Appropriation Authorization Act," November 4, 2002.

21. http://www.aclu.org/SafeandFree/SafeandFree.cfm?ID=11276&c=206.

22. Critical infrastructures are defined under the PATRIOT Act as those "systems and assets, whether physical or virtual, so vital to the United states that the incapacity of destruction of such systems and assets would have a debilitating impact on security, national economic security, national public health or safety, or any combination of these matters" (Title X, Section 1016).

23. Society of Professional Journalists, "Homeland Security Bill Compromises FOI Act," November 13, 2002, http://www.spj.org/news.asp?ref=299.

24. See most recently: Attorney General, "New Guidelines to Share Information Between Federal Law Enforcement and the U.S. Intelligence Community," September 23, 2002. WWW.USDOJ.GOVTDD.

25. Dana Priest, "CIA Is Expanding Domestic Operations: More Offices, More Agents With FBI," *Washington Post,* October 23, 2002, A02.

26. Statement for the Record by Lieutenant General Michael V. Hayden, USAF, Director, National Security Agency, before the Joint Inquiry of the Senate Select Committee on Intelligence and the House Permanent Select Committee on Intelligence, October 17, 2002, http://intelligence.senate.gov/0210hrg/021017/hayden.pdf.

27. Manuel Castells, *The Internet Galaxy: Reflections on the Internet, Business, and Society* (Oxford, England: Oxford University Press, 2001), 10–29.

28. Dr. John Poindexter, Director, Information Awareness Office of DARPA, "Overview of the Information Awareness Office," remarks as prepared for delivery at DARPA Tech 2002 Conference, Anaheim, California, August 2, 2002, http://www.fas.org/irp/agency/dod/poindexter.html. See also John Markoff, "Pentagon Plans a Computer System That Would Peek at Personal Data of Americans," *New York Times,* November 9, 2002; Robert O'Harrow, Jr., "U.S. Hopes to Check Computers Globally: System Would Be Used to Hunt Terrorists," *Washington Post,* November 12, 2002, A04.

29. "Total Information Awareness," *Washington Post,* November 16, 2002, A20.

30. William Safire, "You Are a Suspect," *New York Times,* November 14, 2002.

31. Greg Krikorian, "When in Doubt, Kick Out," *Los Angeles Times,* October 30, 2002.

32. There are also sophisticated encryption systems for hiding messages in the digital coding for pictures, or sound messages, that are even more difficult to flag as suspicious, let alone decipher.

33. *Draft Strategy to Secure Cyberspace,* http://www.whitehouse.gov/pcipb/.

34. Joshua Green, "The Myth of Cyberterrorism," *Washington Monthly* (November 2002).

35. Brendan I. Koerner, "The Security Traders," *Mother Jones* (September–October 2002).

36. Alison Mitchell, "Industry Sees Opportunity in U.S. Quest for Security," *New York Times,* November 25, 2001.

37. Eric Pianin and Bill Miller, "Businesses Draw Line on Security: Firms Resist New Rules for Warding Off Terror," *Washington Post,* September 5, 2002, A01.

4. Secret Arrests and Preventive Detention, *by Kate Martin*

1. Kate Martin has served as director of the Center for National Security Studies, a civil liberties organization in Washington, D.C., since 1992. A graduate of Pomona College and the University of Virginia Law School, she has taught Strategic Intelligence and Public Policy at Georgetown University Law School, and also served as general counsel of the National Security Archive from 1995 to 2002. She has written extensively on national security and civil liberties issues and directed a project on intelligence reform in new democracies in Eastern Europe and Latin America. She has litigated in the field, including successfully suing the CIA for disclosure of the intelligence budget and preventing destruction of White House e-mail messages. She is currently lead counsel in the lawsuit for disclosure of the names of those jailed in secret since September 11.

2. Blackstone, *Commentaries on the Laws of England,* 335.

3. On November 5, 2001, the Justice Department said that 1,182 people had been detained as part of its investigation. After being asked for an accounting, the department stopped keeping a count, but its court filings demonstrate that more than a hundred people were picked up after November 5. Amy Goldstein and Dan Eggen, "U.S. to Stop Issuing Detention Tallies; Justice Dept. to Share Number in Federal Custody, INS Arrests," *Washington Post,* November 9, 2001.

4. The Justice Department refused to disclose how many people had lawyers.

5. Military Order of November 13, 2001—Detention, Treatment and Trial of Certain Non-Citizens in the War Against Terrorism, 66 Federal Register 57833, November 16, 2002; June 9, 2002 order by President George W. Bush to Secretary of Defense Donald Rumsfeld declaring Jose Padilla an enemy combatant.

6. Transcript: Press Conference with Attorney General John Ashcroft, Senate Minority Leader Trent Lott (R-MS), Senate Judiciary Committee Vice Chairman Orrin Hatch (R-UT), Senate Intelligence Committee Ranking Member Richard Shelby (R-AL), October 2, 2001, The U.S. Capitol (available from the Federal News Service).

7. *USA PATRIOT Act,* Pub. L. 107–56, Sec. 412.

8. That provision arguably conflicts with the recent Supreme Court ruling that aliens who have been found deportable, but whom no country is willing to accept, may *not* be jailed indefinitely. *Zadvydas v. Davis,* U.S. Supreme Court, June 28, 2001.

9. Memorandum by Judge Michael Creppy to all Immigration Judges, re "Cases Requiring Special Procedures," September 21, 2001, online: http://news.findlaw.com/hdocs/docs/aclu/creppy092101 memo.pdf.

10. See Ross E. Milloy and Michael Moss, "A Nation Challenged; The Dragnet; More Suspects are Detained in Search for Attack Answers," *New York Times,* September 26, 2001, B3; Karen Abbott, "Government Officials Silent about Detainees," *Rocky Mountain News,* September 26, 2001, A14; William Glaberson, "A Nation Challenged: The Arrests; Detainees' Accounts Are at Odds with Official Reports of an Orderly Investigation," *New York Times,* September 29, 2001, B2; Edward Hegstrom, "Foreign Student Tells of Beating by Inmates in Mississippi Cell," *Houston Chronicle,* September 29, 2001, A31; Macarena Hernandez, "Innocent Muslim Doctor Tells of Arrest, Two-Week Ordeal; In Wake of Attacks, Easily Explainable, Chance Facts Led FBI to Suspect Him," *Seattle-Post Intelligencer,* October 1, 2001, A1; David Johnston, "A Nation Challenged: Security; Detentions May Be Aimed at Deterring Other Attacks," *New York Times,* October 14, 2001, B3; Wayne Washington, "Fighting Terror/Security Concerns the Dragnet; As Probe Widens, Detainee on Hold," *Boston Globe,* October 14, 2001, A31.

11. Dale Lezon, "Passport Issue Becomes a Fiasco; Two Palestinians Wrongfully Jailed File to Recover Court Costs," *Houston Chronicle,* December 25, 2001.

12. Kimberly Hefling, "Evansville Men Released from Custody in Terrorism Investigation," Associated Press, October 20, 2001.

13. Rebecca Carr, "Anti-Terror Tactics Criticized at Senate Hearings," *Cox Newspapers,* December 5, 2001; Testimony of Michael Boyle before the Committee on the Judiciary of the United States Senate, December 4, 2001.

14. See, for example, Marisa Schultz, "Groups Decry Secrecy, Demand List of Prisoners," *Los Angeles Times,* October 30, 2001; Neil Lewis, "Detentions After Attacks Pass 1000 Says US," *New York Times,* October 30, 2001.

15. Letter to Attorney General Ashcroft from Senators Patrick Leahy, Russell Feingold, Ted Kennedy, and Representatives John Conyers, Jerrold Nadler, Robert C. Scott, and Sheila Jackson-Lee, October 31, 2001; and letter from Senator Leahy to Attorney General Ashcroft, November 7, 2001.

16. Attorney General Ashcroft, Press Briefing, November 27, 2001, online: http://www.usdoj.gov/ag/speeches/2001/agcrisisremarks11_27.htm.

17. *Center for National Security Studies, et al. v. Department of Justice* (U.S. District Court for the District of Columbia), No. 01–2500, online: www.cnss.org.

18. *Morrow v. District of Columbia* (U.S. Court of Appeals for the District of Columbia), 417 F. 2d 728, 1969.

19. *Dayton Newspapers, Inc. v. City of Dayton,* 341 N.E.2d 576, 579 (Ohio 1976) (Corrigan, J., concurring).

20. *The Political Writings of Thomas Jefferson: Representative Selections,* ed. Edward Dumbauld (Indianapolis: Bobbs-Merrill, 1955), 93.

21. The Sixth Amendment gives a criminal defendant the right to a public trial; the First Amendment protects the public's right to attend that trial. See Defendant's Reply in Support of Motion for Summary Judgment and Opposition to Plaintiffs' Motion for Summary Judgment, p. 19, *Center for National Security Studies, et al. v. Department of Justice,* online: www.cnss.org. Similarly, the due process clause of the Fifth Amendment prohibits jailing an individual in secret and, accordingly, the First Amendment protects the public's right to know whom the government has arrested.

22. Affidavits of James S. Reynolds and Dale Watson filed by the government in *Center for National Security Studies, et al. v. Department of Justice,* online: www.cnss.org.

23. The government's claim that it had to keep secret the names of nonterrorist detainees because the list would provide a road map to its investigation was further belied by the Justice Department's own repeated press conferences describing, for example, its project of interviewing thousands of Arabs and Muslims, including the questions and results of the interviews. See *Guidelines for Interviews Regarding International Terrorism,* Memorandum for All United States Attorneys, All Members of the Anti-Terrorism Task Forces, from Deputy Attorney General Larry Thompson, November 9, 2001; *5,000 Interviews Status Report,* Department of Justice Press Release, December 21, 2001; *Final Report on Interview Project,* memo to the Attorney and Deputy Attorney Generals from Kenneth L. Wainstein and J. Patrick Rowan, February 26, 2002.

Moreover, while professing concern about releasing the list of September 11 detainees, the government in fact took extraordinary measures to keep secret the names of all immigrants in jail in New Jersey, when there would have been no way of knowing which ones had been jailed as part of the September 11 investigation. When the ACLU of New Jersey sued under that state's open records law for the names of INS inmates in state jails, the Justice Department issued a new regulation ordering New Jersey to withhold the information. See 67 Federal Register 19508–11, April 22, 2002, ordering states to withhold information on INS detainees; *ACLU of New Jersey v. County of Hudson* (New Jersey Supreme Court), No. A-4100-01T5.

24. FBI Director Robert S. Mueller III, Statement for the Record, Joint Intelligence Committee Inquiry, September 26, 2002. Online: http://www.intelligence.senate.gov/0209hrg/020926/mueller.pdf.

25. See, for example, testimony of Attorney General Ashcroft, "Nature of the Terrorist Threat," Hearing of the House Select Homeland Security Committee chaired by Representative Richard K. Armey, July 11, 2002; Remarks of Attorney General Ashcroft at U.S. Attorneys Conference, October 1, 2002, online: http://www.usdoj.gov/ag/speeches/2002/100102agremarkstousattorneysconference. htm.

26. As a result, individuals were arrested and interrogated after they were deported. For example, see stories of Ibrahim Turkmen, Asif-ur-Rehman Saffi, and Syed Amjad Ali described in *Turkmen v. Ashcroft* (U.S. District Court for the Eastern District of New York), 02-CV-2307 (JG); and Steve Fainaru, "U.S. Deported 131 Pakistanis in Secret Airlift; Diplomatic Issues Cited; No Terror Ties Found," *Washington Post,* July 10, 2002, A1.

27. Creppy Memorandum, note 9 *supra.* July 3, 2002, letter from Assistant Attorney General Daniel J. Bryant to Senator Carl Levin.

28. See *North Jersey Media Group v. Ashcroft* (U.S. District Court for New Jersey), No. 02-967; and *Detroit Free Press, et al. v. Ashcroft* (U.S. District Court for the Eastern District of Michigan), No. 02-1437.

29. Statement of Associate Attorney General Jay Stephens Regarding the Sixth Circuit Decision in the Haddad Case, Friday, April 19, 2002, online: www.usdoj.gov/opa/pr/2002/August/02_opa_495.htm.

30. The court ruled that the names must be released under the Freedom of Information Act; it did not decide the constitutional claim. *Center for National Security Studies, et al. v. Department of Justice,* Memorandum Opinion, Judge Gladys Kessler, August 2, 2002. online: www.dcd.uscourts.gov/01 2500.pdf.

31. In *Detroit Free Press, et al. v. Ashcroft,* the Sixth Circuit Court of Appeals declared the closed hearings order unconstitutional; 303 F.3d 681 (Sixth Circuit 2002), online: http://laws.lp.findlaw.com/ 6th/02a0291p.html. In *North Jersey Media Group v. Ashcroft,* the Third Circuit Court of Appeals de-

clared it constitutional; 308 F.3d 198 (Sixth Cir. 2002), online: http://caselaw.lp.findlaw.com/data2/circs/3rd/022524p.pdf.

32. For example: Eunice Moscoso, "Detainees Must be ID'd: Court Rules Against Feds on 9/11 Suspects," *Atlanta Journal-Constitution,* August 3, 2002, Sec A1; Anne Gearan, "Judge: Release Names of Detainees," *Bloomington Herald-Times,* August 3, 2002, A1; Frank James, "Judge Orders U.S. to Name Detainees: Secrecy Called 'Odious;' Government Says It's Vital," *Chicago Tribune,* August 3, 2002, A,1.

33. "The War on Civil Liberties," *New York Times,* September 10, 2002, A24. See also "A Fine Balance," *Fort Worth Star-Telegram,* August 12, 2002; "Names Please: a Judge Orders Identification of Detainees," *Pittsburgh Post-Gazette,* August 7, 2002; "Secret Detentions Violate American Values," *Seattle Times,* August 7, 2002; see also, *Baltimore Sun* and *Boston Globe,* August 9, 2002; *New York Times,* August 6, 2002; *Milwaukee Journal Sentinel,* August 14, 2002; and *Washington Post,* August 10, 2002. The American Bar Association also called for release of the names and condemned the secrecy. American Bar Association Resolution 115B, approved by the ABA House of Delegates at the 2002 Annual Meeting.

34. In his July 11, 2002, testimony to Congress, for example, the attorney general boasted about the terrorism investigation, claiming that it had resulted in some 86 criminal convictions and 417 deportations, but failed to mention that those convictions and deportations were unrelated to terrorism.

35. None of the four declarations filed by the Justice Department in the case claimed that *any* of the detainees was involved in terrorism or even had any knowledge about terrorism. See Reynolds and Watson declarations filed in *Center for National Security Studies, et al. v. Department of Justice.* When the government was forced to tell a court, it was careful to say no more about the detainees than "evidence [initially] suggested they might have connections with, or possess information pertaining to, terrorist activity against the United States."

36. Of the 752 people detained on immigration charges, less than five were charged with terrorism-related immigration charges. See INS Special Interest List filed by the government in *Center for National Security Studies, et al. v. Department of Justice.* The government provided 108 names of individuals charged with mostly minor federal crimes. See Reynolds Supplemental Affidavit and list of criminal defendants filed by the government in *Center for National Security Studies, et al. v. Department of Justice.* Only one individual was criminally charged in the attacks, and he was detained before September 11. Three additional individuals named on the list of criminal defendants were charged with terrorism-related offenses, although not in connection with the September 11 attacks. See Douglas Farah and Tom Jackman, "6 Accused of Conspiracy to Aid in Terror Attacks," *Washington Post,* August 29, 2002, A1.

37. See Amy Goldstein, "A Deliberate Strategy of Disruption: Massive, Secret Detention Effort Aimed Mainly at Preventing More Terror," *Washington Post,* November 4, 2001.

38. District Court Memorandum Opinion, p. 18, *Center for National Security Studies et al. v. Department of Justice.*

39. All but twelve of the criminal defendants have Arabic names, and those twelve include the individuals charged with assisting the hijackers to obtain false documents without knowing their plans. Nearly all of the INS detainees are identified as nationals of Arab or Muslim countries. See INS Special Interest List filed by the government in *Center for National Security Studies et al. v. Department of Justice.*

40. Supplemental Declaration of James Reynolds; Department of Justice Memorandum in Support of Defendant's Motion for Summary Judgment, p. 23, filed in *Center for National Security Studies et al. v.*

Department of Justice. See also Department of Justice, "An Update on Detentions Conducted by the Justice Department Following 9–11," December 11, 2002, online: www.usdoj.gov.

41. The general rule is that an individual may not be jailed before trial unless the government makes an individualized showing that the person poses either a risk of flight or a danger to the community if released on bond. This rule is based on the Sixth Amendment's prohibition against excessive bail, the protection against imprisonment without probable cause of criminal activity, found in the Fourth Amendment's prohibition of unreasonable seizures, and the Fifth Amendment's prohibition of deprivations of liberty without due process of law.

42. See the list of criminal defendants released by the Justice Department in *Center for National Security Studies et al. v. Department of Justice,* listing charges such as credit card fraud, illegal entry into the country, and falsifying information on an asylum application. See, for example, Benjamin Weiser, "Threats and Responses: Sentencing; Ex-Suspect Expects Deportation," *New York Times,* September 19, 2002, A25; Steve Fainaru, "Sept. 11 Detainee Is Ordered Deported; Almarabh Pleaded Guilty to Illegal Entry, Denies Terrorism Links," *Washington Post,* September 4, 2002, A10; Seth Hettena, "Student Suspected of Aiding Hijackers in San Diego Is Sentenced," *Associated Press,* October 2, 2002.

43. Indeed, the Justice Department claimed new powers unilaterally to hold persons in jail pretrial on immigration charges even when an immigration judge had ordered bail. On October 29, 2002, the Department of Justice announced a new rule giving itself the authority to override any decision by an immigration judge to grant bail. The government would no longer have to persuade an appeals panel that bail should be denied while it appealed.

44. See Dan Eggen, "Long Wait for Filing of Charges Common for Sept. 11 Detainees; Delays Reasonable, INS Officials Say," *Washington Post,* January 19, 2002, A12.

45. Attorney General Ashcroft, "Reorganization and Mobilization of the Nation's Justice and Law Enforcement Resources," November 8, 2002, online: http://www.usdoj.gov/ag/speeches/2001/agerisisremarks11_08.htm.

46. Human Rights Watch, "Presumption of Guilt: Human Rights Abuses of Post-September 11 Detainees" (Human Rights Watch, New York, 2002), p. 58, online: http://www.hrw.org/reports/2002/us911/USA0802.pdf; Amnesty International, "Amnesty International's Concerns Regarding Post September 11 Detentions in the USA" (Amnesty International, London), March 14, 2002, pp. 12–13, online: http://www.amnestyusa.org/usacrisis/9.11.detentions2.pdf.

47. The FBI provided a form affidavit to the immigration judges to keep these individuals in jail that relied on a recitation of the terrible facts of September 11 instead of containing facts about the particular individual evidencing any connection to terrorism. The affidavit simply recited that the FBI cannot, at this time, exclude the possibility that the detainee may have some information that could be relevant to the investigation. In the meantime, the individual was held in jail. See affidavit of Michael Rolince filed in *Center for National Security Studies, et al. v. Department of Justice.*

48. ADC Update: Guidance on FBI's DC Area Voluntary Interviews, November 21, 2002, online: http://www.adc.org/index.php?id=1330&no_cache=1&sword_list[]=fbi&sword_list.

49. In October 2001, Malek Mohamed Seif voluntarily returned to the United States after learning that the FBI wanted to interview him regarding the terrorist attacks. During questioning, Seif was forthcoming with information but was then arrested on unrelated charges. See: Rich Connell, "Fearing Escape, Judge Bars Release of Pilot Who Knew Hijack Suspect," *Los Angeles Times,* November 10, 2001; Michael Janofsky, "Middle East Detainee Conducts Hunger Strike," *New York Times,* December 6, 2001.

50. Human Rights Watch Report, "Presumption of Guilt: Human Rights Abuses of Post-September 11 Detainees," August 2002, online: http://www.hrw.org/reports/2002/us911/USA0802.pdf; Amnesty International, "Amnesty International's Concerns Regarding Post September 11 Detentions in the USA," March 14, 2002, online: http://www.amnestyusa.org/usacrisis/9.11.detentions2.pdf.

51. Human Rights Watch, op. cit. pp. 7, 33–45; Amnesty International, op. cit. pp. 16–18. Because many inmates were only allowed one phone call per week, it took several weeks to contact potential counsel. See also Laurie P. Cohen and Jess Bravin, "Denied Access to Attorneys: Some Detainees Are Jailed Without Charges on INS Offenses," *Wall Street Journal,* November 1, 2001, A1. Two lawyers testified before Congress that their clients had been held incommunicado and not permitted to speak to them. Testimony of Gerald H. Goldstein before the Committee on the Judiciary of the United States Senate, December 4, 2001, pp. 1–3; Testimony of Michael Boyle before the Committee on the Judiciary of the United States Senate, December 4, 2001, pp. 4–5.

52. Human Rights Watch, op. cit. pp. 67–87; Amnesty International op. cit. pp. 28–38.

53. See Department of Justice, Office of the Inspector General Report to Congress on Implementation of Section 1001 of the USA PATRIOT Act, July 15, 2002, online: http://www.usdoj.gov/oig/special/patriot_act/index.htm. Cf. *United States v. Awadallah,* 202 F. Supp 2d 55, 61 (S.D.N.Y. January 31, 2002).

54. See material witness statute, U.S.C. Title 18, Sec. 3144.

55. The government has even refused to identify which courts have issued material witness warrants, so that the press and public can challenge any secrecy orders. The trial court in the FOIA case seeking the identities of the detainees ordered the government to release the information, but the government has appealed, note 17 *supra.* See also Steve Fainaru and Margot Williams, "Material Witness Law Has Many in Limbo; Nearly Half Held in War on Terror Haven't Testified," *Washington Post,* November 24, 2002, A1.

56. A federal district court in New York threw out perjury charges against Osama Awadallah—held as a material witness in the post–September 11 investigation—on the ground that his detention was unlawful because Congress had not authorized jailing an innocent person in order to guarantee that he will testify before a grand jury. Another court disagreed, and the issue is currently on appeal.

57. See, for example, the case of Mr. Albasti, note 12 *supra.*

58. Opening Statement by Michael Chertoff, Assistant Attorney General, Criminal Division, Department of Justice, before the Committee on the Judiciary, United States Senate, November 28, 2001, online: http://judiciary.senate.gov/testimony.cfm?id=126&wit_id=66.

59. The rule provides for detention for forty-eight hours or "an additional reasonable period of time" in extraordinary circumstances. 66 Federal Register 48334, September 20, 2001.

60. 66 Federal Register 54909, October 31, 2001. See "Oversight of the Department of Justice," Hearing of the Senate Judiciary Committee, July 25, 2002.

61. Bureau of Prisons, Notice of Rule-making, 66 Federal Register at 55062, October 31, 2001. Apparently, this authority has only been used to date against individuals already convicted of a crime. It is being challenged in court as unconstitutional.

62. Office of Deputy Attorney General, Subject: Guidance for Absconder Apprehension Initiative, January 25, 2002.

63. In some instances, they were able to obtain a lawyer and challenge the proceedings, but under the apprehension order, they were held in jail while proving their entitlement to stay in the United States. See, for example, Susan Sachs, "Traces of Terror: the Detainees," *New York Times,* June 4, 2002.

64. As of January 10, 2003, at least 500 people had been arrested while registering with the INS. See: Teresa Watanabe, " 'Monitors' Target INS Registration," *Los Angeles Times,* January 9, 2003; and Dan Eggen and Nurith C. Aizenman, "Registration Stirs Panic, Worry Some Muslim Foreign Nationals Risk Arrest to Meet INS Deadline," *Washington Post,* January 10, 2003, A1. Men from the following countries required to register with the INS: Afghanistan, Algeria, Bahrain, Bangladesh, Egypt, Eritrea, Indonesia, Iran, Iraq, Jordan, Kuwait, Lebanon, Libya, Morocco, North Korea, Oman, Pakistan, Qatar, Saudi Arabia, Somalia, Sudan, Syria, Tunisia, United Arab Emirates, and Yemen; see online: http://www.ins.gov/graphics/lawenfor/specialreg/index.htm#special.

65. Some brave members of Congress called for immediate suspension of the program. See letter from Senators Russell Feingold and Ted Kennedy, and Congressman John Conyers to Attorney General Ashcroft, December 23, 2002.

66. See note 23 *supra.*

67. Niraj Warikoo, "Arabs in U.S. Could Be Held, Official Warns; Rights Unit Member Forsees Detainment," *Free Press,* July 20, 2002.

68. Military Order of November 13, 2001—Detention, Treatment and Trial of Certain Non-Citizens in the War Against Terrorism, 66 Federal Register 57833, November 16, 2002. This order also authorized the creation of military commissions to try suspected terrorists in secret outside the usual court martial military justice system.

69. The government brought criminal charges in a civilian court against Zacarias Moussaoui for conspiracy in the September 11 attacks, describing him as the "twentieth hijacker," and against Richard Reid, the "shoe bomber," who was arrested on a plane headed for Boston and charged with having explosives in his shoes, and didn't put them before a military tribunal. And the Defense Department regulations, for example, required a unanimous verdict for the death penalty and the presumption of innocence. See online: http://www.defenselink.mil/news/Mar2002/d20020321ord.pdf. Nevertheless, they still failed to assure adequate due process. See statement by civil liberties groups opposing military commissions, online: www.cnss.org.

70. Katharine Q. Seelye, "A Nation Challenged: Prisoners; Believed to Be a U.S. Citizen, Detainee Is Jailed in Virginia," *New York Times,* April 6, 2002, A7.

71. See *Hamdi v. Rumsfeld et al.* (U.S. Court of Appeals for the Fourth Circuit), No. 02-6895, online: http://news.findlaw.com/hdocs/docs/terrorism/hamdirums61902gbrf.pdf.

72. Attorney General Ashcroft, "Regarding the Transfer of Abdullah Al Muhajir (Born Jose Padilla) to the Department of Defense as an Enemy Combatant," June 10, 2002, online: http://www.usdoj.gov/ag/speeches/2002/061002agtranscripts.htm.

73. See *Padilla v. Bush et al.* (U.S. District Court for the Southern District of New York), 02 Civ. 4445 (MBM), online: http://news.findlaw.com/hdocs/docs/terrorism/padillabush62602gmot.pdf.

74. As Nancy Chang points out above, both cases were being decided by the courts as of this writing.

75. See "The War on Terrorism; Guantánamo Prisoners, Military Commissions, and Torture" by Michael Ratner (in this volume).

76. The Bush administration's position ignores the Defense Department's own pre–September 11 rules, which provided that captured soldiers should be afforded a military hearing to determine whether they are entitled to POW status.

77. Relying on this rationale, U.S. forces targeted alleged Al Qaeda members traveling across the desert in Yemen, including a U.S. citizen, and killed them with a missile strike. See Greg Miller and Josh

Meyer, "US Drops Bomb in Yemen, Kills Six Al-Qaida Operatives," *Los Angeles Times,* November 5, 2002.

78. Press reports in December 2002 raised alarming questions about the methods being used by the government in conducting such interrogations. See Dana Priest and Barton Gellman, "U.S. Decries Abuse but Defends Interrogations; 'Stress and Duress' Tactics Used on Terrorism Suspects Held in Secret Overseas Facilities," *Washington Post,* December 26, 2002, A1.

79. See Charles Lane, "In Terror War, 2nd Track for Suspects; Those Designated 'Combatants' Lose Legal Protections," *Washington Post,* December 1, 2002, A1.

80. 18 U.S.C. sec. 4001.

81. *Federalist Papers* 47.

82. Ralph Ranalli and Shelley Murphy, "Reid Says He Will Plead Guilty in Shoe-Bomb Case," *Boston Globe,* October 3, 2002; and Katharine Q. Seelye, "Threats and Responses: The American in the Taliban: Regretful Lindh Gets 20 years in Taliban Case," *New York Times,* October 5, 2002, A1.

83. *United States. v. Ahmed Abdel Sattar, et al.* (U.S. District Court for the Southern District of New York), No. 02 Cr. 325. Also see George Packer, "Left Behind," *New York Times Magazine,* September 22, 2002.

84. John Kifner, Marc Santon, and Susan Sachs, "Threats and Responses: The Buffalo Case; Murky Lives, Fateful Trip in Buffalo Terrorism Case," *New York Times,* September 20, 2002, A1. See *United States v. Yahya Goba et al.* (U.S. District Court for the Western District of New York), No. 02-M-107; *United States v. Mukhtar al-Bakri* (U.S. District Court for the Western District of New York), No. 02-M-108.

85. "Citizens Arrested: Six Indicted for Plotting Against U.S.," October 4, 2002, www.abcnews.com.

86. Manuel Roig-Franzia, "Florida Arrest Renews Debate Over Muslim Charity," *Washington Post,* January 4, 2003.

87. *Federalist Papers* 47.

5. Racial Profiling Post–9/11: Old Story, New Debate, *by Tanya E. Coke*

1. Tanya E. Coke is a former federal public defender and counsel to U.S. Programs of the Open Society Institute, where she consults on issues of race and criminal justice.

2. Gallup Organization, "Racial Profiling Is Seen as Widespread, Particularly Among Young Black Men," December 9, 1999.

3. Gallup-CNN-USA Today, "Terrorism Most Important Problem, but Americans, Remain Upbeat," October 18, 2001.

4. Eric Foner, *Reconstruction: America's Unfinished Revolution* (New York: Harper & Row, 1988), 199–201 (describing sweeping vagrancy laws and other Black Codes enacted after Emancipation in order to control the social behavior and economic labor of former slaves— " 'the vagrant contemplated [by these laws] was the plantation Negro' ").

5. Pat Friend, "Paddy Wagon," at www.allaboutirish.com.

6. 232 U.S. 214 (1944).

7. Richard J. Bonnie and Charles H. Whitebread II, *The Marijuana Conviction: A History of Marijuana Prohibition in the United States* (New York: Lindesmith Center, 1999), 13–14 (noting that opium prohibitions were the first forms of drug legislation to criminalize users in the U.S., and that they origi-

nated in Western states, where "there was little pretense of assimilating the newly immigrated Chinese populations").

8. David F. Musto, *The American Disease: Origins of Narcotic Control,* 3rd ed. (New York: Oxford Press, 1999), 205.

9. Between 1987 and 1999, federal antidrug spending grew from $6 billion to $20 billion. Ted Gest, *Crime and Politics: Big Government's Erratic Quest for Law and Order* (New York: Oxford University Press, 2001), 115.

10. *Id.* at 120 (describing the devising of the 100:1 ratio between penalties for powder and crack cocaine as an arbitrary game of one-upmanship between the House and Senate in response to media hysteria over crack).

11. Martin Smith and Lowell Bergman, producers, "Drug Wars: Part Two," *Frontline* (2001).

12. Although the DEA has never publically disseminated the profile, portions of it emerged through courtroom testimony and journalistic investigations. See Gary Webb, "DWB," *Esquire* (April 1999), 118–127.

13. David A. Harris, *Profiles in Injustice: Why Racial Profiling Cannot Work* (New York: New Press, 2002), 8.

14. *Wilkins v. Maryland State Police,* Civil Action No. CCB-93-483 (D. Md. 1993).

15. David Harris, *Profiles in Injustice,* 62.

16. *New Jersey v. Soto,* 734 A.2d 350 (N.J. Super. 1996).

17. "Inquiry into New Jersey Troopers' Shooting of Three Centers on Claim of Racial Profiling," *New York Times,* May 8, 1998, A25.

18. "Attorney General's Conference on Strengthening Police-Community Relationships: Report on the Proceedings," U.S. Department of Justice (June 9–10, 1999), at 22–23.

19. Gallup Organization, "Racial Profiling Is Seen as Widespread, Particularly Among Young Black Men," December 9, 1999.

20. "Remarks by the President to the National Organization of Black Law Enforcement Executives," Marriott Wardman Park Hotel, Washington, D.C. (July 30, 2001), available at www.whitehouse.gov/ new/releases/ 2001/07/20010730-5.html.

21. See, e.g., *McCleskey v. Kemp,* 481 U.S. 279 (1987) (accepting as true statistical proof showing race was a decisive factor in capital sentencing, but nevertheless rejecting constitutional challenge on the grounds that racial disparities in criminal justice are inevitable).

22. Gallup Organization, "Terrorism Most Important Problem, but American Remain Upbeat," October 18, 2001.

23. *Ibid.* A similar poll by Zogby International, conducted also in October 2001, found that 75 percent of blacks, compared with 64 percent of whites, favored random searches of cars—precisely the kind of stop-first, question-later tactic that has been reviled in the black community. Reuters, "Wide Support for Race-Based Arrests," *New York Times,* November 30, 2001.

24. Ann Scales, "Polls Say Blacks Tend to Favor Checks," *Boston Globe,* September 30, 2001.

25. See Dennis Niemiec and Shawn Windsor, "Arab Americans Expect Scrutiny, Feel Sting of Bias," *Detroit Free Press,* October 1, 2001 (reporting its poll findings that 61 percent of Arab Americans in the Detroit area believe that extra questioning or inspections of Middle Eastern people are justified). Arab

commentators have explained this phenomenon on the grounds that Arabs felt equally fearful as other Americans following the attacks, and that Arabs were eager to show their solidarity with others against terrorism.

26. Dena Burns, "Congress Gets Its First Sister Act Democrats: Orange County Rep. Loretta Sanchez and Sibling Linda Gain Historic Wins for Hispanics and Women," *Orange County Register,* November 6, 2002 ("The Hispanic vote is going to restructure and redefine American politics, not just in California and the Southwest, but the entire country."—Larry Sabato, director of the Center for Politics at the University of Virginia).

27. See Julian Borger, "Bush Boldly Salsas to Latino Tune," *The Guardian,* January 23, 2000.

28. Memorandum for Regional directors, from Michael A. Pearson, INS Executive Associate Commissioner, Office of Field Operations, October 23, 2001.

29. Memorandum from U.S. Department of Justice, Executive Office for U.S. Attorneys, to the Attorney General, from Kenneth L. Wainstein, Director, "Final Report on Interview Project," February 26, 2002.

30. Memorandum from U.S. Department of Justice, Executive Office for U.S. Attorneys, to All U.S. Attorneys, from Kenneth L. Wainstein, Director, "Interview Report," March 19, 2002.

31. Adam Liptak, "In the Name of Security, Privacy for Me, But Not for Thee," *New York Times,* November 24, 2002 (noting the comparative complacency of the American public about terrorism-related incursions on citizen privacy, as compared with more vocal complaints about the consolidation of private information by corporate interests).

32. A comment by Charles Bahn, a professor of forensic psychology at John Jay College of Criminal Justice in New York City, is typical of the political commentary: "You have to use whatever indicators that will bring you the culprit. If somebody from the same group as you has a history of evil intent, then people like that person have to tolerate it for the good of society." Leela Jacinto, "Flying While Arab Profiling May be a Dirty Word, but Some Say Targeting Certain Ethnic Groups Is a Good Thing," *ABC News,* August 14, 2002.

33. ADC Fact Sheet: the Condition of Arab Americans Post-9/11, American Arab Anti-Discrimination Committee, at www.adc.org.

34. See, e.g., Tom Held, "Keating Endorses Profiling for Airport Searches," *Milwaukee Journal Sentinel,* March 12, 2002 ("Instead of pulling a grandmother or a 6 year-old girl from a ticket line, those federal security authorities should watch for the Arab-American, reading the Qur'an and praying before his flight. Random searches contribute nothing to safety at all."—quoting Oklahoma Governor Frank Keating, a former FBI special agent and U.S. Attorney).

35. "That Dirty Little Word Profiling," *Sixty Minutes,* December 2, 2001.

36. Thomas Ambrose, "Profiling's Place on September 11," *Insight,* September 16, 2002.

37. "Wide Support for Race-Based Arrests," Reuters, November 30, 2001.

38. U.S. Department of Health and Human Services, Substance Abuse and Mental Health Services Administration, "2001 National Household Survey on Drug Abuse" (2001)—reporting that 7.2 percent of whites, 72 percent of blacks, and 6.4 percent of Hispanics use illicit drugs.

39. See K. Jack Riley, "Crack, Powder Cocaine and Heroin: Drug Purchase and Use Patterns in Six U.S. Cities," *National Institute of Justice Research Report* (1997), 16.

40. "Drug Policy and the Criminal Justice System," The Sentencing Project (2001), 4–5.

41. www.fbi.gov/mostwant/terrorist/fugitives.htm.

42. Interview with David A. Harris (November 7, 2002).

43. *Ibid.*

44. See Lamberth Consulting, "Racial Profiling Doesn't Work," at www.lamberthconsulting.com/research work.asp (bar graphs from Maryland, New York, London, North Carolina, New Jersey, Oakland, and the U.S. Department of Justice showing consistently higher contraband hit rates for whites than for blacks).

45. *Ibid.*

46. Remarks of the Honorable Norman Y. Mineta, at the Arab Community Center for Economic and Social Services Gala Dinner, Detroit, Michigan (April 20, 2002).

47. Lamberth Consulting, "Racial Profiling Doesn't Work," at www.lamberthconsulting.com/research/ work.asp (showing chart comparing Customs Service hit rates for 1998 and 2000).

48. Interview with Daniel Benjamin, Senior Fellow for U.S. Security Studies at the International Institute for Strategic Studies (November 27, 2002).

49. Jim McGee, "Ex-FBI Officials Criticize Tactics on Terrorism; Detention of Suspects Not Effective, They Say," *Washington Post,* November 28, 2001.

50. *Ibid.*

51. *Ibid.*

52. Interview with Hussan Jaber, associate executive director, Arab Community Center for Economic and Social Services (ACCESS) (November 8, 2002).

53. Interview with James J. Zogby, president, Arab American Institute (November 20, 2002).

54. For a compilation of comments from police in response to this proposed policy, see National Immigration Forum, "Opposition to Local Law Enforcement of Immigration Laws," October 1, 2002, at www.Immigrationforum.org/currentissues/articles/100102-_quotes.htm.

55. "Administration Split on Local Role in Terror Fight," *New York Times,* April 29, 2002. See also "Policing Immigration," *Bergen Record,* April 22, 2002 ("We've been trying to get the immigrants in our town to believe that we're not like many of the governments in their old countries, governments that were corrupt and wanted to railroad them, not serve them."—quoting Sgt. Robert Francaviglia of the Hillsdale, New Jersey, police department).

56. "Ashcroft Comes to His Senses," *Bergen Record,* June 10, 2002. See also "Olson, Rynak Look to Improve Relationship with Somalis," *Minneapolis Star Tribune,* June 7, 2002 ("We want victims of crime to come to us and not fear being turned in to the INS.").

57. Interview with Lorie Fridell, Police Executive Research Forum (November 6, 2002); interview with David Harris (November 7, 2002).

58. Interview with Lorie Fridell, Police Executive Research Forum (November 6, 2002).

59. Lorie Fridell, Robert Lunney, Drew Diamond, and Bruce Kubu, *Racially Biased Policing: A Principled Response* (Washington, D.C.: Police Executive Research Forum, 2001), at 50 (reporting that 12 percent of police departments modified existing policies, and 19 percent adopted new policies, in response to public perceptions of racial profiling).

60. Interview with Lorie Fridell, Police Executive Research Forum (November 6, 2002).

61. "U.S. Weighs Local Role in Immigration," *Chicago Tribune,* April 14, 2002.

6. Living in Fear: How the U.S. Government's War on Terror Impacts American Lives, by Anthony Romero

1. Anthony D. Romero is the Executive Director of the ACLU. He gratefully acknowledges the assistance of Andrew Boyle and Carole Ashkinaze in the research for this chapter.

2. *The Center for National Security Studies, et al. vs. DOJ* (Currently on appeal to the U.S. Court of Appeals for the D.C. Circuit).

3. *Detroit News, Inc., et al. vs. Ashcroft, et al.*

4. *North Jersey Media Group, Inc., et al. vs. John Ashcroft, Attorney General of the United States, et al.*

5. Human Rights Watch, *Presumption of Guilt: Human Rights Abuses of Post–September 11 Detainees* (August 2002); and Amnesty International, *Amnesty International's Concerns Regarding Post September 11 Detentions in the USA* (March, 2002).

6. Bob Cuddy, *Caught in the Backlash: Stories from Northern California* (American Civil Liberties Union Foundation of Northern California, November, 2002).

7. Human Rights Watch, *We Are Not the Enemy: Hate Crimes Against Arabs, Muslims, and Those Perceived to be Arab or Muslim after September 11* (November 2002).

8. Bob Cuddy, *Caught in the Backlash: Stories from Northern California* (American Civil Liberties Union Foundation of Northern California, November, 2002).

9. Jack Chang, "Liberties Tested After September 11: ACLU Report Details Northern California Residents' Experience of Losing their Freedoms, as well as their Peace of Mind," *Contra Costa (California) Times*, November 18, 2002.

10. Dave Lindorff, "When Neighbors Attack," *Salon*, August 6, 2002. http://archive.salon.com/news/feature/2002/08/06/tips/index_np.html.

11. Ann Davis, "Post-September 11 Watch List Acquires Life of Its Own," *Wall Street Journal*, November 19, 2002.

12. New York, Georgia, Idaho, Michigan, New Jersey, North Carolina, Ohio, Oklahoma, South Carolina, South Dakota, Tennessee, Utah and Virginia.

13. State of New York, "Anti-Terrorism Act of 2001," September 17, 2001.

14. *States Enacting New Crimes, Penalties Related to Terrorism.* National Conference of State Legislatures. August 30, 2002, http://www.ncsl.org/programs/cj/terror.htm.

15. United States Congress. USA PATRIOT Act, Sec. 802 A-C. December 6, 2001.

16. *Consolidated Government of Columbus, Georgia vs. Roy Bourgeois and Jeff Winder, both individually and as representatives of the School of Americas Watch, Eric Lecompte and Ken "Doe."*

17. *Ibid.*

18. Sara Wunsch. ACLU of Massachusetts. Phone conversation regarding meeting between John Roberts of the ACLU of Massachussets, city officials, and city residents.

19. Janis Heaphy, Graduation Speech at Cal State–Sacramento, December 15, 2001.

20. *Class Action Complaint, American Friends Service Committee vs. City and County of Denver*

21. Denver City Council. *Resolution No. 13-02: Expressing the Commitment of the City and County of Denver to Civil Rights and Liberties.* 2002.

22. Roger Cisneros, Jean E. Dubofsky, and William G. Meyer, *Report of Panel Appointed to Review Denver Police Department Policies for Collection and Retention of Criminal Intelligence Information,* June 28, 2002.

23. Ford Fessenden and Michael Moss, "Going Electronic, Denver Reveals Long-Term Surveillance," *New York Times,* December 21, 2002.

24. *Ibid.*

25. *The People of the State of New York v. Robert Steele Collier, Defendant.*

26. Michael Moss and Ford Fessenden, "New Tools for Domestic Spying, and Qualms," *New York Times,* December 10, 2002.

27. *Ibid.*

28. *Jewish Community Action et al. vs. State of Minnesota Department of Public Safety* (Currently in the Minnesota Court of Appeals).

29. Chief Bob McDonell. President of California Police Chiefs Association. Letter. April 10, 2002.

30. David Firestone, "Administration to Delay Aid to Local Law Enforcement," *New York Times,* December 3, 2002.

31. Jim McGee, "Ex-FBI Officials Criticize Tactics on Terrorism," *Washington Post,* November 28, 2001.

32. *Ibid.*

33. Ann Davis, "Some Colleges Balk at FBI Request for Data on Foreigners," *Wall Street Journal,* November 25, 2002.

34. City Council of Takoma Park, Maryland. Resolution No. 2002-82. 28 October 2002.

35. ACLU Washington National Office eyewitnesses.

36. Sherry M. Kelly. City Clerk, Berkeley City Council. Letter to George Bush, President. April 22, 2002.

37. Ann Arbor City Council. *R-18-1-02, Resolution in Support of Due Process for All Members of the Ann Arbor Community,* January 7, 2002.

38. Aldermen of Carrboro, North Carolina. *Resolution No. 186/2001-02: A Resolution Regarding the USA Patriot Act and the Protection of Civil Rights and Liberties,* June 25, 2002; and Cambridge City Council. *Cambridge City Council Resolution,* June 17, 2002.

39. Amherst Town Meeting, "Civil Rights and Civil Liberties," *Amherst Town Meeting Warrant Article,* April 24, 2002.

40. *Ibid.*

41. Michael Janofsky, "Cities Urge Restraint in Fight Against Terror," *New York Times,* December 23, 2002.

42. Pauline Maier, *American Scripture: Making the Declaration of Independence* (New York: Alfred A. Knopf, 1997).

7. The War on Terrorism: Guantánamo Prisoners, Military Commissions, and Torture, *by Michael Ratner*

1. Michael Ratner is president of the Center for Constitutional Rights.

2. John Mintz, "Extended Detention in Cuba Mulled," *Washington Post,* February 13, 2002, A16.

3. *Id.*

4. Frank Davies, "U.S. Readies Tribunals for Terrorism Trials," *Miami Herald,* December 26, 2002, 15A.

5. Greg Goldin, "Assault on America II," *L.A. Weekly,* November 30, 2001, 110.

6. *Id.*

7. Secretary of Defense Donald Rumsfeld, DOD News Briefing on Military Commissions, March 21, 2002; "Guantánamo Forever? Preparing for Long-Term Detentions," *Miami Herald,* December 3, 2002, 6B.

8. Rumsfeld News Briefing, *supra* note 7; Douglas Waller, "Ready for the 50-Year War?" *Time* magazine, December 31, 2001, 28.

9. *Rasul v. Bush,* 215 F. Supp. 2d 55 (D.D.C. 2002).

10. *Id.*

11. David Rohde, "Threats and Responses: The Detainees; Afghans Freed from Guantánamo Speak of Heat and Isolation," *New York Times,* October 29, 2002, A18.

12. FDCH Federal Department and Agency Documents, Regulatory Intelligence Data, January 10, 2003.

13. Katherine Q. Seelye, "A Nation Challenged: At Guantánamo," *New York Times,* April 3, 2002, A13.

14. "Respondent's Motion to Dismiss Petitioners First Amended Petition For Writ of Habeas Corpus" in *Rasul v. Bush,* at http://campxray.net/03.18.02%20Gov't%20response%20to%20Writ.PDF.

15. Dr. Reginald Shareef, "Ashcroft on a Slippery Slope," Roanoke.com, November 19, 2001, at www.roanoke.com/columnists/shareef/4041.html, citing *Nightline* (ABC television broadcast, November 18, 2001); Vice President Dick Cheney, defending the idea of military commissions for terrorists, said that terrorists "don't deserve the same guarantees and safeguards" of the American judicial system. "Bush Officials Defend Military Trials in Terror Cases," CNN, November 15, 2001, at http://www.cnn.com/2001/LAW.

16. Davies, *supra* note 4.

17. Neil A. Lewis, "Threats and Responses: Military Justice; Administration's Position Shifts on Plans for Tribunals," *New York Times,* November 2, 2002, A8.

18. Ronald Dworkin, "The Threat to Patriotism," *New York Review of Books,* February 28, 2002:
    The government should be embarrassed to appeal to the *Quirin* decision [upholding a military tribunal] as justification for its treatment of aliens now, because that decision, like the Court's 1944 decision permitting the detention of Japanese-Americans, is widely regarded as overly deferential to the executive and, in a crucial part, wrong. (Justice Frankfurter, in a bizarre and embarrassing memorandum to his fellow justices, had pleaded with them to ignore legal niceties and do what Roosevelt asked as part of the war effort.) The case is a useful reminder of how shortsighted and, in the long run, self-defeating the appeal to judges to show unity with the executive often is.

19. The Center for Constitutional Rights and I have received a great deal of hate mail because of our representation of the Guantánamo detainees. The content of this mail demonstrates that many people appear willing to set aside the Constitution with regard to the detainees at Guantánamo. Two examples of the scores of letters and e-mails make the point:
    I believe that you are misguided. As a U.S. Citizen, I do not believe that there is any legal or moral necessity to give the rights granted by the U.S. Constitution to those detained at Camp X.

The more these persons are questioned, the less future WTC-type incidents will occur. There are 6 billion persons outside our borders; do you wish to grant them our constitutional rights?

Stop coddling the murderers at Guantánamo and spend your time doing something worthwhile for society. They are entitled to exactly the same consideration they gave the workers at the World Trade Center and Pentagon. Why don't you try doing pro bono work for the families of the victims rather than advocating the so-called "rights" of the barbarians who would end our way of life?

See, e.g., David B. Rivkin, Jr., and Lee A. Casey, "It's Not Torture, and They Aren't Lawful Combatants," *Washington Post*, January 11, 2003, A19; Joshua Muravchik, "The European Disease: Irrational Anti-Americanism Takes Root Across the Atlantic," *American Enterprise*, December 2002, 24; Ruth Wedgwood, "The Case for Military Tribunals," *Wall Street Journal*, December 3, 2001, A18.

20. *Padilla v. Bush*, 2002 U.S. Dist. LEXIS 23086 (S.D.N.Y. 2002), on reconsideration, *Padilla v. Rumsfeld*, 02 Civ. 4445 (MBM) (S.D.N.Y. March 11, 2003); *Hamdi v. Rumsfeld*, 2003 U.S. App. LEXIS 198 (4h Cir. 2003).

21. The court in the *Hamdi* case required the government to file an affidavit setting forth some facts underlying the basis for his designation as an "enemy combatant." *Hamdi v. Rumsfeld, supra* note 20. In the *Padilla* case, the federal district court held that the government needed to support its designation of Padilla as an enemy combatant with "some evidence." The court also allowed a consultation with his attorney. On the government's motion for reconsideration the court amplified and upheld its decision. *Padilla v. Bush, supra* note 20.

22. One news story described the prisons as "three dank and overcrowded cell blocks, with a stench of unwashed bodies and from which erupt monotonous pleas for help and mercy, that more resemble cattle sheds or ill-kept stables than a jail." "258 Afghan Taliban Soldiers Released," *Reuters,* March 23, 2002, at http://www.dawn.com/2002/03/24/top11.htm.

23. Carlotta Gall, "A Nation Challenged: The Missing; Families Try to Trace Thousands of Missing Taliban, Many Forced to Fight," *New York Times,* February 21, 2002, A14.

24. Susan B. Glasser, "Malnutrition, Disease Rampant at Prison for Taliban; Red Cross Begins Emergency Feeding," *Washington Post,* April 19, 2002, A14.

25. The name accurately describes the camp; the guards can see everything a prisoner does.

26. As I wrote after one of my trips to Guantánamo in 1991:

The conditions, under which they are living, if you can call it that, are out of Dante's inferno—the ninth circle of Hell. For 14 months, they have used portable toilets that are rarely cleaned, that are filled with feces and urine. The camp is bleak—no grass, hardscrabble ground and temporary wooden barracks on concrete slabs. Within those "homes" 15 to 20 Haitians are huddled with only sheets hanging from the rafters. Rain, vermin and rats are other occupants. Michael Ratner, "How We Closed the Guantánamo HIV Camp: The Intersection of Politics and Litigation," 11 Harv. Hum. L. J.187, 201n. (1998).

27. See e.g., Press Release, Amnesty International, "USA: AI Calls on the USA to End Legal Limbo of Guantánamo Prisoners," January 15, 2002, at http://web.amnesty.org/ai.nsf/Index/AMR510092002.

28. Initially most of the Guantánamo detainees were captured in Afghanistan, but by late 2002, the Department of Defense was unwilling to say from where additional captives were captured as the following dialog demonstrates:

Q. "Did they come from Afghanistan?"

Victoria Clarke, Defense Department spokesperson: "Not saying."

Victoria Clarke, Department of Defense Briefing, October 28, 2002.

29. Viola Gienger, "Lawyers Contest Algerians' Handover," *Chicago Tribune,* April 11, 2002, 4.

30. Brown and Root Services, a division of the oil services company Halliburton, which was formerly headed by Vice President Cheney, is constructing the new prison. The contract may amount to $300 million. Charles Aldinger, "Halliburton to Build Cells at Guantánamo Base," *Reuters,* July 27, 2002.

31. Carol Rosenberg, "80 Detainees Placed in Special Steel Cells, Camp Warden Says," *Miami Herald,* September 13, 2002, 9A.

32. Katherine Q. Seelye, "A Nation Challenged: The Prisoners; U.S. May Move Some Detainees to Domestic Military Bases," *New York Times,* January 4, 2002, A15.

33. George Edmonson, " 'Gitmo' Gets A Makeover As POW Camp," *Cox Washington Bureau,* January 8, 2002, at http://www.coxnews.com/washingtonbureau/staff/edmonson/010802TER-GUANTÁ NAMO.html.

34. *Id.*

35. "Rumsfeld: Afghan Detainees at Gitmo Bay Will Not Be Granted POW Status," *Fox News,* January 28, 2002, at http://www.foxnews.com/story/0,2933,44084,00.html.

36. David Rhode, "Afghans Freed From Guantánamo Speak of Heat and Isolation," *New York Times,* October 29, 2002, at A18.

37. *Id.*

38. Article 71 of the Third Geneva Convention states that POWs are permitted to send not less then two letters and four cards monthly; Article 72 of that Convention also allows them to receive individual and collective relief packages containing foodstuffs, clothing, articles of a religious nature, and other similar items.

39. Rhode, *supra* note.

40. *Id.*

41. *Id.*

42. For a short history of the lease, see Ratner, *supra* 11, Harv. Hum L.J. 187 (1998), at 191.

43. *The History of Guantánamo Bay,* at http://www.nsgtmo.navy.mil/gazette/History_98-64/his chp3.htm.

44. Ratner, *supra* note, Harv. Hum. L. J. 187 (1998), at 192 n. 7.

45. *Johnson v. Eisentrager,* 339 U.S. 763 (1950).

46. *Haitian Ctr. Council v. McNary,* 969 F.2d 1326 (2d Cir. 1992).

47. *Haitian Refugee Ctr. v. Baker,* 953 F.2d 1498 (11th Cir. 1992).

48. For a detailed look at the law, see Human Rights Watch, "Press Backgrounder, Background Paper on Geneva Conventions and Persons Held by U.S. Forces," January 29, 2002, at http://www.hrw. org/backgrounder/usa/pow-bck.htm.

49. Press Release, White House, Fact Sheet Status of Detainees at Guantánamo (February 7, 2002), at http://www.whitehouse.gov/news/releases/2002/02/20020207-13.html.

50. See, e.g., on February 8, 2002, the day after announcement of the United States' position, Darcy Christen, a spokesperson for the ICRC, said of the detainees: "They were captured in combat [and] we consider them prisoners of war." Richard Waddington, "Guantánamo Inmates Are POWs Despite Bush View—ICRC," *Reuters,* February 9, 2002.

51. Department of Defense Briefing, *Federal News Service,* June 21, 2002.

52. "Bosnia Suspects Headed for Cuba," *BBC,* January 18, 2002, at http://news.bbc.co.uk/1/hi/world/europe/1767554.stm.

53. Peter Ford, "Fate of 'detainees' hangs on US wording," *Christian Science Monitor,* January 17, 2002, 1.

54. See e.g., Richard Sisk, "Airport Gun Battle Firefight Erupts As Prisoners Are Flown to Cuba," *New York Daily News,* January 11, 2002, 27.

55. Katherine Q. Seelye, "Rumsfeld Backs Plan to Hold Captives Even if Acquitted," *New York Times,* March 29, 2002, A18.

56. Two cases were filed in federal court in Washington, D.C., and consolidated for the argument and the decision: *Rasul v. Bush* and *Al Odah v. United States,* 215 F.Supp2d 55 (D.D.C. 2002). A third case, *Coalition of Clergy v. Bush,* 310 F.3d 1153 (9th Cir. 2002), was filed in California.

57. The Queen on the application of *Abbasi and Anor. v. Secretary of State for Foreign and Commonwealth Affairs,* Case No. c/2002/0617A:0617B (Dec. 6, 2002).

58. Request By the Center for Constitutional Rights et al. for Precautionary Measures Under Article 25 of the Commission Regulations, filed February 25, 2002.

59. Decision of the Inter-American Commission on Human Rights of the Organization of American States, *Detainees in Guantánamo Bay, Cuba* (March 13, 2002).

60. *Id.*

61. The Queen on the application of *Abbasi and Anor. v. Secretary of State for Foreign and Commonwealth Affairs* [2002] EWCA Civ. 1598

62. *Id.*

63. *Id.*

64. *Id.*

65. Rasul, op cit.

66. Press Release, White House, "Detention, Treatment, and Trial of Certain Non-Citizens in the War Against Terrorism," November 13, 2001 at http://www.whitehouse.gov/news/releases/2001/11/20011113-27.html. The order can also be found in the Federal Register at 66 Fed Reg. 57831 (2001).

67. Uniform Code of Military Justice, 10 U.S.C.801 et seq (2002).

68. Alberto R. Gonzales, "Martial Justice, Full and Fair," *New York Times,* November 30 2001, A27.

69. Department of Defense, Military Commission Order No. 1, March 21, 2002.

70. *Id.*

71. For example, Senator Leahy received a letter signed by over 400 law professors from all over the country, expressing their collective wisdom that the military commissions contemplated by the President's Order are "legally deficient, unnecessary, and unwise." Senator Patrick Leahy, Chairman of Senate Judiciary Committee, "The Continuing Debate on the Use of Military Commissions," Senate Floor, December 14, 2001.

72. William Safire, "Seizing Dictatorial Power?" *New York Times,* November 15, 2001, A31.

73. See, e.g., Remarks of Yale Professor Ruth Wedgewood, at http://www.justicetalking.org/shows/show195.asp.

74. Dana Priest and Barton Gellman, "US Decries Abuse but Defends Interrogations; 'Stress and Duress' Tactics Used on Terrorism Suspects Held in Secret Overseas Facilities," *Washington Post*, December 26, 2002, A1.

75. Rajiv Chandrasekaran and Peter Finn, "U.S. Behind Secret Transfer of Terror Suspects," *Washington Post*, March 11, 2002, A1.

76. Priest and Gellman, op. cit.

77. *Id.*

78. Convention Against Torture and Other Cruel, Inhuman or Degrading Treatment or Punishment, art. I (1984), reprinted 23 ICM 1027, and 24 ICM 535 (entered into force for United States Nov. 20, 1994).

79. Priest and Gellman,.

80. 18 U.S.C. §§ 2340 & 2340A (2002).

81. Priest and Gellman.

82. Priest and Gellman.

83. Walter Pincus, "Silence of 4 Terror Probe Suspects Poses Dilemma for FBI," *Washington Post*, October 21, 2001, A6.

8. Breaking the Code: Or, Can the Press Be Saved from Itself?, *by Michael Tomasky*

1. Michael Tomasky is the political columnist for *New York* magazine.

2. Duncan Campbell, "U.S. Buys Up All Satellite War Images," *The Guardian*, October 17, 2001.

3. "Ikonos Images Dealt Exclusively to NIMA," *Satellite Week*, October 29, 2001; also reported in David Corn, "Their Spy in the Sky," *The Nation*, November 26, 2001, 6.

4. "Stampeded in the House," *Washington Post*, October 16, 2001, A22.

5. See, for example, Michael Hirsh and Michael Isikoff, "What Went Wrong," *Newsweek*, May 27, 2002: a 4,000-word article full of devastating particulars about how the Bush administration deemphasized counterterrorism and shifted funds the Clinton administration had been spending on fighting terrorism to other pursuits in the justice, treasury, and defense departments.

6. Douglas Turner, "Anonymous Sources Fueling Push for War," *Buffalo News*, December 9, 2002.

9. Balancing in a Crisis? Bioterrorism, Public Health, and Privacy, *by Janlori Goldman*

1. Janlori Goldman is director of the Health Privacy Project, an independent, nonprofit organization in Washington, D.C., dedicated to fostering privacy in the health care system to broaden access to care and improve the quality of care for individuals and the community. The project focuses on national and state health privacy policy, genetic privacy and discrimination, and bioterrorism, public health, and privacy. All of the project's publications and resources can be found at www.healthprivacy.org. I am deeply grateful to the Open Society Institute, which has funded the Health Privacy Project's work in this area. I thank Dr. Virginia Ashby Sharpe, who read an early draft of this chapter and shared her clarity and pith. And I appreciate Sandra Mullin, associate commissioner for the New York City Department of Health, for her generous insights.

2. For decades, public health advocates have pointed to public health's deteriorating infrastructure; the tepid, uneven compliance with voluntary and mandatory reporting by health care providers; and

a lack of adequate funding. See Laurie Garrett, *The Betrayal of Trust: The Collapse of Global Public Health* (New York: Hyperion, 2000).

3. See CDC report prepared for Senate Appropriations Committee, *Public Health's Infrastructure, A Status Report, 1999,* which includes recommendations for how to bolster public health and better anticipate new threats, available at www.cdc.gov.; Margaret Hamburg, "Addressing Bioterrorist Threats: Where Do We go From Here?", *Emerging Infectious Diseases* (vol 5., no. 4), August 1999.

4. See Lawrence O. Gostin, Scott Burris, and Zita Lazzarini, "The Law and the Public's Health: A Study of Infectious Disease Law in the United States," 99 Colum. L. Rev. 59, 125–26 (1999).

5. Lawrence Gostin, *Public Health Law: Power, Duty, Restraint* (University of California Press: Berkeley, Los Angeles, London, 2000); Wendy Parmet, "Health Care and the Constitution: Public Health and the Role of the State in the Framing Era," 20 Hastings Const. L.Q. 267 (1992).

6. http://www.cdc.gov/aboutcdc.htm#mission.

7. For a different perspective, see Amitai Etzioni, *The Limits of Privacy* (New York: Basic Books, 1999), in which he argues for a communitarian approach that often subsumes individual privacy for the common good.

8. The modern version of the oath, as written by Louis Lasagna in 1964 and administered as part of an oath to graduating medical students is, in part, relevant, "I will respect the privacy of my patients, for their problems are not disclosed to me so that the world may know." Available at www.pbs.org/wgbh/nova/doctors/oath.html. See also Crawshaw, Rogers, Pellegrino, et al. "Patient-Physician Covenant" *JAMA* 1995;273:1553. For a discussion of how the lack of privacy impacts health care, see Janlori Goldman, "Protecting Privacy to Improve Health Care," *Health Affairs,* Nov/Dec, 1998.

9. California HealthCare Foundation, *National Survey: Confidentiality of Medical Records* (January 1999). Available at www.chcf.org.

10. *Ibid.*

11. A 2001 Harris poll commissioned by BioGen, Inc., documents that four out of ten people with multiple sclerosis lied or failed to disclose the diagnosis to family members, friends, or colleagues because they feared job loss and stigma. A 1997 survey by the National Center for Genome Research found that 63 percent of people would refuse to take a genetic test for a disease for fear that employers or insurers could access the results. These survey results, and others, are available at <www.healthprivacy.org/resources>.

12. For a compilation of reported cases in which peoples' medical privacy has been violated, see www.healthprivacy.org/resources.

13. Rick Weiss, "Ignorance Undercuts Gene Tests Potential," *Washington Post,* 12/2/00, A1.

14. J. Bacon, "AIDS Confidentiality," *USA Today,* 10/10/96, A1.

15. Gina Kolata, "Boston Univ. Found Company to Sift Leading Heart Data," *New York Times,* 6/17/00, A10.

16. R. Rosenberg, "Questions Still Linger on Heart Study Access," *Boston Globe,* 2/21/01, D4.

17. Elizabeth Wolfe, "As Pentagon Computerizes Medical Records, Contractor Suffers Theft," AP, 12/31/02.

18. See Robert O'Harrow, "Hacker Accesses Patient Records," *Washington Post,* 12/9/00, E1. (At University of Washington Medical Center, a hacker downloaded health records and Social Security num-

bers on over 5,000 patients.); "Black Eye at Medical Center," *Washington Post* 2/22/99, F5. (University of Michigan Medical Center mistakenly posted thousands of patients' medical records on the Internet for two months.) As more health information is collected and shared in electronic form, and more networks are developed that give entities outside of the direct health care system access, safeguarding security becomes increasingly difficult. As a National Academy of Sciences report concluded, it is impossible to assure 100 percent security for electronic health information. Thus it is important to be mindful of the risks, and take precautionary measures to limit access, create enforceable privacy rules and policies. See NAS, *For the Record,* 1997.

19. Janlori Goldman, "Protecting Privacy to Improve Health Care," *Health Affairs,* Nov/Dec, 1998.

20. C. Dreifus, "The Fear Factor Meets Its Match: A Conversation with David Ropeik," *New York Times,* 12/3/02, D2.

21. The USA PATRIOT Act, passed six weeks after the September 11 attacks, was rushed through over the strenuous objections of civil liberties groups. To quell concerns that civil liberties were being sacrificed; the act includes a sunset provision of 2005 on some of the most troubling provisions.

22. HIPAA primarily addresses the ability of people to maintain health benefits after they change jobs, but the privacy mandate is bundled into the "Administrative Simplification" section of the law, which requires health providers and plans to shift to use standardized, electronic formats for sharing medical information. HIPAA, P.L. 104–191 (August 21, 1996); 64 Federal Register 59918 (1999); The final regulation as issued by the Department of Health and Human Services (HHS) is available at 45 C.F.R. sec. 164.534 (2001) with modifications issued August 2001, available at www.hhs.gov/ocr/hipaa.

23. 429 U.S. 589 (1977).

24. As the Court stated in *Whalen:* "We are not unaware of the threat to privacy implicit in the accumulation of vast amounts of personal information in computerized data banks or other massive government files. The collection of taxes, the distribution of welfare and social security benefits, the supervision of public health, the direction of our Armed Forces, and the enforcement of the criminal laws all require the orderly preservation of great quantities of information, much of which is personal in character and potentially embarrassing or harmful if disclosed. The right to collect and use such data for public purposes is typically accompanied by a concomitant statutory or regulatory duty to avoid unwarranted disclosures. Recognizing that, in some circumstances, that duty arguably has its roots in the Constitution, nevertheless New York's statutory scheme, and its implementing administrative procedures, evidence a proper concern with, and protection of, the individual's interest in privacy. We therefore need not, and do not, decide any question which might be presented by the unwarranted disclosure of accumulated private data—whether intentional or unintentional—or by a system that did not contain comparable security provisions."

25. *U.S. v. Westinghouse,* 638 F.2d 570 (3d Circuit 1980). For a full discussion of information privacy law, see Janlori Goldman, "Privacy and Individual Empowerment in the Interactive Age," in *Visions of Privacy: Policy Choices for the Digital Age,* ed. Colin Bennett and Rebecca Grant (Toronto: University of Toronto Press, 1999).

26. Congress set a deadline on itself to enact comprehensive privacy legislation by August 1999, and when it missed that date, the mandate shifted to HHS to issue the privacy rules. For a more complete history of the medical privacy regulation, see Peter Swire and Lauren Steinfeld, "Security and Privacy after September 11: The Health Care Example," 86 *University of Minnesota Law Review* 101 (2002): 122.

27. See Janlori Goldman, *Oversight of Medical Privacy,* testimony before the U.S. Senate Committee on Health Education, Labor and Pensions, 4/16/02, p. 16, citing White House Office of Management and

Budget (OMB) report that concludes that implementing the privacy regulation, along with other HIPAA rules relating to standardized healthcare transactions, will ultimately result in substantial cost savings. www.healthprivacy.org/resources.

28. The regulation defines protected health information broadly and includes information about the past, present, or future physical or mental health or condition of an individual (including genetic information), the provision of health care to an individual, or the past, present, or future payment for the provision of care. 45 C.F.R. Sec. 164.501 (2001).

29. Peter Swire and Lauren Steinfeld, "Security and Privacy after September 11: The Health Care Example," 86 *University of Minnesota Law Review* 101, 122. (2002).

30. See Pritts et al., *The State of Health Privacy: An Uneven Terrain*, (Health Privacy Project, Washington, D.C., 1999), and 2nd edition, 2002, available at www.healthprivacy.org/statelaw.

31. The Public Health Threats and Emergencies Act, 2002.

32. P.L. 107–188.

33. C. Park, "Health Powers Act," *Chattanooga Times*, 1/24/02, A1. "Consideration of the [CDC's Model Act] also will ensure Tennessee a chance at getting $865 million Congress has appropriated [to the CDC]," quoting Tennessee Representative Kathyrn Bowers.

34. The model Public Health Emergency Powers Act, drafted for the CDC by the Center for Law and the Public Health, is available at http://www.publichealthlaw.net.

35. The Homeland Security Act, Public Law 107-291 (enacted November 25, 2002), available at www.thomas.gov.

36. Democrats were chiefly concerned about the lack of job protection for the government workers within the new department.

37. Julie Rovner, "Questions Raised over Moving Bioterror out of CDC, NIH," *Congress Daily*, 7/16/02; C. Anderson, "Security Plan May Create Public-Health Conflict," *Philadelphia Inquirer*, 6/26/02, quoting Representative Henry Waxman and GAO head Janet Heinrich as critical of the Bush administration's plan to move bioterror responsibility out of CDC and into new Homeland Security Department. "It may seriously affect our ability to respond to serious health threats of the American people," said Waxman. See also Victor Sidel et al, "Bioterrorism Preparedness: Cooptation of Public Health?" *Medicine and Global Survival*, 12/01, Vol. 7, No. 2, p. 84.

38. The APHA resolution was voted on at its November 2002 annual meeting, and passed with 95 percent support.

39. For more on the Homeland Security Act, see the Web site of the Center for Democracy and Technology, www.cdt.org.

40. See Janlori Goldman, "Government Plan Disregards Privacy Protections," *iHealthBeat*, 12/11/02, available at http://www.ihealthbeat.org/members/basecontent.asp?contentid=24232&datevalue=12/11/2002&collectionid=541&program=13&contentarea=105238.

41. See John Barry, "Big Brother Is Back," *Time* magazine, 12/2/02, p. 33.

42. The Model Act (December 21, 2001 draft), Section 104 (m), available at www.publichealthlaw.net.

43. The Model Act (December 21, 2001 draft), Section 301–303.

44. See Swire and Steinfeld; G. Annas, "Bioterrorism, Public Health and Civil Liberties," *New England Journal of Medicine*, 346:1337–42, 4/25/02.

45. Letter from the New England Coalition for Law and Public Health, November 13, 2001, available at www.healthprivacy.org/resources.

46. *Review of the Model State Emergency Health Powers Act,* Center for Public Health Law, University of Missouri Kansas City School of Law, 11/30/01, available at www.plague.law.umkc.edu/blaw/bt/MSEHPA_review.

47. See letter from Health Privacy Project to Professor Larry Gostin, 11/7/01, available at www.health privacy.org/resources.

48. Sarah Lueck, *States Seek to Strengthen Emergency Powers: Movement Is Raising Privacy and Civil Liberties Concerns,* 1/7/02, p. A26, citing meeting.

49. A co-author of the Model Act stated in a presentation at a Consumer Coalition for Health Privacy briefing that they did not intend privacy to be a part of the Model Act because it was outside the scope of their charge from the CDC.

50. Gostin, et al., "The Law and the Public's Health: A Study of Infectious Disease Law in the United States," 99 *Columbia L. Review 59* (1999). "Legally binding assurances of privacy and security should attach to all personally identifiable public health information. The collector of the data should bear a legal duty to maintain their confidentiality, to store the data in a secure system, and to use the data only for the purposes for which they were collected. Significant penalties should be imposed for breach of these assurances." Gostin, at p. 126.

51. Duane Parde, "CDC Proposal Is Extreme," *USA Today editorial,* April 26, 2002, p. 14A; Matthew Mosk, "Anti-Terror Measures Become Law in Md.; Package gives State Broad Emergency Power," *Washington Post,* April 10, 2002, B1, quoting ACLU attorney stating that bill in its original form was improved after intense pressure from civil liberties groups, removing a proposal to impose criminal penalties on bioterror victims who failed to accept immediate care. The final bill allows the state to isolate and quarantine victims against their will, but not to charge them with a crime.

52. See footnote 30.

53. P. Sloca, *Despite Concerns, Senate Approves Bioterrorism Bill,* AP, 2/21/02, citing Missouri legislator concerns over civil liberties and privacy issues raised by version of the Model Act; AP wire story, "Council to Recommend Changes in State Health Laws in Case of Bioterrorism Attack," 12/5/01, reporting on South Carolina's effort to enact a bill that "legal and medical experts say . . . would give the state broad powers and civil liberties could be abused," quoting concerns of doctors and law professors in the state.

54. Public health emergency preparedness and response (5/15/02), www.bt.cdc.gov.

55. see http://www.cdc.gov/mmwr/.

56. See "Bush Plans Early Warning System for Terror," *New York Times,* February 6, 2002.

57. U.S. Dept. of Health and Human Services, *HHS News,* June 6, 2002.

58. "Texas Launches Electronic Network to Improve Public Health Reporting, Surveillance," Health-Beat, August 12, 2002.

59. HAN is a nationwide program of the CDC, in partnership with NACCO, ASTHO, and others, to establish the communications, information, and organizational infrastructure that will link local health departments to one another and to other third parties.

60. Catherine Greenman, "Tracking an Outbreak Minute by Minute," *New York Times,* January 4, 2002.

61. Lois Collins, "Retain Health Watch," *Desert News,* Utah, April 25, 2002, B1.

62. Catherine Greenman, "Tracking an Outbreak Minute by Minute," *New York Times* on the Web, July 4, 2002.

63. Experience shows that it is unlikely that any limits on the use of this large database of patient data will hold, given that the temptation to use it for other purposes (i.e., law enforcement, research) will be viewed by the courts and policy makers as compelling. See Jerry Berman and Janlori Goldman, "A Federal Right of Information Privacy: The Need for Reform," in *Computers, Ethics and Social Values,* ed. Deborah Johnson and Helen Nissenbaum (Upper Saddle River, New Jersey: Prentice Hall, 1995).

64. Heather Hollingsworth, "Computerized Hospital Records Could Find New Use Combating Biological Attacks," Associated Press wire story, February 23, 2002.

65. Created by the Homeland Security Act, Public Law 107–296, November 25, 2002.

66. Total Information Awareness program, www.darpa.gov, John Markoff, "Pentagon Plans a Computer System That Would Peek at Personal Data of Americans," *New York Times,* 11/9/02, A10; John Barry, "Big Brother Is Back," *Newsweek,* 12/2/02, 33; Editorial, "A Snooper's Dream," *New York Times,* 11/18/02, A22.

67. See Bill Miller, "Outdated Systems Balk Terrorism Investigation," *Washington Post,* June 13, 2002, A12.

68. John Markoff, "Pentagon Plans a Computer System That Would Peek at Personal Data of Americans," *New York Times,* November 9, 2002, p. A10.

69. For the full text of the plan, see www.cdc.gov. Also see Lawrence Altman and William Broad, "State Officials Question Smallpox Timetable," *New York Times,* 12/13/02, A1, for reaction to the plan.

70. Ceci Connolly, "2 Hospitals Refuse Call to Vaccinate Workers," *Washington Post,* 12/18/02, A2, citing decisions by Grady Memorial Hospital in Atlanta and Virginia Commonwealth University in Richmond. The article also cites other large hospitals as leaning against vaccinating employees.

71. www.rwjf.org.

72. Donald McNeil, Jr., "Mixed Reaction to Inoculations but Doubts Raised," *New York Times,* 12/15/2002, A23.

73. Rene Sanchez, "For Medical Workers, Smallpox Vaccine No Easy Remedy," *Washington Post,* 12/15/02, A36.

74. Leonard Cole, "When Smallpox Failed," *New York Times,* 12/2/01"; George Will, "War and Health," *Washington Post* editorial, February 8, 2002, A25.

75. Statement of Dr. Lisa Rotz, a medical epidemiologist at the bioterror program at the CDC, quoted in "Medical Conditions Create Vulnerability to Vaccine," by Denise Grady, *New York Times,* 9/24/02, A1.

76. Sheryl Gay Stolberg and Lawrence K. Altman, "New Plan to Meet Smallpox Attack: Each State Urged to Vaccinate Up to 1 Million in 10 Days," *New York Times,* 9/24/02, A1.

77. Lawrence Altman, "Smallpox Vaccine Knowledge Found Lacking," *New York Times,* 5/10/02.

78. Statement of James Koopman, quoted in "How Devastating Would a Smallpox Attack Really Be?" *Science,* Martin Enserink, 5/31/02 (296 (5573):1592).

79. For a discussion of a policy recommendation to offer the uninsured free access to care, without negative social and economic consequences, in the event of a bioterrorist attack, see Lawrence Gostin and Matthew Wynia's "Uninsured May Spread Bioterror Germs," *Science,* May 2002.

80. Lawrence O. Gostin, *Public Health Law: Power, Duty, Restraint* (Berkeley: University of California Press, 2000), 207.

81. Tuberculosis (TB) was once the cause of nearly 20 percent of the deaths in the United States striking people of different ages, genders, and socioeconomic classes equally. But the treatment of TB sufferers was anything but equal, as historian Sheila Rothman documents. See *Living in the Shadow of Death: Tuberculosis and the Social Experience of Illness in American History* (New York: Basic Books, 1994). In the late 1800s and early 1900s, public health officials exercised coercive police powers almost "exclusively against the vagrant, the poor, and the immigrant, who were thought careless in their hygiene and 'fractious and intractable' in their behavior" (Gostin, *Public Health Law,* p. 207).

The public health response to typhoid fever—a life-threatening bacterial illness spread by typhoid carriers handling food, or through untreated drinking water contaminated with sewage—offers another cautionary tale. The most famous U.S. case involved "Typhoid Mary" Mallon, a young Irish immigrant who worked as a cook in New York and was an asymptomatic carrier of the disease. Mallon was taken, tested, and imprisoned twice against her will, held for a total of more than twenty years without a trial, and in the absence of violating any criminal law—largely, according to historian Judith Waltzer, because of prejudice against the Irish and antipathy for a defiant woman of low economic status. See Judith Walzer Leavitt, *Typhoid Mary: Captive to the Public Health* (Boston: Beacon Press, 1996).

82. See Thomas Stoddard and Walter Reiman, "AIDS and the Rights of the Individual: Towards a More Sophisticated Understanding of Discrimination," *Millbank Quarterly* 8 Supp. 1 (1990), 143–174; N. Hunter and W. Rubenstein, eds, *AIDS Agenda: Emerging Issues in Civil Rights* (New York: The New Press, 1992); Laurie Garrett, *Betrayal of Trust* (New York: Hyperion, 2000); Randy Shilts, *And the Band Played On* (New York: St. Martin's Press, 1987).

83. *Ibid.,* Garrett, at pp. 400–01.

84. *Ibid.,* Gostin, *Public Health Law,* at p. 208.

85. *Ibid.,* Gostin, at p. 401.

86. Ceci Connolly, "Workers Exposed to Anthrax Shun Vaccine, Low Participation Is Blamed on Confusing Signals from U.S. Health Authorities," 1/8/02, A5. Further, a highly critical fifty-page report by the General Accounting Office (GAO) put into question the safety of the anthrax vaccine and the credibility of government officials who have withheld information about the vaccine's serious health risks. *Insight* magazine reports GAO's criticism is based on the findings of its randomly selected survey with 843 reservists from the U.S. Air Force and National Guard. "Alarmed service personnel are avoiding the shots by leaving the military at an alarming rate, and those who submit to the shots are becoming ill at a far greater rate than the Pentagon claimed. According to the GAO, between September 1998 and September 2000 about 16 percent of the pilots and aircrew members of the Guard and reserve had transferred to another unit . . ." "Of those who changed status or quit, 69 percent said it was because they didn't want to take the anthrax shots." The GAO's findings contradict the claims of the manufacturer (BioPort) and the Pentagon: "The overall rate reported for adverse reactions was nearly three times that published in the vaccine manufacturer's product insert, which claimed only 30 percent would experience some adverse reaction." In fact, 85 percent of those who were vaccinated reported experiencing some type of reaction. "Of those experiencing side effects, 24 percent had adverse effects considered serious enough for the shots to be discontinued."

87. http://snltranscripts.jt.org/01/01dashcroft.phtml. Kudos to Professor Marilee Lindemann, who reminded me, as she constantly does, that humor is truth and *Saturday Night Live* speaks it.

10. The Public Health Fallout from September 11: Official Deception and Long-Term Damage, *by Joel R. Kupferman*

1. Joel Kupferman is executive director and senior attorney for the Environmental Law and Justice Project, in New York.

2. Barasch, McGarry, Salzman, Penson, & Lim, *Firefighters Newsletter,* December 2002.

3. Conversation with Dr. David Parkinson of the Long Island Occupational and Environmental Health Clinic in Port Jefferson, New York, March 2002. Dr. Parkinson had examined the nurses where they work at NYU–Beekman Hospital in downtown Manhattan.

4. Toxic Targeting, Inc., "Toxic Targeting Computerized Report—WTC Complex New York New York 10048, September 11, 2001," September 18, 2001. Produced for the New York City Department of Design Construction.

5. EPA press release, "EPA Initiates Emergency Response Activities, Reassures Public About Environmental Hazards," September 13, 2001, http://www.epa.gov/wtc/stories/headline_091301.htm.

6. *Ibid.*

7. EPA press release, "NYC Monitoring Efforts Continue to Show Safe Drinking Water and Air," September 21, 2001, http://www.epa.gov/wtc/stories/headline2_092101.htm.

8. Stephen Levin, medical director, Mount Sinai-Selikoff Center for Occupational and Environmental Medicine, quoted in Christine Haughney, "Health Effects at World Trade Center Debated," *Washington Post,* January 6, 2003, 1.

9. EPA press release, "EPA, OSHA Update Asbestos Data, Continue to Reassure Public about Contamination Fears," September 16, 2001, http://www.epa.gov/wtc/stories/headline_091601.htm.

10. Kenneth R. Bazeinet, "WTC Trucks Had Wrong Dust Filters," *New York Daily News,* August 14, 2002.

11. NIEHS WETP National Clearing House for Worker Safety and Health Training, press release, "NIEHS WETP Response to the World Trade Center (WTC) Disaster: Initial WETP Grantee and Preliminary Assessment of Training Needs," October 23, 2001.

12. NYC Council, "Report from the Committee on Environmental Protection: Air Quality and Environmental Impacts due to the World Trade Center Disaster," December 2001.

13. White Paper "Lower Manhattan Air Quality," March 2002.

14. Remarks of EPA Administrator Christine Todd Whitman at Town Hall meeting, Libby, Montana, September 7, 2001, http://yosemite.epa.gov/administrator/speeches.nsf. Also, USEPA Region VII memorandum, from Christopher Weiss, senior toxicologist, to Paul Peronard, on-scene coordinator: "Amphibole Mineral Fibers in Source materials in Residential and Commercial Areas of Libby Pose an Imminent and Substantial Endangerment to Public Health," December 20, 2001.

15. Jim Carlton, "Buck-Passing Delayed EPA in 9/11 Cleanup," *Wall Street Journal,* May 9, 2002.

16. R. Radhakrishnan, PE, director, Asbestos Control Program, NYC DEP, "Notice to Building Owners Located South of 14th Street, Manhattan," May 11, 2002.

17. Conversation with Russell Peunies, attorney, DEP Legal Affairs Bureau, January 24, 2003.

18. Flyer, DOH, "Recommendations for People Re-Occupying Commercial Buildings and Residents Re-entering their Homes," undated, at www.ci.nyc.ny.us/html/doh/html/alerts/wtc.3.html.

19. This is required under the Clean Air Act's National Emissions Standards for Hazardous Air Pollutants (NESHAP) Regulations (40 CFR, Part 61) and under the Asbestos School Hazard Detection and Control Act (AHERA), OSHA Standards 20 CFR 1926.1101.

20. "Preliminary Report on Health and Safety Evaluation of the Fresh Kills Landfill Project Supporting the WTC Disaster Recovery," by Emilcott Associates for the NYC Detectives' Endowment Association, September 27, 2001. OSHA's respiratory protection standard 29CFR1910.134 requires fit-testing of all tight-fitting respirators.

21. Testimony, New York State Assembly Standing Committees on Environmental Conservation, Health and Labor, November 26, 2001.

22. Conversation with Dr. Stephen Levin, January 24, 2003.

23. Quoted in Michael Ellison, "Heroes of Ground Zero at Risk Breathing Toxic Cocktail," *The Guardian,* October 27, 2001.

24. Dr. Cate Jenkins, "3/6/02 Draft: Asbestos in Settled Dust and Soils," March 6, 2002. Dr. Jenkins, PhD, is an environmental scientist with the Waste Identification Branch, HWID, Office of Solid Waste, at U.S. EPA.

25. Quoted in Dan Fagin, "Tests Not a Danger Here," *Newsday,* September 15, 2001.

26. This information only came out a month later, with the release of documents requested under FOIA.

27. Dr. Cate Jenkins, memo March 6, 2002, and memo "Libby v. Manhattan Different Asbestos Testing Methods," February 14, 2002.

28. I used a plastic spoon and Ziploc bags, but this method does not affect the quality of the sampling in terms of discovering its toxic content. (I also dressed in protective gear.)

29. Conversation with local lab director, late September 2001. And conversation with Dr. Robert Simon, director, ETI Lab, Fairfax, Virginia, September 29, 2001. Dr. Simon's lab had also confirmed our test results.

30. 51 FR 15728.

31. *Ibid.*

32. Alyssa Katz, "Toxic Haste: New York's Media Rush to Judgment on New York's Air," *The American Prospect,* February 25, 2002.

33. *Ibid.*

34. Testimony, Patricia Clark, regional administrator, U.S. Department of Labor, OSHA, before the New York State Assembly Standing Committees, November 26, 2001.

35. NIEHS WETP report, op.cit.

36. Quoted in James L. Nash, "Cleaning Up after 9/11: Respirators, Power and Politics," *Occupational Hazards,* May 10, 2002.

37. NYC Department of Health press release, "NYC Department of Health Releases Community Needs Assessment of Lower Manhattan," January 11, 2002.

38. Barash, McGarry, Salzman, Penson, & Lim, "Firefighters Newsletter," Vol. I, December 2002.

39. Paul J. Lioy et. al., "Characterization of the Dust/Smoke Aerosol that Settled East of the World Trade Center(WTC) in Lower Manhattan after the Collapse of the WTC 11 September 2001," *Environmental Health Perspectives,* July 2002, 703–712.

40. The newspaper's front page carried Gonzalez's article on October 26, with the headline "Toxic Zone."

41. Email from Louise Munster, Freedom of Information Officer, NYS DEC, Region 1, to the Environmental Law and Justice Project, September 24, 2001.

42. *Daily News*/New York 1 poll, at http://www.732-2m2m.com/tt/2002March_articles.htm.

43. EPA method number 600/j-93/167.

44. Howard Bader, environmental engineer, quoted in Cate Jenkins memorandum, "Stuyvesant High School Testing," August 29, 2002.

45. Conversation with Deputy Schools Chancellor Klasfeld, September 4, 2002.

46. NYC DEP memo to New York City landlords dated May 11, 2002.

47. Memo from Salvatore J. Cassano, chief of operations, NYFD Bureau of Operations, August 2, 2002.

48. *Ibid.*

49. Conversation with Lieutenant Colonel Douglas W. Sarvel, Army Corps of Engineers—NY District, October 2002.

50. OMB Watch keeps a list of information removed from government Web sites. See www.omb watch.org/article/archive/104.

51. Attorney General John Ashcroft, *Memorandum for Heads of all Federal Departments and Agencies,* at http://www.epic.org/open_gov/foiagallery/memorandum.html.

52. Conversation with Russell Pecunies, January 24, 2003.

53. 42 USC Sec 9601-9674 CERCLA empowers the EPA to act to prevent environmental contamination and to ensure that, when contamination occurs, it is thoroughly cleaned up, both with short-term measures and with long-term remedial action to provide a permanent remedy.

54. See J. Echeverria and Julie Kaplan, *Poisonous Procedural "Reform": In Defense of Environmental Right to Know,* Georgetown Environmental Law and Policy Institute, gelpi@law.georgetown.edu.

55. The National Contingency Plan gives the EPA and other agencies great powers to collect data and mitigate environmental trauma. 42 USC 9604. 40 CFR 300. Acknowledging the EPA's power and responsibility in the WTC crisis, Whitman testified to the Senate Appropriations Committee that her agency is "assigned lead responsibility for cleaning up buildings and other sites contaminated by chemical or biological agents as a result of terrorism." Testimony, November 28, 2001.

56. Andrew Schneider, "White House Office Blocked EPA's Asbestos Cleanup Plan," *St. Louis Post-Dispatch,* December 29, 2002, A1.

57. Designation Under Executive Order 12958 Federal Register, Vol. 67, No. 90.

58. Robert Martin, resignation letter to Governor Whitman, April 22, 2002.

59. Eric Schaeffer's resignation letter is at www.ewg.org/reports/cpa/schaefferltr.html.

60. Testimony, March 7, 2002.

61. ABT Associates, "Particulate Related Health Impacts of Eight Electric Utility Systems," prepared for the Rockefeller Family Fund, at www.rffundorganization.com. Eric Schaeffer now heads this organization's environmental enforcement project.

62. Christopher Lee, "Whistle-Blower Case at Issue: Senators Decry Intervention by Labor Department Solicitor," *Washington Post,* October 25, 2002, A27.

11. Axis of Antagonism: U.S.–European Relations and the War on Terrorism, *by Gary Younge*

1. Gary Younge is the New York correspondent of *The Guardian* and author of *No Place Like Home: A Black Briton's Journey through the Deep South* (Jackson: University of Mississippi Press, 2002).

2. Jean-Marie Colombani, "We are all Americans," *Le Monde*, September 12, 2001.

3. John Hooper, "Clashes as Bush Lands in Berlin," *The Guardian*, May 23, 2002.

4. "Habits of Alliance," *Washington Post*, January 19, 2003.

5. John Hooper, "Schroder Races Ahead in Polls," *The Guardian*, September 14, 2002.

6. Haig Simonian, "A Megaphone Diplomat," *Financial Times*, September 14, 2002.

7. John Hooper, "U.S. Snubs Conciliatory Schroder," *The Guardian*, September 24, 2002.

8. Kemal Ahmed, "No War Without U.N. Approval Warns Poll," *The Observer*, September 29, 2002.

9. Adrian Hamilton, "The Pathetic Mythology of British Influence," *The Independent*, October 25, 2002.

10. Quentin Peel, "Allies at Fork in Road to World Order," *Financial Times*, September 10, 2002.

11. David E. Sanger, "Rivals Differ on U.S. Role in the World," *New York Times*, October 30, 2002.

12. Martin Woollacott, "Bush Team Think We, the Allies, Crave U.S. Leadership," *The Guardian*, December 15, 2000.

13. Quentin Peel, op cit.

14. Editorial, "What Common Foreign Policy?" *The Economist*, September 21, 2002.

15. Peter Kilfoyle, "Defending Ourselves," *The Guardian*, September 23, 2002.

16. Peter Norman, "Low Vote May See Less Abrasive Assembly, *Financial Times*, June 14, 1999.

17. Ivo Daalder, "Widening the Gap," *Washington Times*, July 20, 2001.

18. Christopher Olgiati, "Rough Justice: The White House via Death Row," *The Guardian*, 12 October 1993.

19. Editorial, "Chilly in the West, Warmer in the East," *The Economist*, May 25, 2002.

20. Pedro Calvo Hernando, "Bush Braves Flak to Cross Atlantic," *The Guardian*, June 16, 2001.

21. Le Monde, "Bush Braves Flak to Cross Atlantic," *The Guardian*, June 16, 2001.

22. Robin Young, "When Churchill Championed Poison Gas," *The Times (London)*, January 3, 1997.

23. *Ibid.*

24. Clinton Cox, "From Columbus to Hitler and Back Again," *Race and Class*, January 1, 2002.

25. Klaus-Dieter Frankenberger, "Bush Braves Flak to Cross Atlantic," *The Guardian*, June 16, 2001.

26. Matthew Engel, "A Galaxy Far Away," *The Guardian*, February 26, 2002.

27. Gary Younge, "War against the Weak," *The Guardian*, October 1, 2001.

28. The bombing of Amoagh in August 1998, alongside subsequent isolated incidents, showed that terrorism could not be eliminated completely, since a few dedicated people can cause enormous havoc. But the political settlement showed that with the will and negotiations in good faith, you can limit the odds of acts of terrorism taking place, marginalize violence from a political culture.

29. Editorial, "Chilly in the West, Warmer in the East," *The Economist,* May 25, 2002.

30. *Ibid.*

31. "German Foreign Minister Criticizes U.S. Foreign Policy," *Associated Press,* February 12, 2002.

32. *Ibid.*

33. David E. Sanger, "Allies Hear Sour Notes in Axis of Evil Chorus," *New York Times,* February 17, 2002.

34. Gerard Baker and Richard Wolffe, "Powell Shurgs off European Dismay over Axis of Evil," *Financial Times,* February 14, 2002.

35. *Ibid.*

36. *Ibid.*

37. Julian Borger, Suzanne Goldenberg, and Michael White, "Can Blair Hope to Sway Bush?" *The Guardian,* January 16, 2003.

38. Gavin Cordon, "Straw Puts Pressure on U.N. to Accept New Iraq Resolution," *Press Association,* October 18, 2002.

12. The "War on Terror" and Women's Rights: A Pakistan-Afghan Perspective, *by Farida Shaheed*

1. Farida Shaheed, a sociologist based in Pakistan, is a coordinator of Shirkat Gah-Women's Resource Centre, which aims to promote women's rights to social justice and social justice for women's rights. Her particular responsibility is the Women Law and Status program, which combines grassroots capacity building with policy advocacy. She is also a Core Group member of the Women Living Under Muslim Laws network of information, solidarity, and support.

2. For example, Israel's immediate actions in the West Bank and Australia's announcement in late 2002 justifying preemptive strikes in Southeast Asia.

3. Quoted in Nikki Craft, "A Call on Feminists to Protest the War Against Afghanistan," in *September 11, 2001: Feminist Perspectives,* ed. Susan Hawthorne and Bronwyn Winter (Melbourne: Spinifex Press Pty Ltd., 2002), 151–155.

4. WLUML—*Dossier d'information sur la situation en Algérie—Resistance des femmes et solidarité internationale. (Compilation of information on the situation in Algeria. Women's Resistance and Solidarity around the World.)* March 1995: WLUML and Shirkat Gah-Women's Resource Centre newspaper clippings files, *The News* and *Dawn,* various dates.

5. Arundhati Roy, *The Algebra of Infinite Justice* (New Delhi: Viking, 2001), 258.

6. Nikki Craft, op. cit. p. 155.

7. Revolutionary Afghan Women's Association (RAWA), "Statement on the US Strikes on Afghanistan," RAWA listserv (October 11, 2001).

8. Afghan Women's Network; Resolution of AWN meeting held in Peshawar, November 7, 2001, sent to Shirkat Gah-Women's Resource Centre on November 9, 2001, and further circulated by WLUML as an Action Alert.

9. Representatives of Afghan Women's Network and Afghan Women's Resource Center at Workshop for Heinrich Böll Foundation Board of Directors, Lahore, November 23, 2002.

10. Afghan Women's Council: *Women Rebuilding Afghanistan—Building the Future with Women: The Challenges of Reconstruction of Afghanistan;* Post Mission Report; December 2002, listserv.

11. Participant in the *Consultation with Afghan Women;* Lahore, November 29–30, 2001—organized by Shirkat Gah and WLUML.

12. Human Rights Watch, "All Our Hopes are Crushed: Violence and Repression in Western Afghanistan," Vol. 14, No. 7(C), October 2002; www.hrw.org/rdeports/2002/afghan3, p.1 of summary; printer-friendly copy [pdf, 54 pages].

13. *Ibid.,* Human Rights Watch, p. 2 of summary.

14. In these attacks, British forces provided some political cover for the U.S. but played a marginal role.

15. "Report of October 17, 2001, National Consultation on NGO Attacks," prepared by Shirkat Gah on behalf of the Joint Action Committee for Citizens' Rights and Peace (JAC) and the Pakistan NGO Forum (PNF) and circulated on October 18, 2001. (At the request of NGOs in NWFP province, Shirkat Gah organized the meeting on behalf of the two coalitions, JAC and PNF, of which it is a member. The meeting brought together some ninety representatives of NGOs, including the seven organizations attacked on October 8, 2001.)

16. Under the new electoral system, sixty additional seats in the National Assembly are reserved for women elected by members elected on general seats.

17. In terms of votes, the situation is somewhat less alarming, with combined politico-religious candidates raising their vote share from 7 percent of votes polled in 1993 to 10 percent in 2002. Analysts believe one-third of the 1.5 million-vote increase is due to the natural population growth of their support base (*The Friday Times,* October 18–24, 2002). The lowering of the voting age from twenty-one years to eighteen years also benefited these political parties who were able to mobilize the sizeable student bodies of their *madrassahs* (schools).

18. Daily press briefings on military action in Afghanistan, by Donald Rumsfeld, U.S. Secretary of Defense and other officials, telecast on CNN, October–December 2001.

19. The MMA's success in the Punjab, where the majority of Pakistan's people live, is marginal, and its presence in the second most populous province, Sindh, is also largely confined to the city of Karachi.

20. *The News,* November 20, 2002. An MMA member of Parliament also raised Kasi's execution in the inaugural session of the National Assembly.

21. *Daily Times,* November 20, 2002.

22. *The News,* January 2, 2003, front page; "Operations Against A1 Qaeda Resume," *The Friday Times,* January 17–23, 2003.

23. Zbigniew Brzezinski, national security adviser to President Carter, cited in Sonali Kolhatkar, "By Any Standards This Is a War Against Afghans," *September 11, 2001: Feminist Perspectives,* ed. Susan Hawthorne and Bronwyn Winter (Melbourne: Spinifex Press Pty Ltd., 2002), 207–214.

24. Charlotte Bunch, an eminent American feminist, calls U.S. foreign policy "military-and-corporate-driven." See Bunch, "Whose Security?" *The Nation,* September 23, 2002. See also Karen Talbot, "Afghanistan, Central Asia, Georgia: Key to Oil Profit," in Hawthorne and Winter op cit., 285–301.

25. The *chador* is a large shawl and was made compulsory over the lighter smaller shawl, *duppatta,* which is a part of the national dress worn by almost all women in Pakistan, even if only slung on a shoulder.

26. Amongst the grievances of the tribal lords and religious authorities who took up arms in 1978 was that the government was forcing girls to go to school, and had prohibited the sale of women and the levirate—the custom of marrying a widow to her previous husband's brother.

27. Sudha Ramachandran, quoting Soraya, an Afghan woman she interviewed, in "Behind the Veil of Oppression," Hawthorne and Winter, op cit. 142. First printed in *The Hindu* Sunday magazine, November 4, 2001.

28. *Ibid.*

29. Pervez Hoodbhoy, "Musharraf and the Jihad Industry," unpublished version of article for newspapers sent out on his listserv (October 2, 2002).

30. In Algeria, so-called Islamists captured women and turned them into slave-prostitutes and sometimes raped virgin women before executing them. See, for example, Zazi Sadou, "Algeria: The Martyrdom of Girls Raped by Islamic Armed Groups," in *Without Reservation: The Beijing Tribunal on Accountability for Women's Human Rights,* ed. Niamh Reilly, Center for Women's Global Leadership (New Brunswick: Rutgers University, 1996), 28–33.

31. Derek Brown, "New Afghanistan Carries on Grisly Game of the Old," *The Guardian,* May 4, 1992, p. 7, quoted by Valentine Moghadam, "Women, the Taliban, and the Politics of Public Space in Afghanistan," in Hawthorne and Winter op cit, p. 272.

32. Shahla Zia, "Some Experiences of the Women's Movement: Strategies for Success," in *Shaping Women's Lives—Laws, Practices and Strategies in Pakistan,* ed. Farida Shaheed et al. (Lahore: Shirkat Gah, 1998), 371–414.

33. Pakistan signed with a declaration stating that accession "is subject to the provisions of the Constitution of the Islamic Republic of Pakistan" and reserved on paragraph 1 of Article 29 of the Convention (relating to dispute between states parties).

34. Mai Yamani, Saudi Arabian scholar, BBC Special, *World Debate on Iraq,* November 24, 2002.

35. This formulation is from Philip Cunliffe, "The Double Death of Fundamentalism," *The Week*—ending November 10, 2002, at the_week@hotmail.com.

36. This is not to imply that imperialism is antiwomen. Indeed, traditionally, anti-imperialist movements have been pro-women.

37. For example, Feminist Majority president Ellie Smeal and Mavis Leno—see Nikki Craft op. cit. p. 151.

38. *Consultation with Afghan Women: November 29–30, 2001—Lahore,* organized by Shirkat Gah and WLUML and bringing together forty-nine women from dozens of Afghan organizations, interview with Palwasha Hassan, coordinator, Afghan Women's Network, December 2, 2001.

39. Quoted in Rosalind Petchesky, "Phantom Towers: Feminist Reflections on the Battle between Global Capital and Fundamentalist Terrorism," in Hawthorne and Winter op cit. p. 320.

13. Human Rights, the Bush Administration, and the Fight against Terrorism: The Need for a Positive Vision, *by Kenneth Roth*

1. Kenneth Roth is executive director of Human Rights Watch.

2. Adam Clymer, "World Survey Says Negative Views of U.S. Are Rising," *New York Times,* December 5, 2002; the Pew Research Center for the People and the Press, "What the World Thinks in 2002: How

Global Publics View: Their Lives, Their Countries, The World, America," http://people-press.org/reports/display.php3?ReportID=165.

3. Geneva Convention Relative to the Treatment of Prisoners of War of August 12, 1949 (Third Geneva Convention), Article 5. The United States ratified the convention in 1955.

4. Taliban detainees should have been eligible for POW status under Article 4(A)(1) of the Third Geneva Convention, which grants such status unconditionally to "[m]embers of the armed forces of a Party to the conflict." The same should have been true for Al Qaeda detainees who had belonged to a militia "forming part of" the Taliban forces. *Id.* However, Al Qaeda members operating outside of Taliban structures would have to meet a separate four-part test under Article 4(A)(2) of the convention—having a responsible chain of command, wearing a distinctive sign, carrying arms openly, and respecting the laws and customs of war. Because these Al Qaeda members would likely fail one or more of these requirements, they would probably be ineligible for POW status.

5. Third Geneva Convention, Article 118.

6. Brian Whitaker and Duncan Campbell, "CIA Missile Kills al-Qaida Suspects: US Admits Involvement in Yemen Attack by Drone," *The Guardian,* November 5, 2002; see also James Risen and David Johnston, "Bush has Widened Authority of C.I.A. to Kill Terrorists," *New York Times,* December 15, 2002; "No holds barred: Yemen and the War on Terrorism," *The Economist,* November 9, 2002.

7. The *New York Times* quoted unnamed U.S. officials stating that the CIA and FBI would "seek to capture terrorists when possible and bring them into custody": see James Risen and David Johnston, "Bush Has Widened Authority of C.I.A. to Kill Terrorists," *New York Times,* December 15, 2002, but no such formal pronouncement was made publicly.

8. For more on the Bush administration's abuse of immigration laws to conduct criminal investigations, see Human Rights Watch, *Presumption of Guilt: Human Rights Abuses of Post–September 11 Detainees,* August 2002, http://www.hrw.org/reports/2002/us911/Index.htm#TopOfPage.

9. Protocol Additional to the Geneva Conventions of August 12, 1949, and Relating to the Protection of Victims of International Armed Conflict (Protocol I), Article 75. Although the United States has not ratified Protocol I, the requirements of Article 75 nonetheless bind the United States because they reflect customary international law.

10. Third Geneva Convention, Article 102 (POWs can be "validly sentenced only if the sentence has been pronounced by the same courts according to the same procedure as in the case of members or the armed forces of the Detaining Power").

11. Third Geneva Convention, Article 130 (defining "grave breaches," or war crimes, to include "willfully depriving a prisoner of war of the rights of fair and regular trial prescribed by this Convention").

12. Human Rights Watch conversations with State Department. See also Human Rights Watch, "Kazakhstan: Turkmen Dissident in Grave Danger of Deportation," September 13, 2002; http://www.hrw.org/press/2002/09/kazakh0913.htm; Glenn Kessler and Peter Slevin, "Cheney Is Fulcrum of Foreign Policy; In Interagency Fights, His Views Often Prevail," *Washington Post,* October 13, 2002.

13. Remarks by the President on U.S. Humanitarian Aid to Afghanistan, The White House, October 11, 2002, http://www.whitehouse.gov/news/releases/2002/10/20021011-3.html.

14. Human Rights Watch, *"We Want to Live As Humans": Repression of Women and Girls in Western Afghanistan,* December 2002, http://www.hrw.org/reports/2002/afghnwmn1202; Human Rights Watch, *"All Our Hopes Are Crushed": Violence and Repression in Western Afghanistan,* October 2002, http://hrw.org/reports/2002/afghan3/.

15. Linda D. Kozaryn, " 'On the Edge' with Rumsfeld in Afghanistan," *American Forces Press Service,* May 3, 2002, http://www.vnis.com/vetnews/usdefense/usdefense2002/usdefense2002-018.htm#7; see also Glenn Kessler, "Study Cites Repression by Afghan Governor," *Washington Post,* November 5, 2002.

16. President Tours Area Damage by Squires Fire, Ruch, Oregon, August 22, 2002, http://www.white house.gov/news/releases/2002/08/20020822-1.html.

17. *Id.*

18. For a copy of the Taft letter, see http://www.hrw.org/press/2002/08/exxon072902.pdf. For a discussion of the lawsuit, see Human Rights Watch, "U.S./Indonesia: Bush Backtracks on Corporate Responsibility," August 7, 2002, http://www.hrw.org/press/2002/08/exxon080702.htm.

19. The United States has ratified the International Covenant on Civil and Political Rights; the Convention Against Torture and Other Cruel, Inhuman or Degrading Treatment or Punishment; the International Convention on the Elimination of All Forms of Racial Discrimination; and the Convention on the Prevention and Punishment of the Crime of Genocide. It has not ratified the International Covenant on Economic, Social and Cultural Rights; the Convention on the Elimination of All Forms of Discrimination Against Women; and the Convention on the Rights of the Child.

20. Protocol I.

21. For a discussion of the methods that the U.S. government has used to prevent judicial enforcement of human rights treaties, see Kenneth Roth, "An Empire Above the Law," *Bard Journal of Global Affairs,* Fall 2002; Kenneth Roth, "The Charade of US Ratification of International Human Rights Treaties," *Chicago Journal of International Law* 347, Fall 2000.

22. See, e.g., Dana Priest and Barton Gellman, "U.S. Decries Abuse but Defends Interrogations: 'Stress and Duress' Tactics Used on Terrorism Suspects Held in Secret Overseas Facilities," *Washington Post,* December 26, 2002.

23. For more on the human rights record of these countries in 2002, see Human Rights Watch, *World Report 2003,* 216–29 (China), 350–59 (Russia), 382–90 (Uzbekistan), 459–72 (Israel). See also Human Rights Watch, "Russia: Clock Running Out for Displaced Chechens in Ingushetia," December 26, 2002, http://www.hrw.org/press/2002/12/russia1226.htm; Mike Jendrzejczyk, "Condemning the Crackdown in Western China," *Asian Wall Street Journal,* December 16, 2002; Reuters, "China steps up call to fight Muslim separatists," December 23, 2002.

24. *World Report 2003,* 488–96.

25. Human Rights Watch, *"By Invitation Only": Australian Asylum Policy,* December 10, 2002.

26. *World Report 2003,* 127.

27. Human Rights Watch, "Uganda Attacks Freedom of the Press: Closes Main Independent Newspaper," October 11, 2002, http://www.hrw.org/press/2002/10/uganda1011.htm.

28. Human Rights Watch, "Leading Liberian Journalist Re-Arrested: Facing Possible 'Terrorist' Charges," July 4, 2002, http://hrw.org/press/2002/07/liberia0704.htm.

29. Fred Hiatt, "Truth-Tellers in a Time of Terror," *Washington Post,* November 25, 2002. See also Human Rights Watch, "Opportunism in the Face of Tragedy: Repression in the Name of Antiterrorism," http://www.hrw.org/campaigns/september11/opportunismwatch.htm#Eritrea; Human Rights Watch, "Eritrea: Cease Persecution of Journalists and Dissidents," May 16, 2002, http://hrw.org/press/2002/05/eritrea0516.htm; Human Rights Watch, "Escalating Crackdown in Eritrea: Reformists, Journalists, Students at Risk," September 21, 2001, http://www.hrw.org/press/2001/09/eritrea0921.htm.

30. Human Rights Watch, "Opportunism in the Face of Tragedy: Repression in the Name of Anti-terrorism," http://www.hrw.org/campaigns/september11/opportunismwatch.htm#Zimbabwe.

31. On February 14, 2002, Milosevic delivered his opening defense at the International Criminal Tribunal for the Former Yugoslavia, in The Hague: "The Americans go right the other side of the globe to fight against terrorism—in Afghanistan, a case in point, right the other side of the world, and that is considered to be logical and normal. Whereas here the struggle against terrorism in the heart of one's own country, in one's own home, is considered to be a crime." http://www.un.org/icty/transe54/020214IT.htm, 248–49.

INDEX

Abbasi, Ali, 145
Abourezk, James, 125
Absconder Apprehension Initiative, 84
Accountability, 79–80, 184, 189
Accuracy in Media (AIM), 153
ACLU. *See* American Civil Liberties Union
Activism, 39–41, 202, 204, 227, 233
Adams, Jan, 117
Administrative detention, 23–24
Administrative process, 14, 21–29
Advocates, civil rights, 4, 6
Afghanistan, 84, 86, 87, 89, 135, 136,
    140–144
    bombing of, 209, 228
    human rights in, 245–246
    prisoners from, 239
    USSR in, 230
    war in, 252, 253
    women's rights in, 222, 224–226,
      231–233, 236
Afghan Women's Council (AWC), 225, 234
Afghan Women's Network (AWN), 225,
    234
African Americans, 91–94, 100
African National Congress (ANC), 17, 19
The Age of Sacred Terror (Daniel
    Benjamin), 104
Agronsky & Co., 153
AHERA (Asbestos Hazard Emergency
    Response Act) standards, 196
AIDS, 177, 179, 180
AIM (Accuracy in Media), 153
"Air-gapped," 70

Airline passenger screening, 97–98, 121
Airports, 97–98, 103, 121
Air quality, 185, 186, 189, 190–191,
    193–194, 196, 198, 200, 201, 205–206
Albasti, Tarek Abdelhamid, 77
Albright, Madeleine, 214
Algeria, 224, 248
Algerians, 136, 143, 242
Al-Harethi, Qaid Salim Sinan, 242
Alice in Wonderland (Lewis Carroll), 133
Alien and Sedition Acts (1789), 21, 30
Alien Registration Act (1940). *See* Smith
    Act
Al Jazeera network, 152
Al Qaeda, 19–20, 27, 53, 68, 79, 89, 95, 100,
    101, 104, 135, 136, 138, 141–143, 146,
    151, 156, 157, 229, 241, 242
Alvarez, Oswaldo, 126
Ambrose, Thomas, 98
American Booksellers Foundation for Free
    Expression, 65
American Civil Liberties Union (ACLU), 4,
    65, 96, 112–115, 117–119, 123–125,
    127–129, 172
American Declaration of the Rights and
    Duties of Man, 144
American Friends Service Committee, 125
American League for Peace and
    Democracy, 25
American Muslim Alliance, 116
American Public Health Association, 169
America's Most Wanted (television show),
    119

Amherst, Massachusetts, 130
Amin, Hafizullah, 230
Amnesty International, 82
Analytical deficit (on information
    collection), 68
Anarchism, 30, 35
ANC. *See* African National Congress
Anfal genocide, 252, 253
Ann Arbor, Michigan, 7, 129–130
Anthony, Antonia, 125
Anthrax, 176, 179–182
Antiprofiling legislation, 108
Antiterrorism and Effective Death Penalty
    Act (1996), 17, 19, 41
Antiterrorism laws, 218
Antiwar rallies, 123
AP (Associated Press), 157
Appeals, court, 133–134
Arab-American communities, 106
Arab-American groups, 98
Arab American Institute, 102, 106
Arab Americans, 91, 95
Arab communities, 105
Arab Community Center for Economic
    and Social Services, 106
Arabs, 76, 78–83, 85, 89, 94, 96, 98, 102,
    104, 106, 112
Arbitrary detention, 140
Armed conflict, 140
Armey, Richard, 7, 51, 119
Army Corps of Engineers, 203
Arnold, Thurman, 25
ARPANET, 67
Article II (Constitution), 50
Article IV (International Covenant on
    Civil and Political Rights), 143–144
Article IV (Third Geneva Convention),
    141, 142
Article V (Third Geneva Convention), 141,
    142
Aryan Nation, 100

Asbestos, 184, 187, 188, 190, 191, 194–197,
    199, 201–204
Asbestos Hazard Emergency Response Act
    (AHERA) standards, 196
Ashcroft, John, 244
    antiterrorism acts advocated by, 33
    on civil liberties as support for
        terrorists, 8
    detention of foreign nationals by, 30
    discriminatory detentions ordered by,
        80–81
    on dissent and patriotism, 122
    and "enemy combatants," 86–87
    on FISA victory, 61, 62
    on FOIA vs. security, 204
    on foreign surveillance, 44
    and hate crimes, 95
    immigration law used by, 27, 28
    information withholding advocated by,
        36
    intelligence gathering advocated by, 40,
        41
    on investigatory detention, 47
    on Jose Padilla, 242
    and preventive law enforcement, 13
    secret arrests ordered by, 76
    secret detentions/immigration
        proceedings of, 2–3
    and secret immigration hearings, 75
    and terrorism threat, 101
    on terrorists, 133
Assembly, 117–118, 122–125
Assets, freezing of, 28–29
Associated Press (AP), 157
Association, 89, 90
Asthma, 189, 192
ATC Associates, 195
"Aunt Molly question," 98, 104
Austin, Texas, 128
Australia, 251
Australians, 145

AWC. *See* Afghan Women's Council
AWN. *See* Afghan Women's Network
"Axis of evil" speech, 219–220, 234
Aziz, Amir, 229

Baader Meinhof Gang, 217
Bailey, Dorothy, 25–26
Barriers, surveillance, 63, 66, 69
Barth, Alan, 26
Bartlett, Paul, 193
Basque country, 217
"Battlefied detainees," 143
Behavior, 102–103
Belarus, 239
Bellow, Bonnie, 194
Benevolence International Foundation, 29
Benjamin, Daniel, 104
Berkeley, California, 7, 129
Betrayal of Trust (Laurie Garrett), 180
Bill of Rights, 47, 123, 128
Bin Laden, Osama, 225, 229
Biological Weapons Convention, 240
Biomedical Security Institute, 174
Bioterrorism, 161, 168–176, 182
    fear of, 162
    and health information networks, 173–176
    and Homeland Security Act, 169–170
    and Model State Emergency Health Powers Act, 170–173
    preparedness for, 174
    and smallpox, 176–179
Birmingham church firebombing, 100
Black church burnings, 100
Black Codes, 91
Black Panthers, 126
Blair, Tony, 210–211, 217, 220
Bombs, cluster, 252
Bonior, David, 118
Booksellers, 45, 63–65

Borough of Manhattan Community College, 201
Bosnia, 136, 242
Bosnia-Herzegovina, 140, 143
Boston Globe, 94
Boston University, 164
Boundaries, surveillance, 54–58. *See also* Barriers, surveillance
Boyle, Michael J., 78
Brandenburg v. Ohio, 16, 40–41
Bridges, Harry, 30
Broadcasting ban (UK), 218
Brookings Institution, 214
Brown, A. J., 118
Brown, Ralph, 13, 15, 26
Buffalo News, 157
Building cleanup (NYC), 190, 202
Burger, Warren, 5
Burma, 239
Burqa, 232, 233, 236, 245
Buses, 203
Bush, George W., 6, 33. *See also* Bush administration
    "axis of evil" speech of, 219–220
    on Britain, 210–211
    court-packing by, 51
    detention authority claimed by, 86
    and expiration of USA PATRIOT Act, 36
    foreign policy of, 32, 211–213
    and Homeland Security department, 34
    military tribunal order of, 31
    on Pervez Musharraf, 226
    press perceptions of, 156, 157
    racial profiling decried by, 94
    SDGT executive order by, 28
    "Signing Statement" of, 64–65
    in Spain, 214–215
    and terrorists as enemies of freedom, 8
    vigilantism/hate crimes resisted by, 3, 95, 112

Bush, George W. (*cont.*)
  war on terrorism declared by, 52
  and women's rights, 224
Bush, Jeb, 97
Bush administration:
  and accountability mechanisms, 67
  antiterrorism executive orders issued by,
    34–35
  Ashcroft controlled by, 9
  and censorship, 13
  FISA amendments by, 60
  on Geneva Conventions, 141
  and human rights, 238–240
  preventive detentions used by, 76
  and privacy rights, 163
  on profiling, 100–101
  secret government of, 36–39
  security-industrial complex growth in,
    70, 71
  surveillance barriers broken down by, 58
  visa checks imposed by, 96

Cable News Network (CNN), 115,
    153–155
Cairo Programme of Action, 249
California, 115–116
California Police Chiefs Association, 128
Cal State—Sacreamento, 124
Cambridge (MA), 123–124, 130
Camp Delta (Guantánamo Bay, Cuba), 136
Camp X-Ray (Guantánamo Bay, Cuba),
    135, 219
Canada, 56
Capital punishment, 122, 214–215
CAPPS II. *See* Computer Assisted
    Passenger Pre-Screening System
CAPS. *See* Computer Assisted Passenger
    Screening System
Carlin, George, 125
Carnegie Mellon University, 174
CARNIVORE search engine, 57, 59, 64

Carrboro (NC), 130
Castaño, Carlo, 244
Catholics for a Free Choice, 223
Caught in the Backlash, 115–116, 119
CBO (Congressional Budget Office), 167
CDC. *See* Centers for Disease Control
CEDAW. *See* United Nations' Convention
    on the Elimination of All Forms of
    Discrimination Against Women
Censorship, 13, 15, 41, 116, 197
Center for Constitutional Rights, 202
Center for National Security Studies, 78
Centers for Disease Control (CDC), 162,
    165, 168–174, 181–182
Central Intelligence Agency (CIA), 46, 53,
    66, 67, 126, 242
CERCLA (Compensation and Liability
    Act), 204
Cerner Corporation, 175
Chador (veil), 231
Chafee, Zechariah, 15
Charitable organizations, 18–19
Chechnya, 217, 218, 247, 250
Checks and balances, 50, 67, 75
Chemical weapons, 253
Cheney, Dick, 137
Chertoff, Michael, 83
Chicago, 7, 125, 126
Chicanos, 92
Children, 115, 248–249
China, 239, 240, 247, 249, 250
Chinese, 92
Churchill, Winston, 215
CIA. *See* Central Intelligence Agency
Cipro, 181
Citizens, 76–80, 86–88, 115, 134
Civil disobedience, 40
Civil lawsuits, 38
Civil rights:
    communities adopting resolutions for
      protection of, 7, 51

documentation of violations of,
113–115
preserving, 7
Civil Rights Division (DOJ), 91
Civil rights movement, 35
Civil Service Commission, 25
Civil society groups, 227
Clark, Marjorie, 202
Clarke, Richard, 69–70
Classified information, 148
Clean Air Act, 190, 206
Clinton, Bill, 28, 93, 155, 158, 218
Clinton administration, 69, 156–157, 167,
214, 224
"Clipper Chip," 69
Cluster bombs, 252
CNN. See Cable News Network
Coalition for Peace and Justice, 123
Cocaine, 92
Coffin, William Sloane, 1
Cohen, David, 126
COINTELPRO, 31
Cold War, 13, 15, 26, 31, 35, 53, 57, 70, 238
Cold War Internal Security Act (1950),
23–24
Cole, David, 110
"Collateral damage," 228
Collier, Robert, 126
Colombia, 244–245, 251
Colonialism, 215–216
Columbus, Georgia, 123
"Combatant's privilege," 141
Communes, 24
Communications, 38, 59, 84
Communist Party, 15–16, 22, 25, 30
Communists, 24–26, 31, 35
Community activism, 202
Community resolutions, 7, 51, 128–131
Community Right-to-Know Act, 204
Compensation and Liability Act
(CERCLA), 204

"Competent tribunals," 141–142
"competent tribunals," 144, 241
Comprehensive Environmental Response,
204
Computer Assisted Passenger Pre-
Screening System (CAPPS II), 121
Computer Assisted Passenger Screening
System (CAPS), 97–98, 121
Congress, U.S.:
Alien and Sedition Acts passed by, 30
anthrax in, 181–182
antiterrorism acts passed by, 33–34
bioterrorism initiatives funded by,
168–169
Bush administration's lack of
cooperation with, 38
citizen detention prohibited by, 88
civil liberties protections adopted by, 4,
5
detention plans of, 23–24
drug legislation by, 92
expiration of USA PATRIOT set by, 36
and FISA amendments, 60, 61
Al Gore in, 156
HIPAA passage by, 167
Homeland Security Act passed by, 7, 51
human rights funding by, 249
Justice Department reporting to, 64–65
passage of USA PATRIOT set by, 76
and public health policies, 182
release of detainees' names demanded
by, 78
TIA funding held up by, 68
in World War I, 15
Congressional Budget Office (CBO), 167
Connecticut, 122, 180
Constitution, U.S., 36, 78–80, 123, 162, 206
Contagion, 176
Convention Against Torture, 149
Convention on the Rights of the Child, 248
Conyers, John, 64, 99

Cook, Robin, 214
Cooper, Bill, 116
Cooperation, agency, 60, 66, 67
Corporate sector, 56
Corvallis, Oregon, 128
Council of Islamic Ideology, 234
Court of Appeals for the Sixth Circuit in Cincinnati, 37
Court of Appeals for the Sixth Circuit in Philadelphia, 37–38
Court orders, 59
Courts, 50–51
    civil rights receptivity of, 4–5
    and "enemy combatants," 134
    federal, 6, 145–146
    Guantánamo role of, 132–133, 139–140, 145–146
    role of, 75, 88
Courts-martial, 141, 146–147, 243
Cox, Clinton, 215
Crack cocaine, 92, 99
Craft, Nikki, 224–225
Creppy, Michael, 37–38
Crimes, war crimes vs., 146
Criminal investigations, 59
Criminal justice, preventive justice vs., 14
Criminal law, 88–90
Culture, 223
Currency, 212
Custody rule (INS), 48
Customer records, 43, 59
Cyber Security Enhancement Act, 62
Cyberterrorism, 70

Daalder, Ivo, 214, 216
D'Amato, Alfonse, 154
"Dark Winter" project, 177
DARPA (Defense Advanced Research Projects Agency), 67
Daschle, Tom, 181

Databases, 42, 54, 55, 63, 84, 85, 127, 175, 204
Data-mining, 41, 46, 63, 67, 120–121, 170
"Dataveillance," 55
DEA. See Drug Enforcement Agency
Dearborn, Michigan, 106
Death penalty, 147, 148, 215
Debs, Eugene, 15
DEC, 200, 204
Declaration of Independence, 130–131
Declared emergency, 144
Defense Advanced Research Projects Agency (DARPA), 67
Defense Department. See U.S. Department of Defense
DeLay, Tom, 155
Deloria, Vine, 125
Democracy, 213
Democratic National Committee, 5
Denmark, 213
Denver, Colorado, 124–125
DEP. See NYC Department of Environmental Protection
Department of Homeland Security. See U.S. Department of Homeland Security
Department of Justice. See U.S. Department of Justice
Department of Transportation. See U.S. Department of Transportation
Deportations, 21, 23, 31, 79, 106, 113
Detention(s), 21–22, 27–28, 30, 35–38
    administrative, 23–24
    and anti-U.S. feeling, 229
    of Arab/Muslim immigrants, 95–97, 114, 243
    arbitrary, 140
    court role in, 132–133
    Creppy directive on, 37–38
    criminal treatment of immigrants in, 83–85

discriminatory nature of, 80–82
investigatory, 47–50
and local police departments, 107
military, 85–88
preventive, 75–76, 81
and rights violations, 82
Detroit, 80, 128
Diallo, Amadou, 94
Diario 16, 214
Digitization, 55
Directorate for Information Analysis and
    Infrastructure Protection, 46
Discrimination, 80–82
Dissent, 117–118, 122–125
Documentation (of civil rights violations),
    113–115
Document fraud, 81
DOH. *See* NYC Department of Health
DOJ. *See* U.S. Department of Justice
Domestic intelligence gathering, 40, 41, 60,
    67, 125–127
"Domestic terrorism," 40
Dostum, Abdul Rashid, 137
DOT. *See* U.S. Department of
    Transportation
Driver's licenses, 127
"Driving While Black" (DWB), 93–94
Drug Enforcement Agency (DEA), 91, 93,
    103
Drug war, 92–93, 99–100
"Due diligence," 62
Due process, 16, 48, 76, 84, 113, 242, 243,
    250
Durham Technical Community College
    (North Carolina), 118
Dust, 184, 186–189, 191, 192, 195–201
DWB. *See* "Driving While Black"

Eastern Kentucky University, 129
East Timor, 246
ECHELON system, 57–58, 66

E-commerce, 69
Economic sanctions, 28–29
The Economist, 212, 214
Economy, 186–189
Eczema, 178
Egypt, 100, 149, 239, 251
Ehrlich, Dorothy, 119
Einstein, Jethro, 127
Eisenhower, Dwight, 70
Electronic medical records, 164, 167
Electronic Privacy Information Center, 65
Electronic surveillance, 58–63, 125
E-mail, 57, 59, 61, 63, 65
Emergencies, 144, 164, 171–173, 185
Encryption systems, 69
Enemy Alien Act (1798), 21–22, 27
Enemy aliens, 21–23
"Enemy combatants," 27, 35, 38, 50, 75,
    86–87, 134, 142, 239, 243
Envirofacts databases, 204
Environment, 184–206
    agency information about, 198–201
    and decontamination/health, 201–203
    EPA response to WTC, 186–193
    testing by EPA of NYC, 193–198
    USA PATRIOT Act affecting, 204–205
Environmental justice, 185
Environmental Law and Justice Project. *See*
    New York Environmental Law and
    Justice Project
Environmental Protection Agency (EPA):
    knowledge of, 198–201
    policies of, 184
    testing/reporting by, 193–198
Equal Protection Clause, 49
Eritrea, 251
Ernest Harrowden (fictional character),
    209
Ethnicity, 77
Ethnic profiling. *See* Racial profiling
EU. *See* European Union

Euro, 212, 213
Europe, 56, 209–221
  and "axis of evil," 219–220
  divergent interests of U.S. and, 211–214
  and human rights, 214–216
  and Iraq, 220–221
  and terrorism, 216–219
European Parliament, 57–58
European Union (EU), 212–213
Evidence, rules of, 147
Exxon Mobil, 246

FAA (Federal Aviation Administration),
  97
Face-matching technologies, 68
Fallout (Juan Gonzalez), 197
Farmer, John, 98
Fatwa (religious edict or opinion), 232
Fauci, Anthony, 181–182
FBI. *See* Federal Bureau of Investigation
FDNY, 203
Federal Advisory Committee Act, 34
Federal appeals court in the Third Circuit,
  113
Federal Aviation Administration (FAA),
  97
Federal Bureau of Investigation (FBI):
  and Arab-American community, 82
  CARNIVORE search engine of, 57, 59,
    64
  CIA cooperation with, 66
  databases used by, 121
  datamining by, 63
  detainees cleared by, 28
  detentions of Muslims by, 112–113
  dissent monitored by, 124
  domestic intelligence gathering by, 40,
    41
  foreign students targeted by, 129
  foreign surveillance by, 44
  illegal activities of, 39

  immigrant group relationships with,
    106
  informants used by, 25, 112
  intelligence-gathering technology
    needed by, 53
  library records sought by, 64
  "Magic Lantern" virus sent by, 69
  Middle Eastern men interviewed by, 105
  misuse of wiretaps by, 61
  Most Wanted Terrorists list of, 100
  "no-fly" list of, 117–118
  as personal information source, 46
  political spying of, 24
  and preventive law enforcement, 13
  Project Lookout of, 46–47, 120
  and racial profiling, 110
  secret arrests by, 76
  and surveillance costs, 68
  and terrorist investigations, 79
  and torture, 149–150
Federal courts, 6, 145–146
Federal Education Rights and Privacy Act
  (FERPA), 4
Federal Emergency and Management
  Agency (FEMA), 189
Federal funding, 128–129
Federalist No. 84 (Alexander Hamilton), 75
Feingold, Russell, 7, 34
FEMA (Federal Emergency and
  Management Agency), 189
FERPA (Federal Education Rights and
  Privacy Act), 4
Fiberglass, 195
Fifth Amendment, 16, 35
Fifth Asian and Pacific Population
  Conference, 249
Filters, HEPA, 189
Financial Crimes Enforcement Network
  (FinCEN), 57, 58
Financial institutions, 62–63
Financial markets, 187, 188

Financial Times, 211
FinCen. *See* Financial Crimes Enforcement Network
Fire engines, 203
Firefighters, 184, 186, 188–189, 191, 198, 201, 203
Fires, 187, 188
Firewalls, 54, 56
First Amendment, 35, 37, 39–41, 44, 60, 61, 64, 65, 78, 89–90, 118, 158
FISA. *See* Foreign Intelligence Surveillance Act
Fischer, Joschka, 219
Fitzpatrick, Jane, 129
Flagstaff (AZ), 7
Florida, 89, 125, 127, 180
"Flying while brown," 94–99
FOIA. *See* Freedom of Information Act
FOIL (Freedom of Information Law) (NYS), 200
Ford, Gerald, 4
Foreign intelligence agencies, 66, 67, 149
Foreign intelligence information, 43, 59–60
Foreign Intelligence Surveillance Act (FISA) (1978), 39, 43–44, 60–61, 65
Foreign Intelligence Surveillance Court, 39, 43, 61
Foreign Intelligence Surveillance Court of Review, 43–44, 61
Foreign nationals, 30–31
Foreign relations, 106
Formal declaration of war, 21–22, 27
Fortas, Abe, 25
Fort Benning (Georgia), 123
Fort Campbell (Kentucky), 77, 78
Fourth Amendment, 35, 42–44, 48, 50
Fourth Circuit Court of Appeals, 50
Fourth Geneva Convention, 142
Fox Network, 119, 155, 156
Framingham Heart Study, 164

France, 58, 209, 212, 215, 220
Frankenberger, Klaus-Dieter, 216
Frankfurter, Felix, 26
Frankfurter Allgemeine Zeitung, 216
Freed, Katherine, 202
Freedom of Information Act (FOIA), 4, 34, 36, 65, 78, 113, 117, 185, 193, 198, 204
Freedom of Information Law (FOIL) (NYS), 200
Freedom to Read Foundation, 65
Freeing up resources, 19
Free speech, 117–118, 122–125
Free trade, 213
Freezing of assets, 28–29
Fresh Kills landfill (Staten Island), 191
"Fundamentalism," 223

"Gag orders," 42
Galeano, Eduardo, 236
Gallup Poll, 94
Gandhi, Mohandas, 40
Garrett, Laurie, 180
Geneva Conventions, 87, 133, 140–144, 148, 239, 241, 254
Georgia, 97
Germany, 209, 210, 212, 215, 217, 219, 220
Gingrich, Newt, 224
Giuliani, Rudolph, 94, 188, 195
Globalization, 53, 55, 57, 58
Global Relief Foundation, Inc., 29
Gonzalez, Juan, 195, 197, 200
Gordon, Rebecca, 117
Gore, Al, 156, 158
Gostin, Lawrence, 173, 179
Government misconduct, 78
Graham, Bob, 97
Grand jury secrecy rules, 83
Greece, 212, 220
Green, Penny, 218
Green, Sugako, 116
Gross, Oren, 31–32

Guantánamo Bay, Cuba, 27, 86, 87,
    132–150, 219, 242, 254
  court jurisdiction for, 132–133,
    139–140, 241
  detainees at, 136–138
  and Geneva Conventions, 140–144
  legal challenges to, 144–146
  living conditions at, 135–136
  military commissions at, 146–149
  and torture, 149–150
  U.S. sovereignty over, 138–140
The Guardian, 151, 211, 219, 220
Guilt by association, 14–20, 26, 31
Gujarat, India, 3
Gulf of Tonkin, 157
Gulf War (1991), 241, 252, 253
Gunn, Joe, 127

Habib, Mamdouh, 138
Hackensack, New Jersey, 107
Hackers, 62
Haddad, Rabih, 80
  "Hague Invasion Act," 250
  Haitian refugees, 135, 139–140
  Hamdi, Yasser, 27, 50, 86, 87, 113, 134
  Hamdi v. Rumsfeld, 50
  Hamilton, Adrian, 211
  Hamilton, Alexander, 75
  "Handschu agreement," 125–127
  HAN (Texas Health Alert Network),
    174
  Harris, David, 102, 103
  Harvard University, 123–124
  Hate crimes, 115–117
  Head covering, 116
  Health, public. *See* Public health
Health and Human Services. *See* U.S.
  Department of Health and Human
  Services
Health information networks,
  173–176

Health insurance, 179
Health Insurance Portability and
  Accountability Act (HIPAA) (1996),
  162, 166–168, 170
Health Privacy Project, 172
Healy, Robert W., 123–124
Heaphy, Janis, 124
Henderson, D. A., 178
Henshaw, John L., 189
HEPA filters, 189
Heritage Foundation, 156
Hernando, Pedro Calvo, 214–215
HHS. *See* U.S. Department of Health and
  Human Services
Hijab (head covering), 116
Hillsboro, Oregon, 128
HIPAA. *See* Health Insurance Portability
  and Accountability Act
Hippocratic oath, 163
HIV, 177–180
HLP (Humanitarian Law Project), 20
Hoagland, Jim, 210
Holmes, Oliver Wendell, Jr., 22
The Holy Land Foundation, 29
Homeland Security. *See* U.S. Department
  of Homeland Security
Homeland Security Act (2002), 46, 51, 119,
  182
  electronic surveillance provisions of, 62
  FOIA exemptions in, 46–47
  passage of, 33, 34
  public health provisions in, 169–170
  Section 225 of, 62
  Section 891 of, 62
  TIPS dropped from, 7
Homeland Security Information Sharing
  Act, 62
Homosexuals, 180
Hoover, J. Edgar, 3, 8, 35, 41
House Un-American Activities Committee
  (HUAC), 15, 26

HRCP (Human Rights Commission of Pakistan), 114
HRW. *See* Human Rights Watch
HUAC. *See* House Un-American Activities Committee
Hudood Ordinances (1979), 231
Hughes, Tiffany, 77, 78
Humanitarian aid, 41
Humanitarian law. *See* International human rights law
Humanitarian Law Project (HLP), 20
Human rights, 237–254
 Europe's position on, 214–216
 international fora on, 247–250
 terrorism affecting, 238–240
 of terrorist suspects, 240–244
 U.S. foreign policy regarding, 244–247
 and war on Iraq, 252–254
 and "war on terrorism," 250–251
 women's. See Women's rights
Human Rights Commission of Pakistan (HRCP), 114
Human rights treaties, 247–250
Human Rights Watch (HRW), 82, 117, 226, 245
Hussein, Saddam, 157, 234, 252–254

Ibrahim, Anwar, 247
Ibrahim, Saadeddin, 251
ICC. *See* International Criminal Court
Identification cards, 127
IEEPA. *See* International Emergency Economic Powers Act
Ikonos satellite, 151–152
Ill treatment, allegations of, 135
IMF (International Monetary Fund), 228
Immigrants/immigrant communities:
 criminal treatment of, 83–85
 driver's licenses for, 127
 racial profiling of, 91–92
 relationships with, 105–108, 128–129
 war on terror affecting, 112–115
Immigration and Naturalization Service (INS), 28, 36, 47–49, 77, 80, 95–96, 101, 107, 127
Immigration/immigration law, 22–23, 27–28, 30, 75
 local police enforcement of, 128–129
 national-origin-based discrimination in, 100–101
 secret hearings on, 79–80
 uniqueness of, 84
 violations of, 81, 96, 106, 107
Immune systems, compromised, 177–178
The Independent, 211
India, 3, 248
Individual rights violations, 82
Indonesia, 104, 226–227
Informants, unidentified, 25, 26, 105
Information:
 access to, 206
 collection of, 41–47, 56, 218
 for environmental activism, 204–205
 medical, 161, 163–164
 personal, 46, 54, 56
 protected health, 167
 sharing of, 46–47, 62
Information Awareness Office (DARPA), 67
Information networks, health, 173–176
Infrastructures, 65–66, 70, 161, 174
Inmate communications, 38, 84
INS. *See* Immigration and Naturalization Service
Intelligence agencies, 66, 67, 149
Intelligence gathering, 40, 41, 105–107, 125. *See also* Domestic intelligence gathering
Intelsat, 57
Inter-American Commission of the OAS, 144–145

International Committee of the Red Cross, 136

International Covenant on Civil and Political Rights, 143–144, 148

International Criminal Court (ICC), 249–250

International Emergency Economic Powers Act (IEEPA), 28–29

International human rights law, 140, 142–145, 149, 240, 241, 248

International Monetary Fund (IMF), 228

Internet, 57, 59, 62, 63, 67

Interpreters, 106

Interviews, 85, 106

Iowa, 127

IRA. *See* Irish Republican Army

Iran, 96

Iran-Contra affair, 42, 67, 68, 121

Iraq, 96, 118, 142, 209, 210, 220–221, 234, 252–254

Irish Republican Army (IRA), 19, 217, 218

Iron workers, 186

Irvine, Reed, 153

Islam, war against, 228

"Islamization," 230–231, 233

Israel, 239, 247, 250

Italy, 220

Jaber, Hussan, 106

Japanese descent, U.S. citizens of, 21, 26, 31, 35, 52, 92, 97, 98, 116

Jefferson, Thomas, 78, 130

Jenkins, Cate, 194, 202

Jewis extremist groups, 28

Johns Hopkins Bloomberg School of Public Health, 172

Jordan, 149

Justice Department. *See* U.S. Department of Justice

"Kalashnikov culture," 230

Karzai, Hamid, 241

Kasi, Aimal, 229

Katz, Alyssa, 197

Kaufman, Hugh, 205

Kazakhstan, 244

Keith, Damon, 113

Kelly, Ray, 126

Kerry, John, 38, 154, 157

Kessler, Gladys, 37

Khan, Ismail, 245

Kilfoyle, Peter, 213

Kilpatrick, James J., 153

King, Martin Luther, Jr., 24, 40, 124

Kirsanow, Peter, 85

"Knock and announce," 45

"Knowledge is Power," 67, 170

Korean War, 240

Korematsu v. United States, 92

Kosovo, 253

Kroeker, Mark, 107

Kurds, 20, 252, 253

Kuwaitis, 145

Kyoto Accord, 211, 214, 240

Kyrgyzstan, 244

Lackawanna, New York, 20, 89

Laird v. Tatum, 5

Landlords, 190–192, 194, 202

Language, 105

Leahy, Patrick, 78, 181

L'effroyable Imposture, 220

Le Monde, 209, 215

Le Pen, Jean-Marie, 215

Levin, Stephen M., 189, 192

Libby, Montana, 190, 205

Liberia, 251

Libraries, 45, 63–65

"Library Awareness Program" (FBI), 64

Libya, 96

Limbaugh, Rush, 156
Lindh, John Walker, 89, 104
Lindorff, Dave, 119
Lioy, Paul J., 199
Lippy, Bruce, 198
Living conditions (at Guantánamo Bay, Cuba), 135–136
Living Wage Campaign, 123–124
Longaker, Richard, 24
Los Angeles, 127
Louisiana, 125
Louisville, Kentucky, 129
Loyalty and security program, 13, 15
Loyalty review procedures, 25–26

Madison, James, 38–39, 88
"Magic Lantern" virus, 69
Mahmood, Syed, 116
Maier, Pauline, 130–131
Malaysia, 247
Mal-e-ghanimat, 224
Malvo, John Lee, 102, 103
Mankiller, Wilma, 125
Maqtari, Ali al-, 77–78
Marijuana, 92
Martin, Robert, 205
Maryland, 93, 103, 125
"Material support," 15, 17–20, 89
"Material witnesses," 49–50, 77, 82–83, 86, 115, 242
McCarthy, Joseph, 3, 5, 8
"McCarthyism," 8, 52
McDermott, Jim, 118
McKinley, William, 30
McQuillan, Peter, 126
McVeigh, Timothy, 100, 110
Medical information, 161, 163–164
Medical personnel, 186
Micro-vacuum testing, 194
Middle Eastern people, 94, 96, 100–102, 104, 105

Military commissions, 133–134, 141, 144, 146–149, 239, 243–244
Military detentions, 85–88
Military-industrial complex, 70
Military tribunal order, 31
Milosevic, Slobodan, 251, 253
Mineta, Norman, 97–98, 103
Minorities, targeting vulnerable, 14, 30–31
Misconduct, government, 78
Mitchell, John, 3
MMA. See Mutahida Majlis Amal
Model State Emergency Health Powers Act (CDC), 165, 168–173, 182
Mohamad, Mahatir bin, 247
Money laundering surveillance, 57, 58, 62–63
Montana, 190
Morbidity and Mortality Weekly Report (CDC), 174
Morehead State University, 129
Morocco, 149
"Mosaic theory," 37, 79
Mount Sinai—I.J. Selikoff Center for Occupational and Environmental Medicine, 192
Moussaoui, Zacarias, 48, 113, 148
Mueller, Robert, 79
Mugabe, Robert, 251
Muhammad, John, 102
Mujahideen, 224, 225, 230, 232, 233
Mukasey, Michael, 49–50, 243
Muller, Danny, 118
Museveni, Yoweri, 251
Musharraf, Pervez, 226, 246
Muslim charities, 17, 29, 89
Muslim communities, 95, 105
Muslims, 76, 78–83, 85, 89, 96–98, 101, 102, 106, 228
Muslim societies, 223
Mutahida Majlis Amal (MMA), 227–228, 234

Nadler, Jerrold, 190, 202, 205
Namibia, 215
National Advisory Committee for Acute
  Exposure Guidelines Levels (AEGLs)
  for Hazardous Substances, 204
National boundaries, 54
National Conference of State Legislatures
  (NCSL), 172
National Contingency Plan, 204–205
National Crime Information Center
  (NCIC) database, 84
National Guard, 77
National Hazmat Program, 198
National health information policy, 167
National identification system, 51
National Imagery and Mapping Agency
  (NIMA), 152
National Institute of Environmental
  Health Sciences (NIEHS), 189, 198
National Institutes of Health (NIH),
  169
Nationality profiling, 100–101, 104
National origin, 100–101
National Public Radio (NPR), 115
National Security Administration (NSA),
  46, 57, 66, 67, 69
National Security Entry-Exit Registration
  System (NSEERS), 49
National Strategy to Secure Cyberspace
  (White House), 69–70
National Toxicology Program, 195
NCIC (National Crime Information
  Center) database, 84
NCSL (National Conference of State
  Legislatures), 172
NESHAP standards, 190
New Deal, 162
New England Coalition for Law and Public
  Health, 172
New Jersey, 93, 98, 103, 124, 180, 188
Newspapers, 65, 78, 80

New York City, 93–94, 125–127, 180,
  184–206
New York Committee on Occupational
  Safety and Health (NYCOSH), 202
New York Daily News, 195, 197, 200
New York Environmental Law and Justice
  Project, 191, 193, 195, 197, 198, 200,
  203
New York Observer, 158
New York Police Department (NYPD),
  125–127
New York Post, 154, 197
New York State, 122, 124, 166, 185, 192,
  198, 206
New York State Department of Health, 195
New York Stock Exchange, 187
New York Supreme Court, 126
New York Times, 1, 5, 7, 61–62, 115, 121,
  125, 127, 130, 137, 152, 153, 155, 197,
  219
NGOs. *See* Nongovernmental
  organizations
NIEHS. *See* National Institute of
  Environmental Health Sciences
NIH (National Institutes of Health), 169
NIMA (National Imagery and Mapping
  Agency), 152
9/11 Environmental Action, 202
Niqab (veil), 116
Nitrogen oxide, 206
Nixon, Richard, 1, 3, 5, 8
No Equal Justice (David Cole), 110
"No-fly" list, 117–118
Noncitizens, 76–80, 86, 133, 134
Nongovernmental organizations (NGOs),
  226–227
Northern Ireland, 217–218
NPR (National Public Radio), 115
NSEERS (National Security Entry-Exit
  Registration System), 49
Nurses, 184

NYC Department of Education, 201–202
NYC Department of Environmental
    Protection (DEP), 190, 193, 202, 204
NYC Department of Health (DOH), 189,
    191, 198, 200, 201
NYC Detectives' Endowment Association,
    191
NYCOSH (New York Committee on
    Occupational Safety and Health), 202
NYPD. See New York Police Department

OAS. See Organization of American States
Observing behavior, 102–103
Occupational Safety and Health
    Administration (OSHA), 189, 191,
    193, 194, 198, 199, 203
Odors, 189
Office of Information and Regulatory
    Affairs, 205
Office of Management and Budget
    (OMB), 167, 205
Office of Regulatory Enforcement, 205
Office of the Ombudsman (EPA), 205
Oklahoma City, 177
Olshansky, Barbara, 202
Olson, Theodore, 88
OMB. See Office of Management and
    Budget
Omnibus Crime Control and Safe Streets
    Act (1968), 60
Online monitoring, 64
Online research, 63
Openness in government, 36
Open Society Institute, 172
Operating engineers, 186, 188
Operating engineers union, 189, 198
Operation Enduring Freedom, 32
Operation Pipeline (DEA), 93, 103
Opium, 92
Optional Protocol to the Convention
    Against Torture, 248

Organization of American States (OAS),
    144–145
Orion (computer company), 125
OSHA. See Occupational Safety and
    Health Administration
Overload dust finding, 201

Padilla, Jose, 27, 50, 86–87, 104, 113, 134,
    242–243
Padilla, Tomas, 107
Padilla v. Rumsfeld, 50
Pakistan, 114–115, 136, 138, 222, 225–231,
    233, 234, 239, 246, 248
Palestinian organizations, 28, 247
Palmer, A. Mitchell, 3, 22, 30
Palmer raids, 22, 26, 27, 91–92
Passenger screening, 97–98, 121
PATRIOT Act. See USA PATRIOT Act
Patterson, David, 202
Peace for Action, 117
Peaceful resolution of conflict, 41
Pearl Harbor, 35
Peel, Quentin, 211, 212
Pennsylvania, 174
Pen registers, 59–63
Pentagon Papers, 5
Personal information, 46, 54, 56
Peru, 134
Philadelphia Inquirer, 154
PHI ("protected health information"), 167
The Picture of Dorian Gray (Oscar Wilde),
    209
Pleasantville, New Jersey, 123
PLO, 19
"The Plumbers," 1
Poindexter, John, 2, 9, 42, 67, 68, 120–121,
    153, 170
Poisonous gas, 215
Police departments, local, 99–100,
    105–108, 128–129
Police Executive Research Forum, 108

Police Foundation, 108
Police officers, 186, 188, 191
Political activism, 39–41
Political office, 116
Political speech, 89
Political surveillance, 6
Politico-religious parties, 227–228, 231, 235
Porter, Paul, 25
Portfolio program (Justice Department), 23, 24
Portland, Oregon, 107, 128
Portugal, 212
Post, Louis F., 22–23
Pound, Roscoe, 26
Powell, Colin, 152, 219, 220
Power, government and, 38–39
POWs. *See* Prisoners of war
Press, 151–158
    human rights coverage by, 251
    and immigration hearings, 37
    trial access by, 148
    women's rights coverage by, 235
    WTC environmental risk coverage of, 186, 188, 195, 197–198
Prevention of Terrorism Act (UK), 218
Preventive detentions, 75–76, 81
Preventive law enforcement:
    with administrative process, 14, 21–29
    with guilt by association, 14–20
    HUAC hearings as, 26
    by targeting vulnerable minorities, 14, 30–31
Prisoners, 219, 239, 253
Prisoners of war (POWs), 133, 141–143, 148, 240–241
Privacy, 54–55, 79
    customer, 59
    laws about health, 165–168
    and medical records, 175, 182

and Model State Emergency Health Powers Act, 171–172
    and public health, 161–183
    rules about, 161
    and smallpox vaccination plan, 177
Privacy Act (1974), 4
Privacy concerns, 6, 41–47
Private sector, 54, 69–71, 175
Probable cause requirement, 42–44
Profiles of Injustice (David Harris), 102
Profiling. *See* Racial profiling
Program on Medicine as a Profession, 172
Project Lookout (FBI), 46–47, 120
"Protected computers," 62
"Protected health information" (PHI), 167
P.S. 58, 201
Public emergency, 185
Public health, 161–183
    future of, 182–183
    historical lessons about, 179–182
    privacy and risk to, 163–165
    privacy laws regarding, 165–168
Public health emergencies, 164, 171–173
Public health law, 179
Public Health Security and Bioterrorism Preparedness and Response Act, 168
Public safety, 2
Punishments (for terrorism), 121–122
Putin, Vladimir, 247

Qatar, 152
Quiñones, Rodrigo, 245

Race and Class (Clinton Cox), 215
Racial profiling, 7, 47–48, 91–111
    defining, 99
    and "Driving While Black," 93–94
    drug-war, 92–93, 99–100
    and "flying while brown," 94–99
    foreign relations affected by, 106
    future of, 107–109

as "heads up" to terrorists, 104–105
intelligence gathering undermined with,
    105–107
and nationality profiling, 100–101, 104
observing behavior vs., 102–103
selective enforcement of, 99–100
and terrorism threat, 101–102
tolerance for, 110–111
Racism, 215
Rahman, Omar Abdel, 14
RAWA. *See* Revolutionary Afghan
    Women's Association
RCRA (Resource Convservation Recovery
    Act), 204
Reagan, Ronald, 42, 238
Real-Time Outbreak and Disease
    Surveillance (RODS), 174–175
Recession, 187
Rector, Ricky, 214
Red Cross, 136, 138
Red Scare (of 1919), 35
Registration of immigrants, 85, 96, 101,
    106
Rehnquist, William, 5, 43
Reid, Richard, 89, 104
Reliable Sources (television show), 153–154
Religion, 77, 223
Religiosity, 231
Religious associations, 89
Religious speech, 89
Reporting:
    Justice Department, 64–65
    public health, 173–176
"Representative sampling," 193–195
Repression, 239, 250
Reproductive rights, 223, 249
Republican National Convention, 95
Rescue workers, 188–189, 192, 201
Resolutions, community, 7, 51, 128–131
Resource Convservation Recovery Act
    (RCRA), 204

Respiratory disorders, 184, 192, 198, 206
Revell, Oliver, 129
Revolutionary Afghan Women's
    Association (RAWA), 225, 234
Rhode, David, 137
Richardson, Texas, 128
Ridge, Tom, 70
Rights violations, 82
Robert Wood Johnson Foundation, 176
RODS. *See* Real-Time Outbreak and
    Disease Surveillance
Roosevelt, Franklin D., 162
Rossol, Monona, 195
"Roving surveillance," 60–61
Rumsfeld, Donald, 3, 132, 137, 144, 210,
    245
Russia, 217, 218, 220, 239, 247, 250

Sacramento, California, 107
Sacramento Bee, 7, 124
Safire, William, 67–68, 121, 148
St. Paul, Minnesota, 127
Salon.com, 119
Samar, Sima, 226
San Francisco, 128
San Jose, California, 128
Satellites, 57, 151–152
Satellite Week, 152
Saturday Night Live (television show),
    181–182
Saudi Arabia, 100, 230, 232, 239, 248
Scales v. United States, 16, 19
Scalia, Antonin, 51
Schaeffer, Eric V., 205–206
Scheindlin, 49, 50
School of the Americas (SOA) Watch,
    123
Schools, 188, 201–202
Schroder, Gerhard, 209, 210
Scientia est potentia (knowledge is power),
    67

SDGTs. *See* Specially Designated Global Terrorists
SDTs. *See* Specially Designated Terrorists
Search engines, 57, 59, 63, 64
Searches, 45–46, 60, 61
Secrecy, 148
Secret arrests, 76–83
Secret Service, 112, 118, 187
Security, 148
"Security Index" (FBI), 24
Security-industrial complex, 70–71
Security standards, 71
Sedition law, 15
Selective enforcement (of racial profiling), 99–100
Self-censorship, 41, 116, 197
Self-regulation, corporate, 56
Sensenbrenner, James, 38, 64
Separation of powers, 88
September 11, 2001 terrorist attacks, 1–4, 7–9, 17, 28, 33, 48, 52–53, 58, 94, 184
Service providers, 57, 59, 62
Sharon, Ariel, 219
Shearson Lehman, 201
Shi'a, 252, 253
"Shoe bomber," 89
Shufro, Joel, 202
Side effects, 177–178
"Signing Statement," 64–65
Sikhs, 98, 115
Sinn Fein, 218
Sixth Amendment, 35
60 Minutes (television show), 98
Smallpox, 176–179
Smith Act (1940), 15, 16, 19
Smoke, 187, 192, 199
Smuggling, 103
"Sneak-and-peek searches," 45–46, 65
Snipers, Washington, D.C., 102–103
SOA (School of the Americas) Watch, 123
Society of Professional Journalists, 65

Sodhi, Balibir Sing, 115
Sodhi, Sukhpal Singh, 115
Somalia, 248–249
South Asia, 223
South Asians, 98, 112
South Korea, 235
Southwest Africa, 215
Soviets, 233
Space Imaging, 151–152
Spain, 212, 214–215, 217
Speaking out, 5, 15
Specially Designated Global Terrorists (SDGTs), 28–29
Specially Designated Terrorists (SDTs), 28, 29
Specter, Arlen, 84
Speech, 30, 89, 122–125
Spock, Benjamin, 1
Spying, 5, 24, 31, 39, 51, 60, 119, 120
Stark, Fortney "Pete," 116
State public health emergency laws, 175, 182
State sunshine laws, 80
Steinfeld, Lauren, 168
Stewart, Lynn, 89
Students for a Democratic Society, 24
Styuvesant High School, 201–202
Subversive speech, 16
Sudan, 96
Sulfur dioxide, 206
"Sunset" provisions, 36, 45, 61
Sunshine laws, state, 80
Superfund sites, 190
Supreme Court, 5, 50, 243
  on alien rights, 23
  and courts-martial, 147
  and guilt by association, 18–20
  and immigration law, 84
  and loyalty review procedures, 26
  on medical records privacy, 166
  and military commissions, 146

on political dissent, 40–41
and sedition law, 15
on subversive speech, 16
on wartime threat by immigrant groups, 92
Surveillance, 41–47, 52–71
application of, 63–66
of Arab nationals, 101
bills expanding/limiting powers of, 125–127
boundaries in, 54–58
capacity for, 56–57
costs of, 68, 70
electronic, 58–63, 125
electronic powers of, in USA PATRIOT Act, 58–63
FBI use of, 105
on individuals, 83
political, 6
and public health, 166, 170
Survival of principle, 31–32
"Suspicious activity reports," 62
Swire, Peter, 168
Syria, 96

Taft, William H., IV, 247
Tajikistan, 244
Takoma Park (MD), 129
Taliban, 89, 135–137, 140–141, 143, 144, 224, 225, 232, 241, 245
"Tangible items," 64, 65
Targeting vulnerable minorities, 14, 30–31
Taylor, Charles, 251
Technology, 56–57
communication, 53
face-matching, 68
finance, 57
limitations of, 68–69
and privacy issues, 55
surveillance, 6, 42–43
Temple University, 93

Terrorism Information and Prevention System (TIPS), 7, 51, 119
Terrorists/terrorism:
European/American responses to, 216–219
human rights affected by, 238–240
human rights of suspects of, 240–244
punishments for, 121–122
racial profiling as "heads up" to, 104–105
and repression, 239, 250
threat of, 101–102
as unique crime, 89
Testing, environmental, 193–198
Texas Health Alert Network (HAN), 174
Third Geneva Convention, 141–142, 148, 241
Third-party records, 42, 43, 56
Thomas, Clarence, 51
Thompson, Tommy, 172, 174
Thoreau, Henry David, 40
TIA Project. See Total Information Awareness Project
Times, 215
TIPS. See Terrorism Information and Prevention System
Title II (USA PATRIOT Act), 42–46
Title III (Omnibus Crime Control and Safe Streets Act), 60
Title III (USA PATRIOT Act), 42
Title V (USA PATRIOT Act), 42
Tolerance, 124
Torricelli, Robert, 153–154
Torture, use of, 149–150, 248
Torture Convention, 248
Total Information Awareness (TIA) Project, 2, 9, 41–42, 67–68, 120–121, 153, 170, 175, 182
Tourists, 187
Toxic Substances Control Act, 197

Transaction space, 67, 69
Transit Workers Union, 203
Transportation Department. *See* U.S.
    Department of Transportation
Trap-and-trace, 59–63
Treasury Department, 29, 57
Trotha, Lothar von, 215
Truman, Harry, 15
Trust, 163, 164, 172, 206
Tunisia, 250
Turkey, 20, 253
Turkmenistan, 224, 244
Turkmen v. Ashcroft, 48
Turner, Douglas, 157
Tyranny, 36, 88

Uganda, 251
Uighurs, 247
Ujaama, James, 113
UK. *See* United Kingdom
UKUSA network, 57, 66
Ultrasonication method, 201
Ummah, 235
U.N. *See* United Nations
U.N. Commission on Human Rights, 248
U.N. General Assembly Special Session on
    Children, 248–249
U.N. Security Council, 220
Undercover agents, 105
Uniformed Firefighters Association, 203
United Kingdom (UK), 69, 145, 210–212,
    215, 217–218, 220
United Nations' Convention on the
    Elimination of All Forms of
    Discrimination Against Women
    (CEDAW), 231–233
United Nations Population Fund (UNPF),
    249
United Nations (U.N.), 222, 223, 248
United Self Defense Forces of Columbia,
    245

Uniting and Strengthening Americal by
    Providing Appropriate Tools
    Required to Intercept and Obstruct
    Terrorism Act. *See* USA PATRIOT Act
Universal Declaration of Human Rights,
    239
Universities, 129
University of California at Berkeley, 116
University of Illinois, 45
University of Missouri, 172
University of Münster, 210
University of Pittsburgh, 174
Unocal, 224
UNPF (United Nations Population Fund),
    249
Urban environmentalism, 185
Uribe, Álvaro, 251
U.S. Army, 1, 5
U.S. Civil Rights Division, 107
U.S. Court of Appeals for the Armed
    Forces, 147, 243
U.S. Court of Appeals for the Sixth Circuit
    in Cincinnati, 113
U.S. Customs Department, 103, 188
U.S. Department of Defense, 35, 41, 50,
    68, 86, 121, 146, 147, 151–152, 164,
    243
U.S. Department of Health and Human
    Services (HHS), 162, 168, 182, 195
U.S. Department of Homeland Security,
    34, 46, 65–66, 165, 169, 170, 175
U.S. Department of Justice (DOJ), 36–38,
    91
  civil rights policies of, 98
  criminal treatment of detainees by,
    83–85, 106
  detentions used by, 27, 28, 35, 95, 113
  dissent monitored by, 124
  FISA amendments by, 60
  and FOIA, 36–37
  hate crimes enforced by, 95

immigation law changed instituted by,
84
immigrant group relationships with,
106
and local police departments, 107
Portfolio program of, 23, 24
racial profiling investigated by, 93
reporting to Congress by, 64–65
secret arrests ordered by, 76–81, 114
TIPS wanted by, 119
warrants for wiretaps/searches by, 42–43
U.S. Department of Transportation
(DOT), 97
U.S. District Court for the District of
Columbia, 113
U.S. embassy bombings in Africa, 88
U.S. embassy in Sarajevo, 136
U.S. Labor Department, 206
U.S. Naval Base, Guantánamo Bay, Cuba.
See Guantánamo Bay, Cuba
U.S. Postal Service, 180–182
U.S. State Department, 98, 106, 239
USA PATRIOT Act (2001), 2
electronic surveillance powers in, 58–63
environment affected by, 204–205
expiration of surveillance provisions of,
36
foreign nationals targeted by, 30–31
IEEPA amendment in, 29
material support provision of, 17
passage of, 33–34
preventive detention provisions in,
75–76
quick passage of, 7
Section 213 of, 45–46
Section 215 of, 44–45, 64
Section 216 of, 59
Section 218 of, 43–44
Section 412 of, 48
Section 802 of, 39–40
special provisions of, 38

surveillance of Arab nationals under,
101
terrorism defined in, 122
Title II of, 42–46
Title III/V of, 42
U.S.S. *Cole,* 242
USSR, 230, 232
Uzbekistan, 239, 244, 250

Vaccination plans, smallpox, 176–179
Vagrancy laws, 91
Vedrine, Hubert, 219
Vehicles, 202–203
Veil, 116, 231
Venegas, Arturo, 107
Vietnam, 142
Vietnam War, 241
Virginia, 125
Voices in the Wilderness, 118
"Voluntary departure," 114
Vulnerable minorities, targeting, 14, 30–31

Wallace, Mike, 98
Wall Street Journal, 120, 156, 190
Walton, Kenneth P., 105, 129
War:
formal declaration of, 21–22, 27
international law definitions of, 143
laws of, 87, 146
theater of, 140
time of, 88, 92
War crimes, 141
War of 1812, 21
War powers, 50
Warrants, 59
War Times (periodical), 117
Washington, D.C., 102–103, 180
Washington Committee for Democratic
Action, 25
Washington Post, 1, 5, 67, 129, 149, 153,
155, 206, 210

Watergate, 6
Water quality, 185, 188
Wawinger, Vigine, 117
Weapons of mass destruction, 253
We Are Not the Enemy (Human Rights
    Watch), 117
Webster, William H., 105
West Bank, 250
Whalen v. Roe, 166
Whistle-blower laws, 206
Whitman, Christine Todd, 93, 188
Wilde, Oscar, 209
Wilkins, Robert, 93
Wilkins v. Maryland State Police, 93
Williams, Hubert, 108
Wilson, Woodrow, 30
Winter Olympics (2002), 174
Wiretaps, 42–43, 60, 61, 83
WLUML (Women Living Under Muslim
    Laws), 223
WNBC, 154
Women Living Under Muslim Laws
    (WLUML), 223
Women's rights, 222–236
    in Afghanistan, 231–234, 236
    Bush administration's position on,
        249

in Pakistan, 226–231, 233, 234
and past abuses, 230–234
and war on terror, 224–226, 233–234
Woollacott, Martin, 211
Workers' compensation, 186
World Bank, 228
World Trade Center (WTC), 148, 184–206
World War I, 15, 21, 91
World War II, 21, 92, 146, 148
WTC. *See* World Trade Center
"WTC cough," 184, 189
"WTC Disaster Site Worker Injury and
    Illness Surveillance Update" (DOH),
    198
Wu, Charlotte, 116

Xinjiang province (China), 247, 250

Yamani, Mai, 234
Yemen, 242
Yemenis, 96, 136, 143
Yugoslavia, 214, 251, 252

Zia-ul-Haq, 230–233
Zimbabwe, 239, 251
Zogby, James J., 102, 106
Zonolite insulation, 205